THE WAY IT WAS

by Herb Plambeck

With My Best Wishes, Always
Herb Plambeck

Published by
Sigler Printing and Publishing
Ames, Iowa

© 1993 First Printing
Sigler Printing and Publishing
Ames, Iowa, USA

Library of Congress Catalog Card Number 93-086282
ISBN Number 0-9635812-2-8

This Book Is Dedicated To The Memory Of

CLARENCE S. HILL

Master Farmer — Community Leader
Agricultural Innovator — Popular Humorist
Proud Father and Grandfather
Recognized Critic and Happy Tormentor
and
Dear Friend To A Countless Number

    A number of years ago, Mr. Hill originally suggested that a book entitled, "THE WAY IT WAS" be written featuring all columns. Although he was my most persistent critic and favorite tormentor, he was completely serious in suggesting such a compilation be published. Thus it is fitting this book be dedicated to his memory.

— Herb Plambeck

An interesting column about Clarence Hill is found in Chapter II of this book.

PREFACE

For 57 years, he has been recognized as the voice of Iowa agriculture. His radio farm reports have been beamed across the state daily. He was a war correspondent in three wars, served in the Secretary of Agriculture's office in Washington, and has traveled far, conducting thousands of interviews in the interest of agriculture. If you have been involved with Iowa agriculture in any form during the last six decades, you know his name.

Herb Plambeck has touched the lives of countless Iowa families. For the last 16 years, has drawn on a lifetime of experiences and friendships to pen, *"The Way It Was"* columns for *WALLACES FARMER*. And that's what this book is all about.

The compilation of columns selected for publication is more than nostalgic — they represent a piece of our great state's agricultural heritage. Herb has brought to the pages of *WALLACES FARMER* the people of the land who are that history. He has sought out the interesting, the colorful, the meaningful, the lighthearted stories to chronicle.

It was Herb's idea to write about the "Golden Agers" who have made such great contributions to farming, to their communities, to their states, to their country. "We'll target folks 75 years of age or more." said Herb. "An intriguing idea," I responded, "okay, let's give it a try." That was in January of 1978, some 175 columns ago. Herb has traveled more than 70,000 miles within the state searching out the exceptional story. He has interviewed more than 350 Iowans in 82 counties, and talked with folks in 15 other states and many different countries.

Among his favorite interviewees are those persons who have celebrated 100 birthdays or more. Edith Smith, at 107 years, gets credit for the most candles to date. You'll read about the Panora Iowan and many other interesting families and individuals in the 300 pages that follow. The accompanying photographs, which graphically depict the period he writes about, are absolutely fascinating.

As you skim the 16 chapters, you'll find stories about farm families who have made a difference. There are Master Farmers, Master Farm Homemakers, congressmen, senators, state legislators, 4-H and FFA members, leaders, innovators, champions in sports, and just "everyday" folks. Their stories offer a broad glimpse of Iowa spanning the decades. There are memories of "pioneer" days, the first tractors, development of hybrid corn and the introduction of soybeans. There are recollections of farming during the 1930s Depression, and the financial crisis of the 1980s. Other accounts focus on diverse subjects from farm programs to the Pope's visit, to "revolutions" in agriculture.

Herb calls it a "recognition of representative 'Old Timers' to whom we are all grateful." Most of all, they are people you will enjoy reading about. You can learn from them, and relive days past. "They are all wonderful, beautiful people," says the author.

One thing I'll bet, whether you're a young person or a senior, if you're interested in agriculture, you'll like this book, where Iowa history comes to life.

Herb tells it like *"The Way It Was."*

You can be sure the author will continue to do that in *WALLACES FARMER* as well. There are many more stories to search out and write.

Now, allow me to tell you a little more about the author.

Herb's first book, *"NEVER A DULL MOMENT"*, was published in 1990, and is now in its third printing. The popular offering tells about those nearly 60 years as a professional communicator. In it he talks about the fascinating times he experienced as a writer, broadcaster, editor, speaker, war correspondent, government official and international tour leader.

In his 33 years with WHO radio, he originated programs and news columns from 50 states and 78 foreign countries. After his four years of "time out" to serve Secretaries of Agriculture Hardin and Butz, 1960-1964, he returned to be heard on WHO programs for seven more years. Since then, his voice has been heard in farm commentaries on WMT, Cedar Rapids, every week. In addition, he and his wife conduct weekly garden broadcasts on KRNT, Des Moines.

Herb has met ten U.S. presidents and with every secretary of agriculture since 1932. He has received 125 major awards, including the prestigious Henry Wallace Plaque and the American Farm Bureau Federation's Distinguished Service Citation.

He's also a family man with a daughter and son. "And, of course, I have the world's three greatest grandchildren," he avows. After 44 years of marriage, Herb was left a widower in 1981. In 1991, he married long-time friend, Laura Hicks, who is now his partner and companion.

There's much more than can be said about the author's accomplishments, service and dedication. We'll just conclude with: "Congratulations, Herb. Not bad for an eastern Iowa farm boy who continues to plant a straight row. And, that's the way it is."

Monte Sesker, Editor, Wallaces Farmer

ACKNOWLEDGEMENTS

In acknowledging the many persons who have had a significant part in the completion of this book, I am reminded of Edward Markham's familiar poem entitled, "A *Creed*", which I have often quoted in speeches made throughout the nation —

"There is a destiny that makes us brothers.

None goes his way alone.

That which we send into the lives of others,

Comes back into our own."

The words "none goes his way alone" are particularly applicable to my efforts in writing *"THE WAY IT WAS."* Dozens of persons have had an especially important part in completing this work, and hundreds of others who are featured within these pages have made possible the finished text. I am profoundly grateful to all.

To the late **Clarence Hill,** highly respected Dallas County Master Farmer, initial thanks are due for his original, and continued insistence *"THE WAY IT WAS"* be written, and to whose memory the book is dedicated.

Similar special gratitude must go to **Monte Sesker,** Editor of *Wallaces Farmer,* who encouraged me to start writing columns many years ago and has seen fit to continue to include them in the widely read magazine almost every month since January, 1978. I also appreciate Monte's willingness to write a preface for this book. Meanwhile, **Frank Holdmeyer,** Managing Editor, merits similar appreciation for his untiring patience in originally checking and editing every one of the more than 175 columns appearing in this book.

Five lovely ladies must also be given full credit and appreciation for their priceless help. **Frances,** my wife of 44 years, was a patient and helpful "sounding board" during the first several years the columns were written. That ended only with her untimely death in 1981. Until other work precluded her writing for me, **Mrs. Hazel Link,** a long-time secretary, spent many hours at her typewriter providing finished copy for the

Frank Holdmeyer

magazine. Since then, **Mrs. Ruth Schultz** has undertaken the challenging task and has employed her word processor for every single sentence in the present book. Her assistance has been exceedingly valuable.

The two other ladies to be acknowledged are my sister, **Mrs. Irma Wilson,** a former English teacher, who did her utmost to assure readers the correct sentence structure, etc., and my new loving wife, **Laura,** who has spent endless hours encouraging me and helping complete this demanding task, as well as proofreading almost every word. Moreover, she is also business manager of the book — a king-size undertaking.

Special thanks also go to **Ron McMillen,** owner of Sigler Printing and Publishing Company of Ames and now publisher of all my books, whose advice and cooperation is much appreciated; and to **Dave Popelka,** also with the Sigler firm, who has supervised all of my input. They have both been most helpful.

There are many others at the publishing company, and at *Wallaces Farmer,* and elsewhere, who have also been very helpful, and many friends who have suggested names of possible *"The Way It Was "* articles, but their names are just too numerous to mention.

Still others have also helped, including farm and civic officials, community leaders, fellow editors, women's club members, military veterans, athletic directors, AGR fraternity brothers and friends at the Farmhouse fraternity, livestock breed association officers, crop specialists, fair managers, and a host of others.

Last, but by no means least, my heartfelt gratitude goes to all those friendly, meaningful men and women I have been privileged to feature or recognize in my magazine columns and in this book. The total now must exceed 300 — possibly 400. Obviously, without their cooperation and participation, there could have been no columns and would be no book. My sincerest appreciation is extended to all.

Much gratitude must also go to family members of persons featured in the columns for their help in providing photos and special facts for this book.

It should be added that while the goal all of us had set was to have a column in *Wallaces Farmer* every month — and at times, two or more — this was not achieved completely. For various reasons, an occasional month was skipped.

Every effort has been made to include every column written for *Wallaces Farmer* in this book. However, because of neglect on my part, one or two columns have been lost or mislaid. For this I am deeply sorry and extend my apology.

All in all, however, I am proud to present this, my ninth book, for your interest and approval.

Irma Wilson	Laura Plambeck	Ruth Schultz
Editorial Assistant	*Business Manager*	*Secretary and Typist*

TABLE OF CONTENTS

CHAPTER I - 1978   PAGE

January - From $10 an Acre to $3000 for Iowa Land 2
Albert Weston

February - This is Your Life-V.B. Hamilton 4
V.B. Hamilton

March - A Veteran Farmer Remembers 6
Carl Anderson

April - 88-Year-Old Farmer Helps Develop Major League Stars 8
Otis and Royal Tuttle

May - May Beef Month Originator Interviewed 9
J.C. Holbert

June - Soil Conservation was Helming's Life 11
Edwin Helming

July - Durk Offringa - Holland Native, American Patriot 12
Durk Offringa

September - State Fair Honors Guthrie County Couple 13
Mr. & Mrs. Carl Peters

October - Carl Marcue, 87, Handicapped, But Still Going Strong 14
Carl Marcue

November - Husking Champion Remembers 16
Ben Grimmius

December - Christmas Letters - A 27-Year Tradition 18
Mr. & Mrs. William Yungclas

CHAPTER II - 1979   PAGE

January - He Remembers WWI Land Boom 22
B.W. Lodwick

February - Ruth Sayre Led Farm Women for 40 Years 23
Ruth Buxton Sayre

March - Clarence Hill, Master Farmer, Happy Retiree 24
Mr. & Mrs. Clarence Hill

April - Ag Teacher Recalls Birth of Iowa FFA 26
Bud Hoopes

May - Ray Pim - Veteran Stockman Enthusiast, Beef Promoter 27
Ray Pim

June - Pioneer Dairy Promoter 29
Chet Schoby

July - Leading Iowa Horseman Exhibits at Big Fairs 31
Herb Schneckloth

August - 88-Year-Old Ready for National Plowing Matches 33
Jack Raines

September - 101-Year-Old Still Enjoys Gardening 35
Ernie Tompkins

October - Pope's Visit Recalls Ligutti's Granger Project 36
Monsignor Luigitti, Mr. & Mrs. Charles Kohler, Mrs. Battini, Tom Sosky, Mr. & Mrs. John Loma, Herman Danti, Cleo Bermda

November - Paul Taff, Youth Leader for 70 Years 38
Paul Taff

December - Christmas Memories from Long Ago 39
Rose Storm Summers, Mae Kennedy, Platt Taylor, Mrs. Ruth Livingston Mills, Homer Gardner, Lt. Gen. Ray Fountain

CHAPTER III - 1980

January - H.R. Gross Retains Interest In Politics 42
H.R. Gross

February - Martin Mosher, Iowa's First County Agent 43
Martin L. Mosher

March - J.M. Steddom - Master Farmer, Master Pork Producer 45
Mr. & Mrs. J. Marion Steddom

April - Egg Factory Succeeds as Total Family Project 47
Mr. & Mrs. Dwight Smith & family

May - Pride in Beef 49
Addis Greiman

June - Over a Half Centure of Dairy Farming 50
Mr. & Mrs. Howie Lang & family

July - Goode Family Holds Exceptionally Good Family Reunions 52
Mr. & Mrs. Victor Goode & family

August - Triggs has Enjoyed 70 Years In the Show Ring 54
J.W. & Merritt Triggs

September - Hosts Relive Past Farm Progress Shows 55
Bill & Ed Fry, Mr. & Mrs. Earl Elijah, Richard Elijah, Art Ride, Dwayne Gerlach, Mr. & Mrs. Willard Gerlach, Mr. & Mrs. Bill New, Robert Jones, Ed & Keith Stuart, Otto Thompson, Maurice Crawford

November - Memories Treasured by a 1928 Master Farm Homemaker 58
Mrs. Mabel Smith

December - The Spirit of Christmas Past 60
"Uncle Henry" Wallace

CHAPTER IV - 1981   PAGE

January - Beeghly Reflects on Gains by Farm Co-Ops 64
Milford Beeghly

February - Eighty Years of Animal Health Improvement 66
Drs. James Carey

March - Frank Crabb - Dean of Iowa Legislators 67
Frank Crabb

March - 1947 Master Farmer, Dairyman & Conservationist 69
Mr. & Mrs. Earl Lyon

April - VEISHEA Originator Looks Back 71
Wallace McKee

June - The Wrights, 50 Years of Dairy Leadership Together 73
Mr. & Mrs. Ernie Wright

July - Threshing Time Nostalgia 74
The Wood Brothers, Robert & Franz

August - State Fair Chaplain 75
Rev. John Clinton

September - Hintz Will Help Harvest His 72nd Corn Crop 77
Irving Hintz

September - Two Iowa Cornhuskers Defend National Titles 78
Bob Ferguson, Lorence Hanson

October - Champion Cornhusker Recalls Rags To Riches 79
Mr. & Mrs. John Middlekoop

November - A City Girl Becomes a Master Farm Homemaker 81
Mrs. Gladys Teachout

ix

CHAPTER V - 1982   PAGE

January - Old-Timers Recall Hard Iowa Winters 86
H.L. Felter, B.K. Williams,. Paul Waite, Fred Metzger, Henry Duin, Mrs. Flossie Slick, Clarence Gage

March - Farmer, 96, Must Choose Between Field Work and Travel 88
Francis Glaspey

March - Born to the Land 90
Richard "Dick" Stephens

June - A Very Large Family, with Four Generations Raising Jerseys .. 91
Fred Metzger

July - Ag Program Sign-Up Worries Pioneer Committeman 93
H. Laurel Dieterich

July - Fifty Years with the Iowa State Fair 94
Harry Duncan

September - Robinson, Architect of Iowa Crop Improvement 96
Dr. Joe Robinson

September - Iowa Corn Authority Became a Diplomat 97
Dr. Earl Bressman

November - Master Farm Homemaker Recalls Hard Times 99
Mrs. Helen Willey

CHAPTER VI - 1983   PAGE

January - Farmer Legislator Recalls Floor Battles 102
Charles Strothman

February - Finds Profits in Lambs 103
John McMahon

March - Master Farmer was Farm Credit Leader 104
Bill Davidson

April - Farmer Turned Preacher 106
C.C. "Cob" Glenn

May - 100 Years of Shorthorns 107
Wayne Neely & Keith Kinyon

June - Dairyman Recalls 80 Years of Progress 108
Russell Bentley

July - Several Generations of State Fair Showmen 110
Hethershaw's & Goecke's

August - A Thresherman for 80 Years 111
Milo Matthews

September - Show Hosts Remember Early Days On The Farm 112
Mr. & Mrs. Lamar Dostal, Helen Hoskins, Lloyd Taube, Cliff Burns

October - Veteran Farmer's Union Members Speak Out 114
Charles Svoboda, Dwight Anderson

November - Master Farm Homemaker of 1951 Remains Active 115
Mrs. Walter Neubaum

December - 30,000 Christmas Trees On One Farm 117
Everett Weigle

CHAPTER VII - 1984   PAGE

January - He's Treated Everything From Oxen to Ocelots 120
Dr. Lester Proctor

February - Farm Wife's Columns Are Basis for Book 121
Mrs. Inez Faber

March - Retired Master Farmers Continue Their Leadership 122
G.D. Bellman, Howard Hill

x

CHAPTER VII - 1984 Continued

April - Conservation Pioneers Recall Early Years 124
    Hilmer Orvella

June - Nine Decades Dairying 125
    Ira Jipson

July - Solar Farmhouse Unveiling at Living History Farms 127
    Dr. & Mrs. William Murray

August - Pioneer Hall - A Major Attraction at Iowa State Fair 128
    "Doc" Dockendorff, Hilda Mercer, Mr. & Mrs. Gerald Van Zante

September - Curtis' 24-Horse Hitch Thrilled Thousands 129
    Roy Curtis

October - Bachelor Farmer Sets Up Junior Youth Camp 131
    Harvey Rickert

November - Master Farm Homemaker Wrote Creed for Women 132
    Mrs. H.L. Witmer

December - 55 Christmas Reunions for the Becks 133
    Mr. & Mrs. Henry Beck & family

CHAPTER VIII - 1985   PAGE

January - Octogenarian Talks to the World Via Ham Radio 136
    Harold Pace

February - Veteran Legislators Foresee Tough Session 137
    Sen. Lee Holt, Rep. Richard Welden

March - Master Farmer Recalls Farm Crisis of the 1930s 138
    Leigh Curran

April - Reflections of a Quarter Century Raising Sheep 140
    Mr. & Mrs. Charles Morgan

May - Cattlemen's Cattleman Upset by Decline in Numbers 141
    Orville Kalsem

June - A Lifetime In Dairying 142
    Herman Eggink

July - Veteran Farm Leader Discusses National Farm Programs 143
    Dwight Meyer

August - Long-Time Exhibitor Reflects on the State Fair 146
    Ralph Bright

September - Ames Landowner Enjoys Same Tenant for 48 Years 147
    Clinton Adams, Carroll Jacobson

November - A Visit with a 92-Year-Old Master Farm Homemaker ... 148
    Mrs. Bessie Newcomer

December - Farm Couple Makes Christmas Merrier 150
    Mr. & Mrs. Virgil Marshall

CHAPTER IX - 1986   PAGE

January - Many Remember 1910 Visit of Halley's Comet 154
    Lena Moffitt, Pearl Ingram, Myrtle Cassell, Nella Eihle, Ida Griffith

February - Dewey Jontz...Involved with Sheep for Seven Decades 155
    Dewey Jontz

March - Master Farmer Offers Hope in Farm Crisis 156
    Herb Campbell

April - Two Iowa Tulip Festivals Nationally Acclaimed 158
    Mrs. Leonora Hettinga, Martha Lautenbach, Peter Gaass,
    Mr. & Mrs. Arie Vander Stoep

May - Clinton County Cattleman Deplores Decline in Numbers 159
    Leo Gannon

CHAPTER IX - 1986 Continued

June - A Half Century of Soil Conserving Efforts 161
    Bill Davis, Alvin Van Zee, Lowell Johnson

July - Fred Schwengel...U.S. Capitol Historian 162
    Fred Schwengel

August - Some Things About the State Fair Stay the Same 164
    Leah & Maurice Keeler

September - Farm Progress Show...History of Farms Recalled 165
    Mr. & Mrs. Noble Twedt, Martha Stall, Mildred Holland,
    Ruth Donaghy, Loren Hildreth, Kathryn Law

September - Farm Progress Show...Second National Farm Event 166
    George Barnes

September - Farm Progress Show...Two Show Hosts Have
Ringside Seats 167
    Loren Hildreth, Ruth Donaghy

October - Town of Cooper Honors its Retirees at a Party 169

November - 36-Year Veteran...Master Farm Homemaker
Continues to be Active 170
    "Flossie" Rankin

December - 107-Year-Old Recalls Christmases Past 171
    Edith Smith

CHAPTER X - 1987   PAGE

January - Weather Observers Recall January Records 174
    Paul Waite, Ross Forward, Earl Slife, Mrs. May Scheer,
    Mrs. Dorothy Pope, Mr. & Mrs. Alton Stohlmann

February - Iowa's Oldest Master Pork Producer 175
    Ben Knutson

March - 1949 Master Farmer Pioneered Conservation 176
    Dale Blackwell

May - German Immigrant Became Successful Cattle Feeder 177
    Lorenz Bahnsen

May - 139-Year-Old Windmill Symbolizes Danish Heritage 179
    Mr. & Mrs. Harvey Sornson

June - Allamakee County Dairymen Celebrate June Dairy Month 180
    Mr. & Mrs. Karl Simmons, Willard & Harold Fritz, Walter Winke

July - Ninety-Year-Old Reflects on Several Careers 181
    J.R. Underwood

August - Indianola Gardener Remains Veteran State Fair Winner 183
    Mr. & Mrs. Vince Pemble

August - Master Farm Homemaker Serves on World Missions 184
    Evelyn Livingstone

September - Tons of Food Ordered for Farm Progress Show 186
    Greg Stensland

September - Veteran Show Exhibitors Recall Past Experiences 187
    Don Mills, Dennis Tatge, Leo Olson, Earl O'Rourke

October - World Ag Expo Topic 189

October - Northeast Iowa Couple Recalls Barn Raising 191
    Mr. & Mrs. Dave Flage

November - WWI Veterans Recall Armistice Day 193
    Amil Laschonsky, Raymond Brock

December - Christmas Reunions Since Early 1900s 194
    Mrs. Laura Nelson, Mrs. Francis Slater, Mrs. Mabel Tomlinson,
    Mrs. Edna McCullough

CHAPTER XI - 1988   PAGE

January - Veteran Master Pork Producer Salutes New Honorees 198
   Joe Ludwig

February - 10th Anniversary "The Way It Was" 199

February - Amana Colonies will Showcase American Agriculture 200

March - "King Corn" Special Trains in Early 1900s 202

March - International Attraction - World Plowing Match 204

April - Iowa Farmer Degree Won 60 Years Ago 206
   Ralph Gruenwold

May - Women's Club Celebrates 90th Year 207
   Mrs. Henry Wallace, Pauline Wipperman

May - Special Events Added to World Ag Expo 208

June - Guernsey Heifers Instead of Wages 212
   Clyde Core

July - Amana's Early Years Recalled 213
   Rudolph Blechschmidt, Helena Rind

August - Pearson Recalls a Half Century of Plowing Matches 215
   Bill Pearson

September - Master Farm Homemakers 216
   Mrs. Lorene Robie

October - Farm Safety Leaders Help Save Lives 217
   Dr. Dale Hull, Mrs. Clarence Miller

November - She Has Voted in Every Election Since 1920 219
   Mrs. Helen Schooler

December - Christmas Reunions Outgrew Farm Home 220
   Mr. & Mrs. Ober Anderson

CHAPTER XII - 1989   PAGE

January - Iowa's Smallest Bank One of the Safest 224
   Gerald "Jerry" Baker

February - Veteran Seeds Man Recalls Wallace's Advice 225
   Mr. & Mrs. Carl Blom

March - Franklin County Cheese & Crackers Club 226
   Willard Latham, Verald Brown, Clarence Thompson

April - Thoughts from the Governor's Grandmother 228
   Mrs. Hazel Branstad

May - Book Written from Mother's Farm Journals 230
   Mrs. Edith Zobrist

June - Master Farmers Contribute to 4-H 231
   Wayne & Margaret Northey, Joe & Duffy Lyon, Howard & Lois Hill

July - Barger Recalls 75 Years of Extension Work 233
   Paul Barger

September - Town Girl Became a Master Farm Homemaker 234
   Mrs. Howard Hefferman

November - Tenant Purchase Pioneers on Same Farm 50 Years 235
   David & Grace Williams

December - Family Quilt A Treasured Christmas Gift 236
   Blanche Hildreth

CHAPTER XIII - 1990   PAGE

January - Family History Fascinates Lew Morris 240
    Lewis Morris

February - Veteran Lawmakers Express Their Concerns 241
    Rep. Wendell Pellett, Sen. Joseph Coleman, Sen. Norman Goodwin

March - The Delicate Balance 242

April - Manders Recalls Major League Baseball Career 244
    Hal Manders

May - Hagen A Leading Dairy Promoter 246
    Al Hagen

June - Koos is Conservationist & Historian 247
    Ervin Koos

July - Clarion Rural School Birthplace of 4-H Emblem 248
    O.H. Benson

August - Bee Exhibit a State Fair Attraction 249
    Glen & Loyd Stanley, Andy Andriano

September - Amana Couple Married 70 Years Interested in
Farm Progress Show 251
    Mr. & Mrs. Philipp Mittlebach

October - Husking Champion Converts Corn to Fuel 253
    Elmer Carlson

November - Aaberg Helped Conquer Animal Diseases 254
    Herman Aaberg

December - Ninety-Eight-Year-Old Kate Plambeck Recalls
Christmas Past 255
    Mrs. Kate Plambeck

CHAPTER XIV - 1991   PAGE

January - WWI Veteran Recalls Severe Northwest Iowa Winters 258
    Orval Barnes

February - Iowa Ornithologist Identifies Hundreds of Birds 260
    Mrs. Gladys Black

March - War Museum Will Recall Iowans Military Exploits 261
    Gen. Edward Bird

April - Winslows Have the Best of Two Worlds 263
    Mr. & Mrs. Francis Winslow

May - McNutt One of Many World Pork Congress Volunteers 264
    Paul McNutt

June - 1954 Master Farmer Assumes Many Responsibilities 266
    Wayne Keith

July - Hammerly's Contributions Span Eight Decades 267
    Lawrence Hammerly

August - Iowa State Fair A Horseshoe Pitching Mecca 268
    Marion Lange

September - Master Farm Homemaker "Carries On" the Tradition .. 270
    Mrs. Caroline Ingels

October - Bachman Husked 271 Bushels of Corn In a Single Day 271
    Earl Bachman

November - Millions Raised for Southeast Iowa
Churches & Parishes 272

December - A Century of Memories 274
    Rona Schaff

CHAPTER XV - 1992　　　　　　　　　　　　　　　PAGE

January - Hagen One Of Iowa's First Master Swine Producers 278
　Walter Hagen

February - Leap Year Birthday's - A Source of Much Fun 279
　Mrs. Lillian Buckley

March - A Vermeer Family Legacy 281
　Vermeer family

April - 105-Year-Old Farm Wife Recalls Pioneer Days 283
　Effie Greiner

May - H.B. Wallace & His Arizona Cactus Ranch 284
　H.B. Wallace

July - County Extension Director Thrives on Variety 286
　Mr. & Mrs. Marvin Smart

August - Veteran Exhibitors Prepare for State Fair 288
　Mr. & Mrs. Harold Goecke

September - Antiques Fascinate Master Farm Homemaker 289
　Mrs. Maxine Gray

October - Community Leader Before & After Master Farmer Award 291
　Elmer Hamann

November - 100-Year-Old Iowan Recalls Serving in WWI 293
　Bill Boian

December - Iowa Communities Spread Christmas Joy 295
　Fred Meyer

CHAPTER XVI - 1993　　　　　　　　　　　　　　　PAGE

January - Record of Past Columns 299

February 299
　Mrs. Herbert Johnson, Collins Bower

March 300
　Mr & Mrs. Lawrence Peters

April 301
　"Bill" Yaggy

May 302
　Raymond Baker

June 303
　Merle Travis

July 304
　Mrs. Armetta Keeney

August 305
　Harold Peterson

September 305
　Amana Colony Residents

Other Columns Planned for 1993 306

Future Plans & Hopes 309

The way it was . . .
1978

FROM $10 AN ACRE TO $3000 FOR IOWA LAND
January 28, 1978

Realizing my first story would probably make or break me as a Wallaces Farmer *columnist, I would have to choose my guest wisely. I knew Albert Weston, 90, a retired farmer and a member of my Colonial America Tours, had a keen mind, a sense of humor, and a very good memory. I selected him as our first guest. He proved to be an excellent choice.*

At the recent national Farm Progress Show, Albert Weston, retired farmer now living in Perry, stood alongside a huge tire on a $125,000 tractor and mused: "Looks as though they've made some progress lately."

And Weston should know. His life has spanned nine decades and his memory takes him back to when Indians stopped at Iowa farm homes. He speaks of his father's attempt to claim a homestead by plowing one endless furrow around 160 acres. There are vivid memories of when all farm work was done by hand or horsepower. Little wonder that the veteran farmer referred to "progress" as he stood near one of eight tires, all taller than himself, each valued at $1000 or more, and all supporting one immense 525-HP tractor.

One of 11 children born to a pioneer Audubon County family, he recalls turning the blue stem prairie into wheatland, breaking colts to harness, and hauling grain to market over swampy, bottomless roads. There was the first of Rural Free Delivery, $10 an acre choice farmland, long days in the fields, and the terror of diphtheria.

But Albert Weston does not dwell on memories. He believes life is a continuous challenge, and that one must stay informed. His daily conversation and writing eloquently displays what he professes.

An example of how he lives life to the fullest was evidenced recently when he observed his 90th birthday aboard a jet airliner enroute home from Washington, DC. As two pretty stewardesses and fellow passengers joined in a "Happy Birthday" song, he said, "Things keep getting better and better all the time."

Weston, and several other Iowans, were returning home after a session with USDA officials and Iowa congressmen Neal Smith and Charles Grassley. Many questions had been asked. And when it came to the tough ones about set asides, the energy crunch, and inflation, Weston was one of the chief interrogators.

The Perry man is a strong believer in education. In an era when few farm boys went to high school, and none to college, he managed to get some high school training and to take college courses. He has never stopped adding to his storehouse of knowledge.

During his active farming days, he seldom missed a Farmer's Institute or opportunity to learn new techniques. When Iowa State College first offered winter short courses for farmers, Weston took advantage of them.

He never misses a Farm Progress Show or similar event and was one of the first to sign up for a chartered bus tour to the 1977 event near Washington, Iowa. Moreover, he talked his daughters, Mrs. William Sampson, wife of an air force colonel, and Mrs. John Maddy, wife of a leading Iowa soil conservationist, to accompany him.

Romance was as evident in the days of Weston's youth as it has been before and since. In rural areas, whenever a new lady teacher came, it was an instant signal for young men to take notice. Prospective suitors paid well to learn the markings on the teacher's entry at box socials.

Weston himself was always one of the first to look over new teachers. So it was that when a beautiful young woman from Story County came to the Viola Center School, Albert lost no time making certain Miss Arvilla Bates was duly impressed. "In those days," he explains, "a fast team and a sporty buggy were the equivalent of today's Stingrays." His own team, "Jessie" and "Dilly", was one of the best in the area. And somehow, he frequently drove by as Miss Bates was leaving school.

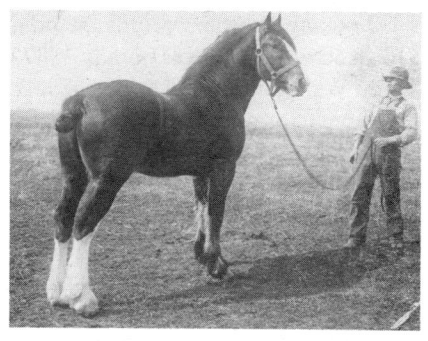

Weston with one of his prizewinners.

All went well, but, as Weston explains, "I nearly blew it once." He explains how he bought a fancy new cutter, and on their first spin, he and teacher upset and landed in a snowbank. Nevertheless, wedding bells rang.

The union was blessed with the two daughters and a son, Paul, an ISU graduate who farmed the home place many years, following a stint in the Soil Conservation Service. The marriage lasted for more than half a century before Mrs. Weston passed away two years after their Golden Wedding celebration.

For several years after their wedding in 1911, the Westons farmed 400 acres in Audubon County, raising purebred Shorthorn cattle and Clydesdale horses, along with hundreds of hogs. Young Weston was an ardent livestock producer and a keen showman. Many top awards were won at county, district, and state fairs.

In 1917, the Westons sold their Iowa holdings for $235 an acre and moved to a choice farm in Cedar County, Nebraska. However, drought and other adversity struck. Twelve years later, after only five good crops, they returned to Audubon County.

The stock market crash in 1929 also left its mark on the Westons and other farmers. Corn brought a mere 13¢ a bushel, and land prices tumbled to new lows. Bank failures and farm foreclosures were common. The Farmer's Holiday movement was termed "frightening."

Weston recalls the introduction of Henry Wallace's hybrid corn and the swing to more mechanization as major developments following the grim, depressing years. He also praises the corn/hog program and the warehouse loans. He remembers serving on one of the early AAA committees, having a hand in pioneering Farm Bureau and 4-H programs.

Weston is a strong booster for soil and water conservation and is deeply concerned about fence row to fence row farming. He also has grave misgivings about escalating farm prices. Asked for his opinion, he said, "I don't see how you can come out on land that costs more than $750 an acre." Similarly, he is convinced that many a young farmer has gone too far in debt buying equipment.

Looking over his records, he points out Iowa farmland went for about $10 an acre when he was born in 1887 to more than $500 an acre in the post-World War I boom, only to plunge to $100 an acre in the 1920s and '30s and skyrocket to as much as $3000 an acre in this past year.

His records show that in 1905, corn was 40¢ a bushel; oats, 24¢; mature cattle, $30 a head; farm labor, 75¢ a day; a work shirt cost just 50¢; and good land averaged about $50 an acre.

Weston believes in farm organizations, but doubts if farmers will ever unite. He predicts the failure of the farm strike. "Farmers are too independent to ever unionize," he says.

As for current farm problems, the veteran farmer strongly favors a set aside. He asks: "If we don't reduce our acreage, what will we ever do with our overproduction?"

On the subject of marketing, no one is more convinced than Albert Weston that increased foreign sales of farm products are essential. "It's agriculture's greatest hope," he says. And with real conviction adds, "If we are to keep on producing more, we simply have to sell more."

THIS IS YOUR LIFE — V.B. HAMILTON
February 25, 1978

The Weston column in January was a winner. Both the editors and readers liked it. My problem now was to find another interesting subject. V.B. Hamilton, well-known leader in farm circles, quickly came to mind. Then I learned he was terminally ill. Nevertheless, he agreed to be interviewed. I dreaded going to him at the hospital, but once I got there, I was relieved to find him eager to see me and to provide me with fascinating information and real inspiration.

When the Franklin County, Iowa, Historical Society opens its doors for the 1978 season, visitors will find a new treasure among memorabilia on display.

Latest acquisition is the Hamilton collection. It's an assemblage of papers, pictures, plaques, and other mementos obtained from V.B. Hamilton, widely known for his statewide leadership in extension, Farm Bureau, agribusiness, and educational circles.

Three voluminous scrapbooks, a notebook containing major speeches, and several drawers filled with gavels, medals and other trophies make up the collection. All will be housed in the society's building in Hampton.

Credit for acquiring the Hamilton collection goes to Joel Esslinger, president of the county historical group.

Volumn 1 begins by telling how Hamilton, a native Tennessean, came to Iowa in 1917. Sole purpose was to enroll in ag courses at Iowa State College.

Greatly interested in livestock, he soon gained a place on the college livestock judging team and went on to win several national and international championships. He and classmate, J.R. Mills, founded Block & Bridle, a national association for ag science students.

Hamilton as a county agent.

Favorably impressed by Iowa's progressiveness, the young Tennessean decided to stay in Iowa a year before returning to his native state.

Ironically, his first venture proved disastrous. Armed with their new diplomas, Hamilton and three classmates — B.W. Lodwick, J.R. Hollingsworth, and Earl Bressman — rented 320 acres near Onawa. Here they tried producing Hubam, an annual sweet clover. Too little capital and too many weeds helped doom the project.

Lodwick became Worth County agent and recommended Hamilton for a similar position in Franklin County. Hamilton, now 80, recalls, "I took the job for only one year, but it didn't turn out that way."

Soon after his appointment, the young county agent wooed and won a bride, the lovely Mildred Brown, daughter of a Franklin County farmer.

Next came endless challenges — forming 4-H clubs, hog cholera eradication, testing cattle for TB, culling chickens, introduction of hybrid seeds and commercial fertilizers, etc. Before a year had passed, he was also working with farm youths in a livestock judging program.

The scrapbook reveals Hamilton's remarkable understanding of livestock and crops, and his ability to transmit that knowledge to his judging team.

Pictures and newspaper accounts show that of some 50 teams coached over a 10-year period, 22 were winners of district, state, regional, national, or international titles.

Their greatest victory came in 1925 when he took his national champion team to England. There they won the gold International Challenge Cup at the Royal Stock Show.

Volume 2 includes references to other important chapters in Hamilton's life. Most memorable are his 11 years as secretary-treasurer of the Iowa Farm Bureau. His philosophy resulted in increasing membership from 19,000 to 50,000 or more and instituting insurance, farm supplies, management, and other affiliated companies under the Iowa Farm Bureau banner.

Another chapter in Hamilton's busy life relates to his 1946 move from Farm Bureau to a challenging Agri-Business venture. It tells how he became a partner in the Farmers Hybrid Company, and how the Farmers Hybrid Hog Company, first commercial hybrid hog firm in the nation, was formed.

Hamilton says, "We were convinced that the science of genetics could be applied to swine — a major breakthrough." By 1960, 20,000 breeding hogs were being produced.

The third volume in the Hamilton collection includes nostalgia and retirement activities. Mentioned are rose-growing, 54 years of Rotary membership, and weekend horseback rides on a pair of Tennessee walkers. A sad note speaks of Mrs. Hamilton's passing in 1970.

There's an interesting yellowed clipping recalling boyhood days and early interest in farm achievement.

Its faded words tell about the Tennessee lad gaining national attention when he grew a record 134 bu. of corn on an acre of his father's farm. Breaking ground with mules on a walking plow, cultivating seven times, transplanting, "gathering" in October, and a production cost of 30¢ a bushel is revealed.

The final volume also gives a special place to the American Farm Bureau's Meritorious Award, highest honor to come to the Iowa farm leader.

One other aspect of Hamilton's illustrious career reveals itself throughout the collection — his nomination to the Board of Regents.

He considers his assignment one of the most awesome of all. He sums it up, "This enabled me to make what many considered my greatest contribution — getting my former college classmate and long-time friend and idol, James Hilton, to accept the presidency of Iowa State University."

Asked recently about his assessment of six decades of farm progress, Hamilton replied, "It's wonderful to have had a small part in it, but let's remember agriculture's greatest advances are still in the future."

A VETERAN MASTER FARMER REMEMBERS
March 25, 1978

With both the Weston and Hamilton columns well received, "The Way It Was" seemed on its way to becoming a regular Wallaces Farmer feature. To maintain the high standard, I chose Carl Anderson, a pioneer Master Farmer and Iowa's first Master Swine Producer, as my March guest. My visit to Anderson's Washington County farm quickly revealed why he was twice so highly honored.

Named a Master Farmer 51 years ago, 80-year old Carl Anderson of Washington, Iowa, has some sage advice for the 1978 group of "Masters".

A former state senator who has received many recognitions during his long lifetime, Anderson says: "Being designated a Master Farmer is one of the highest honors that can come to an Iowan, and one that denotes heavy future responsibility. Some neighbors will laugh, and you will always be on the spot, but the honor will continually challenge you to do your best."

Anderson was one of 16 outstanding Iowa farmers chosen for the high award in 1927, the second year the recognition was accorded by Wallaces Farmer. He, along with Roy Pullen of Waterloo, are the only two survivors of that pioneer group.

Now, as one of the two "deans" among Iowa's Master Farmers, the Washington County man takes great pride in looking back over more than a half century as a member of the state's most select farm fraternity.

Including those currently named, only 280 men and one woman have been so honored over the years.

"It was a total surprise," says Anderson as he recalls his designation for the award. He tells how he had just finished husking a load of corn by hand and was scooping it into the crib when Jay Whitson, a Wallaces Farmer fieldman drove up in the late autumn of 1926. "He asked me a lot of questions about cropping practices, livestock management, land use, etc." says Anderson, who also recalls inviting Whitson to come to the house for supper.

Mrs. Anderson says she remembers that well. She adds, "I was terribly embarrassed because I had prepared a large pot of sauerkraut to go with pork for that evening." Fortunately, Whitson liked sauerkraut.

Born in 1889, the son of a town merchant, Anderson spent his early boyhood in Slater and then was moved to Madrid's "Swedesburg". The oldest of seven children, his summers were largely devoted to earning 50¢ a day in a local brickyard.

Eventually, a neighboring farmer, Del Kennison, hired him to do farm chores. The work was hard, but fascinating. Very soon, the town boy resolved that farming would be his life, a decision he has never regretted.

Carl and the attractive Clementine, whom he met in a University of Iowa biology class, were married in 1912. The bride's father gave them their chance to farm 280-acre Three Oaks stock farm, which was to be their home for the next 63 years. That's where their daughter, Helen, now Mrs. O.W. Hammond of Des Moines, was born in 1917.

Except for some short courses at Ames, Anderson had no formal agricultural training. But soon after he started farming, he became a farm innovator. When cholera threatened to wipe out the neighborhood hog population in 1914, he was the first to vaccinate. In 1916, he was credited as being the first alfalfa producer in Washington County, a venture that led, by necessity, to the use of limestone and inoculants. By 1918, Anderson was already experimenting with superphosphates. Reeds, canarygrass, and other new grasses and legumes were also tested.

Hog production was Anderson's trump card, and again he set the pace. One of Iowa's first advocates of the "clean ground" system, the Washington County farmer attributes his success in pork production mainly to this practice. In more than 60 years of raising hogs, he did not suffer a single serious disease outbreak.

A strong believer in continuous upgrading of the herd, Anderson used nothing but top quality boars in his breeding program involving Duroc, Poland China, Yorkshire, and Hampshire sires. Only the best gilts were saved for breeding purposes.

Records kept by Anderson show more than $1 million worth of hogs raised and sold during his career. In 1942, he was the first Iowan to be named a Master Hog Producer, an honor subsequently accorded to 683 other outstanding hog raisers.

Sheep were also raised on "Poverty Ridge", as Anderson jokingly called his farm. "And those sheep always made money for us," he adds.

Extension service programs rate high marks from the veteran Washington County farmer. The Andersons were also pioneers in Farm Bureau work. Good neighbors and dependable hired hands also get prominent mention.

Conservation has long been practiced on the rolling Anderson acres. The farm, now totaling 440 acres, saw its first terraces in the mid-'30s. Waterways, buffer strips, stock ponds, and contouring were soon added.

The Andersons now live in Halcyon House, an attractive retirement home in Washington. Pictures of their daughter, their grandson and granddaughter, and three great grandchildren, two of whom live on Colorado ranches, are prominently displayed, as are innumerable awards and mementos.

In looking back at his period of service as a state senator, the Washington County Master Farmer regards it as "a great experience and an opportunity to do some real good." While in the senate, he was the author of several bills.

In recalling the Master Farmer recognition event of 1927, the Andersons both smile and for good reason. It marked the beginning of lifelong friendships and happy reunions. And it provided the start of many exchanges of useful ideas. It also brings back a special memory Carl and many others have enjoyed over the years. It seems when Anderson was seated at the head table, the man next to him appeared rather quiet and thoughtful. In an effort to make conversation, Anderson introduced himself and asked, "And who are you?"

The answer was: "I'm Henry A. Wallace." With that, both had a good laugh, and another memorable Master Farmer friendship was formed.

88-YEAR OLD FARMER HELPS DEVELOP MAJOR LEAGUE STARS
April, 1978

The Major League baseball season always begins in April. For that reason, it seemed logical to write about Otis Tuttle of Norway, Iowa, that month. Tuttle, along with his brother Royal, both retired farmers and enthusiastic sports fans, had much to do in starting a half dozen or more Norway high school baseball stars on their way to the Majors. This column told the story.

The familiar call "play ball" brings happy anticipation to most Americans, but to 88-year old Otis Tuttle and his 83-year old "kid" brother, Royal, Benton County Iowa stockmen, it also brings back more than three-quarters of a century of exciting and pleasant memories.

The two veteran Norway, Iowa, farmers are among Iowa's most enthusiastic sports fans and have made countless contributions to athletic endeavors on community, high school, college, American Legion, and national levels. Although never outstanding players themselves, the Tuttles have encouraged dozens of youths to achieve stardom.

Names like Trosky, McVay, Kimm, Elliott, Stumpff, Bodicker, and others — all claiming Norway as their home base — have become familiar to Iowa fans. All speak of the Tuttles as their greatest boosters. Appreciation plaques, autographed baseballs, pictures and clippings in the Tuttle homes attest to the way Otis and Royal are regarded by their "boys".

Grandsons of Osmond Tuttle, who left his native Norway in Scandinavia in 1837, the brothers are proud of their heritage. In discussing "the way it was", they tell how their grandfather first settled near Norway, Illinois. Then, when Illinois land skyrocketed to $18 an acre, he moved to Iowa in 1854 to file a claim on $1.25 an acre land and plot out the town of Norway.

Tuttle with baseball memorabilia.

Farm pioneers in their own right, the brothers started a farming partnership on 500 acres right after World War I, in which Otis was an army infantry lieutenant, and Royal, a pilot in the fledgling U.S. air force. Fond memories come back to them as they speak of harnessing up 26 horses every morning, paying $1200 each for two cows which would become foundation stock for an outstanding Hereford herd, and feeding 400 hogs a year.

Their interest in athletics dates back to the early 1900s when they walked eight miles with their father to play ball. They watched their doctor and preacher, along with business leaders and farmers, perform on a good Norway Iowa team, thereby laying the foundation for future high school championship teams.

In speaking about Norway's sports heroes, Otis enjoys telling about Hal Trosky, famed Cleveland first baseman, who along with another great Iowan, Bob Feller, was with the Indians during that team's glory years.

Otis says, "The Trojousky family lived across the field from us and we exchanged work. Hal was a big-rawboned, farm boy — a good kid with a consuming interest in baseball. We knew he was good, so as school board president, I approved his going to a tutor so he could graduate early and go to spring training. It was a good decision."

Dozens of mementos bespeaking gratitude for athletic contributions adorn Otis Tuttle's living room, sharing places of honor with citations and awards for his work in Selective Service, REC, PCA, rural telephone, and Farm Bureau. There are Hereford Association honors, Eastern Star, Legion, 4-H, Living History Farms, AGR Fraternity, and ISU. A "Friend of Education" trophy is his proudest possession.

Otis philosophizes, "Unless you continue to make new friends among young people, you will become a stranger in your own midst." With his continuing interest in their education, athletics, and other activities, Norway's young people will never regard Otis Tuttle as a stranger.

MAY BEEF MONTH ORIGINATOR INTERVIEWED
May 27, 1978

May is "Beef Month" and the man who originated the nationwide effort to make May an annual beef promotion extravaganza, J.C. Holbert, was one of my college professors. Because I knew "J.C." well as a student and a broadcaster, he consented to be my guest for this month. Here are some of the interesting things he told me.

May is "Beef Month". The nationally acclaimed Iowa cattleman who originated the idea 25 years ago smiles broadly as he reflects on the impact beef promotion has had ever since on the nation's cattle industry.

J.C. Holbert, now 78, of Scott County, vividly remembers the night "May is Beef Month" began. It was in May, 1953. As president of the Iowa Beef Producers Association (IBPA), he was to speak to Clinton County cattlemen. He was working on a folder urging greater beef consumption after he had a long, hard day on the farm with his cattle. He says, "I was in an impatient mood so I told those cattlemen we were doing a lousy job of promoting our product and that we darn well ought to do something about it."

He well remembers the reaction. "They all agreed, but they doubted the money could be raised from hard pressed cattle feeders. Nevertheless, the next day $1600 was raised in a drive led by the late John Mommsen, so we were on our way."

J.C. Holbert, originator of "May Beef Month".

Originating a beef "month" is, however, only one of a myriad of contributions Holbert has made in beef promotion. The Iowan labored long and hard for the beef checkoff and points with pride at the millions now being raised annually for research, consumer education, and beef promotion.

On beef imports, he was one of the first to recognize their effect on U.S. cattlemen and an early advocate of the international quota system eventually adopted.

Crossbreeding, disease control, feed additives, and other livestock industry questions, have also received his attention.

Nor has "J.C.", as he is affectionately known by thousands of former students and fellow breeders and feeders, been alone in his efforts. Encouraging, assisting, and supporting him every step of the way is his attractive wife of 52 years, Mary. One example of this is the way Mrs. Holbert persuaded the National CowBelles to undertake an annual "Beef For Father's Day" promotion.

In the early '30s, the Holbert's bought a small farm near Ames. Sunset Knoll Farms soon became a down-to-earth laboratory for the ISU professor to test genetic theories and prove classroom teaching. Practical economics were applied and it became a home and workshop for students.

On leaving the classroom in 1943, Holbert became associated in a cattle feeding enterprise with the late Clyde Turkington of Letts. Later, he took over the business to handle as many as 70,000 feeder cattle a year.

Over the years, thousands of purebred Angus bulls and heifers, often in lots of 30 or more, have also been sold from the Holbert farms near Davenport and Washington.

Organizational responsibilities shouldered by the Iowa stockman are many. Honors, awards, and citations received by the Iowa stockman are almost countless.

Now approaching his 79th birthday, Holbert reluctantly foresees the time when he must part with his beloved Angus and give up his place of influence in the livestock industry. "I love livestock," he emphasizes, and then goes on to philosophize, "Livestock teaches patience, calls for planning and concentration, demands a man's best, and constantly challenges him to accept and adjust to change."

SOIL CONSERVATION WAS HELMING'S LIFE
June 24, 1978

By June, 1978, soil conservation had become a universal challenge. Soil erosion had become an alarming problem. Nowhere was this more evident than in Iowa, with 25% of the nation's Grade A land. Edwin Helming, a farmer conservationist, aware that a century of careless farming had caused the loss of inches of precious top soil, became a pioneer soil-saving advocate. This column saluted him.

Edwin Helming, veteran Woodbury County, Iowa, — farmer-conservationist and Master Farmer, loves the land. Now semi-retired, he reflects on nearly three-quarters of a century of Iowa farm developments and is convinced that soil and water conservation remain one of our major challenges.

Old timers recall how Indians regarded the Missouri Valley as a Promised Land. Prairie grass grew as far as the eye could see. Buffalo, deer, and wild turkeys were plentiful. But they also recall pioneers with mule teams plowing boundary lines through the rich prairie and that, when the rains came, those furrows became ugly ditches.

As time progressed, the gullies deepened. Spring downpours saw torrents of water tear away fences, roadbeds, and bridges. Floods caused great loss. Millions of tons of precious topsoil went cascading down the river.

It was in this grim setting Ed Helming found himself some 43 years ago.

Prior to 1935, he had lived and farmed near Schaller in Sac County. As a boy, he paid little attention to conservation. In recalling "The Way It Was" then, he speaks of small farms, six horses on the gang, and work in fields from daylight to dusk. Extra money came from stacking straw at $2 a day and husking corn at 2¢ a bushel.

Then young Helming met, courted, and married Almira Peters, a pretty school teacher. Soon, the young couple moved to Woodbury County.

As he looked around his new surroundings in 1936, Ed saw gullies 200 ft. wide and deep enough that stock sometimes plunged to their death in them. Buildings were being endangered. Some farms had already lost half their top soil. Crops on a lowland farm Ed was farming for his father-in-law were inundated. Drainage ditches were filled with sedimentation.

Determined to do something about it, Helming joined with his new neighbors in the local drainage district efforts to hold soil on hillsides. Next, a soil conservation district was formed to undertake conservation practices. Ed was named chairman. Fifty-two watersheds were formed during his tenure.

A greater challenge was yet to come. The Little Sioux Watershed, one of 11 federally

Helming, pioneer conservationist.

11

endorsed pilot watersheds, was formed and again Ed was named chairman. More than 4200 square miles totaling more than 2,881,000 acres subject to erosion were involved.

The magnitude of that responsibility can best be put in focus by pointing out that in 1952, when the watershed was created, 22% of the land within its boundaries had already lost half of its topsoil, and the remainder had lost 25% or more. Incalculable tons of silt were being dumped on the flood plain, filling drainage ditches, and polluting streams.

Helming and his fellow committeemen, likewise all unpaid, worked tirelessly with SCS, army engineers, ACP, and others to have conservation practices adopted on more than 4300 farms in the watershed.

Success was not achieved overnight, but persistence paid off. Within a decade, more than 3300 basic farm plans had been approved, 4700 miles of terraces built, 623 dams constructed, 435 small lakes created, and 160 subwatersheds established.

Work on the Little Sioux River watershed is proceeding at an accelerated pace.

Helming looks at the future optimistically with faith in the young. He believes new conservation challenges can be met, but, "We have to keep working at it continuously."

Ed Helming can take a long bow for his part in this nationally recognized Iowa conservation achievement. Friends say Helming, who was honored as Iowa's Watershed Man of the Year in 1964, has given as many as 40 or more days a year to the cause of conservation.

DURK OFFRINGA — HOLLAND NATIVE, AMERICAN PATRIOT
July 22, 1978

July includes Independence Day when Old Glory is flown high and patriotism abounds. Few native Americans, however, could possibly be more patriotic than Durk Offringa, a native of Holland, who became an American citizen. The beloved "Big Dutchman", as he was known, overcame many obstacles to become a recognized Iowa farm leader and never missed an opportunity to sing the praises of his adopted America.

Independence Day earlier this month found thousands of Iowans proudly displaying our American flag. However, for 86-year old Durk Offringa, a native of Holland, unfurling the Stars and Stripes on holidays only is not enough.

Deeply appreciative of the freedom and opportunities the U.S. has given him, he flies Old Glory daily from the balcony outside his retirement room home in Des Moines.

For many years, Offringa was a county extension agent in Bremer and Linn Counties, and once a candidate for Iowa Secretary of Agriculture.

Recalling his boyhood in Holland, he tells how he got up at 3:30 every morning, crossed the dike, milked 20 cows, and then delivered milk by dog cart to the nearby creamery. He also remembers how the family and the cows shared

Offringa, left, with Iowa's first county extension agent, Martin Mosher.

the same building in winter months, and how hay and potato fields demanded endless hard labor. Many other fond memories flood the Iowa octogenarian's mind. A great admirer of H.A. Wallace, he called on him regularly when Wallace was editor of Wallaces Farmer. Later, he worked with him when Wallace became secretary of agriculture. Then, when Wallace became vice president, Offringa had a memorable experience.

"I was in my office in Waverly when the vice president called, suggesting a breakfast meeting on food conservation in Bremer County. You can be sure I agreed, but on one condition, and that was, I was going to pay for H.A.'s breakfast. I wanted to tell my grandchildren I once took the Vice President of the United States to breakfast."

In emphasizing the untold opportunities this country has given him and millions of others, Durk Offringa says: "When a European immigrant like myself can have all the benefits enjoyed by native-born Americans, and is privileged to touch the lives of countless thousands of fellow citizens, he can truly sing ' God Bless America.'"

STATE FAIR HONORS GUTHRIE COUNTY COUPLE
September 9, 1978

For many of us, the month after the State Fair is just a time to "let down" or to reflect on a prize ribbon or two, but for Mr. & Mrs. Carl Peters, Iowa sheep raisers, September's State Fair recollections were much more than that. They basked in the joy of the recognition given them for 50 years of continuous exhibiting — and the countless winning awards.

At this year's state fair, a veteran Guthrie County, Iowa, sheepman, 81-year old Carl Peters, along with his wife, Esta, and family, experienced a rare thrill.

Peters, a stock exhibitor since boyhood, and his "bride" of 59 years, were recognized at the fair for a half century of continuous participation at the annual Iowa exposition. The entire 1978 state fair sheep show was dedicated in their honor and a plaque was presented to them. Dewey Jontz, president of the Iowa Sheep Council, paid a glowing tribute to the Peters' achievements. Fellow exhibitors and state fair officials honored them at a reception.

Peters vividly recalls "the way it was" when he was a small boy at the turn of the century. When he was only "knee high to a grasshopper," he helped his father and brothers show Holsteins at the Guthrie County show. "In those days, we drove the cattle 13 miles on foot to the fair," he says.

After Carl and Esta were married, their farming soon centered on sheep production. Since then, four breeds of sheep have found a happy home on the Peters farm. Shropshires were the first and were kept until a Minnesota breeder insisted on buying the entire flock. Hampshires were then their mainstay for many years. A foundation ram, Beau Geste 3rd, was imported from England. Owned in partnership with Roy Warrick of Monroe, the big open-faced ram sired dozens of champions and set the pattern for the breed. A few Cheviot lambs were also raised, "but mostly for looks," says Peters.

In 1950, the Panora sheepman's operations expanded to include Suffolks, the breed with which he continued to win top awards at this month's state fair.

The Carl Peters with prize sheep and state fair championship trophy.

Working together has been the Peters' credo since the beginning of their farming. It often meant long hours, especially during lambing time and during the county and state fair seasons.

The Peters' efforts in exhibiting have been highly successful. Dozens of trophies and plaques and hundreds of ribbons overflow their small farm home. A quilt made in the early '30s boasts more than 500 prize ribbons. Since then, countless additional state fair awards, along with county and district fair winnings, have been stored in huge boxes.

In addition to sheep, the Peterses also raised Angus cattle, hogs, and poultry. Mrs. Peters speaks proudly of selling 900 chickens a year, all raised by setting hens. In 1929, it was her "chicken feed" that bought their new Chevrolet.

"The sheep business has been good to us," says Peters. Both Carl and Esta believe lamb is becoming more popular and wool will always be in demand. They are convinced the future for sheep raisers is promising. In unison, they say, "If we had another 60 years to farm, we'd stay in the sheep business."

CARL MARCUE, 87, HANDICAPPED, BUT STILL GOING STRONG
October 14, 1978

Some people spend much time looking forward to retirement. However, Carl Marcue, in his fourth major career, seemingly just never gave retirement a second thought. Moreover, he kept right on going despite a handicap that would totally stop almost anyone else — the loss of both legs. Here is his story of courage and dedication.

All that talk about mandatory retirement at 70 sounds like a big joke to 87-year old Carl Marcue of LeMars, Iowa. Every weekday since his 70th birthday has found Marcue on the job at the LeMars Savings Bank where he serves as agricultural consultant. What is even more remarkable is that he is a double amputee.

Although the loss of his legs has interfered a little with his getting around to farm homes the way he used to, it has not slowed him down much. By way of a garage ramp and "sliding board," he deftly transports himself and his wheelchair into the cab that arrives at 9 a.m. each morning. After a full day at the bank, Marcue returns home where he lives alone.

Carl Marcue in his office.

Marcue started farming in 1911. After 25 years as a farm innovator, he was asked to join the Farmers Home Administration (FmHA), where he worked over a quarter century.

Marcue recalls that his father came from Dubuque County and rented land for $2 an acre, then bought it for $45 an acre.

Carl's mother was raised at West Branch, and was one of Herbert Hoover's childhood classmates. Several items now at the historic Hoover home site came from Carl's maternal grandmother's estate.

Memories of farming and livestock activities take Carl Marcue back to 1898 when as a 7-year old, he started a Milking Shorthorn herd. He says, "I remember Dad getting two Bates bred heifers and one of them calved on my birthday." That heifer calf, "Caroline," became the foundation of his herd. When he sold out in 1936, every female in the herd traced her pedigree back to Caroline.

Young Marcue took on countless tasks to pay his way at college. A pioneer Iowa 4-H leader, Carl speaks proudly of his Plymouth County Corn Club organized in 1915 where seed selection was stressed.

In 1917, he wed Maria Whiting, from a well-known western Iowa farm family. They raised one son, Bruce, who for many years was Woodbury County extension director, and is now Iowa Beef Processors public relations director. There are two grandchildren. Carl quips, "My wife was Scotch-Irish and I'm French-German, so that makes my grandchildren All-Americans."

A pioneer conservationist, Marcue is credited with being the first in Plymouth County to lay out conservation lines, first on his own farm in the early '30s, and later in his FmHA assignment.

Marcue was a pioneer in commercial fertilizer application. He says, "It looked like tankage, but it produced results."

Marcue was named director of what was called The Human Subsistance Program. And when the Tenant Purchase Program came into being in 1939, Marcue was again in the forefront. "That's one of the best programs ever to come along," he says.

In the farm organization field, Carl Marcue was a charter member of the Plymouth County Farm Bureau. Carl has been a worker in community programs and projects. He is one of the few remaining charter members of LeMars Rotary.

As a pioneer and an innovator in northwest Iowa farming who started with one team of two horses, then moved on up to 6-horse hitches, and eventually to the tractor era, Carl Marcue has continually kept pace with farm progress.

HUSKING CHAMPION REMEMBERS
November 11, 1978

Corn husking by hand is pretty much a thing of the past except for some nostalgic contests still being held. For Ben Grimmius, November always brought its memories of the 1920s, when he was one of Iowa's husking champions. This column told of some of the near superhuman feats Grimmius and others accomplished with their husking hooks or pegs.

Back in the early 1920s, during the height of every corn harvest season, the late Henry A. Wallace, then editor of Wallaces Farmer, received many reports of remarkable husking feats. Determined to separate fact from fiction, Wallace, in an editorial written in the fall of 1922, challenged the fast huskers to come forth.

Among the first to answer the call was a tall, strapping, Grundy County, Iowa, farm youth, 17-year old Ben Grimmius. Today, 56 years later, Grimmius, now a comfortably retired, successful farmer, smiles knowingly and pleasantly, as he recalls "the way it was" back then.

He clearly remembers Wallace's 1922 editorial wherein the future U.S. secretary of agriculture and vice president sought to determine the state's best husker, based on certified reports of the most corn husked in a single day.

The response was amazing. An Iowa County husker, John Pederson, was credited with 220 bushels in 10 hours and 45 minutes of steady husking. Lee County's Louis Curley shucked 205 bushels in 9~ hours.

Several others were near the 200 bushel mark. Grimmius had a big day, but had to settle for seventh place.

Remarkable as the achievements were, they did not end the claims and controversies. Wallace, along with several skeptical readers, felt that yields, amounts of corn left in fields, weather conditions, and other factors could make a big difference in final results.

Wallace issued a second challenge, inviting the ten best huskers in the "one day" contest to meet in a side-by-side post season contest under identical time limits and rules. Pederson and Curley quickly agreed to compete, but most of the others declined, except young Grimmius, who accepted and remembers that day vividly.

"It was December 8, and bitterly cold," says Ben, and adds, "the ground was frozen solid. There had already been some snow, temperatures were down toward zero, the cold wind whipped right through us, and my fingers felt like icicles."

As expected, Curley was the winner. It was the Grundy County youth, however, who sprang the surprise of the day. His net was close to the winner's load, and well ahead of Pederson.

The following year, in a state match on the Newlin farm near Des Moines, young Grimmius again placed second in a contest won by John Rickleman, a seasoned Lee County husker. More than a thousand persons attended the 1923 match, signalling the rapidly growing interest in husking contests.

Grimmius, champion corn husker.

In 1924, Ben Grimmius did some serious "practicing" for the state meet. One day he picked 220 bushels in 10 hours and 20 minutes. When the state contest was over, the 19-year old husker was Iowa's winner, thereby laying his first claim to the "All American Corn Husker's" citation he subsequently received.

The year 1924 also marked the staging of the first of 19 annual interstate and national contests. The event was held near Alleman on another bitterly cold day. As Iowa's champion, all eyes were on Grimmius who led the field of six Iowa, Illinois, and Nebraska huskers. Ben ended up in fourth place, while another Iowan, Fred Stanek of Ft. Dodge, won the first of his four national titles.

The Grundy County husker, however, was always the "man to beat," consistently placing among the top huskers and again winning state runnerup honors in 1928.

Grimmius also recalls other husking highlights, including balky horses, stormy days, "the luck of the draw", and warm friendships formed through the matches. He speaks kindly of his home area rivals, Clarence Bockes and Elkie Hendricks, and others in the husking fraternity — Rickleman, Curley, Stanek, Ruel Harmon, Lee Carey, Clyde Tague, and others. "They were all good, hard working men, and good friends," says Grimmius.

Mrs. Grimmius also remembers the state and national matches well. They were married in 1927; and because Ben was either a competitor or interested spectator, Mrs. Grimmius found herself taking care of the milking and other chores at home while Ben was "in his glory."

Now 75, Ben Grimmius continues his keen interest in his farming activities. A son, Willis, now operates the large acreage the family has put together. A daughter, Shirley, is a Des Moines teacher. There are six grandchildren and two great-grandchildren.

Referring to the revival of hand husking matches in recent years, Ben Grimmius says he is pleased to see this happen, but feels it's a far cry from today's 30-minute tests compared to those grueling 80 minute contests of stamina and strength back "the way it was" when he won the state championship 56 years ago.

CHRISTMAS LETTERS —
A 27 YEAR TRADITION
December, 1978

Christmas letters may not be advocated by Ann Landers and others who try to thrust their views on the rest of us. Nevertheless, many people are delighted when they receive a Christmas letter or card from a relative or friend. Mr. and Mrs. William Yungclas have done more than their share of spreading Yuletide cheer. This report told of their many years of composing and mailing delightful Christmas letters.

1978 holiday season greetings are now filling rural mailboxes to overflowing. Christmas cards, with their good wishes from near and far, are universally welcomed. Christmas letters also are frequently included, although sometimes received with mixed emotions. However, there are some notable exceptions. Such is an annual epistle postmarked Webster City and smilingly called the "Yungclas Yuletide Yammer" now in its 27th year.

Composed by William Yungclas, an Iowa Master Farmer in 1951, it is judiciously edited by Ethel, his "bride" of 57 years. Painstakingly written, it is packed with fascinating family news and farm developments and generously sprinkled with down home philosophy, wry humor, clever poems, meaningful sayings, and carefully chosen sketches.

An accomplished writer, Yungclas has a wealth of resource material in the persons of seven children and their spouses, 22 grandchildren, and three great-grandchildren. Scores of other relatives and friends also come in for mention, as does Wayside Farm, the 120-year old Yungclas family farm, now incorporated, with Bruce and Tom, the two oldest sons, actively in charge of the 580-acre crop/livestock operation.

The five other living children and their families are scattered far and wide. Don is a minister in Wichita, Kansas; Virginia is married to Roger Wold, a California banker; Gretchen's husband is Roger Forrester, a food chain manager in Illinois; Kreg and his family have a Denver construction firm; and the youngest, Bill, Jr., is Iowa State University admissions director. The goings and comings of the entire clan, now numbering 41, provide an abundance of Christmas letter grist for "Bill's Mill."

Mr. & Mrs. William "Bill" Yungclas with pictures of grandchildren in background.

Both Ethel and Bill are now entering their 80s. Blessed with generally good health and excellent memories, both vividly recall "the way it was" during their youth and early marriage, as well as the ensuing half century. Much of this comes through in the Christmas letters and in numerous unpublished manuscripts written primarily for the family.

A quick look at the file of Yungclas holiday letters reveals a kaleidoscope of community and family history. Spiced with witty comment, the letters chronicle a quarter century of activities, achievements, triumphs, and tragedy.

Few Golden Agers could be more active or happier than Ethel and Bill Yungclas in their sunset years. Nor could anyone have a pleasanter, more optimistic outlook on life as spelled out in one of their Christmas letters where the blessings of time are linked with the joy and peace of Christmas. The closing words in that letter are, "There is no greater joy than glimpsing the first shining rays of God's new day. Greet it joyously, use it tenderly, share it abundantly, and dismiss it reverently. Tomorrows are wonderful. Use them well. Merry Christmas."

The way it was . . .
1979

HE REMEMBERS WWI LAND BOOM
January, 1979

The second year of our "The Way It Was" columns began on an interesting note. It recalled another time when land prices had skyrocketed. I well remembered that similar earlier period and personally knew the pain land "booms and busts" can cause. B.W. Lodwick, a close friend and college fraternity brother, had gone through the same trying times. Mindful of this, I chose "Lod", as we all knew him, who had made helping deserving young farm couples his life's work, for my first 1979 column guest.

As inflation looms larger, and as land prices, production costs, and interest rates go ever higher, many veteran farm observers wonder what it will eventually lead to. Among those who vividly remember "the way it was" during the boom period right after World War I — and its aftermath — is B.W. Lodwick. He was a pioneer county agent and first director of Rural Resettlement and Farm Security Administrations in Iowa.

Lodwick, now 82, learned adversity early in life. Born near Mystic, Iowa, where his mother died before he was two, he was raised on what he terms "the poorest farm in one of the state's poorest counties." Recalling those trying boyhood years working on farms and in nearby coal mines, Lodwick says, "Had it not been for Grandfather's Civil War pension of $30 a month, we would all have starved."

On graduation, after working his way through Iowa State College, an ill-fated Hubam seed venture with three classmates caused Lodwick to turn to county agent work in the "boom and bust" period of the 20s. He served Poweshiek, Worth and Fayette Counties with distinction; and while in Worth County, he married attractive Alva Gaarder.

By 1953, effects of the 1929-32 depression, coupled with a widespread drought, hit hard in Iowa. In connection with nationwide emergency relief administration efforts, Lodwick was drafted to head Iowa's Rural Resettlement Corporation, later called the Farm Security Administration.

The loan applicants, many of them former hired men, were at the bottom of the economic totem pole, unable to get credit anywhere else. Lodwick says, "All were deserving, and they numbered in the thousands."

One of Lodwick's most memorable experiences was the 1936 Governor's Drought Conference convened in Des Moines by President Roosevelt and attended by governors of seven drought stricken states, including Governor Landon of Kansas, 1936 GOP presidential nominee. Lodwick vividly remembers being seated directly behind the President and noting FDR's awareness of drought and conservation problems and his confidence and decisiveness in facing the issues.

B.W. "Lod" Lodwick

In 1937, the Iowa FSA director was drafted to the agency's regional office in Indianapolis to help with the resettlement of farmers whose land had been taken by the government establish a five-state Tenant Purchase Program. In this assignment, Lodwick directed the purchase of 170,000 acres of land by deserving tenants.

RUTH SAYRE LED FARM WOMEN FOR 40 YEARS
February, 1979

Since the very beginning of modern agriculture — and even before — the role of a farm wife was largely limited to being an unsung, silent partner. However, when I first met Mrs. Ruth Buxton Sayre in her farm home, I realized that pattern had changed a lot; and by the time I wrote this column, I realized how much she had done to elevate the status of country women.

ERA and other women's right leaders are now constantly in the news. Farm women, however, regard Bella Abzug and other activist women's libbers as "Joannie Come Latelies." Long before NOW and similar women's movements were underway, rural homemakers had already organized to help bring farm women into the mainstream of civic action.

Sixty or more years ago, farm homemaker groups, extension service units, home economics and 4-H clubs, and other programs were already advocating participation in public affairs. And for more than half a century, an Iowa farm wife was the guiding spirit in these efforts.

Ruth Buxton Sayre of Indianola, an Iowa Master Farm Homemaker, looks back on "the way it was" when she first pioneered programs for farm women. In 1918, while teaching Latin, history, and English, she was married to Raymond Sayre, a young Warren County farmer then in WWI service. The next year, the couple borrowed money to buy machinery and stock to start farming.

Mrs. Sayre vividly recalls helping make hay, shock oats, drive horses, plant garden, and handle setting hens. "But I never did the milking." she adds.

As a new bride, she especially remembers her concern about serving meals to 15 hungry men in their threshing crew, fully realizing that she would be judged solely on her cooking ability. She also recalls the new chick incubator, linoleum, and kitchen curtains, as well as the party telephone line with all its eavesdroppers. She even remembers the Sayre's ring was "two shorts and a long."

Four children were welcomed into the Sayre farm home. As the family grew, more land was acquired and the home enlarged.

Mrs. Ruth Sayre, President Associated Country Women of the World.

23

Meanwhile, Ruth found herself deeply involved in organizing a farm women's club in her local township. She reminisces: "It took a lot of time and work and I heard many excuses, but we succeeded even though some husbands insisted they wanted no part of it for their wives." It was the first step in a 50-year career devoted to inspiring rural homemakers to participate in community, state, and national challenges, and to county, state and national leadership in Farm Bureau women's activities. Beginning in 1921, Mrs. Sayre served as township Farm Bureau women's director. In 1924, she became Warren County's women's chairman, registering countless miles on the family's "Model T" in organizing clubs, an effort that led to her selection as a district committeewoman in 1931 and state Farm Bureau women's head in 1937.

After faster transportation, better communication, and more labor saving appliances came to rural America, Mrs. Sayre urged farm wives to devote more time to group activities, farm legislation, and community affairs. Her enthusiasm and eloquence as Iowa's Farm Bureau women's chairman was soon noted by American Farm Bureau and other leaders. By 1938, she had been named midwest regional director of the Associated Country Women of America. Ten years later, she was elevated to the ACWA presidency.

As the dynamic spokesman for more than a million American farm homemakers, Mrs. Sayre's influence was felt around the globe. She became active in Associated Country Women of the World, the international farm women's organization, and was later named the ACWW president. In the meantime, her husband had passed away.

CLARENCE HILL, MASTER FARMER, HAPPY RETIREE
March, 1979

Few columns have been more challenging to write and summarize than the one featuring Clarence Hill, in whose memory this book has been dedicated. A master farmer, master craftsman, master conversationalist, master humorist, and master of much else, Hill always delighted in giving me a "hard time". Especially was this true when I tried to summarize all his achievements, and those of his charming (and patient) wife and delightful family.

When *WALLACE'S FARMER's* 1979 class of Master Farmers was honored in Des Moines, March 22, many of those recognized in previous years were present to applaud the new inductees into the state's most prestigious farm group.

Among the best known and most popular of the "alums" present was a Dallas County couple, Mr. and Mrs. Clarence Hill. In earlier years, his father and brother, Howard, had been similarly recognized.

Ag innovator, able manager, community leader, wood craftsman, writer, speaker, and humorist, Hill and his "bride" of 45 years received the Master Farmer recognition exactly a quarter century ago. Devoted parents of a family of five, proud grandparents of 13, pacesetters in farming, active in church and school, and enthusiastic community workers, the Dallas County pair symbolize the creed,

"Good Farming - Clear Thinking - Right Living", and has set a significant example for all to follow.

Now 77, and remarkably active despite two coronaries and a mild stroke, Hill is eloquent testimony that creative hobbies and a desire to share skills and teach others is all important.

A well-equipped woodworking shop, along with an abiding interest in the family's farm and the community youth, have kept him young, alert, and active. Meanwhile, Mable, her husband's "guiding light," not only helps with his hobbies, but has several of her own centered around church activities, CROP projects, and the goodies made in her inviting farm kitchen.

Hill in Granddad's workshop amid two of his 87 grandfather clocks.

"Prepare ahead," are key words in the Hills' retirement success. Not only does this apply to the woodcraft and other hobbies, but also to the family's estate planning. In that regard, Hill says he is shocked at how many people are not preparing either for retirement or the settling of their estate.

The Hills have worked out a plan that recognizes needs for the present and the future. With the full cooperation of all five children and their spouses, they have devised an estate settlement plan equitable to all, and one that assures family continuity on the farm where "grandfather" J.B. Hill first settled in 1866.

Harold Hill, youngest of four sons, and his wife, Carol, purchased the homestead in 1974 and immediately formed a partnership much like the enduring arrangement Clarence and Mable themselves developed in 1940. In addition to Harold on the home farm, Edwin, a twin, is a University librarian in Wisconsin. Art, the other twin, is a Methodist minister at Bagley. Bob is farm manager for a Sycamore, Illinois, bank, while Eleanor, the youngest, is a Glenview, Illinois, housewife. All five hold college degrees, as do their spouses.

A heart attack in 1972 further accentuated Hill's interest in his favorite hobby. Always a lover of trees and an admirer of fine wood, Clarence naturally turned to wood crafting. Accordingly, he converted an old garage into what has been appropriately named "Grand Dad's Clock and Hobby Shop", bought a full line of woodworking tools, and started all manner of wood crafting.

Soon thereafter, he settled on a challenging and satisfying specialty — building grandfather and grandmother hall clocks. Much painstaking effort goes into every clock, along with precise, delicate works obtained from Germany.

Since 1970, some 60 of these clocks with the Hill emblem have been finished. Family members and neighbors have acquired some, but a sales board shows others have gone to California, Georgia, Texas, Ohio, and other distant points.

Looking back on a half century of active farming, Hill recalls "the way it was" in the days of horsepower, hand husking, and bottomless dirt roads.

In the years before tractors, the Minburn farmer pioneered in large hitches, using as many as 12 horses. Today he misses the thrill of such horsepower because, as he points out, "there was a kindred feeling between man and beast."

Hill also was a pioneer in the use of surface silos wherein silage was piled above the ground and covered with soil seeded to rye.

Frequently, he was called upon to publicly promote this innovation statewide. And therewith hangs a tale. One evening, shortly before a surface silo demonstration was scheduled for the Hill farm, an eastern Iowa woman called to say they had heard of the hay and silage piles and planned to come to the open house, but first she wanted to make certain that Hill was "the man with the piles." Clarence assured her he was and subsequently played that pun to the hilt.

Church activities receive top priority on the Hills' community service agenda. The family has a deep and traditional involvement in the Minburn Methodist Church, organized exactly 100 years ago with Grandmother Rhoda Hill, a founding member.

Quick to give his wife full credit for the family's accomplishments, Clarence says Mabel has been the balance wheel throughout their 44 years of marriage. He sums it up succinctly by saying, "She has been my inspiration while I've been her consternation."

Others, however, leave no doubt they also hold Clarence in high regard. In 1975, when Iowa State University honored him with a distinguished alumni award, the accolade in the Honors Day brochure included:

"Clarence Hill's life has been dedicated to service and to making any part of the world he could influence a better place for all. A farmer first and foremost, he has an outlook of humanism, humor, and perceptiveness and an ability to express himself articulately. He has done much through his writing and speaking to promote a general understanding of the farm.

AG TEACHER RECALLS BIRTH OF IOWA FFA
April, 1979

We all respect and admire pioneers — innovators who were first to be somewhere, or to do something, whether it be in agriculture, industry, education, medicine, in space, or in any other area. This column recognized someone I deeply respected as a pioneer in FFA — the Future Farmers of America.

Iowa's Future Farmers of America was entering its second half century of achievement at the Waterloo convention late this month. And a retired Muscatine County, Iowa, educator and farmer reflected on his part in launching the dynamic youth organization.

Lindley Hoopes, now 83, was one of a small handful of men presiding over the birth of FFA. He has watched its amazing growth from less than 50 boys in two chapters to more than 14,200 in 257 units now.

Recalling "the way it was" back then, Hoopes, known best as "Bud," became a pioneer vo ag teacher at Muscatine in 1922. Four years later, he organized Iowa's first Ag Club which, on August 14, 1929, became the nucleus for Iowa's oldest FFA chapter.

Lindley "Bud" Hoopes, outstanding Vo Ag teacher.

Twenty-one charter members made up that first Muscatine FFA unit. Later Hoopes was to see the number grow to as many as 98 members in a single year.

Early programs centered largely on livestock judging and production. Later, emphasis shifted to personal development with public speaking, parliamentary procedure, farm safety, and leadership stressed. There was also training in soil conservation, farm management, record keeping, veterinary medicine, floriculture, landscaping, animal nutrition, and the like. City youths, as well as farm boys, were attracted.

Under Hoopes's leadership, Muscatine FFA soon became a model for other Iowa chapters. This unit helped organize other chapters. Hoopes takes great pride in the accomplishments of his boys. State office records show Muscatine's FFA chapter has boasted four state FFA presidents, six vice presidents, three American Farmer degree winners, and 83 Iowa Farmer degree winners, - 44 of them under Hoopes's tutelage.

Hoopes' own two sons were also in his classes and have brought special pride to their parents. Joe became a vo ag teacher at Monroe and Tom has taken over the home farm in Muscatine.

On August 14, many of Hoopes's former students will return to Muscatine to celebrate the chapter's 50th anniversary and to honor their long time ag instructor and friend. In summing up his many years as an advisor and supporter, Hoopes says, "It's gratifying to have been so deeply involved in the formation of FFA in Iowa. Future farmers have a glorious, golden past, and I am certain they can look forward to an even brighter future in the next half century."

Gerald Barton, state FFA advisor, has known Hoopes for many years. He says, "It was men like Lindley Hoopes, C.E. Bundy, and the late Hampton Hall who laid the foundation that has enabled FFA to become such a strong force in agriculture. Hoopes has inspired thousands of young men and women to assume a greater role in citizenship and leadership."

RAY PIM — VETERAN STOCKMAN ENTHUSIAST BEEF PROMOTER
May, 1979

Cattle feeding has long been a major undertaking in the Midwest and it has seen remarkable advances over the years. Back home in my youth, we fed cattle the old fashioned way. When I learned of how closely Ray Pim's early experiences paralleled mine, and how he had changed to modern ways, I resolved his career as a stockman would make a great May Beef Month story.

May "Beef Month" found a veteran Lucas County stockman, 82year old Ray Pim, recalling three-quarters of a century in the cattle industry and reflecting on "the way it was" in the early 1900s, and the dramatic changes since then.

Back in 1902, Ray was already helping his father feed cattle. Ear corn carried in baskets was broken over edges of homemade wooden bunks. Yards were small and muddy. On feed were 20, 4year old Red Poll steers averaging over 1700 lb. Sale prices were at $3.50 per cwt.

This year Pim is still helping feed stock, but the contrast with 1902 is great. Instead of wading through mud, he gets around in a new pickup. Small dirt feedyards have changed to large paved lots with 250 cattle at long rows of prefab cement bunks.

Instead of lumbering Red Polls, today's crossbreds — Angus, Hereford, Limousin, etc., marketed at 1100 lb. Broken ear corn has given way to alfalfa haylage, shelled corn, and carefully mixed concentrates. Scoop shovels have been replaced by tractor powered loaders and selling prices are around $70 a cwt., a 20-fold increase from 1902.

Pim with Iowa Cattlemen's Hall of Fame Award.

Pim has a rich heritage in stock raising. He is the grandson of William Pim, a Pennsylvania blacksmith who, in 1858, loaded his wife and children — and $4000 in gold — on a homemade Conestoga wagon and made the long trek to Iowa "Indian Country."

On arrival in Iowa, the grandfather bought 120 acres near Lucas for $6 an acre. Next he purchased some Scotch Shorthorns to start Prairie View Stock Farm. In time, he owned 1100 acres.

Then in 1885, the elder Pim's youngest son, Frank, father of Ray, took over. Hornless Red Poll cattle and new farming methods were introduced. The holdings were increased to 1500 acres.

Ray was born in 1897, a stockman through and through. As a youth, he literally "lived in the saddle" helping oversee his father's cattle. On graduation from high school, he enrolled in animal husbandry at Iowa State College and studied under C.F. Curtis and H.H. Kildee. He served in WWI for a year before graduation, after which he joined his father in farming and raising cattle.

"Things were different then," says Pim. He recalls going to Kansas City in 1921 where 1000 lb. steers were selling at a nickel a pound. The 80 head purchased were put on grass and stalk ground and fed ear corn, oil meal, and timothy-clover hay. By the next August, they averaged 1400 lb. and brought $8.50 per cwt. He also tells of driving cattle to the nearest shipping point and how troublesome dogs attacked the largest steer in the lot and how "Old Red" went after the dogs. When the battle was over, the steer had won, but his sale weight had been reduced to a mere 1980 pounds.

In 1926, Ray married Carolyn Deyo, pretty and popular Lucas teacher. They took up housekeeping in the old farm home, then already 70 years old. Two children — Robert, now with the Farmers Home Administration in Washington, DC, and Ruth, now Mrs. Aurel Van Echaute of Moline, Illinois — were welcomed. Both continue to have an active interest in the farm now incorporated as the Pim Stock Farm.

A purebred Hereford herd was established during the '30s. Beginning with the purchase of two $40 cows, the purebred enterprise grew rapidly, eventually numbering 170 brood cows. In 1952, one of Pim's bulls sold for $1065 and nine of their offerings averaged $712 at the Iowa Hereford sale.

Ray Pim's contributions in his community and to the industry are many. He served two terms as a state legislator, and was active in state and national Hereford Association programs. He also served on the National Cattlemen's Association and county and state beef producer boards where he helped introduce the "Top of Iowa" steak.

Ray has also been a "May is Beef Month" speaker. He has purchased prize winning 4-H steers and given them to the ISU football training table, and has provided meat for Rotary Club and other beef barbeques.

A classic example of the Pim family interest in promoting Iowa's beef industry is seen in their operation of the Iowa State Fair Beef Palace.

Despite his 82 years, Pim continues to take an active part in the state fair project. Asked whether he thinks the Beef Palace is worth all the effort, Ray leaves no doubt. He says, "It's our way of helping promote beef and stay in the cattle industry. And it's a wonderful opportunity to meet fine people, many of whom are stockmen like ourselves."

PIONEER DAIRY PROMOTER
June, 1979

This is the story of an Iowa farmer who suffered tragedy and adversity, and who struggled through the worst farm depression a number of years. I observed him rather closely, and noted how he overcame the cruelest of hardships, to become a national leader and promoter for American dairy farmers.

Back in the early 1920s, when the first shock waves of depression struck, C.R. "Chet" Schoby, then a young Kossuth County, Iowa, corn-hog-cattle raiser, went into dairying. It was his first step toward a long career in dairy production and promotion.

His purchase of a boxcar load of Wisconsin Holstein heifers in 1921 launched him on the road to national dairy leadership. This culminated in the presidency of the American Dairy Association.

"You might say I entered dairying by necessity," explains the veteran Iowa dairy leader, now 85 and still going strong. Times were beginning to get rough on America's farms. Debts had accumulated since he started farming in 1916. Prices for

Chet Schoby, master dairyman.

hogs and cattle were not good. Personal tragedy had already been suffered. With three small children to raise, financial obligations had to be met. Summing up, he says, "I had to have a regular, dependable income and monthly cream checks were the answer."

On graduation from high school, Chet worked full time on his father's farm; but for extra money, he taught country school during winter months. Among his pupils was a pretty little 5th grader, Bernice Nelson, who later became Mrs. Schoby and one of his most ardent supporters in dairy promotion.

After his father's untimely death in January, 1915, Chet assumed full responsibility for operating the home place. A year later, he began farming on his own. His first years were demanding and difficult. However, after the purchase of those 30 Wisconsin heifers, income became more stabilized.

During the late '20s, agriculture's problems worsened. Chet well remembers 10¢ corn, $2.95 hogs, and 15¢ butterfat. Many farmers had to give up. Schoby was among those forced to hold a dispersal sale. However, he overcame that blow by buying back some of his best young stock and starting over. Proven sires further upgraded the herd. Cow testers culled out below average producers. Dairy Herd Improvement Association policies were adopted. Eventually, 48 cows were in production, averaging more than 400 lb. butterfat.

The '30s brought more farm grief. Prices hit all time lows. The '34 and '36 droughts, chinch bugs, grasshoppers, and burning heat spelled crop failures. Nor was Chet happy about the overall dairy picture. Imports, surpluses, declining per capita consumption, all worried him.

Dairy product promotion seemed woefully lacking to this dairyman. To prove his concern, he put up large "Drink More Milk" signs on his barns and installed a dairy bar in his basement.

He preached dairy promotion wherever he could, and vividly remembers that first Iowa June Dairy Month meeting held in a haymow near Ames. The late Ed Estel and many other state dairy leaders were present, discussing plans to promote dairy products and dealing with questions centered on funding a promotion campaign.

"That's where I came into the picture," confides Schoby. "I was convinced more emphasis on selling was our answer." He adds, "I felt strongly we must have a statewide checkoff and that I could do the most good for the cause by convincing my fellow producers this was the way to go."

The task was not easy. Countless meetings had to be attended. Legislative committees had to be persuaded. Eventually, however, an annual two-week, statewide checkoff was enacted.

The mandatory set aside was a victory for Iowa dairymen, but Schoby and others soon realized funds from the May checkoff were not enough. A voluntary set aside to supplement the mandatory program was then proposed to run all through June Dairy Month. It was enthusiastically adopted and gave an enormous boost to nationwide dairy promotion.

World War II added to the burdens and problems of dairymen as it did to all other aspects of American life, but for Schoby it also meant another personal tragedy. In 1943, his only son, Frank, who had been taking care of the dairy herd, enlisted as a naval flyer. Less than a year later, his plane went down somewhere in the South Atlantic to add Frank's name to the list of Gold Stars on the nation's Roll of Honor.

It was a terrible blow and to overcome the heartbreak, Chet plunged himself back into the activity on the farm with his dairy, and in dairy promotion.

Schoby's tireless work in Iowa before WWII did not escape the attention of national leaders. As president of the Iowa Dairy Commission, he was one of three Iowan's asked to meet with dairy leaders from Minnesota, Wisconsin, and other states to form the American Dairy Association (ADA) in 1940. Presently, the Iowan found himself to be on the ADA Board of Directors, then an officer of the Association, and, in 1949, elevated to the presidency.

As national president, Chet became America's foremost dairy spokesman. He and Bernice travelled throughout the nation constantly addressing crowds of dairy farmers and always stressing that farmers should pay their own by doing things for themselves. "Selling our way to success" was one of his favorite themes.

The Iowan never missed an opportunity to say, "Dairymen's salvation lies in dairymen spending their own money to promote their own products."

The Algona farmer's success as a national leader is evidenced in a number of ways. Records show that during his four-year term as ADA president, dairy product consumption increased several billion pounds. Meanwhile, budgets for promotion jumped from $3 million annually, to $8 million.

Plaques, trophies, cowbells, and many citations laud Chet Schoby's services as a builder of American dairy markets.

Two visible evidences of the way Mr. Schoby's activities were appreciated are seen. One is a large cowbell entitled the "ADA Distinguished Service Award." The inscription is, *"To Chet Schoby for Distinguished Service to the American Dairy Industry as ADA President 1949-1953."* The other is a plaque presented in Chicago in 1965 with an inscription which includes the words, *"For dedicated service in the business of market building for America's dairy farmers."*

Chet's own assessment of the awards and inscriptions is somewhat simpler and less imposing. He concludes. "Along with thousands of others, we did our best, and as a result, all Americans have benefitted from the nutritious dairy products we have promoted."

LEADING IOWA HORSEMAN EXHIBITS AT BIG FAIRS
July, 1979

Farming with horses has long been almost forgotten. Yet, long ago back in Scott County, I watched closely as our good neighbor, Herb Schneckloth, continued his interest in raising horses. He also became a community leader and Master Farmer, but despite everyone else's fascination with tractors, he bred prize winning Belgians for half a century. Today, his son, Don, is carrying on the tradition of winning national honors, and, along with his wife, Elaine, was chosen as host for President Clinton's Iowa farm visit during the height of the 1993 Mississippi river flood crisis.

Iowa State Fair visitors will see many familiar signs. Those going to the horse barn will see one banner that has been there many years. It bears the name "Sunny Lane Farm Belgians, Schneckloth and Sons, Davenport, Iowa."

Herbert Schneckloth, a Master Farmer now 85, has been involved with horses since the early 1900s, and has been a Belgian breeder for more than half a century.

Master Farmer Herbert Schneckloth with son, Don, and granddaughter, and two of their prize Belgian mares and their colt.

He and his sons, Merle and Don, also Scott County farmers, along with several grandchildren, have been exhibiting at the state fair since the early 1930s.

When *WALLACE'S FARMER* designated him a Master Farmer in 1939, news articles noted Schneckloth was the youngest of the five named, operated 300 acres, had three children, served his community well, bred purebred Belgians, grew a record average of 85 bu. of corn per acre, raised 60 litters of hogs a year, and "knew when and how to feed and sell cattle."

Schneckloth started farming for himself in 1918, right after he married Lenora Lensch, a neighbor girl. Most of the 12 horses in his own stable were mares. And a number of colts were raised every year.

In the mid-'20s, he joined a colt club centered around a Belgian stallion named Major Farceur. This led to greater interest in Belgians. In 1928, he bought two purebred mares from the Hazard and Stout firm of Osage. Two fine colts arrived the next spring.

Schneckloth and his sons, both active in 4-H work, started winning awards at the Mississippi Valley Fair at Davenport. Later, they entered the colt show at the Iowa State Fair and again placed high. This marked the beginning of 45 years of exhibiting in the Des Moines exposition.

Largest number of Belgians on Sunny Lane farm was 75 head in 1940. Today, the number is smaller, but the demand is greater than ever.

Since taking over the home farm and the Belgians, Don and his wife Elaine, and their children, have assumed most of the work and responsibility with the horses and crops.

A daughter, Fern, (Mrs. Harry Hahn) mother of four, lives on a farm near Davenport and was named an Iowa Master Farm Homemaker in 1959.

Don is quick to point out also that he attributes his own success to his early 4-H training and the interest and support of his father and other members of the family. Most of the credit clearly goes to his father. "Without his guidance and help, we couldn't have done the job and we wouldn't be going to the 1979 Iowa State Fair."

88 YEAR OLD READY FOR NATIONAL PLOWING MATCHES
August, 1979

Farmers in their eighties rarely are seen in national competition, but the 1979 National Plowing Matches had a smiling, winning 88-year old entrant. Moreover, the equipment with which "Jack" Rains, the Iowa octogenarian, had won the state title was close to 50 years old.

When the state and national Plowing Matches are held near Marshalltown, August 28 and 29, one of the participants can boast of having more than 80 years of plowing experience. He is Arno Johnson Rains, who will mark his 89th birthday on November 1, and who first reached up to walking plow handles when he was an 8-year old farm boy.

Champion plowman Jack Raines.

Rains, known as Jack to everyone, will represent Iowa in the first annual National Antique Plowing Match. The match is scheduled August 29 and is expected to be a major attraction on the Agri-Power Days program. Cliff Parker of Marshall County, president of the Iowa Plowing Association, in charge of the National Plowing Festival, says Rains will be the oldest competitor ever to compete in the 40-year history of the National Plowing Matches.

Thousands of spectators are expected to watch the veteran plowman perform against competitors from a number of other states, most of whom will be half his age. Much interest will also be centered on his equipment, a 45-year old IH plow pulled by a Case CC model tractor built in 1934.

The antique plow section in which Rains will perform will be the newest addition to the national plowing competition, first held near Mitchellville in 1939. Horse-drawn plowing competition will also be revived at the 1979 matches slated for the Ottilie Seed Farm, 7 miles north of Marshalltown.

State contests will be held August 28, with the Iowa winners then vying with contestants from most other Midwestern states, as well as Pennsylvania and New York, on August 29. National winners will represent the USA in world competition in Australia next spring.

Other attractions include steam threshing and other old time harvest demonstrations, antique autos, a tent city with more than 200 commercial exhibits, a women's demonstration tent, stage programs, and performances by the "Chuting Stars", a naval precision parachute jumping team. Already established are 150 acres of parking, an airplane landing strip, and a helicopter port.

Stage programs and other daily highlights are scheduled. President Carter and former Secretary of Agriculture Earl Butz have been invited as principle speakers.

The Panora octogenarian was one of twelve children. He was raised on a farm near Fairfield and then moved to Missouri — a trip he will never forget because the teams were mired down in mud two feet deep.

After seven years in the Show Me State, Rains returned to Iowa where he found employment in Guthrie County, helping break colts, feed cattle, and operate threshing machines.

As a youth, Rains and another young farmer traded a team of mules and $500 for a threshing machine. "The fellow we bought from was a little drunk at the time," explained Jack. The two young men used the machine several years — to thresh from July through October. Jack vividly remembers pulling the separator between four large stacks of wheat where six spike pitchers and two grain haulers were kept busy handling the bundles and the threshed grain.

The Panora old timer's smile broadens as he recalls his earliest threshing experience. He was only 5 when he ran away from home to watch threshing on a neighbor's farm.

The engineer was a kindly old man, but just when he was about to pull the whistle for Jack, a gasket blew out and steam poured forth in all directions. All the men and their horses ran pell mell, but Jack stayed put, "I thought it was a lot of fun.".

Later, when repairs had been made, he got to blow the whistle for the biggest thrill of his young life. Still later, he watched that same engine pull large plows.

In 1917, he married Ethel Chasteen. Two children both of whom live in Iowa and are intimately associated with plowing matches. Hilda, the daughter, is Mrs. Owen Jorgenson of Guthrie Center, whose husband has been a state winner. The son, Maurice, of Panora, has participated in several Living History Farms matches and will be in the state contest again this year. Rains says, "I was always there cheering Owen and Maurice on, so I guess now it's my turn."

Recalling "the way it was" when he first rented a 643-acre farm, Rains says he had a stable of 32 horses and often worked 8 horse hitches in his fields. Jack adds, "A lot of them were broncos and plenty wild." He recalls one team that would "almost tear my shoulders out."

Rains has always taken pride in plowing straight furrows and says this was a factor in his winning the state meet last year. "But," he adds, "when they started contouring, that ended my straight furrows."

Rains points out he has bought and sold several hundred horses during his farming years and continued his interest in horses until four years ago when he sold his last team.

After leaving the farm, the Panora horseman began restoring old farm machinery and has a number of refurbished plows, cultivators, wagons, rakes, buggies, mowers, and other equipment in his machine shed. The buggy he is now restoring dates back to 1875. A Sears and Roebuck high wheeled wagon in his collection has often been used in centennial and other parades, and once was converted to a covered wagon for a trip into Missouri.

During winter months when it is too cold to work in his "shade tree workshop" restoring machinery, Rains turns to harness making and finds great demand for his services. Saddles, bridles, collars, and other pieces of harness are repaired with great skill and much patience. "It takes 56 feet of twine to stitch one tug," says Rains.

A touch of arthritis has slowed him up a bit, but his daughter notes that on his 88th birthday, he pitched hay most of the day. That he is constantly on the go will be evident when he is seen in action at the National Plowing Matches, August 29. "And," says Rains, "I have no intention of retiring for at least another 12 years."

101 YEAR OLD STILL ENJOYS GARDENING
September, 1979

That gardening is one of the most healthful, as well as enjoyable, of pastimes was seen in the person of 101-year old E.R. Tompkins. "Ernie", as he was known, annually raised a big garden and enjoyed nothing more than giving away his "veggies" — and helping elect presidents.

It's hard to believe E.R. Tompkins of Winterset, Iowa is 101 years old. He gives the appearance of a man in his 70s. An avid gardener, he supplies his friends with vegetables in abundance, writes a beautiful hand, likes to travel, and can recite poetry by the hour.

Born in Van Buren County, Iowa, Tompkins was one of a family of nine. His father, a skilled carpenter, worked in Lee County at 10¢ an hour. To supplement these lowly earnings, his mother took in washing.

At 12, he was buying his own clothes from money earned delivering groceries and picking berries. At 16, he was a $100 a year farmhand.

When it comes to remembering "the way it was," few Iowans can equal Tompkins' recollections in farming and business, and probably none can recall presidential election races as well.

During winter months, Ernie attended a nearby academy. Among his classmates was Hattie Haney of Red Oak, whom he married in 1900 .

The young couple started farming near Red Oak. Rent was $3.50 an acre, but returns were low. Corn sold at 12¢ a bushel, wheat brought 40¢, and hogs averaged about $4 per hundredweight.

After five years of struggling with drought and low prices, the Tompkinses moved their farming operations to Madison County. The first year's crop was good, and the first of the four Tompkins children arrived. Meanwhile, money was borrowed to buy a 40-acre farm at $85 an acre.

Farming went well, but Ernie foresaw the post World War I decline and disposed of his land for a good profit. With children approaching high school age, Ernie and Hattie bought a home in Winterset, and Ernie became assistant manager of the Winterset Farmers Co-Op Elevator.

Within three years, Tompkins was made co-op manager. Hard times had already struck. Businessmen in the community were not cooperative. Farmers were short of money. When banks were closing in the early '30s, Ernie

101-year-old "Ernie" Tompkins in his garden.

played a dangerous game. He and his bookkeeper stashed $6000 in a storage shed. It resulted in a few sleepless nights, but when the Winterset banks closed down the next week, the Farmers Co-op was one of the few establishments able to stay open.

On retirement at 72, Tompkins started a woodworking hobby. He made ornate tables and other furniture. Greater community service also entered Ernie's life. One church building project alone accounted for 752 hours of time.

Ernie is proud of the accomplishments of his children, grandchildren, and great-grandchildren. A son, Edward Tompkins, became an internationally recognized nuclear scientist.

Since his wife died in 1963, Ernie has kept busy. Every summer, he grows an abundance of vegetables at the Villa West Retirement Center where he lives — most are given to neighbors. This year's produce entries in a garden show were among the prize winners.

He credits his long life and good health to "hard work, no booze, no tobacco, no chasing around, gardening, keeping an active interest in what's going on, and looking forward to the future." On this score, he is already considering the Reagans, Kennedys, Carters, Bushes, Bakers, and other presidential aspirants, and has every intention of entering that voting booth in 1980 to cast his presidential ballot for the 21st time.

POPE'S VISIT RECALLS LIGUTTI'S GRANGER PROJECT
October, 1979

When Pope John Paul II made his dramatic announcement that he would come to the Living History Farms in October, 1979, hundreds of us set to work making preparations for the historic event. Everyone was excited about the Pontiff's visit. And for St. Patrick's parishioners at Granger, it was a dream come true and a time to remember Monsignor Ligutti, founder of the Granger Homesteads project.

When Pope John Paul II made his historic appearance in Iowa earlier this month, countless thousands of farm families were among those cheering the loudest. To them, the pontiff's presence at the Living History Farms and in St. Patrick's 39-family member church nearby, was an unprecedented tribute to rural America.

Undoubtedly, Joe Hayes, the Truro farmer whose letter of invitation sparked the Holy Father's visit, was the proudest of all. However, many others were also bursting with pride.

The 204 parishioners in St. Patrick's gleaming white country parish watched in near disbelief as the Pope walked to their tiny altar to give his blessings. Golden agers wept for joy.

Meanwhile, near Granger another group was equally happy and their pride had a second dimension. They were a dozen surviving original Granger homestead project members.

All are immensely proud of their own link with Vatican — Monsignor Luigi Ligutti, a papal agricultural adviser since 1960, who, as a young parish priest, started the homestead project in the trying early 1930s.

All twelve still live on the acreages they were able to acquire through long-term, low-interest, federal loans in 1935, when many coal miners and farm families were destitute. All were glued to their TV sets or at the Living History Farms to see and hear His Holiness celebrate mass and praise food producers, and all were convinced their own Father Ligutti had been a major architect in the papal visit to Iowa.

Granger friends of Monsignor Ligutti, who was known as Pope Paul's "County Agent" assembled at the time of Pope's Living History Farm visit.

Fifty-one homes, each on a small acreage, were included in the original homestead program, enabling each family to grow vegetables, crops, livestock, and poultry. The project was designed to help overcome poverty, combat unemployment, provide nutritious food, and achieve home ownership.

Those still on the tracts they first settled in 1935 include Tom Somsky, 93, who spoke for all in lauding Ligutti as a priest for the poor, and saying, "Without him, most of us would never have had a place of our own."

John Lami, 83, one of thousands of young men recruited in Italy to work American mines, came to Granger in 1914. He and his wife, Anita, have known hard times. But now, as they prepare to observe their 50th wedding anniversary, they say, "This home is the best thing ever to happen to us, and we have Father Ligutti to thank.

Herman Dante, in his 70s, echoes Lami's sentiments. He says many of those now living on the Granger tracts are descendants of the original homesteaders.

Protestants as well as Catholics shared in the homestead venture. Charles Kahler, 77, and his wife, Malona, both Methodists, recently observed their golden wedding in their attractive homestead house. "Compared to the rented rooms we had when we started out, this is a castle," says Kahler.

Most outspoken of all are Elio Biondi and Mrs. Esther Battini, the two youngest of the original homesteaders. Elio says, "My parents and their ten children had moved 13 times and were deeply in debt to the mine's 'company store' when Father Ligutti entered the picture and invited them to be among his first homesteaders. You can be sure we were grateful." Elio, who with his young wife, also was a homesteader, vividly remembers the visit made to his parents' home by Eleanor Roosevelt, and is proud of a picture of the entire Biondi family with the nation's first lady.

Meanwhile, Mrs. Battini, a widow, remembers their former parish priest for his compassion and kindliness. She says, "When my baby became desperately ill and we had no money for medical care, Father Ligutti insisted on her going to the hospital and paying the bill himself."

Recollections of Monsignor Ligutti's work at Granger are many. Biondi enjoys recalling the beloved priest's arrival in the farming and mining community. "He came roaring in on a motorcycle with two greyhounds in the sidecar, a shotgun, and a fishing rod. He got out, introduced himself to those of us standing there, and then took a long look at the weedy church yard." Biondi adds that in the next minute the priest was asking for a team and mower and announcing, "We are going to start right now making hay."

Ligutti served the Assumption Church 15 years. His work with the Granger homesteaders and his efforts in behalf of farmers, catapulted him into the national spotlight. In 1941, he became executive director of the National Catholic Rural Life Conference with Father Gorman, his successor at Granger. Soon thereafter, as Monsignor Ligutti, he was called to Rome to serve FAO and the Vatican where he became known as the Pope's "county agent," as well as to direct Agrimissio, a world-wide program to encourage greater food production in developing countries.

In his global travels, Monsignor Ligutti frequently found it possible to return to Iowa and Granger. He was always happy to be with his former parishioners and immensely proud of the homesteaders.

He told me during my last visit with him in Rome, "That's where I will come back when I pass on. It's home."

PAUL TAFF, YOUTH LEADER FOR 70 YEARS
November, 1979

Working with and leading farm youths can be a challenging, but highly rewarding, task. For Paul Taff of Iowa State University, it was a privilege lasting almost three quarters of a century.

For 92-year old P.C. Taff of Ames, the National 4-H Congress to be held in Chicago later this month will trigger a floodgate of memories.

Taff can look back on more than 75 years of close identification with farm youth programs, some dating back to Uncle Henry Wallace's boys' corn clubs, and to the Three-H clubs, forerunners of the 4-H program.

In recalling "the way it was" back in the late 1800s, Taff tells about the corn, oats, and swine trains traveling around the state with displays and speakers devoted to improving farming method He also tells about joining Uncle Henry's Corn Club in 1903. By mailing 25¢ to *WALLACE'S FARMER*, a farm boy would receive a quart of Reid's Yellow Dent corn, a new variety highly recommended by P.G. Holden, pioneer Iowa State College extension leader.

Taff planted, cultivated, and harvested the plot, entered a sample in Uncle Henry's corn show and then wrote an essay telling how pleased he and his father were with the yield. He explains, "We won no prizes, but it started my father planting Reid's Yellow Dent and it marked the early beginning of my own career in extension and youth leadership work."

In 1904, at a two-week farm short course at Ames, he met Holden. Later Taff was asked by Holden to help conduct county-wide farm short courses throughout the state.

He enrolled at Iowa State College, working his way with pay as low as 10¢ an hour. He was on the varsity debate and judging teams, served as class vice president, and edited the *"BOMB"*, the college yearbook. In 1913, he received a degree in agronomy. After graduation, he maried Gertrude Canberry of Guthrie County.

Even during Taff's college years, he was active with junior farm clubs. Most of the head, hand, and heart 3-H clubs had given way to 4-H by 1912. A fourth leaf, representing health, had been added to the clover emblem.

By 1914, Taff had been named acting state extension director. Next year he led 43 county junior corn club winners on a trip to the Panama-Pacific Exposition in San Francisco.

In addition to extension duties, Taff was named assistant state leader in 1917, and two years later was appointed state leader.

During his 33 year tenure as state leader, Taff helped inspire hundreds of thousands of young Iowans. He led Iowa 4-H delegates to the first National 4-H Congress at the Chicago Stockyards in 1921.

In 1971, Taff was honored at the Chicago meeting for participating in every congress. Since then, he has missed only one.

The recent visit to Iowa of Pope John Paul II caused Taff to recall rich memories of a beautiful experience.

Taff had a personal audience with the late Pope Paul VI in Rome in 1951. He told the Holy Father how he was involved with the 4-H clubs. The pope replied, "Yes, I know about these clubs. Keep up the good work."

Longtime 4H leader, Paul Taff, right, received special award from ISU president, Robert Parks.

In his years as state leader and the 20 earlier years during which he worked with young people, as well as after his retirement, Taff influenced them to "Make The Best Better." His tenure of leadership will probably never be equaled.

Along with golden wedding pictures with his late wife, their five children and spouses, 14 grandchildren and "nine or ten" greatgrandchildren, a Loras College Doctor of Law degree, and the coveted 1968 Vatican's Knights of St. Gregory Award, Taff displays many significant service awards. But none are more cherished than two Partner in 4-H plaques, eloquent testimonials of the respect and esteem in which countless thousands of former club members hold for Paul Taff, Iowa's beloved, long-time state 4-H leader.

CHRISTMAS MEMORIES OF LONG AGO
December, 1979

Christmas is a time for memories, and there is no better way to share them than with Golden Agers in a retirement Center. Six Scottish Rite Park residents shared their Yuletide recollections with us for this column.

Christmas memories dominate many of our thoughts during the holiday season. Nowhere is this more evident than in a retirement center. At Scottish

Members of Scottish Rite Park Senior Citizens Group gathered to exchange Christmas past experiences.

Rite Park in Des Moines, Golden Agers exchange recollections of long-ago Christmas events.

Rose Storm Summers, 78, widow of Frank, widely known farm management specialist, recalls childhood Christmas joys in the Rockwell City area.

"We loved stringing popcorn and cranberries, riding on bobsleds, finding little toys or an orange in our stockings, and we enjoyed Mother's wonderful cooking."

Mae Kennedy, 87, a Polk County native, is the widow of a former *WALLACE'S FARMER* writer and pioneer county agent, Carl, who also served as Iowa secretary of agriculture. Her happiest childhood Christmases were spent at the home of an aunt near Story City. "We enjoyed Christmas programs and playing with our cousins."

Platt Taylor, 80, born at Villisca, and a WWI veteran, says his Christmas memories started when he was only five. He recalls, "When the parlor door slid open Christmas morning, it was a beautiful sight, with a Christmas tree, old-fashioned candles, a water bucket nearby, some toys, my grandparents, and a pocket watch I carried for years."

Mrs. Ruth Livingston Mills, 83, whose husband Zeller died in 1948, recalls happy childhood Christmases on a Marion County farm. She remembers the merry jingle of sleighbells as she huddled under a buffalo robe enroute to church, and a Christmas tree brought in from the woods.

Mrs. Mills also knew skimpy Christmases. After working with *WALLACE'S FARMER* in 1921, the young couple tried farming near Sioux City, only to see their 75¢ corn plunge to 10c a bushel.

Old soldiers nearly always have keen memories. Homer Gardner, 83, born at Ottumwa, served 23 months in World War I, and later became national president of the famed Rainbow Division.

In 1917, his battalion was near Ft. dePeigney, France. The men bought every toy and trinket in the Langres area to give the children of the war-torn countryside a tremendous Christmas. "We decorated a big tree with everything from colored bandages to shiny mess kits." says Gardner.

Lt. Gen. Ray Fountain, 85, distinguished judge, originally from Missouri Valley, has memories of Christmas in both world wars. In 1917, as a first lieutenant with the 278th Aero Squadron, he flew in "Jennies" and British DeHavilands. One of his men shot a wild boar for their Christmas feast. "It was terrible meat, but the Christmas spirit and thoughts of home pervaded that starlit night in France."

During WWII, Fountain spent three Christmases overseas — Algiers in 1942, Caserta, Italy, in 1943, and Brittany the next year. In December, 1945 he was back home with his wife and son for their happiest Christmas ever.

The way it was . . .
1980

H.R. GROSS RETAINS INTEREST IN POLITICS
January, 1980

"The Way It Was" columns in my third year of writing were opened with a summary of the life and times of H.R. Gross, famed Iowa newscaster in the 1930s and later a U.S. Congressman. Gross was my first radio mentor to whom I will be forever indebted for his teachings and patience. In our Washington visit, I was reminded about H.R.'s fascinating career from boyhood on the farm to the halls of Congress where millions praised him for his fearlessness as the American taxpayer's "watchdog."

In this presidential election year, many a combat scarred veteran of earlier political wars will be watching trends closely. Among them will be the distinguished H.R. Gross, 80, now living in Arlington, Virginia, after serving 26 years as representative of Iowa's 3rd District.

An outspoken critic of ever-growing "big government," Gross is a relentless foe of reckless spending. The feisty former Iowan regards 1980 as a critical year in American history.

As the one time Union County farm boy looks back on "The Way It Was," he can cite ample reasons for his conservatism. Born in Arispe, Iowa, of parents anything but wealthy, and raised on a farm near Creston, he experienced both hardship and hard times.

When only 17, Gross was engaged in the 1916 Mexican border clash and at 18 he was in Chateau-Thierry, the Argonne Forest, and other WWI battles.

He studied journalism at the University of Missouri. Then he worked as a sports editor, news reporter, managing editor, and city editor. While serving as UP bureau chief in Des Moines, he married Hazel Webster of Howard County, Iowa, a personal secretary in the attorney general's office. They celebrated their golden wedding anniversary last June.

Congressman H.R. Gross

By 1930, farmers were badly disillusioned. Under the leadership of farm militant, Milo Reno, the Farmers Union was gaining momentum. Gross was interested in Reno's work and became editor of the *Iowa Union Farmer*. He soon became embroiled in the Iowa Cow War, the Farm Holiday movement, and cost-of-production debates.

In 1934, Gross substituted for Reno on some WHO radio programs. Station management quickly noted his deep voice, gunshot delivery, and conscientious concern for farmers and workers. Soon he took over WHO's news division.

In 1940, Gross was urged to challenge incumbent Gov. George Wilson. Final vote was close, but Gross lost both his gubernatorial bid and his job.

The next eight years were not easy, with two young sons and a wife to support. At station WLW, in Cincinnati, Ohio, Gross became one of the top newscasters east of the Mississippi. Next he served an Indiana station. Then in 1944, he returned to Iowa to become news director for KXEL in Waterloo.

Gross quickly gained a large northeastern Iowa following. In 1948, he successfully challenged the incumbent 3rd District congressman. Once in Washington, it did not take long for his colleagues to learn where he stood.

The nation's taxpayers never had a more eloquent champion. Regarded as one of the hardest working legislators ever to sit in congress, Gross did his homework well.

Fiscal responsibility became an obsession for the Iowa congressman. His vigilance in guarding against irresponsible spending earned him the reputation as "defender of the public purse" and "watchdog over congressional funds."

Gross scarcely missed a single hour on the house floor during his 13 terms of service. Official rolls credit him with a 98% voting record and participation in every roll call and quorum call. Supporters say he saved the taxpayers billions of dollars.

Despite his constant criticism and his charges, Gross won the lasting respect of all his colleagues. At a gala banquet for 600 in his honor, they awarded him a plaque bearing the inscription, "To our beloved and difficult colleague with the genuine esteem and affection of all his fellow members in congress."

Looking at 1980 and beyond, Gross says, "Things seem to be getting worse by the hour." He remains dead set against the government becoming any larger and costlier. He believes conservatism must become the nation's watchword.

MARTIN MOSHER, IOWA'S FIRST COUNTY AGENT
February, 1980

The colossal benefits provided to American farm families by County Extension Agents can never be fully measured. County Agents, as they are called, have constantly been in the forefront in Agriculture's March of Progress. Their advice and service has been worth countless billions. They have given rural America pride and self-esteem. It was my privilege to know and interview Iowa's FIRST County Agent — and here is his story.

Rapidly approaching is the 98th birthday of Martin L. Mosher, Iowa's first county agent. Now a resident of the Mayflower Home in Grinnell, Mosher finds himself with much work yet to be done before he attains the century milestone.

There's another book to be written, farm management records and charts to update, correspondence to carry on, and shop work to do. And, as the number of great grandchildren keeps increasing, additions must be made to family records.

Martin Mosher was born of Iowa farm pioneers on the Edgewood Stock Farm near West Liberty, on April 12, 1882. He has vivid memories of "The Way It Was" in Iowa farming communities during the latter part of the 19th century. These are written in an interesting 214 page compendium, *"It Happened That Way Out Where the West Begins."*

Over 140 pictures, maps and drawings, some dating back to the 1880s, help tell the story of pioneer life in Iowa. The book was completed in 1976 and is considered an authentic historical document.

Until he was 19, young Mosher was never more than 20 miles from home. Then he enrolled in farm courses

Martin Mosher reflecting on a century of farm progress.

at Iowa State College in Ames. An eager student and hard worker, he became closely associated with Prof. P.G. Holden, famed ISC educator M.L. Wilson, "Uncle Henry" Wallace, and other agricultural leaders and editors of the early 1890s.

While an undergraduate, Mosher helped Holden conduct corn research. The extension service came into being just when Mosher graduated. Next year he became a member of the extension farm crops division.

Corn improvement was Mosher's long suit. A college roommate and great admirer of Henry A. Wallace, he subscribed to Wallace's conviction that every county had some farmer with a superior strain of open-pollinated corn.

Among the most exciting chapters of Mosher's life is one centered on an extension service program related to the famed "corn trains" of the early 1900s.

As a young ISC agronomy professor, he was selected to join Holden, Wilson, and other top corn specialists on the whirlwind rail tours conducted by four major railroads throughout the state.

An official corn train summary shows 855 lectures dealing with all phases of corn production given by a team of experts including Mosher and Holden. There were as many as 15 whistle stops made in a single day. Crowds of up to 400 or more attended a single stop. Mosher says, "In the winter of 1905, after a disastrous freeze the previous fall, much of our effort was directed toward germination testing. One of the trains I was on reached 31,780 farmers in a 12 day run."

In 1908 Holden chose Mosher to be ISC's representative in Mexico to help upgrade that country's corn production. Then, as documented by editor H.A. Wallace, he became Iowa's first county extension agent and was sent to Clinton County. During his 3 1/2 year assignment, Mosher devoted much time to crop and livestock improvement.

On moving to Illinois in 1916 to become farm advisor in Woodford County, Mosher's work included the discovery of a superior open pollinated strain on the Krug farm. In time, Krug's corn became almost as well known as Reid's Yellow Dent.

Throughout his service as a pioneer county agent and farm advisor, Mosher saw the need for better farm management.

In his work with farmers, he stressed the value of keeping accurate records and applying business principles to farming. Boosting sweet clover as the best nitrogen gathering organism, seed testing, the McClean ground system for hog production, "Trinity" feed mixtures, ensilage for feeding steers, and accurate accounting were other innovations Mosher stressed.

In 1923, the University of Illinois drafted the former Iowan to serve as Illinois' first farm management specialist. For the next 27 years, Mosher worked with thousands of leading Illinois farmers and continuously preached the gospel of better farm management.

Over the years, the pioneer Iowa farm leader has accumulated countless data. Much of this has now been summarized. Hundreds of charts have been prepared. Presently, he is finalizing his nearly 60 years of work in farm management.

Asked about his overall conclusions after all these years, Mosher replies, "Improved crop yields and livestock efficiency seem to be the two major goals to strive for."

Mosher still spends five or six hours daily at the electric typewriter in his small room in the Mayflower Home. He maintains a steady correspondence with his five children and other family members. Moreover, he keeps tabs on 18 grandchildren, and continues to edit material for a book about his experiences with farmers.

Mosher and his "dream girl", Elva Forman, a West Branch farm girl, were married December 29, 1908. Their five children are all living.

As he works toward his 100th birthday anniversary, Martin Mosher continues to keep his pulse on current events. Presently he is extremely concerned about the growth of inflation.

Recalling the depressions that he has lived through, he says, "I experienced some terribly difficult times in 1893 and 1920, as well as the great depression of 1933. There is only one way we will overcome what may well be another financial disaster and that is by hard work and greater productivity."

"The trouble is," he adds, "today nobody wants to do very much hard work."

J.M. STEDDOM — MASTER FARMER, MASTER PORK PRODUCER
March, 1980

A friendship that extends over 60 years — and a respect that continues to grow with each succeeding year — prompted me to seek out J. Marion Steddom, one of Iowa's most outstanding farmers and community leaders, for an in-depth visit. Here is my report.

Your next issue of *Wallaces Farmer* will feature the announcement of 1980 Master Farmer designees. Six outstanding Iowa families will be recognized for their years of community service and progressive farming.

Expected to be on hand at the award luncheon on March 20, are Mr. and Mrs. J. Marion Steddom of near Grimes in Polk County. Recipients of the award in 1957, the Steddoms have never missed a Master Farmer gathering. Marion Steddom is a nationally known pork producer and an enthusiast for international farm exchanges.

He can look back to the turn of the century when he was a Mahaska County farm boy. His father bought a small farm where Marion and his brother were quickly exposed to thrift, hard work, and hogs.

In 1918, when Marion and his brother reached their middle teens, their father rented 360 acres near Grimes.

Although best known for his accomplishments and contributions in the swine industry, Steddom has also been involved in many other projects. Soon after completing Iowa State College's two-year ag course in 1922, he taught Smith-Hughes ag courses at Storm Lake.

Then he and two young neighbors, Carl and Henry Heidman, teamed up for a debate competition sponsored by Farm Bureau. Editor Henry A. Wallace and attorney John Connolly helped coach the team which twice won the state contest. Topics debated included the McNary-Haugen Bill and its proposal for an equalization fee to subsidize farm exports. Another debate question was, "Will tractors ever replace horses?"

In 1930, the Steddoms' rented farm went up for sale at $80 per acre. Marion invested every cent of his earnings into the farm while his father went deeply in debt for the rest.

He says, "We would have lost it all if it had not been for Henry Wallace's Corn-Hog Program. Corn was 45¢ a bushel when we took the loan, but went to 95¢ during the drought of '34. We sold $5000 worth of corn and saved the farm."

Marion married Gladys Holliday in 1935. He met her about 1914 when they were both at a one-room school in Mahaska County. Marion chuckles when he speaks of buying a ring for Gladys. He says, "I got our 16-foot truck bed, loaded it with hogs, hauled them to market, and got $137 for the whole load — just enough for the ring,"

J. Marion and Gladys Steddom.

Soon after starting to farm on their own, Marion and Gladys became involved in community work. Both were active in the Grimes Presbyterian church. Marion was named township Corn-Hog Program (now ASCS) committeeman and a director of the Polk County Farm

Hog production was Steddom's long suit. Beginning with a couple hundred head marketed annually, the number soon moved up to 1000, then 2000. His records show that more than 9 million pounds of pork were sold during the 43 years, with prices ranging from $3 to $30 per hundredweight.

In 1943 Steddom was one of the first of more than 800 Iowans to be named a Master Swine Producer. In 1949 Steddom was named a director of the Iowa Swine Producers Association. Six years later he became president. During the eight years he headed the Iowa swine group, he joined Wilbur Plager and Keith Myers, both of Grundy County, and others from other states to form the National Swine Council.

Other contributions the Polk County Master Farmer has made to the swine industry include serving on the advisory board of the National Packers and Stockyards Act, member of the USDA Market Type Hog Study Group, helping organize the Iowa Marketing Board, and chairing the Iowa Hog Cholera Eradication Board. Repeatedly, he was asked to speak at state and national swine functions.

In summing up more than 60 years of identification with the pork industry, Steddom says, "In spite of problems, raising hogs has been good for us. It was porkers that paid for the farm."

In recent years his son, John, has farmed most of the land. Meanwhile, Marion approaches 80 years of age. He has gone out of livestock production except for a small herd of Limousin cattle. However, he remains active in community projects, enjoys grandchildren Todd and Heidi, and keeps monitoring national developments. Among his present community interests is serving as a founding director of the Living History Farms, a 600 acre educational historical foundation where Pope John Paul II delivered his historical soil stewardship message.

Internationally oriented, the Steddoms have traveled extensively in Australia Europe, Russia, Mexico, and elsewhere. They have hosted hundreds of foreign visitors on their own farm. Since 1955, when Marion was one of the first 12 Americans to get behind the Iron Curtain, visitors from Russia, Argentina, Australia, Africa, Brazil, Canada, Ceylon, France, Germany, Japan, Switzerland, and several other countries have been entertained at the Steddom Farms.

Latest of Steddom's interests centers on the Self Help Foundation of Waverly. The foundation assembles and ships small, easily operated tractors designed for use by farm people in underdeveloped countries.

In his interest in achieving better international understanding, Steddom says, "It's of the utmost importance. You don't get mad at people you personally know and like. People to people exchanges are our best hope for achieving world peace."

EGG FACTORY SUCCEEDS AS TOTAL FAMILY PROJECT
April, 1980

Farm poultry flocks are now almost a thing of the past. No longer do farms have a few hundred laying hens producing eggs to be exchanged for groceries on what once was the traditional Saturday evening visit to town. However, there are exceptions to every rule. On Dwight Smith's farm located just a few miles from my own Boone County farm, he and his family members still gather eggs daily, and by the thousands. Here's the story.

April and Easter and eggs seem to go together. For egg producers at this time of year, the center spotlight shines on the "incredible edible egg."

Three generations in one Boone County farm family are among the many appreciative of the season's egg promotions.

Comprising this family are 82-year old Dwight Smith and his wife, Elnora, now just turning 80, their son, Glen, and his wife, Leona, and their two children.

More than 10,000 laying hens are housed in the Smith "egg factory" two miles east of Boone. Daily, some 9200 eggs are gathered, washed, cased, cooled, and stored preparatory to twice weekly collections.

Dwight Smith, founder of the enterprise, still does his full share of the chores. Each family has its own large laying house and its own 5200-bird flock. Purchasing of the pullets, feed, and equipment is done cooperatively, but egg payments are made separately to each family.

For the elder Smiths, their present poultry program is a far cry from "The Way It Was" in the chicken business when they were young. Dwight came to Iowa as a small boy, and was raised on an uncle's acreage near Des Moines. He remembers helping care for a mixed flock of Plymouth Rocks, Buff Orpingtons, White Wyandottes, and White Leghorns. "We raised about 100 a year and most of them scrounged for themselves," says Smith.

He also remembers hens laying and hatching eggs in hidden nests and tells how the Leghorns were always roosting in trees. He recalls the 200-egg home incubators, brooder houses, and mixing up a chicken mash of sorts by dumping potato peelings, red pepper, kitchen scraps, and ground corn into a large vat and heating it before scattering it in an old semi-monitor hen house.

Mrs. Smith, the former Elnora Benson, was born on a small farm in Monroe County. She and Dwight, who had joined Rollins Hosiery Mills, were married in 1927 in the Little Brown Church near Nashua. Later Dwight managed the Rollins Silk Baling at Boone.

A Russian Jew who visited the plant predicted the U.S. would be drawn into WW II and Japanese silk imports would stop. Smith took the warning seriously and bought a 100-acre farm near Boone. A few months later, Pearl Harbor was hit and the Boone silk plant closed.

The Smiths started out in general farming. Then an old poultry house was remodeled and a flock of Rhode Island Reds purchased for hatching eggs. Glen, then only 11, took to the project like a duck to water.

The farming operation increased to 260 acres and included dairying, feeding hogs and cattle, as well as handling the large hatching flock.

In 1963, Glen and Leona Haw baker were married. And in 1965, the Smiths began expansion of their egg operation.

Smith points out that in addition to himself and Elnora, Glen and Leona work continuously in the enterprise. And adds proudly that the grandchildren pitch in when needed. "It's a total family farm project," says Smith. "That's the only way producers can achieve success in these times."

The Dwight Smiths at work in their "egg factory".

PRIDE IN BEEF
May, 1980

May is "Beef Month". Originated by my favorite college professor, J.C. Holbert (featured in a 1978 column), it has become one of Agriculture's most successful promotions. One reason is because of men like Addis Greiman, veteran cattleman, who has done much for others in his community and whose integrity as an Angus breeder is known throughout the U.S. and beyond. My respect for this Iowa stockman prompted this column.

Iowa stands tall in all phases of beef production. May Beef Month, now in full swing, spotlights the entire industry, presently contributing $2 billion annually to the state's economy.

Addis Greiman, now 80, senior partner in the Greiman Angus Farms, and his family have long been dedicated to raising Angus Greiman proudly points out how his father, Fred, first became obsessed with Angus back in the 1890s. "In 1898, he and a neighbor each took a load of Shorthorns to Chicago. While there, he saw a display of Angus bull calves from Scotland. Immediately, Father resolved to bring one back to Garner."

Angus breeder Addis Greiman.

But to his dismay, the check for his 24 fat cattle was not big enough to cover the opening bid for one of the imported calves. But he didn't give up his dream.

A South Dakota stockman offered to trade "sight unseen" an Angus bull for a Percheron stallion. "Imagine Father's surprise," says Addis, "when, after loading the 1800-lb. stallion on a box car bound for South Dakota, he went to the depot to find a wild and woolly Angus calf weighing less than 400 lb." But the calf grew rapidly, and later was used as herd bull.

Offspring from the Angus-Shorthorn cross were fast, efficient gainers. When sold, they topped the Chicago market.

Addis quickly became enamored with the "bonnie blacks." As a teenager, he worked full time on the farm and with the cattle. Neither he nor any of his 13 brothers and sisters received any wages; but on turning 21, each child received a 160-acre farm, half of which was a gift, with the remaining 80 acres the recipient's obligation.

Addis married Ruth Schipull of Renwick in 1925. He and his bride settled on the home farm and started paying off the other 80 acres. Shirley, their youngest child, now lives in Connecticut. Sons Don and Cliff, with Addis, operate 900 acres with Angus cattle their major project. Don serves as president of the Iowa State Fair.

During the depths of the Depression in 1932, after having upgraded his herd for seven years, Greiman entered the purebred business. In 1955, Addis and his sons established a partnership.

Throughout his 50 years as an Angus breeder, Addis has infused leading blood lines into the herd, now supplementing with AI, carcass evaluation, performance testing, and indexing are other techniques in helping make Greiman Angus nationally known.

Exhibiting is no longer done on an extensive scale, but the Greiman herd has claimed more than its share of blue ribbons, purple banners, and trophies.

With a reputation for honest dealing, and having performance tested cattle of the right type, the Greimans have made sales in almost every state, plus Canada and New Zealand.

In recent years, a new dimension has been added to the farm's operations and income. A steak fry provided by the Greimans for a group of Minnesota Viking fans made a hit. Result was the start of a custom dressed beef program.

Greiman's sons and daughters-in-law are proud of their agricultural heritage. All the grandchildren have been involved in 4-H or FFA, and seem to share their grandfather's enthusiasm for good livestock. There is every reason to believe the Greiman farm, one of Iowa's Century Farms, will continue to remain in the best of hands.

OVER A HALF CENTURY OF DAIRY FARMING
June, 1980

Strange as it may seem, a WW II visit I made to a dairy farm in Scotland resulted in this report, centered on an outstanding Iowa Ayrshire breeder, 86-year old Howie Lang. Highly successful dairy production and exhibiting by three generations of the Lang family are noted.

While serving as a WW II war correspondent, I occasionally visited with British and Scottish farmers. In Scotland, while looking over James Howie's Ayrshires, I mentioned Howie Lang, Poweshiek County, Iowa, dairyman. Pleased, Jim Howie said, "Howie Lang is one of my kinfolk — and a real credit to the Ayrshire breed."

Howie Lang is 86. He lives on the farm where he was born and is as enthusiastic as ever about Ayrshires. Anyone who has watched him and his family in the show ring, will agree with his Scottish kinsman.

Lang vividly recalls "the way it was" even before the turn of the century. His father had 13 cows, mostly Shorthorns, but also including an old, easy-to-milk Jersey. She seldom kicked, so Howie and his brothers learned to milk her.

Comparing the early 1900s to the modern methods and equipment now found in dairy barns, the veteran Ayrshire breeder says, "Then, women milked cows in the open; today we have pipeline milking systems and carousels. Computerized rations have replaced chopped corn."

Production tested herds of 75 or more are common now compared to a few "duke's mixture" cows in the old days. "And as for waste disposal, the only barn cleaners we knew then were four-tined forks," says Lang.

Lang has also noted vast changes in marketing. He points to the huge 6000 gallon stainless steel tank trucks now hauling milk hundreds of miles, compared to families trading a few pounds of butter for groceries in a nearby town when he was a boy. He also emphasizes that today's $12 a cwt. for milk is a bit different from the few cents a pound his parents received for their cream.

The youngest of three brothers, Howie married a neighbor girl, Stella Hendrickson, in 1917. She laughs about their first meeting. "It was Children's Day at the church. Howie was behind me and pulled my long curls all through the program. I was so mad I told my mother I never wanted to see that naughty boy again and would never go back to that church."

But 12 years later, they were married and have attended that same church ever since.

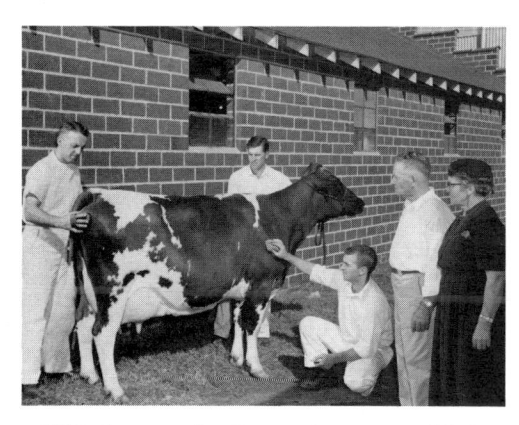

With three sons busily sprucing up one of their prize Ayrshires, Mr. & Mrs. Howie Lang look on approvingly.

Their six children have brought much pride to Howie and Stella. The oldest, Evelyn, now Mrs. Guilford Moore, is on a farm near Grinnell. Irene, of Newhall, married Daryl Gallager. Merle is now state veterinarian. Maynard is an Ayrshire breeder near Brooklyn. Jack bought the Century home farm, while Larry is a West Des Moines dentist. Along with 22 grandchildren, there are 21 great grandchildren and three great-great-grandchildren.

Ayrshires entered the Lang farm picture in a unique way. Howie, with his brothers Allen, who married Stella's sister, and Russell, who farmed near Grinnell, and Henry Hendrickson formed a partnership called "The Big Four Farms". Hampshire hogs were their specialty.

While exhibiting at a national swine show in Peoria in 1922, the Iowans were taken to the Dreamworld Farms to see Hampshire hogs and Ayrshire cattle. Howie and Russell were so favorably impressed by the young Ayrshire heifers that they offered to trade three prize show hogs for three calves.

During their first years in dairying, the Big Four Farms sold cream. Later, during the 1929 Depression, Russell purchased 20 top Ayrshires from an Illinois farm and established a dairy near Grinnell.

A new, modern dairy barn with milking parlor and cooler was built in 1947. Eventually, the herd numbered 90 purebred cows.

Records were meticulously kept. The herd was upgraded for higher production. Artificial insemination was introduced. Production testing and other management procedures found the Langs winning the Ayrshire association's "Most Constructive Breeders" award six times.

Lang Ayrshires were outstanding. Premier breeder and exhibitor banners were won in open shows at the Waterloo Dairy Congress, Iowa State Fair, All Iowa Fair, and national dairy shows at Columbus, Madison, and Indianapolis.

More significant than any show ring awards, however, are the honors accorded Howie for his personal contributions to the Ayrshire breed. He has served as president of the Iowa Ayrshire breeders and twice was named a director of the American Ayrshire Society. In 1967, the society's highest honor - Distinguished Service Award went to Lang.

Although now retired, the elder Lang is still active and continues his interest in dairying. Two sons are following closely in his footsteps. Maynard, now 54, is a well established Poweshiek County dairyman, operating 320 acres and continuing the Ayrshire tradition with a milking herd of 90 top production and show animals. Meanwhile, Jack has about 120 head of dairy stock, 70 of them Ayrshire or Holstein cows.

Asked how he views the future, the veteran dairyman says, "Dairying will continue to be a promising field if we don't overproduce." He emphasizes milk is one of our most nutritious foods, and June Dairy Month is a good time to remember the importance of dairy products.

GOODE FAMILY HOLDS EXCEPTIONALLY GOOD FAMILY REUNIONS
July, 1980

Mr. & Mrs. Victor Goode.

Family reunions are popular wherever and whenever families can get together. Few such gatherings can top the Goode family's annual reunion. My visit with Victor Goode, the family patriarch, revealed that five generations of Goodes come from far and near for the happy annual occasion. Heroic deeds and fascinating achievements, past and present, are told and retold.

Family picnies and reunions are popular activities this month and next. With crops well along and summer farm work under control, there's time to get kinfolk together. The Goode family of Ottumwa is an excellent case in point.

Ever since their forebears, Samuel and Frances Goode, came from England by sailing vessel in 1865, the family has been closely knit. Meanwhile, the present generations are maintaining traditions started a half century or more ago. Each July, the individual families gather for their own special picnic. Then in August, an annual reunion brings all the Samuel Goode descendants together.

To Victor Goode, retired 83-year old Wapello County farmer, the reunion merits the highest priority. Now the family patriarch and reunion chairman, Victor begins planning for the event months in advance.

Large numbers of relatives and in-laws represent as many as five generations and come from as far away as California. At times, well over a hundred persons have registered. The elder Goode recalls one gathering with 37 cousins present.

Huge quantities of tempting food and much reminiscing mark the annual event.

Great-great grandfather Goode heroically and single-handedly extinguished a fire on the U.S. bound sailing ship that carried many immigrants, including his wife and five of their seven children. That story will be retold at this year's meeting, as will anecdotes about pioneer days on Illinois and Iowa farms.

Recollections won't be limited to bygone generations. Victor and his brothers, sisters, and cousins can recount many interesting experiences about "the way it was" during their childhood and early adulthood. Vic, as he is best known, vividly recalls using shovels and horse-drawn, hand-controlled scoops to work out poll taxes. The early days of farming for Vic and his brother, Cyril, will also be recalled. While Vic was "batching it", he says it got so lonesome even the flies wouldn't stay.

In the early '20s, the brothers rented a half section of land to grow crops, milk cows, and feed hogs. Vic remembers driving the fat shoats on foot to Blakesburg and loading them onto cattle cars to ship to Ottumwa where they brought $2.90 per cwt. Getting 80 gal. of milk to Ottumwa daily was quite a chore. Winter blizzards blocked the roads and the only way to make delivery was by shoveling through the drifts by hand.

Goode ran the steam engine on the neighborhood threshing run. He laughs as he reflects about blowing the whistle to scare the girls along the roadside as he moved the big machine from farm to farm.

Vic was one of the first Iowans to adopt soil conservation practices. He used horses to build the first terraces in the state's south central region. Other activities were Triple A committee, school board president, and a church building project. A Farm Bureau member for nearly 60 years, he was county president in 1949-50 and helped host President Truman on one of his Iowa visits.

Victor and Alberta Goode were married in 1929 and raised six children. The oldest, Elbert, farms near Indianola and was once host to President Nixon. The oldest daughter, Margaret, now Mrs. John Sanders, is secretary for the annual Goode reunion and sends out all the notices. Donna is the wife of Cortie Rolison. Two daughters, Deena and Janice, have been widowed. The youngest, James a Vietnam veteran who survived a harrowing sea experience, and now lives in California. There are 17 grandchildren and nine great grandchildren.

Vic and Alberta observed their golden wedding anniversary last fall with many well-wishers present.

The Goodes speak of a number of interesting family coincidences. They tell how both of their sets of parents came from the same community and were married within two weeks of each other. Both couples had eight children. And both couples lived to celebrate their 60th anniversary with the observances in the same church.

Victor continues to be active and alert to current events. He finds inflation puzzling and disastrous and is convinced present exorbitant prices cannot be maintained.

Vic's hobbies include reading, church activities, and calling on old friends and shut-ins.

Alberta enjoys her flowers, model kitchen, church circle, and sending birthday and get-well cards. Her major interest is keeping family records. She has 14 well documented scrapbooks. They are filled with pictures, clippings, poems, family memorabilia, and full accounts of trips made with Vic and others in the family to all parts of the country and to Mexico, Canada, and Hawaii.

All bring back precious memories and are a treasure everyone can enjoy when all the Goodes get together for their 1980 family reunion.

TRIGGS HAS ENJOYED 70 YEARS IN THE SHOW RING
August, 1980

Iowa State Fair exhibitors are a hardy and determined lot. I have known hundreds of them. Some keep on showing produce or stock "forever". One I especially admire is J.W. Triggs, veteran purebred hog breeder. When I learned that, beginning as a lad, he has had 70 years of various show ring victories, and was pointing to his 50th year of State Fair winnings, I was compelled to write this story.

When the Iowa State Fair begins, livestock shows will again claim the central spotlight. Many veteran exhibitors will come back for "just one more try" at coveted purple banners.

Few, if any, pioneer showmen can boast a longer or more interesting record of state fair participation than J.W. Triggs of near Mt. Ayr in Ringgold County. Now in his 80th year, Triggs' interest in livestock breeding and showing extends over nearly seven decades. "J.W.", as he is best known, enjoys telling "the way it was" as he progressed through good times and bad with hogs, horses, and cattle.

John Triggs, Veteran hog producer and showman.

Born just "across the line" in Missouri, he moved to Iowa at an early age. His father raised Durocs. "They were big and lardy in those days," he says.

In 1919, shortly after he married Carrie Hutchinson, a Ringgold County farm girl, J.W. set out to buy some Durocs. However, on the way, he saw three Spotted Poland China gilts. He was so well impressed, he forgot all about the "red ones" and bought the Spots.

Next, he went to Henry Field to buy a pure-bred Spotted boar, hauling him all the way from Shenandoah to Mt. Ayr in a crate on the side of a Model T. "And," says Triggs, "we've raised Spots ever since."

From that small beginning, during a trying time of low prices and other discouragement, Triggs developed one of the best known herds in the state. J.W. has collected trunkloads of ribbons at county fairs, sold breeding stock throughout the Midwest, and been honored in the state fair's Hogman's Hall of Fame.

Many major awards have been won, including some state fair Grand Championships and high places with Belgian horses. While Triggs is proud of all his 8000 prize ribbons and other awards, other considerations loom even larger. "We meet so many wonderful people."

J.W. served on the Ringgold County fair board for many years; and as a founder of the show, was honored earlier this month. His sons are also active as community and church leaders, with Merritt now on the state fair board and superintendent of the hog show.

Merritt Triggs, Iowa State Fair Board member and Hog Show Superintendent.

J.W. says showing stock is a major sales tool and winnings are a good advertisement. His buyers have ranged from California to Virginia and from Minnesota to Oklahoma.

Raising, showing, and marketing the prize hogs has always been a family enterprise. The sons, Merritt and Marvin, and their wives, Lorene and Darlene, are active in the Triggs' hog breeding programs. Grandsons Allan and Kevin will be helping granddad at the state fair this year.

Asked just why he likes Spots so much, the southern Iowa breeder insists they are excellent and prolific mothers, have sound feet and legs, can stand confinement stress well, and gain size and weight rapidly. One of his boars attained a weight of 980 lbs. He adds, "When they develop something better than Spots, I'll change, but that's not likely."

HOSTS RELIVE PAST FARM PROGRESS SHOWS
September, 1980

The annual Farm Progress Show, sponsored by the FARM PROGRESS PUBLICATIONS, *of which* WALLACES FARMER *is one, is always the outstanding single U.S. Agricultural exhibition of the year. I have attended all those held in Iowa and have visited with all the host families. This article summarizes some of their impressions of the shows' highlights 1959-1980.*

When *WALLACES FARMER* and *PRAIRIE FARMER* magazines first combined forces to stage a Farm Progress show in Illinois in 1953, their editors could scarcely visualize the "tiger" they had by the tail. Six-row equipment was considered big in those days. Large acreages were still devoted to oats, and inputs to achieve 150 bu. of corn per acre were limited. Chemicals were still experimental. And soybeans had not yet come into their own.

In 1959, the late Sen. Earl Elijah of Cedar County, along with his wife and two sons, hosted the first Farm Progress Show in Iowa.

Remarkable advances in technology were displayed and demonstrated. Anhydrous ammonia, newly developed herbicides, confinement feeding of hogs, and single cross hybrids were some innovations of vital interest to the thousands of visitors.

Today, as final preparations are being made for the 1980 show to be held near Nevada, Iowa, September 30, October 1 and 2, innovations in agriculture remain the central theme. Nowhere are advances in farming more evident.

The Elijah family hosted the 1959 Farm Progress Show. Shown here are Mrs. Earl Elijah and son.

Mrs. Elijah, now 93, and her son Richard, note the contrast between 1959 and 1980. Richard says, "Herbicides were just appearing then and anhydrous was relatively new." He points out that for many at their show, it was the first time they had seen high moisture corn handling. "It was also their first look at pig parlors, liquid manure, single cross hybrids, picker shellers, fenceline augers, and side unloaders," adds Richard.

Mrs. Elijah speaks fondly of Zoe Murphy, then *WALLACES FARMER's* women's editor, and director of the women's tent with its new microwave cooking demonstrations and mother-daughter style shows. Also recalled is the Prairie Lady model home and the many church ladies who served food to the multitude of show visitors.

Richard points out there will be 700 varieties of corn, soybeans, sorghum, and alfalfa in the 1980 crop displays. This is in contrast to less than 250 at their event.

Elijah adds, "Some of the first two-row picker shellers were used during our show. But this year we'll see $100,000 hydrostatic combines with 12-row cornheads capable of harvesting 240 bu. of corn every seven minutes." He also notes that the pig parlor they built 21 years ago has been dwarfed by today's $125,000 structures.

The Everett Smith family helped host the Farm Progress Show in 1962.

Since 1959, Iowa Farm Progress Show hosts have included Mr. and Everett Smith says, "It was a fulfilling experience — one we wouldn't want to have missed — and highly educational, especially seeing effects of herbicides." He adds, "The look of amazement on the face of the Russian Minister of Agriculture as he was noting American farm technology was something to behold."

All expressed complete satisfaction in the sponsoring magazine's management of the show. "Every promise by *WALLACES FARMER* was fulfilled," says Bill Fry, only person to host the event twice. All hosts praise the show managers: Maynard Bertsch, 1959-71; Chuck Altmann, 1972-73; Frank Holdmeyer, 1974-75; Scott McKinnie, 1976-79, and Steve Cain, who is now in charge.

Rains and knee-deep mud forced two cancellations of the 1965 show on the Fry farm. When the show returned in 1971 was more cooperative. New four-wheel drive tractors, bunker silos, 12-bottom plows, and other new field developments were successfully demonstrated.

In 1968, when the Clause families were hosts, confinement cattle feeding and new harvesting techniques attracted much attention. The Clause brothers sum it up: "A Farm Progress Show is a marvelous opportunity to provide a stage for thousands of farmers to see the latest innovations in agriculture."

The mother of Bob, Rog, Gerald, and three daughters, Mrs. A.R. Clause, now 87, also remembers the 1968 event on their farm. She says, "Our whole family, including 21 grandchildren and several great-grandchildren were excited. Our homes were full of relatives from as far away as Texas. All of them were amazed."

Ricke, who hosted the 1974 show, will again be in charge of field harvesting demonstrations at this year's event. He notes, "It's a power show," pointing out that by 1977 there were close to 50 four-wheel drive behemoths in action, along with an 18-bottom plow, and a four-wheel drive, eight-row combine that "stole the show." A Canadian tractor, rated at 500 hp, was another crowd pleaser.

Mrs. Maurice Crawford, an Iowa Master Farm Homemaker, representing the three host families in 1977, remarks, "We all enjoyed the opportunity and are grateful to everyone who helped." She sums it up, "Farm Progress Show sponsors and visitors make great friends."

Bill Fry and son, Edward, hosted the Farm Progress Show twice, in 1965 and 1971.

Four families will host this year's show. They are Mr. and Mrs. Bill New, Mr. and Mrs. Dwayne Gerlach, Mr. and Mrs. Willard Gerlach, and Mr. and Mrs. Ernie Otto. More than 6000 acres are involved with a 100-acre tent city offering 410 displays with a total value estimated in the many millions.

Show manager, Steve Cain, and Frank Holdmeyer, machinery editor for *Farm Progress Publications,* say one specialty this year will be the energy efficient grain drying operation capable of handling 1000 bu. an hour. Others are two model homes, new machine sheds, an animal health tent that seats 500, gasohol exhibits, an Iowa State University Energy Tent, crop protection projects, a Canadian farm display, along with this nation's largest farm grain storage complex geared to handle 350,000 bu.

Robert and Roger Clause hosted the 1968 Farm Progress Show.

Otto Thompson, 99 years old, owns part of the land operated by the Gerlach brothers. He says the old walking plows and mule teams he remembers as "the way it was" some 90 years ago would look mighty strange alongside one of those $95,000, four-wheel drive, 400 hp air-conditioned, stereo-equipped tractors he will be seeing in action at the show.

MEMORIES TREASURED BY A 1928 MASTER FARM HOMEMAKER
November, 1980

Master Homemakers named annually by WALLACES FARMER *have a wealth of heartwarming stories to tell. In checking, I learned of one member in the first class of honorees chosen back in 1928. She is Mrs. Mabel Smith, now 89, who was more than pleased to share interesting recollections with our readers.*

Iowa's Master Farm Homemakers met in Des Moines November 19 to induct five new members into one of the state's most exclusive organizations. Mrs. Mabel Smith of Conrad found it a day of special memories.

Now 89 and living in a nursing home, Mrs. Smith was the first Iowan to be honored as a Master Farm Homemaker in February, 1928.

Looking back to that eventful day more than a half century ago, Mrs. Smith recalls making an acceptance speech carried by Radio Station WOI. She spoke of her devotion to her family and her dedication to making life ever better for those living in the country. And in a fervent petition, she closed her message with an appeal, "God help us, as homemakers, to use the tools we have to make this world a better, happier, and safer place for all."

Her husband, best known as "J.O.", listened intently to his wife's comments on an old Atwater-Kent radio equipped with earphones.

"I am so pleased *WALLACES FARMER is* continuing the Master Farm Homemaker program. Those of us privileged to receive this recognition believe it's a way to pay tribute to all farm homemakers for their contributions in the home and through community service," remarks Mrs. Smith.

Mabel Mann Smith lived in Marshalltown until she was 20. But even as a child visiting her grandparents' small farm, she resolved she would marry a farmer. "I loved the outdoors, and country living appealed to me from the beginning," says Mrs. Smith.

Recalling "the way it was" when she first became a farm homemaker in 1914, Mrs. Smith speaks of the countless tasks confronting farm wives in the early 1900s. She especially remembers the corn harvest season, when their 150 or more acres of corn all had to be husked by hand.

As many as four "shuckers" were hired every fall. "That was quite a gang to cook for, but I enjoyed doing it. They always enjoyed eating what I prepared," recalls Mrs. Smith. She also tells about keeping the woodburning stove hot every day and baking bread every other night. She washed, dried, mended, and ironed for all the harvest hands, as well as for J.O. The hand-operated equipment she used then was a far cry from the automatic washers and dryers of today.

The 1929 Depression left a lasting impression on Mrs. Smith. She remembers a lot of skimping had to be done. Egg and cream checks were the family's salvation. She adds, "Although it didn't seem that way at the time, I'm glad we had our money in land. Nobody could take that away from us.

Thanksgiving time brings special memories to Mrs. Smith. She points out, "We always had so much to be thankful for." Never extravagant, Mrs. Smith did not buy a Thanksgiving turkey. Instead she would roast one of the chickens she had raised. Guinea hens were also grown on the Smith farm.

An artist with paints and other materials, as well as with the frying pan and sewing needle, Mrs. Smith has done much with watercolors, pastels, and oils. Some of her paintings adorn the walls of the Oakview Nursing Home where she now lives.

Other cherished mementoes for grandchildren include small stuffed animals Mrs. Smith made out of sewing materials left over after a dress or coat was finished. Among the most interesting is a mother kangeroo carrying a tiny little "roo" in her pouch. Another treasure is a pig made from an army shirt worn by her youngest daughter while serving as a combat area nurse with a Field Evacuation Hospital attached to General Patton's 3rd Army in Europe.

Mrs. Smith also made her own holiday greeting cards for many years. And, as the Christmas season approaches, she is again looking forward to displaying her homemade cornhusk doll nativity

At the time she was named Iowa's first Master Farm Homemaker, the February 24, 1928, issue of *WALLACES FARMER* summarized Mrs. Smith's activities by saying, "She has been active in Farm Bureau work, served as 4-H leader, taught Sunday school for 13 years, and is active in other community work." The report also told of Mrs. Smith teaching her children appreciation of country living through nature study and other programs. Mention of family vacations, child training, parent study courses, regular family medical checkups, and hot school lunches was also made.

The Smiths had two daughters, Mary (Mrs. Richard) DeWitt of Winterset, and Ruth (Mrs. Jay)

An Iowa pioneer Master Farm Homemaker Mrs. Mabel Smith.

Miller of near Conrad. Five grandchildren and four great grandchildren have been added to the family. The Smiths had been married 55 years when J.O. died in 1972. Mabel talks of the love and admiration she had for her farmer husband, and the joy they had working together on the farm and in family and community endeavors.

A strong believer in the Golden Rule, Mrs. Smith is convinced that contributions made to worthy causes help build treasures in heaven. As to honors and recognitions, she stresses that with recognition goes responsibility, a policy she has embraced ever since she was named Iowa's first Master Farm Homemaker.

A 1977 publication, *"Grundy County Remembers "*, includes several quotes by Mrs. Smith. "To live abundantly depends on our personal choices, and to increase the range of our active interest increases the range of our lives."

In another statement, Mrs. Smith spoke for all of the 204 Iowa farm wives on whom the special honor has been bestowed since 1928. She writes: "The homemaker is the custodian of the ideas and ideals of the oncoming generation. No civilization can rise higher than the ideals and personal choices of its womanhood."

THE SPIRIT OF CHRISTMAS PAST
December, 1980

Christmastime has always been special in my December column every year. This one is truly about "Christmas Past". It reached back 125 years to Civil War times as reported in the IOWA HOMESTEAD, *predecessor of* WALLACES FARMER, *and continued through the "Gay Nineties". Some years "Uncle Henry" Wallace devoted the magazine's entire cover page to a lengthy "Merry Christmas" greeting and message.*

For 125 years, seven or more generations of readers of *WALLACES FARMER* and its predecessor, *THE IOWA HOMESTEAD*, have welcomed Christmas greetings in December issues of this nationally acclaimed farm publication. Messages of Yuletide cheer have ranged from front page editorials to readers' opinions in the "Hearts and Homes" column and other special departments.

Now, with the Iowa Farm Progress Publications' 125th anniversary celebration nearing its close, it seems appropriate to look back on Christmastime observances reported in the 1800s. A perusal of bound or microfilmed volumes of the *Homestead* as far back as Civil War times and *Wallaces Farmer* issues in the 1890s takes note of "the way it was" back in pioneer days.

Aside from Civil War news and its troubled aftermath, the *Homestead* kept faith with farmers by reporting and imparting much farm information. One holiday conclusion most readers would reach is that money was scarce in the 1800s, prompting the making and giving of many homemade presents. A second impression is that religious convictions about the Christmas season totally overshadowed all the commercial aspects.

Going back nearly 120 years, the *Homestead* was giving much attention to the war between the states. One item headed "Good News" told how the rebels had been stopped near Mobile. The article closed by saying, "Old Stonewall Jackson has finally met his match." Lincoln's Emancipation Proclamation in 1863 was also headlined. The fortunes of war demanded some of the publication's space, but there were also references to Christmas, farming tips, and agricultural news.

Editors spoke about Union and Confederate soldiers returning to their farms for the holidays. Christmas references centered largely around suggestions on roasting turkeys, making pumpkin pudding, and other culinary skills. Except for toys for small tots, there was little gift giving and not much holiday cheer during wartime Christmases.

Family activities, however, remained a central holiday season theme in the mid-1860s. Mrs. C.A. Thomas of Jones County, wrote the *Homestead* in 1864 saying the five sons and three daughters of the Thomas family lived on six farms adjoining the home place.

The whole family, including the in-laws and 15 grandchildren, always made Christmas plans at Thanksgiving. All gathered in one of the seven farm homes on Christmas Day for a turkey dinner at noon, followed by a program of Christmas carols, recitations, and readings, climaxed by lighting the candles and distributing useful gifts tied on the big Christmas evergreen tree.

The so-called "Gay Nineties" evidently were not as carefree as commonly assumed. In the *Homestead's* December 1892 issue, a Central City reader, using only the name "Charity", wrote in the home department. "We have four girls and only one dollar for six Christmas gifts. Our wee one, now three, has just 12¢, but is determined to buy Mommy the "beautifullest present."

"We made remarkably inexpensive purchases including whisk broom, pocket watch, shaving brush, penny dolls, a grape basket cradle, candy, apples, even perfume. Our oldest daughter also traded geranium slips for clothing scraps so she could make a quilt. It will be a very Merry Christmas for the six of us."

Another contributor, who signed herself as "Peter's Wife," offered suggestions on overcoming difficulties besetting the economy in December 1893. She provided directions for making scrapbags, pansy mats, shaving books, tobacco bags, knitting baskets, and scrapbooks.

Toward the turn of the century, conditions evidently improved. At any rate, in the mid-'90s, Emma Powel McCloud reminded readers, "It is more blessed to give than to receive," and gave tips on Christmas shopping. "Little girls," she wrote, "need dressed up dolls, but big girls should be given undressed ones so the little 'mothers' can make clothes for their 'babies.'"

"Little boys," she added, "should also have dolls, but dressed like boys." For school boys, tool kits were suggested. Recommended for teenagers were books like *Pilgrim's Progress, Arabian Nights,* Dickens' carols and Longfellow's poems, all available for 17¢ a copy or less. "Good books," said Mrs. McCloud, "are the best of all investments."

Countless other reminders about what we now term Old Fashioned Christmases are found in many other pre-1900 December issues now carefully preserved in the publication's Des Moines library.

Uncle Henry Wallace was editor of the publications from 1885 to 1916. His son, H.C., and grandson, Henry A., later followed in his footsteps. A former minister and a fluent, prolific writer, Uncle Henry wrote thought provoking, widely read editorials, often with missionary zeal. When the December 1891 issue's publication date happened to fall on December 25, he made the most of his opportunity to write a Christmas editorial.

Entitled, "A Merry Christmas," Uncle Henry's editorial took up the complete front page, beginning with:

"Let the Christmas tree be loaded with gifts, and the table be spread with the most bountiful fare.

"It is a day of gladness and rejoicing, not for the rich or the poor, the American or the Englishman, but for all the world.

"We do not make merry today because of the abundance of our harvest as on Thanksgiving Day, or because a nation was born, as on the 4th of July, but because glad tidings of great joy have come to all the people."

The lengthy editorial concluded with the following observation:

"Christ was reared in a country village. He illustrates the loftiest conceptions by flowers and grass, the sower of seeds, the grinding of wheat, the sweeping of the house and other ordinary tasks. Is it any wonder then that common people have always held fast to Christian teachings?"

And, as if he were writing a Christmas editorial for today, Uncle Henry Wallace finished his Christmas message by saying, "So long as there is a Christian idea of justice and mercy and of the worth of man, injustice will not triumph, and liberty will not perish from this earth."

The way it was . . .
1 9 8 1

BEEGHLY REFLECTS ON GAINS BY FARM CO-OPS
January, 1981

To get my fourth year of "The Way It Was" *columns off to a good start, I turned to a long-time friend for this story. He is Milford Beeghly, outstanding Northwest Iowa farmer and nationally recognized leader of a farm cooperative. Beeghly is still going strong. As a matter of fact, he and his new bride had just returned from their honeymoon in Russia when this introduction was written in 1993.*

When Agri-Industries, a regional farmers cooperative handling 429 million bushels of Midwest corn and soybeans last year, holds its annual meeting in Des Moines January 26 and 27, it will open the floodgates of memory for Milford Beeghly, a veteran northwest Iowa farm co-op leader. Beeghly, now 82, can look back on three-quarters of a century of co-op involvement.

Milford's father, Ezra Beeghly, was one of the founders of the Pierson Farmer's Co-0p Elevator. Today, 76 years later, Milford and his son, Wayland, a Foreign Agricultural Service official stationed in Moscow, are still doing all their business with the Pierson Co-op.

Going back to "the way it was" in co-op efforts shortly after the turn of the century, Beeghly says, "When the other elevators realized my father and his neighbors meant business, one of them quickly sold out to the farmers. Then, when the Pierson Co-op opened for business, wheat went up 50¢ a bushel that same day and corn jumped 8¢.

Soon after he started farming on his own in 1934, Milford became a director of the Pierson Co-op, then was named vice president, and eventually elected president. During the 33 years of his presidency, the co-op branched into production of commercial feeds, lumber supplies, and providing fertilizers, chemicals, and petroleum.

During his presidency at Pierson, Beeghly was elected a delegate to a Ft. Dodge meeting of the Farmer's Grain Dealers Association (FGDA), predecessor of Agri-Industries. Soon thereafter, he was chosen an FGDA director and later named vice president. Then when Oscar Heline stepped down as head of the regional co-op, Beeghly was elected president.

Farm co-op leader Milford Beeghly.

During his 13 years as president of the FGDA, Milford had a hand in many historic co-op developments. Among them was the building of three barge facilities on the Mississippi at Meekers Landing, Muscatine, and McGregor.

"It was a struggle to get that done," points out Beeghly. "Some co-op members were upset about costs while others doubted that increased export trade would develop."

Other accomplishments as head of FGDA included purchase of the six million bushel capacity Avon elevator, installing a sensational full boxcar unloader, buying the 18th Street elevator in Des Moines, and purchasing a Mason City soybean processing plant.

Major achievements however, was helping raise a half-million dollars to join other regional co-ops in acquiring a huge New Orleans elevator and dock facility.

Beeghly smiles when he compares facilities today with those of 75 years ago. He says, "We had room for 40,000 bushel of cash grain then, which wasn't bad for that time, but now our capacity is 750,000 and a lot of hedging is being done."

A life-long farmer, Beeghly has many memories of "the way it was" when he was a youth. The corn and hog markets broke in 1919, resulting in widespread bank failures and rough times for farmers' elevators.

Field work was all done by horses. Twelve head were harnessed every day on the Beeghly farm. A dozen families were involved in the neighborhood threshing ring. Shocking, shredding, and shelling corn also involved much hard work. In the fields, corn was cultivated five times. Potato bugs were picked by hand.

Beeghly was a pioneer in many developments. After two years at Iowa State College, he started working with hybrid corn in the 1920s. On becoming acquainted with H.A. Wallace, then editor of *WALLACES FARMER*, his interest in hybrids increased.

In the early '30s, at a Church of the Brethren near Kingsley, young Beeghly met Dorothy Graham, a school teacher. Soon they were going steady and talking about the future. However, because Milford felt he ought to get established in the seed corn business first, marriage plans were postponed.

In 1934, Milford acquired some single cross seed and planted 20 acres. Visions of a profitable harvest were shattered, however, when hail and a devastating drought struck, reducing fields to a single bushel per acre. The next year, another 20 acres were planted, but an early frost wiped out the crop. Milford tried again in 1936, only to see heat and drought destroy still another harvest.

Undaunted, young Beeghly put in another 50 acres to hybrid seed production in 1937, and this time managed to get a good crop. By 1941, Beeghly Hybrids were well established, enabling the wedding bells to ring for Dorothy and Milford.

Two daughters, Bonnie (now Mrs. Anthony Nigro of Omaha), and Beverly (now Mrs. Jerris McCollum of Pierson), and a son, Wayland, were welcomed into the Beeghly family. Five grandchildren enjoy "Grandpa" Beeghly's 580-acre farm where hundreds of cattle, hogs, and sheep are raised, and where they can see conservation tillage and green fields bespeak love of the land.

Beeghly smiles as he contemplates the Agri-Industries meeting and compares it with those of his boyhood. He comments, "Father thought our Pierson Co-op was doing well when they grossed $25,000 and we were pretty proud when FGDA topped a million the first time. Now Agri-Industries reports a 1980 gross of many, many millions."

Before concluding his co-op leadership service, Beeghly served on the Farm Credit Board for twelve years and with the Central Bank for Co-ops for six years.

Looking back, he lauds Midwest farmers for their foresight in building facilities large enough to take care of their storage and marketing needs and says, "Those towering elevators stand as monuments to the vision of farmers trying to solve their economic problems."

EIGHTY YEARS OF ANIMAL HEALTH IMPROVEMENT
February, 1981

Dr. James Carey is one of the most remarkable professional men I have ever known. When I interviewed him at the age of 89, he could already claim 80 years of involvement in animal health. As a nine year old boy, he accompanied his father, a pioneer veterinarian, in two-wheeled carts as they made calls at farms where sick animals were found.

The 99th annual Iowa Veterinary Medical Association (IVMA) convention, held in Des Moines early this month, was of vital interest to more than 900 Iowa veterinarians and the thousands of farmers they serve.

Most of those present had attended a number of IVMA conventions. Dozens had registered at 25 or more gatherings. None, though, could compare with the record set by 89-year old Dr. James Carey of West Liberty.

Since 1919, when he began his practice, Dr. Carey has not missed a single convention. "And," he points out, "every one of them has been a golden opportunity for professional improvement."

The son of an Iowa veterinarian, Dr. Carey's interest in the profession started more than 80 years ago.

As a small boy, he rode on buggies and buckboards as his father, Dr. Samuel Carey, known as a "horse doctor" in those days, made his calls in the surrounding area.

Communication problems loomed large for veterinarians at the turn of the century and through the 1920s. Carey says, "Father never did use an automobile. Most calls were made with one horse hitched to a top buggy. Two horses were used when snow or mud got deep. So were high-wheeled carts. Sometimes the only way to get through was on horseback."

Dr. James Carey is a member of a three-generation veterinary clinic.

Model T's and other early makes of autos were in the picture by the time James Carey started his practice. But when blizzards struck, or spring rains turned mud roads bottomless, he had to resort to buggy, cart, or saddle.

The two most trying periods the West Liberty veterinarian recalls were a widespread hog cholera outbreak in 1926 and an equine encephalomyelitis epidemic in the late 1930s. Because he had the foresight to stock up on large supplies of serum, Dr. Carey was able to save thousands of hogs.

After his son joined the West Liberty firm, Dr. Carey was able to devote more time to developing surgical procedures, an area in which he excelled and gained national acclaim.

With his son and Dr. Larson handling more of the calls, the elder Carey also found more time to participate in state and national veterinary programs.

Honors accorded the West Liberty practitioner included the presidency of the IVMA, Cattlemen's Hall of Fame award, Iowa State University Alumni Achievement Award, and the IVMA President's Award.

Looking back on eight decades of association with animal health, Dr. Carey says the most pronounced changes included switching emphasis from horses to dairy stock, then to hogs and now beef cattle. The transition from little farms with small herds and flocks to large farms with hundreds of cattle and hogs is also noted, as is the move toward specialization and the greatly improved roads.

Seen as the greatest boon in the profession is the intravenous medication of stock, such as use of calcium derivatives for milk fever and the WW II development of penicillin. Increased attention to small animal practices and the advent of short-wave radio communication are other major advances Dr. Carey lists.

In reviewing his 80 years of connection with the veterinary field, Carey makes another significant point. He says, "Greatest asset any veterinarian can have is a helpful, patient, and understanding wife to handle countless phone calls and answer difficult questions." He makes it clear his mother, and then his wife, Gracie, and more recently, his daughter-in-law, Dorothy, each deserve much credit and praise for the Careys' veterinary successes. Though no longer in practice, Dr. Carey continues to keep up-to-date on professional developments. Meanwhile, he helps look after his family farm holdings and Angus herd, enjoys his six grandchildren and eight great grandchildren, and says, "It's been an interesting life for me, and I know veterinarians will always make a contribution to the well being of both man and animals."

FRANK CRABB — DEAN OF IOWA LEGISLATORS
March 14, 1981

Writing about politics and politicians is not my forte, but developments in Iowa's Legislature always interests me. Because I felt my WALLACES FARMER *readers also wonder about decisions made on "Capitol Hill", I sought out Frank Crabb, a veteran Iowa lawmaker, for this report.*

"We've got to bite the bullet in this session," says Frank Crabb, 77, Denison, oldest member of the 69th Iowa General Assembly. He then adds, "And when we're through with our making cuts and reductions, some people will be yelling louder than a stuck pig."

Crabb, now serving his sixth consecutive term, represents some 28,000 constituents in District 53, comprised of parts of Crawford, Harrison, and

Monona Counties. He leaves no doubt that money will be the overriding issue in the current legislature, as lawmakers strive to keep Iowa's treasury in the black.

"It won't be easy," the Denison legislator emphasizes, "but we have to do it." He says non-revenue producing departments will likely be the first to feel the economic ax.

Rep. Crabb should know. He has personally experienced tough times before. The memory of 1929 and the trying '30s is still vivid. He knows what it's like to try raising hogs for a nickel a pound. He has seen 400 men queue up in a vain search for work. He recognizes the necessity of balancing government and personal budgets.

The Denison lawmaker has a unique and interesting background. Born in Illinois, he has lived and worked in a dozen states. After college, he joined Swift and Company in Chicago, and for the next 44 years was a leader in the meat industry, working for and managing packing plants in Chicago, St. Joseph, Sioux City, Omaha, Pueblo, Indianapolis, Ft. Dodge, Estherville, Denison, and in Australia.

Early in his career, he was superintendent for Swift at Sioux City. After other assignments, he directed Tobins at Ft. Dodge and Estherville, before taking over Farmland Industries' Farmbest plant at Denison.

When he reached the mandatory retirement age, Crabb decided he would rather "wear out" than "rust out", so he threw his hat in the political ring, winning a seat in the Iowa House. Since then, he has been reelected five times.

A lifelong Republican, Crabb's recollections as a legislator are interesting. "It's a fascinating opportunity and a great lesson in human nature," says the 77-year old solon. As a freshman lawmaker in the 63rd Assembly, he vowed to just listen, look, deliberate, and vote. Shortly, however, his long experience in the meat industry caused him to take a more active role.

The first bill assigned to Crabb was the highly controversial meat inspection law. Well-acquainted with federal regulations, he sought USDA counsel, wrote a bill requiring greater sanitation, debated opponents, and saw the measure pass almost unanimously.

In the ensuing years, a dozen or more bills have come under Crabb's guidance. Many responsibilities have also been assumed on agriculture, rules, commerce and labor, and industrial relations.

Asked about other observations in the State House, Rep. Crabb says he enjoys the house and senate joint sessions and waxes eloquently about the recent appearance by Kathryn Koob of Jesup, one of the 52 Americans held in Iran 444 days. "It was an emotional experience for us," he opines. "She is a lovely person, deeply religious, with high praise for her parents and her upbringing, keenly aware of America's real values and deeply appreciative of the freedoms too often taken for granted."

Married in 1931 to Dorothy Ward of Washington, Iowa, Frank and his attractive wife will observe their golden wedding during the time of this legislative session. The Crabbs have a daughter and three grandchildren in New Jersey.

Reviewing "the way it was" in his boyhood, the Denison solon recalls his father dragging dirt roads to work his poll tax, putting in more hours at that than it now takes to drive the interstate across Iowa.

Noting the advancements in mechanization and crop and livestock improvement on farms the past 50 years, Crabb says, "It boggles the mind to imagine what another half-century of progress will bring."

Referring to his legislative years, Crabb feels the changes have also been dramatic. Summing it up, he says, "We've moved from a liberal to a conservative philosophy and from a large treasury surplus to a shortage of money."

Crabb has delighted in the work with the Republicans and Democrats alike and concludes that, "Serving in Iowa's legislature is a privilege and a pleasant way to climax an active career, now extending over some 60 years."

1947 MASTER FARMER, DAIRYMAN AND CONSERVATIONIST
March 28, 1981

There are some people you just can't keep down. Mr. and Mrs. Earl Lyon are in that category. They suffered drought, depression, fire, and loss of land, and yet they came out on top as dairy leaders, conservationists, and Master Farmers. Interviewing them was an inspiring experience, and a lesson in the value of persistence.

Master farmer Earl Lyon and Mrs. Lyon at their retirement home.

If any of the 1981 class of Master Farmers featured on pages 84 and 85 of this issue are interested in emulating a Master Farmer couple named previously, they would do well to get acquainted with Mr. and Mrs. Earl Lyon of Tama County.

The Lyons were accorded the state's highest farm recognition in 1947. Earl, now 85, and Mrs. Lyon, are the personification of *WALLACES FARMER's* long time slogan, "Good Farming - Clear Thinking - Right Living."

Married 57 years ago, Earl best known as "Pete", and Helen, started from scratch. Since then they have worked hard, raised four sons and a nephew, established an outstanding dairy herd, accumulated land, become pioneers in soil conservation, exemplified community service, built a comfortable retirement home, and reveled in 53 grandchildren and great-grandchildren.

His older brother, Bob, had married, and in 1921 invited Earl to join in a partnership that was to last until Bob's untimely death in 1947.

Machinery, livestock, and horses were all jointly owned. A joint checking account was used and mutual interest cemented the relationship.

When Earl and Helen married in 1924, the brothers rented an additional 80 acres. That same year, they bought their first Jerseys, two good heifers purchased from the nearby Sac and Fox Indian reservation, and a bull from the Sherman Nurseries. As the herd increased, the brothers became pioneers in the Cow Testing Association, culled out low producers, and bought Canadian bulls to improve type and production.

With no pun intended, Earl says, "They were our bread and butter during the tough late '20s and '30s when the weekly Hudson Creamery checks were our salvation."

Today, two of Earl and Helen's sons, Howard and Joe, are continuing the dairying partnership on 1100 acres with a herd of 140, many of them Jerseys.

4-H has been a significant influence in the Lyon families. Bob's children enrolled more than 50 years ago. Helen and Earl's four sons and the nephew, Bill Zmolek, were all outstanding in 4-H. Their show ring victories at the Iowa State Fair and the National Dairy Cattle Congress were legion.

Recalling "the way it was" during his early years of farming, Earl will never forget the Depression. Banks had closed, insurance firms were foreclosing on mortgages. Drought stunted crops. Prices were low. Taxes and interest payments on the 120 acres he had purchased in 1928 could not be met.

Nor were drought and rock bottom prices all that concerned the Lyon family in 1934. On October 12 of that year, Helen looked out the window and saw smoke pouring out of the barn. Instinctively, she rushed into the burning building to chase out a calf, some gilts, and a colt.

Recalling the fire, Earl says, "Helen got out just in time. Moments afterwards, the barn exploded and burned to the ground, setting most nearby buildings aflame."

He adds, "1934 wasn't one of our better years. The corn did about five bushels an acre and we got only four loads of oats bundles from 20 acres. Then, when we hauled them into the barn, we lost the whole works in the fire."

Soil conservation came into the picture after Burns Byrum, longtime Tama County extension agent suggested that Earl join the soils district and put soil conserving practices on his rolling farm.

Deeply concerned about erosion on his hillsides, Lyon became the first farmer in the area to get a soil plan, use grassed waterways, establish terraces, and contour and strip crop his fields.

Tremendously impressed by the way conservation practices slowed the loss of topsoil on his farm, Earl started to "preach the conservation gospel" at meetings throughout the area.

Other innovations that this Toledo Master Farmer helped set the pace for include check stripping fields with super phosphate to prove the value of chemical fertilizers, liming, planting hybrid corn, and use of hybrids.

Family ties remain close in the Lyon family and an abiding interest in agriculture prevails, as attested by the farmer sons, Howard and Joe. Durwood, of Oklahoma, is a meat packing specialist and Tom, the youngest, is with Midwest Breeders in Wisconsin. The nephew, Bill Zmolek, one of six nieces and nephews for whom Helen and Earl were guardians, is a veteran Iowa State University extension livestock specialist. All the 33 grandchildren are college graduates, as are many of the great-grandchildren.

Caring for a growing family of lively sons, as well as for her husband, and later trying to keep track of "cousins by the dozens," has kept Helen too busy to do as much community work as her husband.

On the other hand, Earl has given much time to conservation programs, dairy meetings, the Jersey association, Triple A, and school boards. He is an enthusiastic sports fan and watches all the basketball tournaments closely.

An avid reader, Earl enjoys every issue of *WALLACES FARMER*, cover to cover. His wife says, "Sometimes I think it's his 'bible'." Both are exceedingly proud of the Master Farmer honors awarded them 34 years ago.

In looking back over the years, Pete Lyon gives credit to many people for the success he has had. He is particularly grateful to extension and Soil Conservation Service personnel who have helped him. "None of us can do it alone," says Earl.

Asked about vexing questions facing farmers today, and about the April 1 milk price support problem, Lyon says, "We shouldn't tamper too much with a program that has worked well for producers as well as farmers."

He also asks a question of his own by saying, "How many people in this country would trade places with the dairyman and his 365-day, dawn-to-dusk job?" All in all, he believes the future for dairying is good.

Although a Democrat, he wishes President Reagan well, asserting, "If inflation isn't stopped, it will lead us straight to disaster." He has misgivings on the energy situation, saying, "We are all hostages of the big oil companies, whose next round of profits will be staggering." On patriotism, the WWI navy veteran's voice chokes a little as he says, "Look at all those white crosses around the world. Those men died to help make our country better, and we haven't done too well by them."

VEISHEA ORIGINATOR LOOKS BACK
April, 1981

Wallace McKee is a popular farmer and dairyman, often in the forefront of new developments. Therefore, I was not surprised to learn that, as a young college student, he came up with the name "VEISHEA" for Iowa State's annual celebration, now one of the nation's largest university student-directed events of its kind. Here's the story:

Iowa State University's 24,000 students will stage their annual VEISHEA celebration in early May. And it will mark the 60th consecutive year Warren County farmer Wallace McKee will have been on the program - and for good reason.

McKee, now 83, is credited with originating the annual Ames event. As its founder, he has been signally honored several times.

It is fascinating to hear the Carlisle farmer and stockman recollect how VEISHEA came about. As a junior in the animal husbandry division and chairman of the college's annual Ag Day program, he went to the University of Missouri's Farmers Festival to "pick up ideas." During the train trip back to Ames, he pondered the logic of Iowa State College's (ISC) fragmented open house programs, wherein each division had its own special day. "Why not combine all divisional events into one huge student-managed celebration?" he asked himself.

He discussed the idea with the Ag Club, of which he was president. The club's enthusiastic response gave McKee courage to take the plan to college leaders. Most of them were highly favorable. The idea caught on, but it took a year to implement.

A "bare bones" budget was finally raised. A format calling for open houses, a parade, pageant, and other features was adopted. A meaningful, catchy, representative name had to be chosen. A campuswide contest brought up the name, VEISHEA, incorporating the opening letters for Veterinary, Engineering, Industrial Science, Home Economics, and Agriculture — the five major ISC departments at that time.

Wallace McKee and Grandson at McKee farm sign.

Regarded as a smashing success, that 1922 exhibition set the pattern for all future VEISHEAs. The event is now acclaimed as the nation's largest and best student-managed festival of its kind.

McKee happily recalls a personal aspect of the first VEISHEA. Serving as director of the home economics exhibit was a pretty coed, Ruth Pollman of Davenport. Two years later, wedding bells rang for the young couple.

Years later, after all the McKee's five children had been enrolled at ISU, they delighted their parents by their involvement in VEISHEA.

Robert, now president of Brenton National Bank in Des Moines, followed in his father's footsteps as chairman of a major committee, while Margaret (now Mrs. James Hickman of Madison, Wisc.), followed in her mother's steps by chairing a home ec committee. Beverly, an ag student (now Mrs. Lee Newell of Gardnerville, Nev.), worked on Ag Club features. Miriam (now Mrs. John Cerveny, also of Madison), helped in various program tasks, while Jean (now Mrs. Oliver Jervis of Naperville, Ill.), was active with VEISHEA sorority features.

McKee's pride doesn't stop there. Several of his 15 grandchildren have graduated from ISU and participated in VEISHEA. "Now," says McKee, "the great-grandchildren have started arriving and I hope some of them will also get in on the fun."

Asked to comment on 59 previous VEISHEAs he has attended, McKee says, "They've all been great and keep getting better right along." With understandable pride, he adds, "The framework today remains essentially the same as in 1922."

At Ames, ISU students Brett Carter and Dave Bolte are co-chairmen for this year's VEISHEA. Close to 60,000 visitors, many of them graduating high school seniors, will enjoy a mile-long parade, pageants, reunions, demonstrations, exhibits, and "eye-opening" divisional open houses. "It's going to be the grandest of them all," says McKee.

THE WRIGHTS - 50 YEARS OF DAIRY LEADERSHIP TOGETHER
June, 1981

In my work as a writer and broadcaster, I have come across thousands of husband and wife teams. In fact, most farm couples are. Seldom, however, can I recall a husband-wife team to surpass that of Mr. & Mrs. Ernie Wright. Iowa dairy leaders in the fullest sense, they did everything together, and served each other in every undertaking, as this article indicates.

June Dairy Month officials don't have an All-American Dairy Leader's award. If they did, an Iowa husband and wife team certain to be nominated is Mr. and Mrs. Ernest Wright of Black Hawk County.

Ernie, as he is universally known, can recall more than 70 years of association with dairy cattle. His wife of 53 years, Marj, has been her husband's most ardent supporter in every dairy undertaking.

Marj and Ernie Wright, Iowa's foremost dairy promoters.

Now 79, Wright might well be termed "the complete dairyman." At age eight, he started milking. All through his teens, he helped with his father's herd in Linn County. At Iowa State College (ISC), he enrolled in dairy husbandry. College expenses were earned by milking test cows. He also taught dairying, showed dairy stock at fairs, and became cow tester for Boone and Dallas Counties.

Shortly after graduation, Wright became field secretary for the Iowa Holstein Association and an ISC assistant in dairy husbandry. The next year, Ernie was named field secretary of the Iowa State Dairy Association.

In 1933, the Wrights bought a 120-acre farm near Waterloo and started a herd of well-bred Holsteins. Ernie continued his dairy association responsibilities until 1943. Then he was named dairy and farm advisor for Iowa's Board of Control, a post he held 22 years, working with 22 high-producing cows.

Along the way, Ernie also became involved in state and national Holstein Breed Association responsibilities, including the Iowa presidency and serving as a director for the Holstein Friesian Association of America. The Cedar Valley Milk Producers elected him president.

Mrs. Wright, the busy mother of two daughters, Marilyn and Virgina, and a son, Jack, managed the farm and herd whenever her husband's work took him away. She handled much of the state association correspondence, was a 4-H leader, and for 30 years was National Dairy Congress secretary.

A pioneer in June Dairy Month activities, Ernie says, "It's highly appropriate some time and thought be given the dairy cow - Foster Mother of Mankind - and to dairy producers. June Dairy Month serves that purpose."

In comparing today's dairy industry with dairying 71 years ago, Wright sums it up in two words, "utterly amazing." "When I first became field secretary, the U.S. had 24 million cows producing 125 billion pounds of milk. Today we have about 11 million cows providing 126 billion pounds."

After the Wright's first trip to England, accompanying a 4-H judging team to the international contest, they resolved to do more traveling instead of buying more land. Since then, they've been in more than 100 countries around the globe.

Looking ahead, Wright believes dairymen will become even more specialized. "With even larger herds, there will be continued emphasis on efficiency and quality and a never-ending struggle to set a fair price for both producer and consumer," he says.

THRESHING TIME NOSTALGIA
July, 1981

Powerful steam engines and some of the most popular farm threshing machines carried the name of "Wood Brothers." As a boy, I grew up in threshing crews with Wood Brothers "steamers" and "threshers". However, when I was pitching bundles into the feeder, I could never have imagined that in time I would greet Franz Wood, the inventive genius, in church every Sunday. Not only that, there was also his daughter, Helen, my children's Sunday School teacher, whose fascinating history of the giant threshing firm is summarized here.

Early in this century, late July and most of August was threshing time on Midwest farms. Old timers can recall how steam engine operators fired up their rigs during the night, then sounded off with long, melodious whistles at dawn to signal the start of another harvest day.

Introduction of farm tractors in the '20s and combines in the '30s started sounding the death knell for the big steamers and lumbering separators, but threshing nostalgia lives on. Throughout the Grain Belt, dozens of harvest bees are held each summer.

Reminders of Iowa's dominance in pioneer threshing equipment are evident at every such event. Especially is this true of the Wood Brothers steam engines and grain separators dating back some 80 years. And to the daughters of the late Robert and Franz Wood, inventors and developers of the famed line of early threshing tools, there is no limit to their nostalgia.

Cousins Gladys Wood, now 82, and Helen Wood, 77, vividly remember their childhood days traveling with their fathers and brothers from farm to farm. During their teen years, the Des Moines based Wood Brothers factory turned out threshing machines by the trainload.

Robert, the elder brother, was bent toward business and administration. Franz, best known as "F.J.", was the engineer and

Helen Wood at a Wood Brothers' steam engine at a threshing event.

inventor. Between 1898 and 1930, F.J. won patents on more than 20 inventions. A self-feeder he created was an instant success. Soon he was building them for other Minnesota threshermen. In time, the Wood Brothers Self Feeder Company was born, the first step in the long road that eventually led to Iowa and the mammoth Wood Brothers manufacturing plant in Des Moines.

The road was never easy. In 1927, after a fire, a new factory, with a long, fully modern assembly line, capable of handling nine machines simultaneously, was completed. Then in June, when the company fell 300 orders behind, 12-hour shifts were undertaken, enabling daily production of 40 of the huge machines.

1928 was another boom year. In his book, *Wood Brothers in Action*, F.J. recalled shipping 200 threshers to North Dakota on a special train. That same year, F.J. designed a new combine, thereby adding a new dimension to the Des Moines company's line.

By early 1930, more than 1000 combines had been sold, but then disaster struck. The 1929 market crash had shaken the nation. Farmers were unable to pay for the combines purchased. No money was coming in to meet interest obligations on close to a million dollars of indebtedness. Credit ran out. Early in 1930, the banks foreclosed. And all seemed lost.

Despite every obstacle and the bleak outlook, F.J. designed a new threshercombine. Meanwhile, the Roosevelt-Wallace policies had improved the farmer's lot. A bank loan helped the brothers pay off their obligations and reestablish their business, according to Helen, Franz's daughter.

Eventually, after Robert's death, the business was sold; but that did not end F.J.'s interest in threshing. Even though in his 80s, Helen recalls the great delight F.J. took in attending many threshermen's reunions throughout the Grain Belt. She proudly points to the way her father was lauded for his contributions to better farm living; and as the last survivor of that special breed called Iron Men, was acclaimed "Thresherman of the Years."

STATE FAIR CHAPLAIN
August, 1981

If ever there was a modern day "circuit riding preacher", it was Pastor John Clinton. Like thousands of others, I got to know and respect Pastor Clinton for his 66 years in active ministry, his total dedication to the Boy Scouts, and his service as Iowa State Fair Chaplain. This column tells about his tireless efforts preaching the word of God, and the State Fair log church he built on the Fairgrounds as an exact replica of the first church ever built in Iowa.

In serene contrast to glittering Midway attractions, roaring auto racers, shouting hucksters, and bellowing cattle, a simple log church beckons Iowa State Fair visitors. Here you can escape the noise and excitement on all sides and spend a few minutes in worship.

Located just northeast of Ag Hall in the heart of what is called Heritage Village, the church is an exact replica of the first church built in Iowa, in Dubuque, back in 1834.

While the church may seem stark and primitive, its pastor, State Fair Chaplain John D. Clinton, quickly dispels every vestige of austerity. The 88-year old Dr. Clinton, who considers himself "everybody's preacher," radiates unbounded enthusiasm every moment.

Clinton, dressed in the ministerial garb of a century or more ago, always opens the programs with a unique welcome and a challenging comment. But he regularly calls on well-known personalities to do the preaching. This year, Katherine Koob, Iowa's own Iranian hostage heroine; Dolph Pulliam, TV personality; Captain Glenn of the highway patrol; and others have already been scheduled.

John Clinton was named state fair chaplain some 15 years ago. He is a third generation "Iowa circuit rider." His grandfather, John W. Clinton, born in Canada in 1831, came to Iowa as a young teacher-preacher and rode the circuit constantly. Chaplain Clinton's father, DeWitt, pursued the same path, serving in the ministry 50 years.

Rev. John Clinton, everybody's favorite chaplain.

With a deep interest in Boy Scout work, Dr. Clinton has five times served as a chaplain at the nationwide Scout Jamboree at Valley Forge.

Dr. Clinton has preached in open air theaters, written reams of poetry, conducted countless ecumenical programs, directed church ground breaking with yokes and oxen, and raised thousands of dollars for the Living History Farms' Church of the Land and similar worthy causes. He wrote a church historical novel, and was a founding observer delegate at the birth of the United Nations in San Francisco in 1945.

In his Heather Manor study in Des Moines, Chaplain Clinton is surrounded by mementoes and records. Most treasured are pictures of the family.

A record has been kept of all the times Dr. Clinton served his fellow men and women. The totals are staggering in his 66 years in the ministry.

Perhaps Dr. J. W. Dickman, president of Upper Iowa University summed up Clinton's contributions when conferring an honorary doctorate on the State Fair Chaplain. He said, "Because of your exceptional leadership, untiring industry, creative originality, and superior talents — and as a student, author, lover of mankind, preacher to all — you are 'Truly a Servant of God.'"

HINTZ WILL HELP HARVEST HIS 72ND CORN CROP
September, 1981

As a member of the National Farm Institute's founding group, I noted one elderly farmer who never missed a session. He is Irving Hintz, an octogenarian born in the late 1800s, when farming methods were still rather primitive. As the years unfolded, Hintz employed the most modern farm tools in his own operation. And I soon learned his unfailing Farm Institute attendance was because he wanted to be up-to-date on the latest 20th Century national and world farm developments. A brother, Paul, now lives in Des Moines.

On the Bill Hintz farm near Monticello, the corn harvest is on this fall and the man operating the huge modern combine in most of those fields will be Hintz's 82-year old father, Irving. It will be the elder Hintz's 72nd season of involvement in corn harvesting and quite a contrast from early husking days.

"I was about nine when my father first let me help pick," says Irving Hintz. He would work on the down row behind the corn wagon while his mother and father picked alongside the wagon. "In those days, 40 bushels an acre was considered a good crop; so if we worked hard, we could husk and scoop 80 bushels in a long day," says Hintz.

How does that compare with what will be accomplished this fall? Irving answers, "It will be different. If all goes well, on a good day we'll pull out around 5000 bushel." If present yield estimates hold up, Hintz anticipates that he, his son, and his grandson, Lawrence, 25, a former Marine, will combine a little more than 100,000 bushels, compared to approximately 3500 bushels of hand husked corn on his father's "180" back in the early 1900s.

Memories of "the way it was" back in the early 1900s come to Irving Hintz's mind as he maneuvers the huge combine down the field six rows at a time.

He vividly recalls the move from Buchanan County to Monticello in Jones County. The snow was deep and it was bitterly cold. Neighbors with bobsleds took the stock and machinery to railway boxcars for a gruelling two-day trip from Independence. His father rode with the stock while the mother and her sons followed in the caboose.

The new home was not exactly a mansion. The boys'

Irvine Hintz and his combine.

room was unheated and snow drifted in through cracks in the wall. During one blizzard, the snow piled up enough to reveal footprints of the boys' cold, bare feet as they dashed toward the living room heater to dress.

Crop improvement was heavily emphasized during Irving's youth, and the Hintz family was always among the first to adopt new methods. They were pioneers in alfalfa and sweet clover production and among the first to grow hybrid corn. They also were among the early automobile and tractor owners.

A WWI veteran, Hintz took a course in agriculture at Iowa State College. He married, and started farming in 1924, and raised two daughters and a son.

Always a leader in his community, Hintz was one of Jones County's early Farm Bureau presidents, and retains an active interest in all modern developments in agriculture.

One of the activities Hintz enjoyed immensely was the National Farm Institute held annually in Des Moines beginning in 1937. Hintz has never missed a single session. "I enjoyed the discussion and debate so much I just kept going back every year," is the way he expresses it. Then he adds, "The institute served a useful purpose, but now magazines like *WALLACES FARMER* and radio and TV have replaced it."

The elder Hintz spends much time in his study with its coats of arms, family mementoes, and an impressive library. He keeps well abreast of current events, and sees inflation and high interest rates as this nation's greatest threat.

TWO IOWA CORNHUSKERS DEFEND NATIONAL TITLES
September, 1981

A modern version of the old-fashioned "Battle of the Bangboards" is annually reenacted at the Living History Farms near Des Moines. Hand husking contests, so popular in the 1920s, '30s, and early '40s, will have as many as 100 competitors. This report deals with the one held in 1981.

A state contest, open to huskers from all parts of Iowa, is scheduled for the Saturday, Oct. 17, opening of the annual Corn Harvest Festival. Vince King, farm manager for the Living History Farms and chairman of the festival, says classes for novices, women, and huskers 65 or older will be offered, in addition to the open class for men. Winners in each class will represent Iowa in the national competition Sunday, Oct. 18.

State contests have also been scheduled for Minnesota, Ohio, Kan-

Present day husking champ, "Bob" Ferguson.

78

sas, Indiana, and South Dakota. Still other states expected to send entrants for the national contest include Illinois, Nebraska, Missouri, and Texas.

Two Iowans and one Minnesotan will defend championships won near Oakley, Kan., last year. Both of the Iowans, 58-year-old Robert Ferguson of Mahaska country, and 68-year-old Lorence Hanson of Taylor county, will be trying for unprecedented third consecutive national championships this year. Ferguson won the open class and Hanson the old timers division in Ohio in 1979 and in Kansas last year.

The 1980 national winner in the women's division was Esther Pabst of Sanborn, Minn., Irene Quick of Manilla, Iowa, winner of the national title in 1979, was third last year, and is expected to bid again for national honors this year.

Rules for the modern matches vary considerably from those adopted in the 1920s when the late H.A. Wallace, long time editor of *Wallaces Farmer* and later vice president of the U.S., originated the national matches. Until 1941, huskers were required to husk 80 minutes without interruption. Today's open class entrants pick only 30 minutes.

Other Iowans who have won the national open class in recent years are Don Karsjens, Parkersburg; Tony Polich, Des Moines; and Joe Anholt, Fort Dodge.

CHAMPION CORNHUSKER RECALLS RAGS TO RICHES
October, 1981

One of the most remarkable men, and close friends, I will ever know is John Middlekoop, who started life as a poor tenant family farm boy and wound up as a millionaire. This story enumerated many of the necessary and solid steps between the two stations. It was a glowing testimony of the opportunities found in the American Way. It was an exciting story to write and one I am sure readers will enjoy.

From hired man to millionaire, John Middlekoop, former state champion cornhusker, is a classic example of the realization of the American dream.

Middlekoop, a 75-year old retired Jefferson County farmer and seed producer, enjoys reminiscing about "the way it was". Recalling his boyhood, he says, "No one was poorer than we, but it didn't hurt us a bit." From Dutch immigrant parents, John, his brother Martin, also a cornhusker, and two sisters, learned the meaning of hard work early in life.

John was raised on a poor, rented farm. The need to supplement family income ended his formal schooling in the sixth grade. Spading out a basement was his first job at $1 a day. In his mid-teens, he became a hired man. A dependable worker, his salary eventually went up to $52 a month.

In 1927, while still working for others, John married Anna Burbank. The young couple set up housekeeping in a small home on a nearby farm. There, John, Jr., the first of their two sons, was born. Two years later, when hard times developed, Middlekoop was told his wages would be cut to $35 a month. "That's when Anna and I decided to start farming on our own," he explains.

With enough money to buy two horses, a used plow, and other essential machinery, the young couple was able to rent 100 acres. Their first years of farming, however, were discouraging. Drought, insects, and low prices struck hard.

John says, "Our goal was to save $1000 a year, but we didn't even have that much in the bank at the end of six years."

In the meantime, Middlekoop was making a name for himself as a champion cornhusker. While still a hired hand, using a husking peg, he regularly husked and scooped over 100 bushels of open-pollinated corn by noon daily.

During his career, he progressively won six Mahaska and three Jefferson County titles, several district events, and a state crown in 1937. In the national contest that year, he placed eighth.

John Middlekoop, corn breeder, husker, showman and judge.

This October 18, John Middlekoop will be among the most interested spectators at a national revival of hand husking matches at the Living History Farms. "It will be different from my time," says John, pointing out that instead of husking 80 minutes without interruption, as was done in the 1924-41 matches, huskers need to pick only 30 minutes now. "And there probably won't be a single peg husker among them," he says.

By 1943, the Middlekoops had saved enough to make a 50% down payment on a fertile 160 acres priced at $200 an acre. A DeKalb dealership added $3000 a year of much needed income. Soon the $15,000 farm debt was paid off.

Once on his feet financially, John Middlekoop continued to buy land. In 1948, he decided to go into seed production on his own. Starting on a small basis, he grew double cross corn from parent seed. A small processing plant was established and seed deliveries were made in person. Then, in 1952, Middlekoop became a pioneer in producing single cross seed, a move that has resulted in expanding seed production from 52 acres annually to close to 1200 acres on their own farms.

Smiling, John declares, "I guess my middle name really should be 'corn'. I've been involved in all phases of corn production ever since I was a young lad, when Newt Krizer, the famous corn showman, hired me to tip, butt, and hand shell his seed corn for 5¢ a bushel."

Many corn authorities consider Middlekoop as a modern day "Legend in Corn." At 14, he won the Chicago International Corn Show grand championship. Subsequently, he has won innumerable awards, including 12 purple banners at the Iowa State Fair. One of his ten ear samples is now in the Truman

Library. Middlekoop presented the champion exhibit to President Truman in 1949 when Truman visited Iowa.

Even more significant to John is the Iowa Masters Corn Contest trophy for achieving the state's highest corn yield in 1955, and several plaques showing a Middlekoop hybrid as a District winner in the Iowa Corn Yield Contest.

While the Middlekoop saga is a "rags to riches" story, it is also one of compassion and caring. Although reluctant to take credit, the family has contributed generously to many worthy charities. Over the years, donations have totaled high into six figures. But life hasn't been a bed of roses. In 1963, Anna became afflicted with multiple sclerosis and has been confined to a wheelchair the past ten years or more.

Mindful of his wife's condition, John planned and built a modest ranch style home totally adapted to a wheelchair patient's needs. Although still helpful when he can be, John has turned the entire seed enterprise over to his son, Jack, and devotes most of his time to caring for his invalid wife and doing the home chores.

Anna is deeply religious. She enjoys reading and keeping scrapbooks about the grandchildren and family achievements. John's limited spare time is devoted to flowers and a large weed-free garden. He also has a small orchard of dwarf fruit trees. The couple will celebrate their 55th wedding anniversary in a very short time.

What is his secret to success? John Middlekoop quickly points out being at the right place at the right time is important, but opportunity still prevails for those who seek it. On financial borrowing, he says, "Stay fairly close to shore." He adds, "If I have any advice to give to young people, it would be, set a goal, work hard, save, and sacrifice to attain it, and then set another and higher goal.'"

A CITY GIRL BECOMES A
MASTER FARM HOMEMAKER
November, 1981

That a girl raised in the city can become a Master Farm Homemaker is an established fact, and no one is a more eloquent testimony to this than Gladys Teachout of Shenandoah, whom I visited some 55 years after she changed from town girl to a farm wife. When I learned of her accomplishments in the home as a mother and as a farm partner, I just had to chronicle her interesting and challenging experiences.

For five active Iowa farm wives, November 24, 1981, will always be a "red letter" day. It is on that date they are being inducted by *WALLACES FARMER* as Iowa's newest class of Master Farm Homemakers.

Among those vividly remembering her own induction is Mrs. Gladys Teachout, class of 1947, of Shenandoah, now 80, and a widow for many years.

"Before my marriage I had been a city girl and rural teacher," explains Mrs. Teachout, adding that, "never could I have dreamed of such an honor coming my way." She then goes on to say, "I knew there were those who wondered why George chose a town girl for a bride, so I resolved from the first day that I would be the best farm wife I could, even if he and my sisters-in-law might have to give me some on-the-job training."

Mrs. Teachout also well remembers how quickly she was put to the test. She says, "Within two weeks after our wedding day, the ensilage crew came to our farm and I had to prepare meals on an old range for those ten hungry men. I was scared, but I did my best."

Master Farm Homemaker Gladys Teachout amid her many flowers.

Not only did she pass the test, but kindly neighbor ladies, some of whom helped her with that first big challenge, encouraged her with their praise. Soon thereafter, she found herself canning the cherries she and George had picked, baking bread, preserving fruits and vegetables from the farm's big garden and orchard, and helping with the fall harvest.

Six children were welcomed over the next 20 years. Their needs, providing meals for the growing family and hired help, preserving 1000 quarts of food a year, washing and ironing, keeping the five bedroom house tidy, and helping care for large turkey flocks, kept the "town girl" exceedingly busy.

Nor did she have the luxury of today's conveniences. With no electricity, there were no labor saving, push-button appliances. Water was pumped by hand. Washing was done with a gas-powered engine. There were no clothes dryers and no indoor plumbing. Kerosene lamps and lanterns furnished light.

The Fremont County homemaker is quick to acknowledge the advent of electricity in 1946 as one of the happiest days of her life and that she lost no time in buying a vacuum sweeper, refrigerator, and electric stove.

In recalling "the way it was" on the Teachout farm since 1925, depression years quickly came to the southwest Iowan's mind. She says, "We raised almost all our own food, buying only flour, salt, sugar, and condiments. Forty bushels of apples went into the cave and 40 bushels of potatoes into the cellar. Cobs, along with wood from the orchard, provided fuel. I made dresses for the girls and myself from feedsacks."

Despite her busy life as farm wife and mother, Mrs. Teachout found time for volunteerism. She served as township 4-H leader, became chairman of the Fremont County 4-H committee, and was active in the church and in the school, Farm Bureau, and other community projects. Later, as her husband's health began failing, she devoted more time to his care and the farm's management.

In addition to field crops and livestock, the Teachouts raised, processed, sold, and shipped as many as 15,000 turkeys a year. Gladys was involved in every step of the enterprise from feeding the poults, to "unstacking" the flighty creatures after thunderstorms and transferring them from the range into shelter in the fall.

Most of the turkeys were sold locally, but orders for Thanksgiving and Christmas gifts came from all over the U.S. "All through November and December, our phone almost literally rang off the wall," says the Shenandoah woman. Turkeys, however, are no longer a part of the Teachout farm operations.

A brochure, *"Let's Talk Turkey about Teachout Turkeys - Famous For Flavor"* was written by Gladys and included suggestions on buying and roasting the holiday birds, along with her favorite dressing, gravy, and cranberry recipes.

Part of the Teachout land is an Iowa Century Farm. On the death of her husband in 1960, the couple's sons took over all active management. Don, with his wife and family, now lives on the home place. Representing the fifth generation are two of Don's sons, Michael and Chris, now farming with their father. George, 14, is also showing interest in the family farm venture.

Other members of the family are also within easy reach. A daughter, Della, and her family live right in Shenandoah. Another daughter, Ardyth, is in Omaha, Three other children, Robert, Georgene, and Karen, with their spouses and children, are Kansas Cityans.

Although her heart remains on the farm with all its treasured memories, Gladys now again lives in town. She remains active in several study groups, Altrusa, Legion Auxiliary, and other clubs.

A spacious lawn, large vegetable garden, flower borders, shrubs and trees, plus a veritable botanical center of orchids, begonias, geraniums, and other plants in a large, sunlit porch, all enable her to use her "green thumb" talents.

Needlepointing, antique collecting, painting, reading, and keeping tabs on 13 grandchildren and seven great-grandchildren are other hobbies that make each day one of fulfillment for the Shenandoah Master Farm Homemaker.

The way it was . . .
1 9 8 2

OLD TIMERS RECALL HARD IOWA WINTERS
January, 1982

The first chapter of my 1982 columns was written with cold Iowa winters in mind. It centers on the memories of severe winters as recalled by six "old timers", several of them long time acquaintances of mine. Interestingly, this January issue of WALLACES FARMER *reached readers on what turned out to be the coldest day of 1982 — a unique coincidence.*

This month marks the 70th anniversary of what is commonly accepted as the coldest day in Iowa history. On January 12, 1912, a Washta weather observer, the late H.L. Felter, looked at his official weather bureau thermometer in disbelief. A reading of 47° below zero was showing.

After rechecking the instrument several times, he phoned the state meteorologist in Des Moines to report his frigid finding. The amazed state official recorded the Arctic-like reading in the U.S. Weather Register where it remains unbroken.

Today, motorists entering the northwest Iowa town are greeted by a large road sign proclaiming Washta as the coldest spot in Iowa.

Several old timers can recall the day the Cherokee County town gained its unenviable distinction. One of them is the 83-year old former mayor, B.K. Williams, long the editor of the Washta Journal, just 13 when the mercury hit bottom.

Referring to "the way it was" that bitter morning, Williams says, "We bundled up warm, rushed out to feed the stock, and dashed right back into the house to huddle near the stove." He adds that it was a battle to keep tank heaters going and says he will never forget how cold his fingers and toes were on the 2½ mile walk to school. On the plus side, he says, "It was the best winter we ever had for harvesting ice, and we youngsters had a great time skating and sledding."

State Climatologist Paul Waite, points out that Washta had stiff competition. That same January morning, Inwood, Iowa's most northwesterly city, reported 46° below and Alden a minus 42°.

Waite also quickly adds Iowa has had other severe winters, most notably the winter of 1935-36, when temperatures held consistently below 0° from January 18 to February 22, the longest uninterrupted severe cold wave in the state's history. Moreover, 51 inches of snow fell to make the combination of cold and snow the worst on record.

Memorable severe 1800 era winters listed by Waite, since official record keeping was started by army posts in 1819, include 1857, 1875, 1879, 1898, and 1899. In this century, in addition to 1912, standout years include 1917-19, 1928, and 1940, when the Armistice Day storm and temperature drops caused so much tragedy and loss. More recently, the winter of 1961-62 was the snowiest of all with a fall averaging 59 inches.

Ninety-six-year-old Fred Metzger, Rock Rapids, who will be featured in these columns in June, can vouch for the severe winters of northwest Iowa. The

B.K. Williams at a sign welcoming visitors to where temperatures once plunged to nearly 48° below.

pioneer Lyon County Jersey cattleman clearly remembers 1909 when heavy snow fell to last into April, 1910. "It was rough picking corn that winter," says Metzger. But 1912 was worse, though, when Inwood had 46° below and snowdrifts blocked every road.

The former Lester, Iowa farmer recalls taking the family to church by bobsled with shortcuts through fields and over fences on the nine mile ride. Ironically, that summer, he saw the red line push up to 112° on July 4, burning up most crops. As for record snowfall, Metzger points to February 17, 1961, when 32 inches fell to help make the northwest Iowa winter total add up to 90 inches.

Henry Duin, soon to be 85, of George, and who, like Metzger, lives in Lyon Manor near Rock Rapids, says, "1936 was the worst because snow was so deep and temperatures plunged close to 40° below." He remembers shoveling a quarter mile of four foot snow to get the corn sheller through and says bobsleds were used for weeks. He also recalls readings up to 114° above that July.

Duin, who is a 63-year life member of the American Legion and recently received a letter from President Reagan, remembers one winter storm worse than any of those in 1936. He says, "In January, 1975, just before our Golden Wedding, a three day 'hurricane blizzard' struck, piling snow so deep we could only look out of one window."

A central Iowa woman, Mrs. Flossie Slick, formerly of Woodward, thinks the 1940 Armistice Day storm was probably the worst. She points to the tragic loss of human life and the enormous property loss suffered that day when readings fell 30° in two hours and howling winds changed rain into a blizzard.

Mrs. Slick also remembers 1936. She says, "It was starting to snow when I took my daughter, Virginia, to Perry to play in a girl's basketball game. When we got out, snow was knee deep and we had to take the train back to Woodward the next day." She adds that most of Virginia's teammates went with them and the girls had a great holiday. Her husband spent the entire night pulling motorists up the hill with his trusty team of horses.

From northeast Iowa, Clarence Gage, 76, of Charles City, feels there is no question but what 1936 takes the "hard winter" prize, but he can also remember 1912 when, as a small boy, he walked to school with a sister. "I'll never forget that long, cold mile," says Gage.

As for 1936, Gage says, "From January 15 to about February 20, Charles City averaged 6° below zero and the snow was a foot deep.

"H.R. Gross was on WHO radio every night telling how bad it was all over and pleading with us to feed the pheasants."

FARMER, 96, MUST CHOOSE BETWEEN FIELD WORK AND TRAVEL
March 13, 1982

Some people seem able to go on forever doing what they enjoy doing. A case in point is 96-year old Francis Glaspey, who loves spring field work. However, this year he is confronted with quite a dilemma. His son could use him on the tractor this spring, but a daughter has extensive travel plans for him. This may result in corn planting playing "second fiddle."

Ninety-six year old Francis Glaspey of Johnson County finds himself caught on the horns of a dilemma. Not once in over 80 years has he missed a season of fieldwork in this country or in Canada.

This winter, with deep snow and bitter cold prevailing through most of January, the elderly eastern Iowa farmer has been looking forward to spring's arrival more eagerly than ever. He is anxious to get back on his old Case tractor this May and again help his son, Robert, and grandson, Bruce, with seedland preparations and cultivating.

At the same time, however, Glaspey may have the opportunity to make a sentimental journey back to many of the places he worked and farmed, both in the U.S. and Canada.

His oldest daughter, Mrs. Myrl Jackson of Grinnell, has offered to accompany her father on the ambitious trip, but it may have to take place when fieldwork is at its peak here in Iowa. "And that's where the rub is at." says Glaspey.

Flanked by son, Robert, left, and grandson, Bruce, right, 96-year-old Francis Glaspey proudly wears his harvest hat.

The proposed trip sounds very tempting. "It sure would bring back many memories," says Glaspey. However, the journey, if made by automobile or bus, could take eight weeks or even more. "And that might knock me out of plowing corn," he complains.

Cultivating corn is Glaspey's favorite task. Mrs. Jackson says, "We may have to plan the trip around that job." Meanwhile, Francis is somewhat concerned about cultivating work this year because of a slight deterioration in one eye.

Recalling his boyhood, he says, "With my team and walking cultivator, I might plow out or cover a hill once in a great while. That didn't matter much then. But now, with a six-row cultivator hitched to the tractor, every time I goof on one hill, I clobber five others."

If it materializes, the trip might start in Pottawattamie County, where Glaspey was born, go on to other Iowa counties where he spent his boyhood, and then to North Dakota, where as a young teenager, he worked on an older brother's farm several years.

Francis would like to go into Manitoba where, at 18, he worked in harvest fields and contemplated homesteading. Next the journey would take him to Montana where he took a turn at being a cowboy, and then Washington, where he helped with the harvest, then got a job on a 35,000 acre irrigation project.

Later, at 21, he returned to North Dakota to claim a 160 acre homestead site near his brother's spread. However, North Dakota's dry weather, small yields, and big mosquitoes were not for him. So, he came back to Iowa before going on to Chicago to an auctioneering school.

Francis returned to Iowa and married Carrie Mentzer. He started farming in March, 1909.

They raised six children. In addition to Mrs. Jackson, they are Velma Rugesegger, Mitchellville; Meda, now deceased; Robert, who now has the farm near Hills; Katherine Rose, who lives in Florida; and Carl of Arizona, who died last year. There are 20 grandchildren and one great-grandchild. Mrs. Glaspey died a few years ago.

Remembering "The Way It Was" is one of Francis Glaspey's favorite pastimes. During his youth, he says working long days for 50¢ was not unusual. However, during harvest seasons, he got $2.50 a day.

Stacking grain was the vogue in the early 1900s. Glaspey recalls how four stacks were made so a thresher could be set between them. Steam engines on 44 inch separators were used, and the young Iowan found himself a busy man.

Francis's long life is nothing unusual in the Glaspey family. His oldest sister lived to be 99. His youngest sister, Carrie, is now 94. A brother, Jim, is 92.

The Glaspeys are an agricultural family through and through, beginning with the great-great-grandfather who came from Ireland to farm in New Jersey. Robert's son, Bruce, now 24, is a fifth generation American farmer.

In addition to their farm interests, the Glaspeys have taken a fancy to auctioneering. Francis himself is a graduate of the Jones Auction School in Chicago. Three of his brothers, Bert, Bill, and Dick, joined him in crying sales in eastern Iowa. The son, Bob, attended a Mason City auction school and is now an active auctioneer. Bruce, the grandson, is also starting to cry sales.

Francis's daughters, Myrl and Velma, say, "Dad's real hobby is work. We can't keep him out of the fields in the summer and can't stop him from shoveling snow in the winter."

His white geese are his pride and joy. But he takes equally good care of his guinea hens, turkeys, and chickens, just as he formerly did with his horses, cattle, hogs, sheep, and even goats. His special delight now is gathering up to two dozen or more eggs a day, no matter what the weather.

BORN TO THE LAND
March 27, 1982

Farming can be like a roller coaster with endless ups and downs. No one knows this better than Richard "Dick" Stephens, vice president of the Iowa Farm Bureau many years, and later, a State Senator. A fourth generation member of a six generation farm family, Stephens knows how bleak, as well as how rewarding, a farm enterprise can be.

As is true of many other Master Farmers honored by WALLACES FARMER over the years, Richard Stephens of Washington County was born to the land. A former state senator and Iowa Farm Bureau leader, Dick, as he is best known, is the fourth of six generations to till the same farm.

A family history shows that in 1839 Samuel Stephens, Dick's great-grandfather, came to Iowa from Ohio by covered wagon. Three years later, he walked from Crawfordsville to Burlington and back to secure a land patent at $1.25 per acre, signed by President Tyler.

Richard "Dick" Stephens in his extensive library.

Richard Stephens, now 78, has carried on the family farming tradition, starting with a four-horse hitch on a sulky when he was only five years of age. A hired man had suddenly quit, and the elder Stephens was anxious to get the field turned. Accordingly, he placed young Dick on the seat, gave him the reins, and had him help finish the field. Dick says, "I felt ten feet tall and was the proudest kid in Washington County." It's a miracle he got the plow into the ground.

Recalling "the way it was" in his youth, Dick Stephens tells of driving an eight-horse hitch on a $15, three-bottom gang plow and of husking and scooping corn for 2¢ a bushel. One severe winter found him earning money hauling 15¢ corn.

In 1926, Dick married Florence Kraus, his eighth grade classmate and sweetheart. She had gone to State Teachers College (University of Northern Iowa), and taught several years. Dick attended Iowa State College (Iowa State University) before he was called home to help in the family farm operation. In the late '20s, two sons, Allen and Boyd, were born.

Adversity, as well as success, has marked Dick Stephens' career. On returning from Ames, he, his father, and his three brothers signed a note for a land purchase. A few years later, when the bottom fell out of farm returns, the sheriff came to serve foreclosure notice. "With only $80 in my name, and no credit, that was a rough time." says Dick.

The next year, however, he managed to rent a large farm on what was termed a "sliding scale" policy. Stephens was still trying to make a shaky comeback in 1934 when drought struck. He says, "I nearly got wiped out a second time."

As conditions improved, Stephens expanded the enterprise. Eventually, he was handling over 400 acres, producing 30,000 bushels of corn, and up to 400 cattle and 3000 hogs annually. He became a pioneer in confinement feeding, and was named Iowa Master Pork Producer in 1942, one of the first of some 900 hog producers so honored.

Stephens was a pioneer in soil conservation — terracing, contouring, and grassed waterways.

Stephens made many contributions in community and political circles, as well as in agriculture. He has been active in church, school, 4-H, Shrine Hospital, Farm Bureau and other community work. In the political area, he served in the Iowa House eight years and six in the State Senate.

When he was named a Master Farmer in 1948, some of the strongest points in Stephens' nomination were his overall farm management and his penchant for keeping daily records since 1926. Those records show a fascinating story of agriculture's ups and downs.

Originally both the Stephens' sons were destined to farm. However, at age 18, Allen was stricken with polio, leaving him severely handicapped. Gifted with a keen mind, Allen later became his father's principle legislative advisor.

Meanwhile, Boyd, the younger son, went on to operate the Stephens century farm, where he crops 600 acres and feeds up to 700 cattle annually. Boyd's two daughters and a son are the sixth generation on the Stephens' farms.

Recently, Mr. and Mrs. Richard Stephens celebrated their 55th wedding anniversary amid an ocean of memories, including that exciting day in 1948 when they were named Iowa Master Farmers.

A VERY LARGE FAMILY, WITH FOUR GENERATIONS RAISING JERSEYS
June, 1982

Fred Metzger is quite a family man. He has fourteen children, 84 grandchildren, 165 great-grandchildren, and 13 brothers and sisters. And most of that "small army" of Metzgers are in farming enterprises or in the dairy business. I also found the elder Metzger to be one of the most interesting persons I've ever interviewed. This column tells why.

June Dairy Month is a significant nationwide observance for all dairy producers. For 97-year old Fred Metzger of Rock Rapids, it is a special occasion. Metzger is a pioneer northwest Iowa Jersey breeder and the patriarch of four generations of active dairymen.

Five of Metzger's 14 children became Jersey breeders and all but two of the others farmed in Lyon County. Of his 84 grandchildren, most entered farming and a dozen became prominent Jersey cattle producers or were otherwise involved in dairying. Many of 165 great-grandchildren are also following in their great-grandfather's steps in farming or raising Jerseys.

Remarkably alert and active for his age, the elder Metzger now lives in Lyon Manor, a retirement center. He is confined to a wheelchair much of the time. Along with keeping tabs on grandchildren and great-grandchildren, he reads extensively, latch hooks rugs, keeps business records, plays bingo, and entertains visitors. He also keeps up on Jersey cattle developments, repairs old clocks, and cheers up everyone in the manor.

Born in Illinois in 1885 of German immigrant parents, he and his 13 brothers and sisters spent their childhood in eastern Iowa and southern Minnesota.

His early manhood was spent in northern Missouri where he first became enamored with Jerseys more than 75 years ago.

97-year-old Fred Metzger keeping busy.

In 1906, Fred and a brother rented a small Lyon County farm, grew a spring crop, then threshed out grain stacks from August to early November.

One job was on the Knobloch farm near Lester, where Fred quickly noticed one of the family's pretty young daughters. Courtship rapidly followed, and on November 17, shortly after the last bundles were threshed, Fred and Carrie were married. The union was to last 73 years until Carrie's death in 1980.

After acquiring minimal amounts of equipment and stock, the young couple rented a quarter section in early 1908, farmed it several years, then bought 154 acres, at $125 an acre, in 1918.

Then in the mid '20s, with a dozen prospective young milkers growing up, Fred was able to make his dream come true. A consignment of Illinois high grade Jerseys came to Iowa and Fred bought 21 of the best, partially converted the big horse barn to a milking shed, and put each cow's name above her own stanchion. The Metzger Jersey herd soon became among the best in the state.

During the difficult late '20s and early '30s, the Metzgers were glad they had switched to dairying. "When the bottom dropped out of everything else, it was pretty nice for a family of 16 to have a cream check come in every week," opines Fred.

Fred started the foundation herd for what is now almost a Lyon County Jersey dynasty, expanded by some of his sons and grandsons. Altogether, the Metzger Jersey total is now above 1000 head, of which some 395 are actual producers.

After his wife died, Fred moved to his present home in Lyon Manor, where he delights in telling visitors about "the way it was" and of the innumerable changes in dairying since he saw his first Jersey 80 years ago. He says, "We've gone from the three-legged milking stool to Pyrex pipelines and herringbone milking parlors."

An interesting aspect of the Metzger interview is that the family asked Ernie, Fred's oldest son, to be present to correct any errors the 97-year old gentleman might make. Instead of Ernie correcting Fred, it was the other way around. Fred corrected his 73-year-old son three times, then took me to his clock repair room, where a dozen large timepieces, including grandfather clocks, were awaiting his expertise in clock repairing.

AG PROGRAM SIGN-UP WORRIES PIONEER COMMITTEEMAN
July 10, 1982

President Franklin Roosevelt's and Henry A Wallace's government farm programs, their history and merits, as well as concerns about their future, are eloquently voiced by Laurel Dieterich, long time county and state committeeman, fiery champion of the AAA and similar programs, and my guest for this column. A half-century of intense farm program involvement is summarized.

Laurel Dieterich, veteran State Committeeman

In farm circles, one of today's major questions centers on compliance with the 1982 acreage reduction signup. Watching the outcome with great interest is 87-year old H. Laurel Dieterich of Montezuma, a pioneer in AAA and corn/hog programs of the early '30s.

"The 78% signup this spring was gratifying," says Dieterich, and adds, "but if corn prices advance between now and July 30, half of those 118,413 farmers signed up will drop out. That will be a tragedy. The only way to avert disaster in agriculture is to cut production."

Dieterich speaks from long, bitter experience and a unique historical perspective. In 1918, he started farming, struggling all through the trying '20s when hog prices fell to $2.50 per cwt., and into the early '30s when corn plunged to 10¢ a bushel.

Recalling "the way it was" 50 or more years ago, Dieterich says, "Our markets were manipulated. We fought drought, pestilence, crop failure, and low prices, and had little to say about our products. Too often, at year's end there was nothing to show for our labors."

Dieterich's face lights up, though, when he recalls how, out of desperation, the sons of the soil finally awakened. Right after the 1932 New Deal landslide, H.A. Wallace, the WALLACES FARMER editor, was named Secretary of Agriculture. "That's when things started happening for the better," he says.

Wallace, who frequently editorialized about burdensome surpluses, convinced President Roosevelt something had to be done. On May 12, 1933, the Agricultural Adjustment Act was enacted. Shortly, Wallace requested Iowa corn and hog producers meet in Des Moines to organize a state corn/hog committee and asked farmers to administer an emergency hog marketing program.

The plan called for marketing hogs at much lighter weights, thereby relieving the pork glut. It also included slaughtering bred sows and gilts before farrowing. A 4¢ a pound premium was paid to farmers complying with the program. Dieterich was named township chairman of the program. Within a year, he was elevated to district fieldman, leaving his wife and 18-year old son to handle the heavily mortgaged farm.

Some 4000 farmers, all determined that AAA continue, descended on Washington to meet with Roosevelt and Wallace. Roosevelt thanked them for their compliance and asked the farmers to remind city dwellers that "empty farm pocketbooks do not turn factory wheels."

After the AAA was declared unconstitutional, the Domestic Soil Conservation Allotment program was approved. Dieterich was named one of the three state committeemen to administer the plan and head the state's commodity credit program. Dieterich also wrote a history of AAA in Iowa.

Then followed a time of personal tragedy, including the sudden death of his 19-year old daughter, Dorothy, and the breakup of his marriage. The difficult period was climaxed when his defense of employees not able to make political contributions cost him his state committee assignment.

On returning to Poweshiek County, Dieterich was asked to administer the ASCS program until his retirement in 1966. In the meantime, he remarried. Today, he and Margery live in Montezuma, while son Kenneth and his family operate the home farm near Brooklyn.

In reviewing his nearly 50 years of concern with farm program activities, Dieterich says cooperation and compliance with acreage reduction is absolutely essential. He concludes, "If all farmers who signed up to cut production would stay with the program, we could work our way out of this mess in a year or two, thereby guaranteeing profitable returns for everyone."

FIFTY YEARS WITH THE IOWA STATE FAIR
July 24, 1982

As one who has missed only two Iowa State Fairs since 1924 — and those two only because I was in Washington serving as Assistant to the Secretary of Agriculture, Dr. Earl Butz — I love to hear long-time State Fair officials recount their experiences. No one could do that better than Harry Duncan, past president of the annual Iowa Exposition. Here are some of his recollections.

From state fair hog barn helper and ticket taker in 1919 to president of the famed Iowa exposition in 1966 — that's the story of Harry Duncan, Louisa County fair enthusiast.

Duncan, now 85, and far from retired, loves nothing more than to reminisce on "The Way It Was" in farming and fair going the past 70 years or more. Sitting back in his spacious real estate office in Columbus Junction, he enjoys relating his experiences as a farmer and stockman, auctioneer, county fair official, and as an employee, exhibitor, showman, director, vice president, and president of the Iowa State Fair.

Born and bred a stockman, his grandfather Duncan brought some "China" hogs to Iowa in 1847. Later, Harry's father enlarged and improved the Poland China herd. Then in 1916, Harry, youngest of nine children, and his brother, William, started their own Poland herd. The partnership was to last nearly 30 years. Many championships were won at county and regional fairs.

Recalling show ring experiences, Duncan says they used two railroad box cars for their show stock, feed, straw, and other equipment, going by train from one fair to the next. Some weeks, they would clear $100 above expenses.

Duncan's association with the Iowa State Fair started humbly.

A cousin, Jay Duncan, then swine show superintendent for the Des Moines exposition, took Harry and others with him in 1919 to clean pens and enter hogs in the show. A day after the fair opened, ticket sellers at the south gate failed to show. Fair officials quickly enlisted Harry and one of his pals to take over.

The next year Duncan was assigned to the Grand Avenue entrance with its heavy auto traffic. He chuckles when he explains, "We jumped on the running boards of the moving Model Ts, collected the admission, jumped off, and never missed a fare."

Two years later, he was advanced to the main office for admissions, serving in that capacity several more years. However, in 1927, when June wedding bells rang, he gave up state fair duties to concentrate more on farming and showing Polands.

But a few years later, Harry took over the exposition's swine department. He worked closely with the late Lloyd Cunningham, the state fair secretary, and later with Ken Fulk, whom he described as the greatest promoter he has ever known, "whether there was money on hand or not."

Under Duncan's leadership, the Iowa swine show soon was recognized as one of the nation's largest and best.

Harry Duncan, congenial Iowa State Fair President.

In 1949, state fair officials responded by electing Duncan to the board. Then, in the early '60s, he was chosen vice president, and in 1966 was elected president.

Fond recollections of his 26 years of service on the fair board include the Iowa State Fair Centennial, when President Eisenhower was guest of honor. Duncan proudly exclaims, "What a show we put on for him and for all of Iowa that year."

Highest satisfaction, however, came from working with thousands of leading livestock breeders and with FFA and 4-H members. Greatest thrills for both Harry and Mrs. Duncan were hosting grandstand show celebrities.

Their four sons, William, Robert, Paul and Larry, also got to take in the fair, but as livestock barn workers instead of vacationers. "We enjoyed it all, though," says Mrs. Duncan, adding that "all ISF officials and their wives stayed in the old administration building for the fair's duration and became one big, happy family."

As for problems, Duncan is quick to explain coming out on top financially is the greatest concern, while rain, or the threat of it, and refunding money for grandstand seats is the worst fear. Duncan feels the fair is an important institution and a major Iowa showcase.

ROBINSON, ARCHITECT OF IOWA CROP IMPROVEMENT
September 11, 1982

Over the years, thousands of Iowans have had a hand in improving corn, grain, and legume or grass varieties. However, when it comes down to selecting one person for his overall, untiring crop improvement efforts, one of my long-time idols, Dr. Joe Robinson of Iowa State, quickly comes to mind. "Doctor Joe" had worked with almost everyone else in the crop improvement field for over 50 years. His contributions were enormous. This article told about some of those accomplishments.

Dr. Joe Robinson, architect of crop improvement.

Many Iowa farm families owe a debt of gratitude to Joe Robinson, retired Iowa State University seed researcher. Now Robinson looks back on more than 60 years of progress in crop improvement.

Joe has been the driving force in Iowa's seed improvement programs since their inception in 1920. A native Oklahoman, he first came to Iowa State College as an agronomy graduate student in 1916. After a year of service in WWI, and a year of teaching at the University of Wyoming, he, with his bride, the former Ruth Nash, returned to ISC's campus to work on crop production.

Robinson guided seed producer associations, directed state and international grain shows, and designed the famed Iowa Corn Yield Test. He pioneered in hybrid corn production and established Iowa's widely heralded seed certification program. He also successfully combined various corn, grain, soybean, and other seed producing organizations under one umbrella, now called the Iowa Crop Improvement Association.

Even the most conservative estimate on increased value of certified seed, both to producer and buyer, will reveal millions of dollars of added annual income to Iowa farms. This explains why Robinson is universally regarded as "Mr. Iowa Certified Seed."

It is also a major reason why Iowa State University students this year singled out Robinson for their coveted Agricultural Hall of Fame award.

"Recognizing that advances from 35 bushels per acre corn averages to recent 200 bushels "plus" have been achieved the past 60 years, we will need new breakthroughs in plant structure, soil nutrients, water supplies, and other inputs if we hope to duplicate those dramatic improvements," says Robinson.

IOWA CORN AUTHORITY BECAME A DIPLOMAT
September 25, 1982

How one man, who was a confidant of Henry A. Wallace, wrote books about corn, became a diplomat, and single-handedly stopped a war in South America, was detailed in this column about Dr. Earl Bressman. I was almost spellbound as he told me about those and other exploits. The interview took place in one of his Western Iowa cornfields.

It was 60 years ago this fall that Earl Bressman, as Iowa State College (ISC) graduate student, wrote the final paragraphs of a book devoted entirely to corn production. Co-author was H.A. Wallace, editor of *WALLACES FARMER*. Bressman did not realize then that the book would become the first of five volumes he would edit and revise for use in ag college classrooms and on thousands of farms for the next six decades.

Nor could the Hamilton County student, youngest of 11 children from a Swedish immigrant family, dream of the illustrious career on which he was about to embark.

This month, Dr. Earl Bressman, now 88 and a respected western Iowa farmer-banker, daily checks his own bumper crop of corn. He vividly remembers the endless research and tireless writing he did back in 1922. "Much of that work is now obsolete," admits Bressman. Then he adds, "But some of it is as practical today as it was then, and has paid off for me, and thousands of other corn growers for six decades."

Recalling "The Way It Was", Bressman tells about first meeting Wallace. He says, "I was a young WWI veteran enrolled in Ames College as ISU was then known. We were immediately attracted to each other by our mutual interest in corn production and breeding and in persuading Iowa State officials to devote more time and land to corn research. That was 1919 and we hit it off well."

In the early '20s, soon after Bressman had received his BA in agronomy, and had married the daughter of Monona County banker Charles Moorhead, Wallace invited the young couple to Des Moines. Conversation quickly drifted to corn, and to the need for a practical volume on corn production. The result was Bressman agreed to join Wallace in writing a book to be entitled *Corn and Corn Growing*.

Bressman researched and wrote most of the practical material. Wallace dealt with crop economics and provided the tables and charts.

Intended primarily as a textbook for college ag students, the book was equally popular among practical farmers. Two more updated editions were published.

The FDR landslide victory had catapulted Wallace into the Roosevelt cabinet as Secretary of Agriculture; and as soon as Wallace had been confirmed, he sent for Bressman to become his principal advisor.

Although not schooled in politics, Bressman soon found himself in the thick of the action. He and Assistant Secretary Tugwell handled the day-to-day details of the department, with the Iowan in charge of the Beltsville Experiment Station and 20 department bureaus.

Major controversies also flared. In 1935-36, Interior Secretary Ickes, noted for his quick temper and determination, demanded the then Soil Erosion Service be headquartered in his department. Wallace was equally determined it remain in agriculture. Bressman will never forget the hectic weekend when he and several trusted friends wrote a bill advocating a name change to Soil Conservation Service, with the proviso USDA be in charge. Congress quickly approved the proposal, much to Ickes' wrathful dismay and Wallace's satisfaction.

After the interdepartmental feud died down, Bressman took time out to revise and update the corn producers' "Bible" a fourth time.

Although still Wallace's daily confidant, Bressman was being wooed by state department leaders. Given a leave from USDA, he was asked to undertake diplomatic tasks in Latin America, most of them centered on agriculture and economics. One fulfilling reward came when Bressman was accorded Ecuador's Medal of Honor.

It was in South America in early 1938 when Bressman scored his greatest triumph. A bloody war had been raging between Bolivia and Paraguay for three years. Roosevelt, anxious the fighting end, dispatched Bressman to meet with Paraguayan officials.

He met with the Paraguayan president, learned of the country's most pressing needs, and then offered to provide $2 million in loans and aid for education, road building, sanitation, and farm credit, on condition that hostilities end immediately. The Paraguayan dictator agreed, called his generals together, and ordered a cease-fire.

Bressman, U.S. State Department Official who once prevented a South American war.

The next day, President Roosevelt informed his cabinet the South American conflict had been ended by Earl Bressman, the astute, soft spoken Iowa farm boy turned diplomat. His diplomacy resulted in a presidential commendation.

Bressman remained in government service several more years, handling many responsibilities.

He was Inter-American Agricultural Affairs Director for Nelson Rockefeller. On another occasion, he worked with the famed Walt Disney on a Hollywood documentary film about South America. Costa Rican officials called on Bressman to plan and supervise construction of a million dollar Inter-American Institute of Agriculture and serve as its first director.

After nearly 30 years of dedicated and distinguished national and international public service, Bressman returned to Iowa to join his father-in-law in the banking business, and to assist Jay Newlin and Edgar Anderson in revising the fifth and last edition of the book he and Wallace first co-authored in 1922.

The final version of Corn and Corn Growing was in marked contrast to the original book. Published in 1949, the new volume incorporated the latest scientific knowledge on hybridization, harvesting techniques, marketing, and uses of corn and corn products. Inbreeding, single crosses, corn performance trials, production costs, and factors still applicable today were emphasized.

On the death of his father-in-law in 1956, Bressman took over the presidency of the Moorhead State Bank, a position he continues to hold. He and

Mrs. Bressman live in a rambling, beautifully appointed home, each room filled with treasured mementoes of their many years in teaching and in public service, and with pictures of their children, Donna (now the wife of Gen. Richard Beckner of Arlington, Virginia), and Dr. Charles Bressman, a physician, who lives with his wife and four children in Omaha.

Bressman gives credit for his many successes to the inspiration, support, and encouragement from his wife and his late father-in-law, and says hard work and educational preparedness helped him be at "the right place at the right time."

As for his romance with corn, he says, "That flame burns as brightly now as when I wrote the opening paragraphs of Corn and Corn Growing back in 1922. Corn is the greatest plant God has given us, with its ability to provide so abundantly for a world where food remains the first law of life." "Yes," he concludes, "corn will always be the 'King of Crops.'"

MASTER FARM HOMEMAKER RECALLS HARD TIMES
November 27, 1982

Anyone wondering what life could be like for a young Iowa farm couple in the late '20s and early '30s, will find this column very informative and highly interesting. Mrs. Ross Willey recalled what took place on their own farm during those trying years, and some of the more pleasant experiences that followed.

When *WALLACES FARMER* honored Iowa's newest group of Master Farm Homemakers on November 23, many women previously recognized were present. Among them was Helen Willey, class of 1947.

This western Iowa farmwife recalls her own induction vividly. She says, "Zoe Murphy called from Onawa saying she wanted to visit. I was in the midst of canning and was to sing at a funeral a few hours later. There was no time to get things tidied up for so important a visitor."

Nevertheless, Mrs. Murphy, then women's editor, must have liked what she saw. Three weeks later, a letter arrived informing the Monona County woman she was one of five chosen for the state's highest farm homemaking honor.

Mrs. Willey still revels in her role as a farm homemaker. She and her husband, Ross, operate 400 acres near Whiting.

The Willeys met while attending the University of Iowa. They were married in 1928 after Helen had taught for several years and Ross had rented a bottomland farm.

Their first home was large and rambling; but they had to limit their living quarters to the kitchen and one bedroom because their cookstove, fueled by cobs and wood cut from the riverbank, was their only heating element. Water had to be pumped and carried by hand, and there were no modern conveniences or electricity.

A son, Vincent, arrived in 1929, the year of the stock market crash. Their daughter, Ruth, was born the next year when the bottom started dropping out of farm returns.

The drought of '34 and the bitter winter of '36, followed by a blazing hot summer, took its toll. But what the Willeys remember most clearly was the 1952 flood when the mighty Missouri River was 17 miles wide in places.

They had to move the Ayrshire dairy herd to higher ground on a brother-in-law's place while hogs were taken to a Woodbury County friend, and the Angus moved to Turin. They moved what furniture they could upstairs, rolled up the carpets, and put bricks under the stove legs and 10-gallon milk cans under the piano.

Master Farm Homemaker Helen Wiley with special 50th anniversary remembrance.

Along with her housework, caring for two lively children, raising and canning vegetables, and tending a flock of White Rocks, Mrs. Willey helped in the fields and with livestock. She also served her community in many ways, including school, church, Farm Bureau, Eastern Star, and youth.

She describes getting training under Mrs. Raymond Sayre, internationally renowned leader of farm women, as her most enriching experience. Being chosen a delegate to the Copenhagen convention of the Associated Country Women of the World was her greatest thrill.

Following the Copenhagen meeting, Mrs. Willey traveled extensively in Europe visiting farm homes. This experience resulted in the Willeys opening their farm home for vacation opportunities for city visitors from the U.S. and other lands.

Although still interested in many activities, the Willeys now concentrate largely on their seven grandchildren and seven great-grandchildren. At ages 80 and 76, Ross and Helen are still busy farming and have no intention of moving to town.

The way it was . . .
1 9 8 3

FARMER LEGISLATOR RECALLS FLOOR BATTLES
January 23, 1983

The Iowa Legislature begins its annual session in January every year. It seemed logical to choose a legislator as the opening guest for 1983. Although there were many from which to select, I quickly chose Charles Strothman, veteran farmer and legislator. Strothman's abundance of common sense and good advice, based on years of farm and Capitol Hill experience, made him the logical preference.

There are 41 freshman legislators in this year's Iowa General Assembly. Any one or all of this group of newly elected lawmakers would be well-advised to seek the counsel of Charles Strothman, New London farmer and 10-year veteran of service on Capitol Hill.

Strothman, now 81, served during the 60th to 64th General Assemblies. "My first term in the house was in 1963 and I was pretty quiet," explains the Henry County stockman. Then he adds, "But I did a lot of homework and sought advice from experienced legislators."

Strothman suggests to this year's freshmen group, "Be seen and not heard. Observe carefully. Analyze your colleagues. Don't step on too many toes, and be friendly with those in the opposition party as well as those in your own."

Charles Strothman, farmer and legislator.

A long-time livestock breeder and producer, Strothman was placed on the agricultural committee in his first term. The next four sessions, he served as ag chairman and was a member of the appropriations, education, ways and means, and highway and road committees.

The southeast Iowa farmer vividly remembers some of the battles fought on the house floor. He says, "Reapportionment resulted in a hundred different plans before we settled on one." Strothman was in the forefront in beating back union labor forces in right-to-work legislation.

The Henry A. Wallace Agricultural Building was another hotly debated issue while Strothman was in the house. Convinced Iowa needed a central department of agriculture headquarters, he saw "red" when city lawmakers tried to divert ag building funds to other purposes.

He was also a constant champion of tax reform and good roads, and a strong advocate of livestock and crop checkoffs, hog cholera and brucellosis control, and crime prevention.

Looking ahead to legislation in the 70th General Assembly this year, Strothman says the question of tax revenue will get top priority, but proposals to abandon 100,000 miles of Iowa's farm roads must be defeated. He is also opposed to pari-mutuel betting. Strothman feels a uniform grading law must be passed in this session.

Strothman's wife of 54 years was his research assistant during their service in Des Moines. She was an enthusiastic member of the Ladies League and often guided visitors through the capitol.

The former legislator is still active in Strothman Farms with sons, Charles and John, a grandson, and son-in-law, Emmett Messer, whose wife is a district Farm Bureau committeewoman. Three other children are also farm, extension, and agri-business oriented, as are most of his 19 grandchildren and four great-grandchildren.

FINDS PROFIT IN LAMBS
February 26, 1983

Sixty-five years is a long time for anyone to pursue the same undertaking, but one Iowa shepherd gave T.L.C. to his flock of sheep all that while and did not stop even then. John McMahon, 79, was one of the Midwest's most knowledgeable lamb producers. This column tells why.

It's lambing time in Iowa. By April, some 13,000 farm flocks will have produced an estimated 340,000 lambs to maintain Iowa's national leadership in lamb production.

For 79-year old John McMahon of Corwith, lambing time brings no surprises. This marks the 65th season he has served as a round-the-clock "midwife" in his lambing pens.

John McMahon with grandsons and lambs.

McMahon's career as a sheep raiser started in 1918 when his father bought a flock of Shropshire ewes. John explains, "My older brother felt sheep were below his dignity, so my dad turned them over to me. I've been at it ever since."

The veteran sheepman started farming on his own in Hancock County just 50 years ago, raising up to 200 ewes a year. During his career he has produced an estimated 10,000 lambs, he notes.

A dedicated shepherd, McMahon sometimes averages less than three hours sleep a night during the month-long lambing period. "Being there when the little 'bleaters' arrive to make sure they nurse right away is vitally important," he asserts.

Over the years, McMahon has averaged a 130% lamb crop, achieving 150% at times. "If I average $1^1/4$ lambs per ewe, I can show a good profit," he declares.

McMahon devotes less than 40 acres of his 160 to alfalfa and the corn and beans necessary to feed out his lambs in drylot. With corn at $2.47 a bushel, McMahon figures he netted several hundred dollars per acre with sheep last year. "But it wasn't always that way," he quickly adds.

Recalling "the way it was" 65 years ago, he says all sheep were pastured and at the mercy of the weather, parasites, and wolves. None were fed grain. Wool was of poor quality and sold cheap. Very little lamb was served, and mutton was despised by most housewives.

"We've come a long way since that time," remarks McMahon. He says he "got smart" some 25 years ago when he switched to drylot feeding. In addition, he developed a better breeding program, provided good housing, started using well-balanced rations, and went to cooperative marketing.

Feeding punctually at 5 a.m., 12 noon, and 6 p.m. daily without fail is another McMahon ritual.

McMahon believes good rams account for two-thirds of a lamb flock's potential, so he purchases the best purebred Hampshire and Suffolk rams he can locate to use on his cross-bred ewes.

Lambs are finished within 120 days at 110 to 115 lb.

McMahon is a director and grader for Quad County Lamb Co-op. As soon as 400 lambs of like weight and quality are assembled, he and Riley Gillette of Spencer phone a Baraboo, Wisconsin, computerized marketing outlet, where up to twelve packers from throughout the nation bid on the Iowa finished lambs.

A widower since 1978, McMahon now does all his own cooking and baking. Lamb shoulder is his favorite dish, although he also admits to some fondness for chops and leg-o-lamb. He has a daughter, Mrs. Marie Egolf in California, and two sons, James in Alabama and Emmet in New Jersey.

There are eight grandchildren whose annual visits he deeply appreciates, adding, "The four youngest — Sarah, two Johnnies, and Tommy — are just as fond of the baby lambs as Grampa is himself."

MASTER FARMER WAS FARM CREDIT LEADER
March 26, 1983

A community, state, national and international farm leader and spokesman was selected for my third column for 1983. He was Bill Davidson, successful, personable, likeable and extremely knowledgeable Master Farmer. Bill's dedication to the value of farm credit placed him in high positions in this country and in yeoman service overseas.

Wise use of credit has long been a key to success in farming. Nowhere is this more evident than among Master Farmer award winners. "Credit is one of modern agriculture's most valuable tools," says 82-year old William Davidson of Stanwood, named a Master Farmer by Wallaces farmer in 1947.

Bill Davidson not only has seen how essential agricultural credit was on his own family's farm operations, but also as a local, regional, national, and international farm credit official. The Cedar

Davidson was a Master Farmer and international agriculturalist.

County farmer was one of this country's early Production Credit Association (PCA) leaders, and, along with his wife, Lois, served two hitches as an agricultural credit co-op advisor in Africa.

Davidson recalls how his grandfather, driven out of Ireland by the potato famine, walked from Muscatine to Stanwood to claim a 120-acre homestead. Later, after building a cabin along the Davenport stage route, the elder Davidson borrowed money to acquire another 40 acres.

Handling credit became a Davidson family tradition when the grandfather started a country bank in 1890. In the early 1900s, Bill's father became a board member, later to be succeeded by Bill himself.

"We learned about credit the hard way," asserts the Iowa Master Farmer, recalling 1932 when the farm mortgage was due and banks failed.

When Bill married Lois Munn in 1928, he started farming. Difficult times followed. By 1932, farm foreclosures were far more numerous than now. But, they buckled down, spent less than $100 a year for groceries, kept using horses, had a Grade A dairy herd, and fed steers.

His banker advised him to hang on. And when the bank closed in 1933, Davidson still had 150 steers on feed.

"That's when PCA entered the picture," says Bill. The newly organized Davenport PCA lent him 5¢ a pound on his steers, enabling them to be fed out and sold.

Bill was enthusiastic about what PCA had done for him and others, and of its concept whereby borrowers can organize cooperatively, buy stock, and eventually gain ownership. He agreed to serve on the Davenport PCA board the next year. Two years later, he became president and watched its growth from $200,000 in loans the first year to well over $20 million annually now.

In 1952, Davidson was elected to the regional PCA board in Omaha, and in '54 was elected president. Four years later, he was elected a director of the Federal Farm Credit Board.

The Iowan's work in international farm credit circles began by leading a group of Panamanians on a tour of U.S. co-ops. No sooner had he finished that assignment than he was chosen to become an agricultural credit advisor in Libya. After a crash course in Arabic, the Davidsons held their farm sale and flew to Tripoli.

After a stint in North Africa, the Davidsons went to what is now Tanzania to establish branch banks.

The busy Iowa Master Farmer retired in 1968.

FARMER TURNED "PREACHER"
April 23, 1983

It may have been attendance at "Billy Sunday's" long ago revival meetings and hearing the famed evangelist preach that eventually inspired him. In any case, my close friend "Cob" Glenn, long-time farmer and state leader in agricultural, Red Cross, and other wartime assignments, wound up as an ordained pastor. This Easter season feature summarized his fascinating experiences and rewarding life.

When Easter messages were heard earlier this month, few clergymen presented their sermon with greater fervor than a retired 82-year old Mitchellville, Iowa, farmer turned preacher.

Coldren Glenn, now serving the New Virginia Christian church, did not obtain his lay minister's license until he was 67 years old.

Glenn has a rich heritage in both farming and religion. He is the son of a Civil War veteran who came to Iowa in 1855. Today, Glennsdale Farm, owned by Glenn, is on the exact site where that covered wagon trek ended 128 years ago. He is one of a handful of Iowans who was born, and still lives in, a Century Farm home built 100 years ago.

Farmer, preacher, C.C. Glen.

Glenn's parents were founding members of the Mitchellville Christian Church. At age eight, he started attending Billy Sunday's revival meetings.

Glenn entered farming the hard way when he had to take over at age 22 because of a family emergency.

Recalling "the way it was", he speaks of his fondness for horses, big hitches, and breaking colts. He says, "I liked my horses so much I didn't get a tractor until 1941."

As a beginning farmer, Glenn joined the Farm Improvement Association, forerunner of the Farm Bureau. Soon thereafter, he was named a county director, and then became organization director for central Iowa. In the mid '30s, he was active in the Corn-Hog and AAA programs.

Glenn's effectiveness as a speaker and organizer did not go unnoticed.

The National Farm Institute, Chamber of Commerce committee, historical societies, and church groups all sought his services. The Red Cross made him county chairman; and when WW II broke out, he was the unanimous choice for war board chairman.

Now an eloquent speaker, he recalls being terrified at any oratorical assignment during high school. However, while in college, he studied public speaking to help overcome his fear.

In 1931, young Glenn married Alta Riddle. Four years later, their oldest daughter, Mary (now Mrs. David Fuchs of Cleveland), arrived. Martha (now Mrs. Richard Mitchell of Gainsville) was born in 1938. Two years later, she was named the Iowa State Fair's grand champion baby. There are five grandchildren.

Many Iowans remember "Cob" Glenn, as he is best known, for the millions of dollars he helped raise during WW II as state chairman for the war bond division, or as executive director for the Iowa Production and Marketing Administration (PMA). Still others speak of Glenn's leadership in Men's Christian Fellowship circles or as chairman of the first National Plowing Match.

A heart attack in the early '60s slowed him down. After he recovered, he concentrated on Christian Fellowship and then enrolled in the Eureka School of Theology, receiving his license as a lay minister in 1968.

Soon afterwards, Glenn was asked to preach at the New Virginia church. Ever since, almost every Sunday of the year, the Glenns have made the 126 mile round trip to serve a small, but highly appreciative, audience.

Speaking for the congregation, Mrs. Marshall Houlette and Mrs. Don King sum it up. "The Glenns are so dedicated they make every Sunday a special day for every one of us."

100 YEARS OF SHORTHORNS
May 28, 1983

In searching for a meaningful "May Beef Month" story for the May, 1983, issue, I felt I had hit the "jackpot" when I learned of the Neely-Kinyon Shorthorn herd. The deeper I dug, the more excited I became. Here is the resultant article about a 100-year old herd on a 100-year old farm in the 200th year of Shorthorns in America.

Combining a Century Farm with a century of cattle breeding is one of the rarest of farm accomplishments. Here in Iowa, Adair County may be the only county that can make this kind of boast, thanks to the Kinyon family of near Greenfield and Wayne Neely of Maryland.

As we observe May Beef Month, 100 consecutive years of Shorthorn cattle breeding are being celebrated on the Verda Lea farm, so named because Verda Lea means green field.

Wayne Neely and Keith Kinyon with one of their prize shorthorn bulls.

Current principals in the long-established cattle breeding operation are Wayne C. Neely, 79, former Iowan now living in Maryland, and Keith Kinyon, 61, and his wife, Myrtle.

Neely, regarded as one of the nation's leading Shorthorn breed observers tells how it all began. "My grandfather came from Pennsylvania to buy this Adair County farm in 1877. He paid $25.75 for the 80 acres with buildings and $12.50 for an adjourning unimproved 80. In 1883, he registered his first purebred bull."

"Uncle Henry Wallace, founder of Wallaces Farmer, had a major role in establishing our 100-year old herd," says Neely. W.W. Neely, father of the present co-owner, was only 21 when he registered his first Shorthorns. In 1929, when T.M. Neely died at age 91, "W.W." took over the herd. When W.W. died in 1948, his widow brought Neely and Kinyon into the partnership. Since 1951, the herd has been known as Neely-Kinyon Shorthorns.

The Scotch influence in the Iowa herd appeared soon after it was established. A son of an imported bull from the herd of Amos Cruikshank, Scotland's founder of the breed, was purchased in 1888. A cow named Scotch Rose, of almost pure Scotch breeding, was brought to the Neely farm in 1905.

The Neelys have always bought the best bull they could afford. Females, however, have been largely home-bred.

The Neely herd is the oldest Shorthorn herd in Iowa. Research indicates it is one of the seven oldest herds of the breed nationally.

The Neely-Kinyon Shorthorns, when exhibited in 4-H classes by the Kinyon children, made a strong showing. Jim, now wrestling coach at Roland-Story, and Pat, now Mrs. Steve Kline on a farm near Afton, and Carol, a teacher at Murray, all won championships at the Adair County Fair, and scored winnings at the Iowa State Fair and the Omaha Ak-Sar-Ben. Over the years, 4-H Club work has been a significant aspect of the Kinyon family. Earnings from 4-H entries paid half the children's college expenses.

Neely is secretary of the Maryland Shorthorn Association, regularly contributes articles for Shorthorn Country, the breed's national publication, and writes a monthly Shorthorn Breeders newsletter.

Neely and Kinyon are especially pleased that their herd has attained the century mark this year. Not only does their herd boast 100 years of continuous ownership by the same family, but that it was exactly 200 years ago this year when the first Shorthorns were imported from England.

DAIRYMAN RECALLS 80 YEARS OF PROGRESS
June 25, 1983

A railway accident causing 15 cows enroute from New York state to be scattered along an Iowa railway roadbed marked the beginning of O.R. Bentley's 76-year long career as a Guernsey breeder. This June 1983 Dairy Month article told of the amazing success the veteran dairyman had with his outstanding herd.

While June Dairy Month emphasizes dairy promotion, it also provides an opportunity to reminisce about changes in the industry. Few Iowans can comment more authoritatively on some 80 years of dairy progress than 88-year old Russell Bentley, veteran Story County, Iowa, Guernseyman.

When he was in high school, Bentley's father gave him a purebred Guernsey in lieu of a year's wages. "She was a beauty and I've been a dairyman and Guernsey enthusiast ever since." Bentley adds, "I've watched dairying change from our old wooden stanchions, one-legged milk stools, and horse trough cooling to the modern milking parlors, stainless steel pipelines, and 540-gallon cooling tanks like my son now uses. n

The Bentleys were married in 1917. After three years of teaching vo-ag in Aurelia and Dow City, Russell joined his father in a partnership on an 80-acre dairy project. Two years later, Russell and his wife bought land southwest of Ames, took their half of the herd, and started on their own.

Russell recalls: "We named the place Sunnyslope Farm, but all we had was 100 acres of poor land, a hay shed and crib, a burned-down house, and twelve cows.

Russell Bentley, Guernsey cattle breeder.

They then bought and moved an old house that didn't quite fit the basement foundation, built a milking shed, bought rock phosphate and lime to grow alfalfa, worked tirelessly on daily chores and milk deliveries to Campustown, and continued upgrading and enlarging their Guernsey herd.

Their three daughters and a son helped with the dairying and were active in 4-H. Meanwhile, superior bulls were purchased, production records set, showring winnings achieved. and the high quality of Sunnyslope Farm's milk resulted in expanded sales.

Bentley figures the greatest boon in his dairy experience was "the Surge milker I had to get in 1929 when my young helper got sick. We were still farming with horses, milking and bottling by hand, making house-to-house deliveries seven days a week with no vacations or coffee breaks. Believe me, that milker was a labor and time-saving Godsend."

Bentley and his five sisters and brothers were all early Ames College graduates. His children and grandchildren are also college graduates. His son and two grandsons are ISU dairy science grads.

Russell is now a member of the ISU Order of the Knoll and was recently honored by the creation of the Russell Bentley Endowment for Excellence in Dairy Science.

An aerial photo shows how that burned-out house and sheds of 1922 have been replaced with modern dairy buildings and a nice farm home, silos, productive land, and one of Iowa's finest Guernsey herds.

It's a joy to watch Russell Bentley's wrinkled face become wreathed in smiles as he looks toward more than 100 head of beautiful, fawn and white, high-producing, purebred Guernseys grazing in the pasture of Sunnyslope Farm. And when, with twinkling eyes, he says, "Isn't that a pretty sight?" justifiable satisfaction resulting from more than 75 years of dairying achievements is being voiced both in humility and pride.

SEVERAL GENERATIONS OF STATE FAIR SHOWMEN
July 23, 1983

Helping Iowa display its finest farm produce and winning coveted State Fair awards was a tradition inherited by a number of Iowa farm families. Two I knew well were the Hethershaws and the Goeckes. Both families had a rich heritage of blue ribbon awards. Witness these summarizations as chronicled in 1983.

August 10-20 will be Iowa State Fair time when Iowa Agriculture will be "on parade" with the state's finest livestock, grains, fruits, vegetables, flowers, and other products.

Highlight of the fair for many visitors over the years has been the Agricultural Hall, home of the butter cow, lard pigs, conservation exhibits, commodity displays, landscaped gardens, and horticulture, crop and floriculture competitions.

The fair attracts exhibitors from throughout the state. Over the years, tens of thousands of Iowans have participated. Great loyalty has been shown by some families. Two classic examples are the Goeckes of State Center and the Hethershaws of Des Moines.

State Fair Ag Superintendent Ray Hethershaw.

James Hethershaw began showing flowers and vegetables when the State Fair moved from Fairfield to West Des Moines. Later, James' son, Fred became a big winner and went on to exhibit at national and international shows. He is credited with winning gold medals and being an originator of the famed Iowa Horn of Plenty at the 1915 San Francisco World's Fair. He served as State Fair agricultural show superintendent many years.

For the past 60 years, a third generation member of the family, Ray Hethershaw, now 76, has followed in his father's footsteps.

Now retired, Ray says, "It takes a lot of time and patience to prepare a winning exhibit, but there's great pride in helping portray Iowa at its best."

The Goecke show legend can best be told by Frank Goecke, 92, who now resides in Marshalltown's Westwood Care Center. One of six sons and two daughters born to a German immigrant family, Frank first started showing at the fair in the early 1900s. He continued to show and win until 1981, when he retired.

Evidence of Goecke's magic touch as a showman is on every wall in his room. Purple state fair sweepstakes banners emphasize his invincible corn showmanship for many years. Plaques, pictures and large boxes jammed with purple rosette ribbons are added proof.

Not only did Frank and Ernest and their nephew, Harold, claim countless state grain championships, but the Goecke family was equally prominent in livestock winning. In 1939, when all five of Frank's sons — Ralph, Clifford, Robert, Ray, and Calvin — were in 4-H, they each won their respective Hereford baby beef class at the State Fair. Then they went on to win the coveted "group of five" championships.

Still another member of the Goecke family, Clarence, now retired in Waterloo, won the International Stock Show grand championship in 1928.

Summarizing his three-quarters of a century of purple ribbon winning, the hale and hardy elder Goecke says, "There's no money to be made in showing, because it takes so much time. But the friends you make — both old and new — make it all worthwhile. Pride is a big factor, too, and it's fun to show something that's a credit to all Iowans."

State Fair Champion Exhibitor Frank Goecke.

A THRESHERMAN FOR 80 YEARS
August 27, 1983

Threshing grain with big steamers and large separators may be a lost art now, but old threshermen "never die". No one could exemplify that better than 86-year old Milo Mathews. At an Old Settlers' and Threshermen's Reunion attended by 50,000, I watched him regale many with his 80 years of exciting threshing experiences.

Crowds of up to 50,000 are expected to attend the Midwest Old Settlers and Threshers Association's annual reunion in Mount Pleasant beginning September 1. Of all those present, no one will enjoy the threshermen's "spectacular" more than 86-year old Milo Mathews, Mount Union farmer, and last living member of the association's eight founders.

Mathews has a rich heritage of mechanical skills. His great-grandfather helped build the Erie Canal. His father and two uncles were threshing pioneers. Milo has been involved with steam engines for 80 years.

Recalling eight decades of threshing experience, Mathews says, "Father bought an old Case 32-52 for junk in the early 1900s. He and his brothers rebuilt

Steam engines on parade at Midwest Threshers Reunion.

it so well it ran 22 more years in our large neighborhood threshing ring. I was only six years old when they let me help, and it made me feel ten feet tall."

When he speaks of his active threshing years, Mathews' eyes twinkle. He tells of firing up during the night and trying to be the first to blow the whistle in early dawn.

Mathews threshed until 1943. WW II was in progress. His oldest son, Robert, enlisted, never to return. Tears come to his eyes when he says, "By the time Bobby was five years old, he could identify every engine part in the catalog. Now he lies in Punchbowl Cemetery in Hawaii."

Veteran thresherman Milo Mathews.

Speaking of the genesis of the nationally recognized threshing event, Mathews tells how four area steam engine buffs — Ray Ernst, Ted Detrick, Herman Elger and Clark Everts — now all deceased, went to Pontiac, Illinois to a 1949 threshers' reunion. Greatly impressed, they asked Mathews and three other engine owners to join them in founding the Mount Pleasant reunion in 1950.

"With only a dozen engines and separators at work between heavy showers, it wasn't much of a show," says Milo, "but several thousand people came and were so enthusiastic we decided to make it an annual event."

On display during the five-day Mount Pleasant reunion this year, will be 69 restored large steam engines, some weighing 12 tons and valued at over $50,000; 35 small scale model engines; 300 or more antique tractors and autos; horse drawn separators; and steam powered trains operated by Milo's youngest son, Stan.

Mathews has never missed a reunion and owns seven of the huge engines at the show. "When I'm 100 years old, I'll be just as enthusiastic about steam power as I've been the past 80 years. There's something special about a steam engine. They're a little like a good wife. Give them tender, loving care and they'll do anything for you. Mistreat them and you'd better run for cover."

SHOW HOSTS REMEMBER
EARLY DAYS ON THE FARM
September 10, 1983

However amazing farm progress has been in recent times, there are still many farmers with vivid memories of "The Way It Was" in years gone by when horsepower and human muscle preceded tractors and computers. In this column, five old timers recalled how things were long before Farm Progress Shows.

Computerized farming will be a highlight of this year's Farm Progress Show. And emphasizing the trend toward computer technology, one of the major crowd pleasers will be an ISU "computerized" driverless tractor.

Other attractions on the 1300-acre site include no-till demonstrations, terracing, and other soil conservation practices, a "weed garden", a half-billion dollar farm machinery display, harvesting demonstrations, hundreds of corn and soybean plots, herbicide and insecticide tests, and countless other good reasons to attend.

While modern technology will get the spotlight at what is being termed "The World's Fair of Agriculture," several host family members will view the progressive steps in farming portrayed at the show from the perspective of "The Way It Was" when they started farming.

Mr. & Mrs. Lamar Dostal, Farm Progress Show co-hosts.

Mrs. Helen Hoskins, 78, says, "The new Prairie Lady farm home on the Meythaler farm is quite a contrast from the house and appliances I had as a bride." She recalls the oil stove, wash tubs, wood furnace, kerosene lamps, hand-operated washer, outdoor toilet, creaky water pumps, milking by hand, and absence of refrigeration. She concludes, "and we most certainly did not have air conditioning or a jacuzzi type bathtub."

Lloyd Taube, 77, laughs when he compares the way he used to attack weeds in contrast to today's modern herbicide applicators. "We used a sharp hoe and a handful of salt on our Canada thistles," says Taube. He adds that his 1932 John Deere "A" tractor would look rather insignificant alongside the 400hp behemoth to be on display at this year's show.

Clifford Burns, 85, a neighbor to those involved in this year's Farm Progress Show, goes back to an even earlier period. He vividly remembers the big horse hitches and smiles when he says, "In 1927, I paid $575 for my first Fordson. Compare that with what they'll ask for one of those giant 1983 models at the show."

Mr. and Mrs. Lumir Dostal, Sr., 73 and 72 respectively, will achieve a unique record by co-hosting this year's show with their son and his family and neighbors. The senior Dostals were also central hosts to the 1958 National Corn Harvesting Contest. President Eisenhower and the then Senator John Kennedy were headline speakers. Visiting with "Ike" about farming experiences, and having dinner with him, is one of the elder Dostal's most cherished memories.

Dostal also notes the vast changes in farming over the years, saying, "We started in 1932 with two mules on 80 acres, when corn was 10¢ a bushel, hogs $3 per cwt., rent $5 an acre, and corn was cultivated five times."

Later a steel-wheeled IH F12 replaced the mules. However, tractors and more technology followed. "And now," Dostal concludes, "I'm eagerly looking forward to what they're going to show us September 27, 28 and 29 in the way of tools and techniques for the future."

VETERAN FARMER'S UNION MEMBERS SPEAK OUT
October 22, 1983

Farm organizations, their leaders, and their members always made for a good story. In this column, I featured two long-time, staunch Iowa Farmer's Union members, Dwight Anderson and Charles Svoboda, both of whom always spoke out loud and clear.

At their recent statewide Iowa Farmer's Union convention, two veteran members not only spoke out about "the way it was", but also about the way it is now and the way it should be in the future.

Dwight L. Anderson, 82, Agency, joined the National Farmer's Union (NFU) back in 1919, even though officially ineligible. He explains, "You had to be 21 to get on the charter. I was only 19, but joined anyway."

A member of NFU for 64 years now, Anderson says, "This is the only true farm organization. It's neither radical nor rightist, and is a voice for the family farm."

Charles Svoboda

Anderson strongly believes everyone should be active in politics and that those governed the least are governed the best. He has a unique political background himself, asserting, "First I was a Republican, then since 1953, I've been a Democrat."

Proof of the Wapello County farmer's sincerity in being an activist is attested by his serving the Iowa Farmer's Union (IFU) board ten years and challenging Fred Stover for the presidency during the IFU's most trying times.

Financial difficulties now facing many farmers reminds Anderson of what he considers the NFU's finest hour. He says, "It was in the early 1930s when we helped Milo Reno form the 'farm holiday movement' and had 5¢ farm sales to stop foreclosures. We were on the firing line, but we fought hard and won a lot of moratoriums."

His fighting days behind him, Anderson and his wife now enjoy traveling to Central America, Canada, and elsewhere.

Charles Svoboda of Clutier will be 83 November 5. Born on the farm his grandfather bought in 1869, he's always been a diversified farmer, saying, "I raised it all — corn, beans, cattle, hogs, chickens, hemp, barley, oats, wheat, ducks, kids, and cain."

Highly organization minded, Svoboda not only belongs to NFU, but to the American Farm Bureau Federation and National Farmer's Organization (NFO) as well.

In comparing the three, his observation is that the Farm Bureau grew too big and mercenary too fast while the NFO aimed too high to be realistic.

"The Union," he adds, "is the only one to really represent and speak for the family farmer."

Svoboda feels he should know the difference because he joined the NFU in 1920. Four sons and three sons-in-law, are currently IFU members.

Svoboda and his wife are extremely proud that all seven of their children live on diversified family farms; and, in spite of this year's heat and drought, are doing well. And they are even prouder of their 33 grandchildren, many of whom are on farms, and their five greatgrandchildren.

"The way things are going," laughs the Tama County farmer, "there'll be so many Svobodas we'll have to put numbers, instead of names, on them."

Dwight Anderson

MASTER FARM HOMEMAKER OF 1951 REMAINS ACTIVE
November 26, 1983

Master Farm Homemakers seem to have a penchant for carrying on activities in which they were involved before receiving the state's highest recognition for rural women. Mrs. Walter Neubaum was a classic example. Although honored more than 30 years before this column was written, she continued to help in her community, church, and charities, and maintained her farming and gardening interests.

Although Mrs. Walter Neubaum of Barnum was unable to attend the Iowa Master Farm Homemakers luncheon held recently in Des Moines, she recalls a similar event in 1951 when she was one of those honored. "It brought back a flood of happy memories," she says.

Now a widow, Mrs. Neubaum still lives on the farm she and her husband bought in 1942 after farming in western Iowa the previous 12 years. "Those were busy, and sometimes trying, years," she explains as she remembers "The Way It Was" in the '30s, '40s, and '50s.

"Times were rough when we started in Monona County in 1931," recalls Mrs. Neubaum. She tells how they pooled what resources they had, borrowed a little more, bought some horses, a few second-hand implements, and a couple of sows. She adds, "We didn't even have enough left over to have a wedding picture taken."

She also remembers how things were when she was a bride. "We had no running water, no electricity, no modern bathroom, and our house was so cold in the winter that hot water in the teakettle became ice overnight," she asserts.

Hard times, aggravated by drought, befell most farmers in the early '30s. To make matters worse, the bottom dropped out of the hog market, making loan repayments difficult.

Nevertheless, by 1942, they had saved some $2000 to use as down payment on the 160 acres in Webster County. Their son was only a year old when they made the move.

Soon Mrs. Neubaum became involved in community activities. Before long, she was being tapped for leadership roles on the extension council, county PTA, county Farm Bureau, county fair, 4-H, women's chorus, and local school board.

Mrs. Walter Neubaum, pleased to be named a Master Homemaker.

Because of her work as a PTA president, a neighbor nominated Mrs. Neubaum to the school board. She was elected and went on to serve 11 years, six of them as president.

Regarding her selection as a Master Farm Homemaker, Mrs. Neubaum says when the letter came informing her of the honor, she could not believe it. "Here I was receiving the highest recognition an Iowa farm woman can get and it was for activities I greatly enjoyed," she states.

Like most of the other 219 Master Farm Homemakers who have been honored, Mrs. Neubaum has continued with community service over the years, and is still active in church women's groups, Bible study, charity work, Farm Bureau, and on the township election board. In addition, she takes care of her garden, roses, songbirds, and a huge lawn.

An immaculate housekeeper, she seems happiest when she is busy in her home or garden or yard. She also maintains an active interest in the farming operation now directed by her son, Walter, who, along with his wife and four children, lives nearby.

"I enjoy my grandchildren, and especially so during the Thanksgiving and Christmas seasons. A family means so much to all of us," concludes Mrs. Neubaum.

30,000 CHRISTMAS TREES ON ONE FARM
December, 1983

Iowa's more than 150 Christmas tree growers may not agree on everything, but they are unanimous on one thing — that the pre-Christmas period in December is the busiest, as well as coldest, time of the year. One of those growers was Everett Weigle, long-time county agent, who had 30,000 Christmas trees when I visited his farm to get this column.

Later this month, some 300,000 or more Iowa families will celebrate Christmas around a beautifully decorated evergreen produced on an American tree farm. Of these, some 50,000 will be Iowa-grown Christmas trees.

There are now more than 150 tree farms in Iowa growing Scotch, Austrian, Norway, and white or red pines for the Christmas trade. And 107 are members of the Iowa Christmas Tree Association.

Iowa's Christmas tree farms are located in some 35 different counties. One of the largest is Woodland Acres in Winneshiek County, started 24 years ago by Everett Weigle.

Weigle and two friends purchased a badly farmed 180-acre tract near Decorah in 1958. In 1959, the trio did a lot of terracing and planted 3000 pines.

Everett Weigle, Grower of Christmas Trees.

A year later, 8000 more trees were planted. Eventually, Woodland Acres boasted 30,000 trees. However, not until 1967 did the Winneshiek tree farmers realize any return on their sizable investment. First sales were made to neighbors in the community. Later, wholesale outlets were found. A "choose and cut" policy was also undertaken to enable families to select and cut their own trees.

One year, Woodland Acres produced a near perfect ten foot tall Scotch Pine that wound up in the state capitol as a Christmas gift for Governor Ray. A similar, but smaller, tree was presented to Secretary of Agriculture Lounsberry's office.

"It takes about eight years to get a tree to marketable size, says Weigle, now 77. He adds, "In the meantime, you need a good, sharp pruning shears, as well as a lot of patience."

Most of the Woodland Acres tree farm now has a new owner. The remaining 30 acres are still operated by Weigle.

Summing up his tree farm experience, Weigle says, "It's gratifying to see a badly exploited hillside become green again. Our trees not only stopped erosion, but they also added much beauty to the community. In addition, there is a ready market for well cared for, properly sheared trees."

A 1928 graduate of Iowa State College (ISC), Weigle smiles when asked "the way it was" in his youth. He replies, "My first job was at the Omaha stockyards, but when the depression hit, I went back to our Howard County farm to help and to work for a livestock dealer for $15 a week."

He then became Wright and Hamilton Counties' extension youth assistant, and was promoted to Winneshiek County extension director in 1934.

In 1937, Everett married Lenore Thorne, a 1931 ISC graduate. They have a daughter in Vancouver, a son in Minneapolis, and four grandchildren.

During his active tree farm years, Weigle was executive secretary of the Iowa Christmas Tree Association.

As Winneshiek County agent for 35 years, he left an indelible mark in his pioneering efforts in soil and water conservation, 4-H leadership, mutual insurance, rural electrification, fire prevention, farm cooperatives, AI, camping centers, dairy production, and boar test stations.

Weigle has been the recipient of many awards, including the Iowa State University Merit Award for his community service, and the Luther College Community Service Award. Weigle is warmly greeted by both old and young, all of whom seem to be convinced he is the greatest community servant in history.

The way it was . . .
1984

HE'S TREATED EVERYTHING FROM OXEN TO OCELOTS
January 28, 1984

Veterinarians are obviously the best friends animals ever had, but they also are great Agricultural benefactors. Our first 1984 column guest was Dr. Lester Proctor, past president of the Iowa Veterinary Medical Association, in his 50th year of practice when this was written. His story about the number and kinds of animals treated is remarkably interesting.

The 102nd annual Iowa Veterinary Medical Association (IVMA) convention will be held the end of this month. Among those present will be Lester Proctor, 76, Oelwein veterinarian, who will reminisce with his fellow practitioners. Friends and clients believe the number of animals he has treated approaches a half million.

In the 50 years since he first started practicing, he has driven well over 10 million miles and gone through 42 autos in administering to everything from oxen to ocelots.

From boyhood on, Proctor wanted to be a veterinarian. After winning a $100 scholarship, he left for Iowa State College (ISC). Six years later, he had won high school prerequisites and earned his DVM degree.

Immediately upon graduation in 1934, Proctor was asked to serve on the ISC veterinary staff until the Bureau of Animal Industry enlisted him to inspect drought-ravaged cattle from western states shipped to stockyards in South St. Paul, Minn. Of the 800 tested daily, some 5% were relegated to tankage.

That fall, Dr. Proctor bought a practice owned by the widow of a Hazelton veterinarian. He married his college sweetheart, Lucille Wade, and the two of them set forth to become guardians of animal health.

Recalling "the way it was" when he first became a "horse doctor"- a term commonly applied to veterinarians — Doc says there were many horses on farms in those days, especially in the Amish communities.

Sleeping sickness, officially known as equine encephalomyelitis, was a king-sized challenge in '38 and '39 when horse owners were pleading for help day and night. Doc recalls one six-week period with only one night of uninterrupted sleep.

In 1943, the practice was moved to Oelwein, a more central location from which to serve clients in the five counties. Doc hired an associate and added a small animal practice.

In 1952, while serving as IVM president, Proctor made brucellosis the number one priority of his administration.

Dr. Lester Proctor, veteran veterinarian.

A brucellosis committee involving Iowa State University, United States Department of Agriculture, and Iowa Department of Agriculture, and all dairy groups, was established.

The crusade paid off. Legislation was developed to attack the problem with quarantines, indemnities, and education.

The campaign in which Proctor has placed so much emphasis, and given strong leadership, has almost totally eradicated brucellosis in Iowa. "I regard it the major achievement of my career," says the newly retired northeast Iowa practitioner.

As the practice grew, so did the family. Two daughters, Joanne and Donna, and two sons, Ted and Jon, were born. There are also 11 grandchildren and seven great-grandchildren, including newborn triplets.

Summing up his observations after a half century of practice, Doc says, "The contrast between '34 and '84 is almost unbelievable. CB radios, air conditioned autos, paved highways, better instruments, drugs and vaccines have enabled us to conquer most problems facing all creatures "great and small."

FARM WIFE'S COLUMNS ARE BASIS FOR BOOK
February 26, 1984

Not many persons become authors at age 87, but Inez Faber did when she wrote " Down Here On Soap Creek". The whimsical book included parts of columns she had written for Iowa newspapers in the turbulent '30s, fateful '40s, and fabulous '50s.

Soap Creek may not be as well known or as imposing as the Mississippi River or the Missouri River, but to 87-year old Inez McAlister Faber, Moravia, it is the world's most significant stream.

As a young bride, Inez worked with her husband in fields along the banks of the "Soap". Here they fought floods, drought, the Depression, and other adversities. Here, too, is where they raised four sons and where Inez started a career in journalism. That career has culminated in a book called, "Down Here on Soap Creek."

At the age of 13, Inez contracted tuberculosis and moved to a drier climate. Despite her illness, she borrowed books to keep up in school.

After three years, Inez recovered sufficiently to return to Iowa, finish school, help on the farm, and fall in love with the neighbor boy, Richard Faber.

The Fabers began farming in 1922 by renting 90 acres and milking a few cows. Cream checks enabled them to buy several sows and a laying flock. By 1927, they had two sons and had saved enough to buy 100 acres near Moulton, where two more sons were welcomed. Seven years later, they came back home to the Soap Creek area to a larger operation.

Shortly after returning to the Soap Creek farm, Inez started writing a column for the Des Moines Register and Tribune.

Entitled "A Farm Woman Speaks Out," it was an immediate success.

Mrs. Inez Faber, author of "Down Here On Soap Creek."

Soon the *Centerville Iowegian* asked for a similar column headed, "Out Here on Soap Creek," as did the Albia Republican and the Blakesburg paper.

For a time, the busy farmwife and mother was writing nine columns a week. In her columns, she reported on such things as a robin's nest, 4-H, the ladies' Wednesday Club, the demise of a pet cat named Felix, the boys' adventures, a day of fishing, her husband's eye injury, Christmas at grandmother's, and hundreds of similar down-to-earth topics.

An auto accident in 1951 ended Inez's career as a columnist. Serious injuries necessitated abandoning her typewriter. Meanwhile, the sons married and had families of their own. Vaughn, the oldest, took up farming along Soap Creek. Charles became head of education at the University of Kentucky. Bruce joined the Internal Revenue Service. Irvin, the youngest, became a communications officer with Iowa Power in Cedar Rapids. Twenty-one grandchildren and 18 great-grandchildren are in the family.

In 1979, at an elderhostel gathering in Iowa City, a teacher encouraged Inez to write a book featuring the favorite columns in her scrapbook. The family helped with the selection, and son Charles assisted with editing and typing.

Within two years, Inez, then 85, had copy ready. To no one's surprise, the homey material was as relevant in 1982 as it was when written in the '30s, '40s, and '50s. Chapters featured the early years, the difficult 1930s, housebuilding trials, the boys and their escapades, chinch bugs, artists, rainy days, and farming with horses. Other amusing incidents featured such events as Aunt Til's dash through deep snow to elope and enable her lover to escape her father's anger and shotgun.

The title, "Out Here on Soap Creek" was a natural. Acceptance was gratifying. "It was a happy way to close out a long career and a hobby I love," concludes the veteran writer.

RETIRED MASTER FARMERS CONTINUE THEIR LEADERSHIP
March, 1984

Iowa Master farmers have claimed center stage for many years and 1984 was no exception. Four outstanding farmers were named to one of Agriculture's most exclusive clubs. To add our tribute to the observance, we sought out two "Masters" chosen in previous years. They were G.D. Bellman and Howard Hill and this report tells about them.

Including the seven new honorees named this month, the Iowa Master Farmers program, started by Wallaces Farmer in 1926, now boasts 314 members. Largest group numbered 16 in 1927. Smallest was 1946, just after WW II, when only two were selected, G.D. Bellman, Indianola, and Howard Hill, Minburn. Bellman, 89, now spends his winters in Texas. Hill, 75, lives where he started farming in 1931.

Despite his years, Don Bellman joins his tenants, David and Kathy Cummings, in all decision-making on his 300-acre Warren County farm.

Always community minded, Bellman is a lifelong Farm Bureau member, long-time treasurer of the Mt. Hope school board, 30-year member of a county oil co-op, served 20 years on the PCA board, and hosted the first All Iowa Conservation Day in 1947.

E. Howard Hill, Iowa Farm Bureau President.

Hill, in addition to feeding some 500 cattle and 1500 hogs annually, also assumed dozens of leadership positions. For 16 years, he was president of the Iowa Farm Bureau. He also served as president of Iowa's Flying Farmers, Living History Farms, the Iowa Packing Company, as well as vice president of Minburn's Farm Co-op, Iowa Soil Research Association, Iowa 4-H Foundation, and National Independent Meat Packers.

Both men are retired, but their interests in farming and community service continue. Bellman remains champion for soil and conservation and studies new agricultural trends.

Hill serves as a director for a leading Des Moines bank, is a lay leader in the Methodist church, and participates in the 4-H Foundation, soil research, Iowa State University Foundation Board, Iowa Good Roads Association, and Living History Farms.

Bellman started milking and dreaming about being a dairyman when he was 8. He was 12 when his father died. At 18, he developed plans for a modern dairy barn. At 21, he started dairying on his own. Looking back at "The Way It Was" 70 years ago, he has no regrets about his hard work.

Hill's experiences take him back to the days of $2.50 per cwt. for porkers and burned-out crops in the mid-30s. Yet he looks back on that trying period as happy years when there was much family togetherness. Hill says he borrowed $7000 at 6% in '31 to buy his horses, machinery, seed, feed, and household needs. "An unbelievable contrast with what it would take today," says Hill.

Hill's formula for leadership is, "Be a good listener. Appreciate other's views. Don't take yourself too seriously. Lead as long as you make a contribution. Steer clear of belligerence. Above all, be honest with your organization and yourself."

One of Hill's fondest memories was a visit he and two other Iowans, this writer among them, had with President Truman in the White House in

1948. "We were there to invite the President to the National Plowing Matches at Dexter," explains the 1946 Dallas County Master Farmer.

In 1927, Hill's father was named a Master Farmer. In '54, his brother, Clarence, was similarly honored.

Bellman's family is widely scattered: Irene in Vinton; Kathryn in Oklahoma; Robert in Kentucky. There are 13 grandchildren and 16 great-grandchildren.

Hill, twice widowed, has three daughters, Marylyn Hagedorn, Des Moines; her twin, Marjorie Joslin, Minburn; and Mrs. Margaret Northey, wife of a Dickinson County farmer. There are seven grandchildren.

CONSERVATION PIONEER RECALLS EARLY YEARS
April 28, 1984

When this column was written in 1984, soil conservation had already been an obsession of Hilmer Orvella for close to 50 years. Owner of a hilly farm prone to erosion, Orvella became a pioneer in terracing and other conservation practices. In doing so, he soon made "believers" out of dozens of skeptical neighbors.

No-till and similar soil conservation practices are often regarded as significant new developments, but for Helmer Orvella, 90, Decorah, soil conservation is an old story.

As far back as 1938, this veteran Winneshiek County farmer was a pioneer in soil conservation. Using a small track-type tractor and an old road grader, he built terraces on his farm, then invited skeptical neighbors and friends to see the results.

"We started farming in 1922. Our land was hilly and after 15 years of watching the topsoil erode away and wind up in the Mississippi and other waterways, we decided that had to stop, so I put in some terraces," explains Orvella.

Strip-cropping and contour plowing were other early conservation practices adopted by Orvella in the late 1930s. His interest in nailing down the topsoil has never wavered.

Along with Leo Herold and Albert Wommeldorf, Orvella was one of Iowa's first soil conservation district commissioners. All three were loyal disciples of Rev. Oscar Engebretson, pastor of the Washington Prairie Lutheran church. "Nobody ever did more for the cause of conservation," says Orvella.

Skepticism greeted Orvella's first conservation efforts. However, once the doubters saw the way he and his neighbors, William Torgren and Melvin Anderson, were getting

Orvella was a pioneer builder of field terraces.

increased yields, as well as slowing erosion, they soon became converts. "We built terraces right through the line fences," injects Orvella.

Everett Weigle was secretary for the district commissioners during Orvella's two 6-year terms. "No-till is only a recent development in conservation farminwg. Grassed waterways, contouring, strip-cropping, grassed headlands, sediment basins, and diversions are among the many practices adopted since 1938," notes Weigle.

Cost sharing has been another major development. With some $25 million available to Iowa for soil-conserving efforts this year — much of it for cost sharing — an increasing number of farmers will join in the crusade.

Orvella has kept pace with the newer practices, including putting backslope terraces on his hilliest farm. Proof that he has set a good example is seen in two of his grandsons, Larry Orvella and Paul Brubold. Both have carried on the tradition of conservation farming.

Keeping streams and ponds free of silt is a selfish obsession for Orvella. Trout fishing is his hobby. He says, "When you land a 4-pounder, all the effort to keep the silt out of the streams becomes worthwhile."

Orvella has other good reasons for making conservation a top priority. "Exploiting and exporting our top soil is a terrible disservice to our children, grandchildren, and great-grandchildren," says the father of two daughters and a son. "They are my main reasons to keep pushing to save our soil."

NINE DECADES DAIRYING
June, 1984

Ninety-seven year old Ira Jipson had a memory that went back beyond the turn of the century, and dairying was always foremost in his recollections. This report points out his ability to recall comparisons in dairy cattle and creameries from the late 1890s to 1984.

A 97-year old Oelwein area farmer, Ira Jipson, boasts a lifelong career associated with dairy farming and country creameries.

Jipson, who comes from a family of 12, still lives on his farm near Oelwein. His son, Ralph, now actively operates the land and the herd, along with William, his grandson. Nine other of his 17 grandchildren also farm, some in dairying.

Ira Jipson, long-time Iowa dairyman.

Asked about "The Way It Was" in his dairying experience, Jipson vividly recalls the family's move from Dickinson County, in northwest Iowa, to the Oelwein area back in 1895.

Recalling the long trek of 88 years ago, Ira says, "Father went ahead with four boxcar loads of shorthorn cows and calves and a bull or two. The cows had to be unloaded at rail yards a couple of times to be fed, watered, and milked. My father got fellows off the street to help him get the milking done."

A few days later, Ira, with his mother, brothers, and sisters, along with the furniture, machinery, and a hired man, took another train destined for Oelwein. Along the way, Ira remembers changing cars several times, and some bothersome drunks at depots.

"Farms often changed hands in those days," explains the veteran dairyman. He points out that his parents made several moves after coming to Fayette County. He adds, "My father always liked to get a place near a creamery."

Jipson says at the turn of the century cattle were often shipped and bought by the boxcar load. He recalls his father paying $20 per head for a carload of 20 grade shorthorns.

At one time, Ira and two sisters milked 60 head mornings and evenings. He says, "But those cows were poor producers and their lactation period was only about five months, so it wasn't that big a job."

As time went on, Ira persuaded his father to upgrade the herd by crossing the Shorthorn cows with a Holstein bull. Only the best heifers were retained.

Some creameries operated only part of the year, but as the Jipson herd was upgraded, milk production became a year-round project, and the Bakers Corner creamery remained open all year.

In time, additional land was needed. Ira urged his father to buy a nearby 140 acres for $50 per acre with an understanding the younger Jipson would gain title after four more years.

In the meantime, Ira was married, started a family, got a herd of 20 grade Holsteins, bought a registered bull, and was off and running as a dairyman on his own.

Jipson bought one of the first milking machines introduced in the county. "You had to be a master mechanic to run it," he says. Some of the cows were less than willing to take to the mechanical monstrosity, so they were displaced.

A battery-operated Delco plant was also installed in 1939. "That changed our life almost from night to day," opines Ira.

Eventually, the Farmers Co-op Creamery closed, so Jipson turned to whole milk production. The herd was enlarged and a new barn was built in 1952, and a new $1800 cooling tank installed. Whenever higher dairy standards were developed, the Jipson herd met them, and, at times, achieved a 50¢ premium per cwt.

During the more than nine decades he has been on the Iowa farm scene, Ira Jipson has experienced enough unbelievable changes to fill volumes. One was the decline and eventual disappearance of country creameries. "It had to happen," says Jipson, "but for many years they were a valuable service to all of us."

SOLAR FARMHOUSE UNVEILING AT LIVING HISTORY FARMS
July 14, 1984

Celebration of an 81st birthday and the grand opening of a solar home took place at the Living History Farms on the same day in July, 1984. However, there should be no surprise that the two events coincided. The birthday observance was for Bill Murray, founder of the Farms, and the solar home was one of his favorite projects. This report is about the double celebration.

When William Murray marks his 81st birthday Sunday, July 15, it will be a memorable occasion. The nationally recognized agricultural economist has invited several hundred friends to help him and his wife celebrate the event, which will be observed at Living History Farms.

Many prominent individuals will be on hand. Heading the list of celebrities is Norman Borlaug, a native of Cresco and winner of the 1970 Nobel Peace Prize for his work in the Green Revolution. Governor Terry Branstad will head the list of state officials.

Focal point of the event will be the grand opening of the solar farm home.

Completion of the solar farmhouse will be a long-time dream come true for Murray.

Construction was started in 1977 when Murray and others on the Living History Farm's governing board felt a futuristic, energy-conserving structure would round out the historical portrayal of Midwest farm housing from Indian days to the present.

Work on the ambitious project has taken so long because of its innovative nature. However, now that the living quarters and other rooms are nearing completion, Murray and his wife, Alice, plan to "move in" as temporary residents on the evening of the birthday celebration.

Mrs. Murray, the former Alice Van Wert, known throughout the state as the Iowa Farm Bureau women's chairperson from 1960 through 1966, smiles a bit when she emphasizes, "We don't intend to live there very long, but it will be an interesting experiment in ultramodern solar farm home living."

Made of concrete, and known as the Murray Solar Farmhouse, the two-story structure has long sweeping roof lines blending into the surrounding terrain. A three-foot layer of soil, topped with a thick layer of sod, covers the concrete roof to provide added insulation.

Heating will be provided by a solar tank 30 ft. in diameter and 13 ft. deep. Seventy tons of unprocessed salt have been placed in the circular structure to capture heat from the sun's rays during summer months and hold it for release into ducts for winter heating.

Visitors attending the July 15 grand opening will find the lower floor provides for three spacious bedrooms, along with a resource room designed to provide information about solar energy for farms.

Floor plans for the upper story reveal a kitchen, dining room, living room, bathroom, and a modern farm office. The office will house a farm computer, TV set linked to a satellite dish, cordless telephones, calculating equipment,

Living History Farms President, Dr. "Bill" Murray.

market tickertape, and other advanced technology.

Cost of the project has mounted steadily, but grants and gifts have enabled Living History Farms to complete the novel undertaking. Feasibility studies and architectural costs come to approximately $100,000. The building itself has already cost over $500,000.

Dedication of the Borlaug plots will be another July 15 feature event. Borlaug, whose many years of work in Mexico with semi-dwarf wheat earned him the Nobel Peace Prize, is expected to make some comments when the plots are dedicated. The Howard County native will also pay tribute to the late Henry A. Wallace, former Wallaces Farmer editor, who went on to serve as U.S. Secretary of Agriculture, Secretary of Commerce, and Vice President.

PIONEER HALL — A MAJOR ATTRACTION AT IOWA STATE FAIR
August 11, 1984

State Fair attractions number well up in the hundreds. It would be difficult to single out the most outstanding one, but it's not hard to select one of the most unique. It's Pioneer Hall where dozens of antiques and old machines are always on display and where Hilda Mercer, a winning exhibitor for 45 years, and "Doc" Dockendorff, the "Rope Man", held forth year after year.

State Fair visitors interested in "The Way It Was" will find a smorgasbord of nostalgia in Pioneer Hall, a large gleaming white building dominating Heritage Village in the northeast section of the fairgrounds.

Countless antiques, old machinery, historic books, harnesses, pottery, china, glassware, and other reminders of the past will be on display.

Mr. and Mrs. Gerald Van Zante of Monroe are co-superintendents of Pioneer Hall. They expect no less than 125 exhibitors from throughout Iowa to display thousands of items of memorabilia. "Interest in our displays is great," says Mrs. Van Zante. She reports visitors from every county in Iowa, from 33 other states, and 12 foreign countries signed the guest register last year.

Gerald points out Pioneer Hall is only one of the Heritage Village attractions. Others include the State Fair Museum, First Church, a country school, a fort, an Indian Village, totem pole, railway station, and several other exhibits.

Oldest exhibitor entered the past several years is 85-year old Hilda Mercer of Des Moines, who will be attending her 70th annual state fair this year. Mrs. Mercer has been a major heritage exhibit winner many times, exhibiting hand-painted china, candy dishes, bell collections, bottles, cowbells, and many other collectibles. She has also won blue ribbons on her wedding dress, graduation dress, and an old white hat she wore the first time she came to the fair back in 1913.

Mrs. Mercer's participation has not been limited just to Pioneer Hall, however. She has also been a state fair winner in flower arrangements, vegetable classes, and in the culinary division where she has been an exhibitor every year since 1930 except during WW II when the fair was cancelled.

Another senior citizen actively participating in Pioneer Hall programs is 76-year old Mayor "Doc" Dockendorff of Pella who terms himself "the Old Rope Man."

"Doc" Dockendorff.

Doc has been making rope ever since he was a young farm boy, and has demonstrated his skill at the fair the past 15 years. "Jump ropes for boys and girls" are his most popular productions, but he also makes halters, lariats, and other rope products, all from discarded binder twine.

For a number of years, Dockendorff also was Master of Ceremonies for the Heritage Village competitions. Reflecting on the contests, he enjoys recalling some amusing incidents. One of these took place in the tobacco spitting contest when a contestant, after managing a long, suspenseful delay accompanied by unusual facial contortions, finally "let go", only to have his false teeth fly along with the wad of tobacco.

CURTIS' 24-HORSE HITCH THRILLED THOUSANDS
September, 1984

Many of us have heard grandparents tell about using four or six-horse hitches on their farms. I can also personally recall handling six horses on a gang plow. However, when a long-time friend, Roy Curtis, hitched and drove 24 horses to the thunderous applause of thousands of Farmer's Union members at their annual celebration at the Mississippi Valley Fair, it made our four and six-horse efforts rather insignificant.

Farm Progress Show visitors next week will be literally surrounded by endless horsepower. Standard farm tractors rated at 150 or more horsepower will be in action in harvest fields on every side. Meanwhile, leading manufacturers will be displaying units rated up to 450 HP.

While all the big diesels will be of great interest, especially to younger farmers, they will also remind older visitors of times when horsepower came in the form of "oatburners" — powerful Belgians, Percheron, Clydesdales, Shires and grade draft horses. The contrast will be striking.

And for 87-year old Roy Curtis, Princeton, it will bring back exciting memories. Curtis, still remarkably active for his age, will never forget the day in September, 1934, when he was asked to put together a multiple-hitch of

Roy Curtis, skilled horseman.

24 horses and drive them in front of a crowded grandstand at Davenport's Mississippi Valley Fairgrounds.

In an earlier year, Curtis had thrilled a large Farmer's Union picnic crowd by cutting figure eights and demonstrating other driving skills with six and eight horse teams. "But hitching and driving 24 was something else," says Roy.

After accepting the challenge, Curtis first had to line up 14 horses from neighboring farms to add to his own ten. Next he had to find young and fearless friends to help. "It took over an hour to get them all hooked in six columns of four abreast to form a checkerboard pattern alternating the darks and the lights. When we got through, I had 480 feet of reins to handle, six lines in each hand," Curtis explained.

Moving the big hitch over eight miles of country roads and through city streets to the fairgrounds was no small task, but Curtis and his helpers made it safely. Then came the big moment when the 24 horses and wagon moved onto the track.

There were a few tense seconds when the horses, most of which had never performed before, heard the thunderous applause and started to bolt. Miraculously, Curtis quickly gained full control.

For the next 20 minutes, the cheering crowd of 5000 saw one of the greatest demonstrations of horsemanship ever staged in Iowa. Not only did Curtis take the 20 tons of spirited horseflesh down the track at full gallop, but he maneuvered every turn successfully, stopped the huge hitch on command, backed the show wagon into a marked spot and closed out by cutting large figure eights directly in front of the grandstand to the crowd's immense delight.

So popular was the big hitch that Curtis was asked to repeat the performance three more years. Meanwhile, his family, his farming interests, and his purebred Belgian stable were all growing rapidly.

Today the 87-year old Scott County farmer and his six sons operate a large tract of land, while he serves the Belgian Draft Horse Corporation of America as vice president, judges horses in U.S. and Canadian shows, is active in Toastmasters and the Gideon Society, and helps care for the Buffalo Bill Cody homestead on land he has donated to the County Conservation Board.

Eight children, 23 grandchildren, 11 great grandchildren, and many friends helped Mr. and Mrs. Curtis observe their 60th wedding anniversary earlier this year.

24-Horse hitch driven by Roy Curtis brings thunderous applause at Farmers Union celebration.

BACHELOR FARMER SETS UP
JUNIOR YOUTH CAMP
October 27, 1984

When a bachelor becomes the leader of all kinds of children's events and activities, it's a news story worth repeating. That's what this column is all about. Harvey Rickert, a 76-year old bachelor, reveled in the youngsters as much as they enjoyed him.

Harvey Rickert, 76, of near Bellevue is a bachelor, but his interest in young people knows no bounds.

Although now retired from active farming, Rickert continues to take a deep interest in his community, and especially in children involved in Farmer's Union programs.

"We have had a tradition of family meetings which included the children, but I noticed the kids were often bored at these meetings, so I decided to do something about it."

With the help of his sister, Isabel, and some rural teachers, he arranged for the children to participate in each meeting. In time, he worked out youth programs centered around Jackson County Farmer's Union members' children, 5 through 14. The group met once a month and involved as many as 60 youngsters.

Harvey Rickert, friend of youth.

So successful were the monthly gatherings that it soon became obvious the young people wanted a camping experience. The result was the establishment of a junior youth camp on the Rickert farm about 20 years ago.

Conducted during the second week of June every year, the camping program includes hiking, crafts, games, and studies in nature and geology. A shelter house with screens has been built for group meetings. Sleeping is in tents.

Interested parents and high school students, along with school officials, assist Rickert in conducting camp activities and counseling. A teacher, Dorothy Marshall, and a school principal, Virgil Murray, are also on the volunteer staff.

The campsite is surrounded by tree covered hills and lush valleys with a gorgeous view of the Mississippi River. Some 2000 trees are added annually for reforestation.

In addition to its beauty, the Rickert farm is in itself a lesson in Iowa history. Indians formerly roamed the area and Indian artifacts are still unearthed. Within two miles of the camp, Indian mounds can be found in Bellevue State Park.

Pioneering days are put into focus when Harvey tells his young guests about his grandfather coming to the U.S. in the late 1850s and paying $10 an acre to purchase 120 acres during the height of the Civil War.

In 1907, Harvey's father, Henry, Jr., a commercial thresherman, bought the farm for $30 an acre. Harvey, in turn, bought the property in 1948 at a cost of $70 an acre. Soon thereafter, he became involved in farm organizations, holding memberships in the Farm Bureau and NFO, as well as organizing the Jackson County Farmer's Union in 1958.

Rickert is a strong believer in supply management. The Jackson County Farmer's Union official also believes farmers should conduct statewide and nationwide referendums to help assure parity prices through a program administered by farmer-elected committees.

MASTER FARM HOMEMAKER WROTE CREED FOR WOMEN
November, 1984

Most rural residents have heard or seen "A Country Woman's Creed." Some have actually memorized this meaningful essay on country life. Not everyone, however, knows who wrote it. This column tells about the author, Mrs. H.L. Witmer, and how she was inspired to write it during a long career in behalf of rural women.

"I'm glad that I live in the country....I love its beauty and its spirit. I rejoice in the things I can do as a country woman for my home and my community." With these opening words, Mrs. H.L. Witmer of Tipton, one of Iowa's Master Farm Homemakers, wrote the "Country Woman's Creed" back in the late 1940s.

These words preface the credo that has guided Mrs. Witmer's entire career - first as a rural teacher, then successively as a young farm wife, 4-H leader and committee woman, county and state Farm Bureau leader, U.S. delegate to the Country Women of the World sessions, and as a Master Farm Homemaker.

Mrs. H.L. Witmer, author of Country Women's Creed.

The "Country Woman's Creed" was not composed overnight. "I thought about it for a long time," says Mrs. Witmer, "working in our home, tending our children, driving the tractor, and yes, even at meetings. It was always on my mind."

She first started putting the words on paper in 1947. "It sort of spelled out the philosophy of my life."

Toward the close of the creed, Mrs. Witmer expresses a deep conviction. "I believe my love and loyalty for my country home should reach out in service to my community...country people need to be proud of their heritage."

The farmwife first read the creed at a Cedar County meeting attended by more than 100 women, including Mrs. Roscoe Eliason, then state Farm Bureau Women's chairperson, and Louise Rosenfeld of Iowa State University. Those present listened intently through the concluding statement, "This fertile garden we live in brings us closer together and to the Master Gardener who knew and cared for country ways and country folks." No sooner had the applause subsided than Mrs. Eliason and Miss Rosenfeld had asked for copies to distribute.

Within days, national and state publications and radio personalities were publicizing the creed. Farm broadcasters at WMT and WHO voiced it on their programs and provided printed copies to thousands of listeners. Requests for copies came from all over the nation directly to Mrs. Witmer.

That the author lived up to her credo was manifested in many ways.

In looking back on "The Way It Was," Mrs. Witmer makes these comments about her community, state, and national efforts. "I am grateful for my loving husband and family who supported me, the opportunity to write the "Country Woman's Creed", and the privilege of being chosen an Iowa Master Farm Homemaker."

55 CHRISTMAS FAMILY REUNIONS FOR THE BECKS
December, 1984

Family reunions at Christmastime are a universal custom, and the Henry Beck family carried it out to the fullest. When we wrote this feature, they were preparing for their 55th Christmas celebration. From the beginning, it had always been held in their modest, small, farm home which got "smaller" every year as the number of grandchildren and great-grandchildren became larger and larger.

When Henry and Pearl Beck, Lenox, celebrate Christmas, it is always a family event in the fullest sense of the word. Joining the Taylor County farm couple in the happy occasion every year are their son and his wife, three daughters and their husbands, ten grandchildren, and 13 great-grandchildren.

For 55 consecutive years, the Becks have observed Christmas in their modest and attractive farm home. It's a custom every family member enjoys immensely.

"Our home seems to be getting a little smaller every year," says Pearl. She adds, "We had lots of room when the children were young, but when they married and brought their little ones, things became somewhat noisier and more crowded. Now, with the grandchildren and great-grandchildren all with us, it can become quite lively."

Henry, who is 86, adds, "There's always room for a few more." Two newcomers will be welcomed to the yuletide festivities this year. They are Maggie, 6-month old daughter of Denise Robinson, one of the granddaughters, and Andrew, baby son of Janie Wren, another granddaughter.

Despite the crowded conditions, everyone has a great time. And none of the family traditions have been abandoned. There's always a large, beautifully decorated Christmas tree in the living room. Miraculous as it may seem, all 33 celebrants will somehow manage to gather around the tree to sing carols and exchange gifts piled several feet high under the tree.

As is to be expected, the Christmas dinner becomes a major part of the festivities. A 25-lb. turkey serves as a centerpiece, surrounded by a bushel of mashed potatoes, large bowls of gravy, glazed yams, lots of dressing, mince pies, and other trimmings.

Most of the family live in southern Iowa. A daughter, Mrs. Vaunciel Brott, and her husband, along with several grandchildren, are farming close to the 140-acre home place Henry and Pearl bought in 1920. Daughters Marilyn Wren and Caroline Walter and their families live in Indianola. Their son, Dr. Reldron Beck, lives in Las Cruces, N.M., where he is a professor in animal science and range management.

Date of the celebration alternates between December 24 and December 25. In this way, children and grandchildren also have the opportunity to visit the "other side" of their family either on Christmas Eve or Christmas Day.

Mr. & Mrs. Beck.

The Becks have a heritage of operating conservatively. Pearl says, "We watched the pennies closely. I often canned more than 500 quarts of food a year." Henry adds, "We've never spent what we didn't have."

Both have been active in community service. Henry was a county Farm Bureau director, school board member, pillar in the Lenox Methodist Church, and an ASC farmer committeeman for 20 years. Pearl has been active in the church and was once president of the women's society.

Looking back at "The Way It Was" both of them agree that the advent of rural electrification was a high point in their lives. "No more lamp chimneys to clean," recalls Pearl.

Looking ahead, Henry says, "We celebrate Thanksgiving together, too, but our Christmas reunions are always the year's highlight, and they keep getting bigger and merrier every year."

The way it was . . .
1985

OCTOGENARIAN TALKS TO WORLD VIA HAM RADIO
January 12, 1985

Few of us get to talk with people all over the world, but my long-time friend, Harold Pace did so for more than 60 years. A "ham" radio devotee, Pace had interesting International conversations almost every night of the year. This column featured the Muscatine farmer's fascinating hobby.

A Muscatine farmer talks to the world with his little finger. He is Harold Pace, 81, a former Iowa Grange master and community worker, whose hobby is amateur radio.

Pace has been a ham radio operator for more than 60 years. He recalls first hearing wireless time checks in a jewelry store in the early 1920s. Captivated by this, he told his father, who encouraged him to take up the hobby. Within weeks, he had strung some fine wire around oatmeal boxes, made a condenser out of tinfoil, found a vacuum tube, and was receiving and transmitting messages.

Pace was officially licensed in 1925, and for the past 59 years he has talked with tens of thousands of other ham operators in more than 100 countries.

"You name the state or country and chances are I've talked with someone there," says Pace. Australia, Brazil, Cuba, Denmark, France, Germany, Holland, Italy, Japan, New Zealand, Poland, Russia, South Africa, Venezuela, Yugoslavia, and Zambia are only a few of the homelands of his amateur radio friends.

Pace logs every call. Last December he totaled 578 conversations with operators in 47 states and 29 foreign countries.

Former Grange Master Harold Pace talks to the world via ham radio.

During every conversation, he manages to slip in a bit of promotion for Muscatine and Iowa. He often exchanges farm information and other concerns in the U.S. with fellow "hams" all over the world. The stack of cards he has received from those with whom he has talked is reaching toward the ceiling.

Pace says during the first 50 years, he put less than $500 into his hobby. However, since 1975, he has added more sophisticated transmitting and receiving equipment to the tune of around $1000.

Atmospheric conditions are always a factor, both in reception and transmission, explains Pace. "Nighttime is best for foreign contact." He adds that when reception is good he frequently "visits with the world" until 4 a.m. His call letters are WOBTP.

After joining the Sweetland Grange in 1938, he and his late wife advanced to leadership positions both in the state and local organization. He became State Master in 1949, and points with pride to heading 52 subordinate

Granges during his 6-year term. He has attended 44 Iowa and 14 National Grange conventions.

Remembering "The Way It Was" when state master, Pace says, "Road improvements, women's programs, legislative work, good neighbor projects, landscaping church grounds, graveyard rehabilitation, talent programs, and youth leadership were stressed."

Twice widowed, Pace has three sons: Harold, Jr., who carries mail and farms near Muscatine; and twins, Dave, now a Minnesota assistant 4-H leader, and Harlan, a Chicago hospital dietician.

VETERAN LEGISLATORS FORESEE TOUGH SESSION
February 8, 1985

The Iowa Legislature is always going "full blast" in February, and 1985 was no exception. Keeping things on an even track were two veteran lawmakers, 76-year old Richard Welden and 75-year old Lee Holt. Their years of Capitol Hill experience proved valuable in attaining sound legislation,

If the combined wisdom of Iowa's two oldest legislators will be given consideration in the 71st General Assembly now underway, Iowa can expect some overall belt tightening and some new legislation to ease the strain now confronting many hard-pressed farm owners.

Oldest elected representative on the hill is 76-year-old Richard Welden, Iowa Falls. In the Senate, 75-year-old Lee Holt, Spencer, is the senior member. Both vividly recall "The Way It Was" during the Depression of the '30s. They know what goes up must eventually come down — a lesson many younger Americans have yet to learn.

Neither solon is greatly surprised at budget and other state problems now so evident. Both have advocated holding the line in previous assemblies. Both believe this session will have to bite the bullet, either by way of an across-the-board government spending freeze or reducing agencies or employees.

Senator Holt recalls statehouse activities long before he was elected to the House in 1979, and subsequently to the Senate. As a farm worker exactly 50 years ago, he won a position as doorkeeper for the House of Representatives. Before the 1935 session ended, he was promoted to assistant sergeant-at-arms at $3.60 a day.

"Back then, a half century ago, almost all state government employees were housed under this golden dome," says Holt. "But look at us now. We have bureaus and agencies and employees in high rises all over the state," he adds.

Representative Welden, a Hardin County farm owner, now in his 10th consecutive term in the House, quickly spells out the seriousness of the state government's dilemma. He says, "We are already paying $100 million of interest annually on bonds."

Weldon adds, "Debt service on the Board of Regents' bonds comes to $20 million a year. We have to call a halt to further increases."

Although neither serves on the agricultural committee, both men are deeply concerned with the current farm crisis, as well as the state's business climates in general.

Welden says, "If we can't regain more cattle and other livestock numbers, and don't realize more income from crops, there'll be further losses in our work force, and in overall population and revenue." He adds that improving the business climate by more favorable tax planning is highly essential.

As for the lottery as a bailout, both men say that with a Democratic majority it was inevitable, although Holt did not favor it, nor did Welden vote for it in the past. Both agree the current session will be one of the stormiest and most difficult in the state's history.

On improving the business climate, both legislators consider this essential in attracting new — or expanding existing — industries, thus providing more jobs. Both men will support more favorable tax structures.

Taking a hard look at all present agencies, avoiding duplication of services, maintaining a top educational system, implementing a state water plan, repairing roads and bridges, and encouraging small business firms — these are some of the many things Senator Holt and Representative Welden realize they must help solve before the 71st General Assembly becomes history in May. Others are looking at corporation farming, restricting land takeover by foreigners, guarding against moratorium panic, holding the line on state salaries, and protecting the environment.

MASTER FARMER RECALLS FARM CRISIS OF THE 1930s
March 23, 1985

Leigh Curran, Master Farmer.

Most readers know about the farm crisis of the 1980s. For some of us it brought back vivid memories of a similar devastating period in the 1930s. One farmer who could recall from bitter experience was Master Farmer Leigh Curran, nationally known purebred cattle breeder and exemplary community leader.

The current farm crisis, wherein some farm families are facing foreclosure, brings back vivid memories for Leigh Curran, Mason City. The Polled Hereford breeder and former State Senator was named a Master Farmer by *Wallaces Farmer* in 1947.

Now 78, the Cerro Gordo County stockman can look back to "The Way It Was" in the turbulent

'30s when he personally experienced the anguish suffered by thousands during the Depression. His father, a Red Polled cattle breeder who immigrated from Illinois, was confronted with the loss of his 200-acre farm.

"Those were trying times with corn at 10¢ per bushel and forced land sales a common story," recalls Leigh. He remembers the moratorium declared in 1934 and says, "For several years, no one was sure who owned our land."

In the meantime, Leigh met Dorothy Foster of Britt. They were married in early 1937, and quickly resolved to buy farmland. Leigh offered the insurance company holding his father's mortgage $115 an acre to reclaim the homestead. The offer was quickly accepted. More favorable times followed. Within five years, the Curran Stock Farm was theirs, and the happy home for their three daughters, Kay, Jane, and Gail.

Leigh soon realized a larger operation would be better for livestock production. A nearby 120-acre tract, which the Curran family had rented, was on the market. Leigh offered $10 an acre down payment.

Corn the Currans had raised was stored on the place. Leigh sealed his share and when prices moved up dramatically, he reclaimed the corn. And he found the profit amounted to exactly $1200, enough to make the down payment.

While still in his teens, Leigh became interested in Polled Herefords. Convinced the new breed would be far more popular than his father's Red Polls, he introduced a Polled Hereford bull into the herd in 1921. Within ten years, the Currans had upgraded the herd to where they were winning major Iowa shows. Hogs and lambs were also involved in Curran's program.

The herd eventually numbered 200 head of registered Polled Herefords, and championships were claimed at Fort Worth, Denver, and other leading shows, including the Iowa State Fair, where the *Wallaces Farmer* silver trophy was won four consecutive years. Shipments of Curran's cattle were made to Europe, South America, Australia, Canada, and to more than 20 states.

Leigh served many years as a national director for the Breed Association before he dispersed his herd in the late '60s.

In the realm of community service — a criteria heavily considered in designating Master Farmers — few Iowans can surpass Leigh Curran's contribution. He served in the Iowa Legislature eight years as a State Senator and two years in the House. He sums up this service by saying, "It was costly for us, and often frustrating, but rewarding in many ways."

Curran has also served on the Iowa National Resources Council, Iowa 4-H Foundation, and the Iowa State University Ag Advisory Committee.

In his own community, Curran's contributions have been almost endless — the North Iowa Fair Board, North Iowa Medical Board, Mason City Riverfront Commission, Senior Citizens Board, Methodist Church Conference, Chamber of Commerce Ag Committee, Rotary Club, the Clear Lake Handicapped Village, and numerous other local and regional boards.

Asked how he has served so many community, state, and national organizations so well and so long, Curran quips, "I don't play much golf."

REFLECTIONS OF A QUARTER CENTURY RAISING SHEEP
April 13, 1985

Starting all over after losing a farm must be difficult. However, Charles and Ruth Morgan did it after having to give up their land during the 1930s. This article tells how they met the challenge by working together with the help of a lot of good lambs.

Charles Morgan, Outstanding Sheepman.

Unlike most farmers, Iowa lamb producers are cautiously optimistic about their 1985 profit picture. Sheep and lamb numbers are down and lamb prices are somewhat higher than in recent years.

Among those expressing that optimism are Charles and Ruth Morgan of near Colfax, whose 42 Suffolk ewes had 73 lambs this spring, including three sets of triplets. Charles, 75, says, "I wish I could sell today." He remembers when lambs brought $30 or less.

Charles and Ruth were married in 1929. "We do everything together, and have for 56 years," says Ruth. Her husband adds, "And it hasn't always been easy."

The Morgans can personally relate to the farm crisis now so evident. Recalling "The Way It Was" over half a century ago, Charles explains, "We had both saved so we could buy a nearby 100 acres for $200 an acre."

"We worked hard," says Charles, "but when hog prices dropped to $2.50 in 1933 and cattle to $5, we couldn't pay the interest and had to give up." Ruth adds, "It was tough, but we were young and in good health. The only thing to do was start over."

After going through the agony of foreclosure in 1933, the Morgans were able to rent, then buy, 40 acres for $150 per acre in 1937, and another 40 acres for the same price a year later. After paying off the 80 acres, they bought 120 acres more in the early 1950s for $300 an acre, another 80 acres in 1954, and still more since then, bringing the total to 335 acres. "And it's all ours," asserts Ruth proudly.

Commenting on their piece-meal acquisitions of land, stock, and equipment, Charles says, "We decided we couldn't buy some expensive item everytime the moon changed."

As for their interest in lambs, Morgan laughs about how they got into the sheep business. He says, "We used to raise cattle, hogs, and chickens, but I hated the hens. One day while we were cleaning out the smelly henhouse, I said, 'Ruth, why don't you get rid of these dumb chickens and convert this into a sheep shed?' To my surprise, she agreed."

The hens went to market that week and the Morgans bought their first ewe at the nearby sale barn. That was 26 years ago. Soon they added 11 more. Ruth says they were "just sheep," but did well. Eventually the flock increased to 100 ewes.

The flock is smaller now and the Morgans rent out their land on a crop share basis. Their flock of well-bred Suffolks is a perfect retirement project. They take turns serving as "midwife" to the ewes day and night during lambing season.

About a week after lambing, the Morgans work together in vaccinating, docking, worming, etc., the little "woolies." Self-feeders make chores easy. A careful record is kept on every animal. Replacement ewes come from their own flock. Except for those for 4-H projects, the lambs are sold at 120 lb. at the sale barn.

Proof of the quality of their stock is seen in the results of the Albert Lea, Minn., 60-day lamb test where the Morgans won on 1.8 lb. of daily gain.

They are proud of ribbons won in shows in Minnesota, South Dakota, and Iowa. Charles says, "We like ribbons, no matter what color they are."

CATTLEMEN'S CATTLEMAN UPSET BY DECLINE IN NUMBERS
May, 1985

When it came time to recognize May Beef Month in our 1985 "The Way It Was" schedule, there was no doubt about who to select. Orville Kalsem, a second generation Master Farmer, feeding cattle on a Century Farm, was the unanimous choice. This story dealt with this cattleman's feeding methods and achievements, and his concern about the industry.

May is Beef Month, but that whimsical, smile-provoking question so popular on TV a year ago, "Where's the beef?" still persists. Here in Iowa, a related question, "Where are the beef cattle?" remains.

During the past 16 years, Iowa's annual slaughter cattle numbers have plunged from 4.6 million to less than 2.5 million, a staggering 44% drop.

Deep concern is felt throughout the state, and no one is more upset than 78-year old Orville Kalsem of Huxley, often referred to as a "Cattlemen's Cattleman." "It shouldn't be this way," says the Story County Master Farmer.

Orville Kalsem, a cattlemen's cattleman seen at right wiith sons, John and David.

He adds, "We can feed cattle better and cheaper than any other state, and Iowa corn-fed beef is the nation's choicest meat."

Kalsem's 680-acre enterprise near Huxley, where he, his sons, John and Dave, and his grandsons finish out close to 1100 head a year, is solid proof that cattle feeding can be done successfully.

A "born" cattleman, representing the third of five generations of feeders, Kalsem recalls that his grandfather came from Norway to start farming on what is now a Century Farm. Only a few head of cattle were being fed 100 years ago, but when Orville joined his father, Ole, in 1930, the number soon increased to 200.

Orville and his wife, the former JaVerne Ersland, have lasting memories of "The Way It Was" when they started farming during the Depression. "I well remember breaking bushel after bushel of ear corn right at the feed bunks," says JaVerne. Orville broke colts for $25 each to help meet farm expenses. Especially vivid are memories of a bank closing in the mid-thirties when Orville found himself with only $3 in his pocket and a carload of horses to ship.

As the years unfolded, the number of cattle on feed gradually increased. Horse barns had to be converted to cattle feeding sheds. Cylindrical silos were replaced by bunkers, one of them 200 ft. long, 45 ft. wide, and 12 ft. deep. Pole barns were built and lots paved. Sophisticated feed mixing and hauling equipment were purchased. Implants were introduced. A 12 x 14 scale was installed. Automation was undertaken, and today 1000 head can be fed in 1½ hours.

In 1970, the family enterprise was incorporated into Kalsem Farms, Inc.

Teamwork has been a major factor in the Kalsem Farms' success. Orville continues to direct much of the buying and marketing. John is the authority on cattle health and feeding. Dave is the crop man and accountant, and his wife, Cheryl, keeps the records.

Service to the community and to the cattle and horse industries has been an obsession with the Story County Master Farmer. He organized the county Cattleman's Association, became president of Iowa's Beef Producers, and vice president of the American Cattleman's Association. He also chaired Iowa's Marketing Board, remains active in his church, and is a nationally recognized judge. Dozens of citations adorn his basement office walls.

Highest tribute, however, is seen in the number of visitors hosted annually by the Kalsems. In the past 20 years, no less than 4000 persons from 23 countries have come to note "how it's done right" at Kalsem Farms.

A LIFETIME IN DAIRYING
June, 1985

Immigrants from Europe and Asia have repeatedly become successful American farmers and stockmen. Herman Eggink, who left Holland when he was only 20, is a prime example. His humble beginnings as a hired man and his rise to state leadership in dairying makes an interesting success story.

June Dairy Month seems an appropriate time to review accomplishments of some old-timers in the dairy industry. One such veteran is Herman Eggink,

81, Sibley, a long-time Holstein breeder and well-known northwest Iowa dairy industry leader.

Eggink was born in Holland. At age 20, the young Dutchman bade a tearful farewell to his parents and nine brothers and sisters and traveled to America to fulfill his dream of becoming a dairyman.

He soon found himself at work on a South Dakota farm in a community populated by Russian, Norwegian, Swedish, and German families.

Asked how and why he came to Iowa, Eggink explains, "The family I worked for moved from South Dakota to Iowa in 1928. I had met their pretty daughter, so I came with them to Osceola County ostensibly to husk corn, but mainly to see her. Two years later, Nettie and I were married and started farming and dairying on a rented farm near Melvin."

Reflecting on "The Way It Was" in the early '30s, Eggink says, "It was rough — low prices, severe drought, bitter winter cold, and depression panic."

What he describes as a "scrub herd" was put together in 1931. Ten years later, with three sons and a daughter to provide for, the Egginks purchased 80 acres near Sibley. By 1941, they had a good start on a high producing herd of registered Holstein-Friesians.

By 1940, the Egginks had switched from selling cream to bottling milk for the Osceola County Creamery. Soon thereafter, the Egginks put in an electric cooler and other new equipment to become the first dairymen in their neighborhood to market Grade A milk.

Eggink soon took on leadership roles — first as Osceola County Creamery secretary, then president of the Iowa Holstein Association and the Osceola County Fair. He has also been very active in the First Reformed Church, and more recently, has written many inspirational and historical articles. Mrs. Eggink was a 4-H leader for more than 30 years.

As for the future of dairying, Eggink says, "It's good for dairymen who are dedicated to their herds." He is opposed to high support prices, asserting, "Good managers can survive without high subsidies. Poor ones should not be supported."

VETERAN FARM LEADER DISCUSSES NATIONAL FARM PROGRAMS
July, 1985

One man's obsession with avoiding corn and other surpluses translated into sounder government farm programs for everyone. Dwight Meyers, who served as Iowa Production and Marketing Administration chairman, lived and breathed crop adjustment as the major answer to farm prosperity. This column summarized some of his efforts, as a community, state, and national leader.

If Dwight Meyers of Odebolt could be induced to write a book, it would serve as a fascinating history of farm developments in this century. Meyers, now 83, has lived the "ups" and "downs" of farming since the early 1900s. Commenting on "The Way It Was", he speaks of the drudgery of chores by lantern light, single row cultivators, six-foot horse drawn grain binders, and "lots of scratchy, itchy wheat and barley beards."

After graduating from Iowa State, where he was a champion wrestler and participated in baseball, football, track and other sports, he married pretty Helen Rochyo, whom he first met at a church leadership retreat near Boone. Right after their Thanksgiving Day marriage in 1925, the young couple took over the Meyers homeplace.

Their first five years saw relatively good years in farming, but that changed quickly when the Depression struck. By then, four of their five children had arrived. "Believe it or not, just keeping the family properly fed was my biggest concern in the early '30s," says Dwight. By 1937, things had improved enough for the Meyers to buy the 185 acre homestead at $125 an acre.

Dwight Meyers

An "innovator" in every sense of the word, Dwight began keeping accurate farm records from the outset of his farming operations. In the early '30s, he was one of the first to test and sell hybrid corn. He dropped out of the neighborhood threshing ring to become the first combine owner in his community. With the advent of rural electrification 50 years ago, he was one of the first to help get rural America "out of the dark." After helping organize the Sac County REC, he headed both the Corn Belt and Iowa REA Boards.

Federal farm programs quickly found him in the vanguard of practical farm leaders. Back in the Depression era, when Henry Wallace first advocated farm controlled crop adjustment programs, Dwight Meyers was on his township Corn-Hog Committee, helping buy "piggy" sows. He also measured corn acres and checked farm compliance for the Agricultural Adjustment Act.

When the Supreme Court declared the Triple A unconstitutional, Meyers considered it a major setback for American agriculture, but quickly helped organize crop adjustment and corn sealing programs.

PMA (Production Marketing Administration) was the successor of the Crop Adjustment programs. Meyers, having completed three terms in the Iowa Legislature, was named State PMA Chairman in 1953, a difficult time when numerous irregularities had to be corrected. So effective were his Iowa PMA efforts that national leaders called him to Washington in 1956 to become Deputy Director of the USDA's Soil Bank Division. Three years later, he was named Director of the Civil Defense Food and Materials Division.

A firm believer that production adjustment is essential for the nation's agricultural economic well-being, as well as for soil resources, Meyers says he is pleased that the ASC, successor to PMA, has stressed contouring, terracing, strip cropping, waterways and tiling, all of which he considers significant contributions to soil conservation. However, he is concerned about efforts toward high price supports, saying, "They will only build up more surpluses, and disposing of that burdensome overproduction is our biggest problem."

Asked as to what Congress, the White House, and the USDA should do in shaping up the 1985 Farm Program, the veteran Odebolt farm leader says, "They've got to put more emphasis on production adjustment. We must prevent further buildups of corn, wheat, soybean and other U.S. stocks. Disposing of our price depressing surpluses must get priority. Farmers don't want handouts; all they ask is a fair shake."

However great an effort Dwight Meyers has put forth in township, county, regional, state and national leadership roles, and however successful he has been as a farmer, many will say his greatest contributions have been in community service. Beginning with campus and Adelante fraternity activities at ISU, and continuing as soon as he started farming on his own 60 years ago, he has been a community booster every step of the way.

Space permits listing only some of the projects and programs in which Meyers has been deeply involved.

Aside from his serving as a State Legislator three terms, and assuming major responsibilities with the fledgling REA and Federal Farm Programs, Dwight served ten years as a township 4-H leader; organized the widely recognized Sac City and Odebolt Farmers Night Schools; was a charter member and Board Chairman of the Colonial Manor Nursing Home in Odebolt; chaired the Odebolt Community Betterment Committee, as well as the Odebolt Council; was a lay leader and chairman of the Trustees, as well as state conference delegate and Sunday School teacher in the Odebolt United Methodist Church; was the first president of the Sac County ISU board; was on the Board of Directors for the Peoples State Bank; was on the State Extension Advisory Committee; and helped organize the N.W. Iowa Farm Business Association. He has also been president of the Odebolt Rotary Club and of AARP (American Association of Retired Persons).

In farm organization circles the veteran Odebolt farmer was especially active in Farm Bureau work since 1926, including several terms as township director, county president, and member of the State Resolutions Committee.

Honors accorded him are many. A few of the dozen or more framed citations on the wall above the work desk in his study include: ISU citations, the Odebolt Community Betterment Leadership Award, and the plaque signifying Meyers as the winner of the 1942 State Corn Yield Test with a 10-acre yield average of 151 bushels. Meyers recently was honored by ISU as an outstanding 1925 graduate. While in college, he was a member of two honorary scholastic fraternities, Alpha Zeta and Gamma Sigma Delta.

Dwight Meyers' five children are Mary Thompson, Odebolt; Barbara Johnson, Cedar Falls; Clyde Meyers, Ames; Lois Moffitt, Minneapolis; and James, who is on the home farm, where he is a nationally recognized hog producer and is active in computerizing dozens of Northwest Iowa farming operations. Sixteen grandchildren help brighten the Odebolt octogenarian's life. Mrs. Meyers passed away earlier this year, not long after the couple noted their 59th wedding anniversary.

LONG-TIME EXHIBITOR REFLECTS ON THE STATE FAIR
August, 1985

There are almost as many ways to get into farming as there are farms, but Ralph Bright, who wound up being one of the nation's premier Brown Swiss dairy cattle breeders, probably had the strangest — and hardest — way of all. In this column, we told about that rough beginning and what it led to in recognition, respect and reward.

When the Iowa State Fair opens its 10-day run on August 15, Ralph Bright, 75, an experienced Brown Swiss breeder of Eldora, will reflect on a treasure trove of memories.

Bright, his wife, and four children participated in over 150 shows. During their half century of exhibiting, they took part in shows in Illinois, Ohio, Wisconsin, Nebraska, Oregon, and California, as well as the Iowa State Fair, All Iowa Fair, and National Dairy Congress.

"Considering the time and expense involved, you don't make any money showing," says Bright, "but it gives your herd tremendous exposure." He has sold cattle to 37 states and several foreign countries, including Italy and Columbia. Biggest sale was for $10,000 when the Rockefeller family bought a prizewinning bull.

Ralph Bright, top Brown Swiss cattle breeder and showman.

Bright's rise to the top was by no means easy. A northeast Iowa farm boy, and the youngest of 11 children, he left home at 15 to fend for himself, drifting from one place to another, seeking any kind of work.

"I was in tough company much of the time," says Bright, "and had to learn to defend myself." During his rough and tumble life in Dakota's wheat fields, he took up boxing, knocking out most of his opponents, many of them highly touted professionals, and earning from $10 to $100 per exhibition. He explains, "I needed money to start farming."

Married to his grade school sweetheart, Iola Davis, in 1930, Bright recalls using his boxing and other earnings to buy four horses and used machinery in 1931, including a corn planter for which he paid $4.

After the purchase of their first purebred cow in 1934 (bought for $37 when she was ten years old), the Bright's Brown Swiss herd expanded rapidly. In time, a total of 85 head were involved.

All four of the family's children — LaRita, Delores, Karen, and Lonnie — won state and national 4-H honors. Karen also was named Iowa Dairy Princess, and as a 2-year old toddler, Lonnie won the Iowa State Fair Champion Baby contest.

Equally, or more meaningful than show winnings, were some of the production records achieved by the herd, including better than 23,000 lb. at 4.3% milk in a single year by one of the top producers.

A church tither and community leader, as well as a champion dairyman, Ralph Bright proudly lists 22 charities among his beneficiaries, most of them church-oriented.

In community efforts, Ralph is especially proud of the $45,000 Hardin County Youth Center he helped originate and build. The center now serves many organizations. He was president of his breed association and of DHIA, superintendent of churches, Hardin County 4-H chairman, and was named Iowa Distinguished Dairyman.

For the past two decades, health problems have plagued both Bright and his wife. "Even with our problems, I've been a very fortunate man," philosophizes the Hardin County Master Dairyman.

AMES LANDOWNER ENJOYS SAME TENANT FOR 48 YEARS
September 28, 1985

Landlord-tenant relations sometimes become horror stories, but they were anything but that for Clinton Adams, Ames owner of four farms. That Adams and his tenants enjoyed working with each other is indicated by Carroll Jacobson and his family. The Jacobsons had already been on an Adams farm for nearly a half century when this was written.

Favorable landlord-tenant relations have long been a goal in rural America. In Iowa, where nearly 50% of the land is farmed by tenants, improving owner-operator relations is a continuing challenge. In years past it has often been disheartening.

Greedy absentee landlords, inequitable cash rent arrangements, exploitation of soil by tenants, failure to make repairs and improvements by landlords — these are only some of the problems causing mistrust and creating financial and emotional strains between owners and operators. On the other hand, completely harmonious arrangements between landlord and tenant can also be found.

A classic case of happy and satisfactory land stewardship centers around an Ames landowner, 80-year old Clinton Adams. As owner of four Boone and Story County farms, Adams has achieved a remarkable record of tenant continuity.

In what must be some sort of tenure record, Carroll and Edith Jacobson, 73, have rented a 170-acre farm near Roland from Adams for 48 consecutive years. Moreover, the highly successful partnership has been achieved without the benefit of any written lease or contract.

Adams and his tenant agree that a lease is advisable from a legal standpoint, but in their case, it has not been necessary.

"We had planned to draw up a lease," says Adams, "but by the time we got around to it, we had such confidence in each other, we didn't bother."

Clinton Adams, farm owner, and Carroll Jacobson, tenant.

The Jacobson livestock-grain enterprise, currently operated by Bob and Cindy, Carroll's son and daughter-in-law, has been a profitable venture for all concerned. The 50-50 crop share plan, augmented by a $20 per acre cash rental fee for non-crop acres has been in effect from the outset, and applies to all four of Adams' farms.

Pride in ownership is eloquently expressed by Adams in the manner in which all buildings on all four of his farms are maintained and painted, and capital improvements added when logical. Pride in residency is equally expressed by the Jacobson family and other tenants in the perfect order evidenced around the farmsteads. A manicured lawn, beautiful flower borders, and an immaculate home all reflect that pride.

Asked what he considered the key to harmonious land-tenant relations, Jacobson answers: "It's 100% trust in each other." Adams totally agrees with that philosophy, asserting, "The things I seek in a tenant are trustworthiness, honesty, diligent work, and pride in the fields, farmstead, etc."

That Adams has been successful in his quest is seen not only in Carroll Jacobson's 48-year tenure, but also on other farms. On a Boone County farm bought 53 years ago, Fred McHone was operator until he retired because of his health. Then Dave Snyder came 36 years ago and still farms it with the help of his son, Steve. On the other Boone County place, Carl Lee became the tenant 50 years ago. After he died, a nephew, Millard Lee, took over in 1948 and operated the 400 acres 30 years, to be succeeded by his son, Eugene, the past seven years. Meanwhile, on the Adams' 314-acre holding near Gilbert, Millard's brother, Merle, has rented that farm for the past 25 years.

The Ames landowner says, "It's my conviction a person should not own or operate a farm unless he takes good care of it. My tenants are all good stewards."

He says, "I want my tenants to have all the conveniences and improvements that I enjoy in my own home."

A VISIT WITH A 92-YEAR OLD MASTER FARM HOMEMAKER
November 23, 1985

In case anyone thinks a farm wife's role has to be limited to raising the children, doing the cooking, housework and gardening, and helping in fields and barns, they ought to have known Mrs. Ralph Newcomer, an Iowa Master Farm Homemaker. This account told of the talents, activities, and achievements this remarkable woman had.

Teacher, artist, writer, poet, women's leader, sheep breeder, Master Farm Homemaker, and genealogist — these are just some of the activities and recognitions Bessie Short Newcomer, a *Wallaces Farmer* Master Farm Homemaker of 1948, can include in her resume.

Now 92, and a resident of the Bloomfield Manor Care Center, the Davis County nonagenarian is keenly alert and loves to reminisce about her pioneer background as well as all the teaching she did in Iowa, Missouri, and Nebraska.

A 1912 Drake University graduate, she served as a Latin and English teacher until she married Ralph Newcomer, a Wabash Railway official, in 1922. The couple then moved to a 130-acre farm where Bessie took care of the field work and a flock of sheep while her husband continued his work with the railroad. Two sons, Ralph and Robert, were raised on the farm near Moulton.

By the time the oldest boy, Ralph, was 12, the Depression had already taken a heavy toll. Hardship had affected almost everyone. "The farm problem and depressed prices had become a serious economic and political issue. The need for organization was urgent," recalls the southern Iowa homemaker.

Mrs. Bessie Newcomber, on Farm Bureau Women's Committee.

A born leader, Mrs. Newcomer soon found herself the county Farm Bureau women's chairperson and a delegate to the American Farm Bureau convention in Washington, D.C. Inspired by the need for more organization, she accepted the challenge of District Committee woman for ten southern Iowa counties and served with distinction for 12 years.

During all those years, Bessie, as she is popularly known, continued her active farm work including a sizable flock of sheep. "My people liked me because I was a working farm wife and often told them I was direct from the sheep shed," laughs Mrs. Newcomer. However, her interests were by no means limited to the fields and flocks, or farm organization leadership.

Writing articles for state and national publications was one of her favorite activities. One memorable editorial was a strong statement opposing federal aid for education. Another, entitled *"Uncle Sam's Pinup Girls"* stressed the interdependence between agriculture, industry, and labor. An authority on taxation, she often pointed out tax inequities. In one case, she asked, "Why is it that 'old Bessie' will be taxed at $3.50 at one end of our pasture, but $7.50 if she's on the opposite side?"

Nor has Mrs. Newcomer stopped writing. Last year, at age 91, she composed *"Creed Of A Country Woman"*, spelling out in beautiful prose her belief in the land and its people.

A talented artist, the walls of her room are enhanced with country scenes she has painted in oil and watercolor.

Genealogy is one of her favorite pastimes. She is determined to have her grandchildren and great-grandchildren know their great-great-great-grandparents came from Virginia to Ohio by covered wagon.

Although now confined to a wheelchair, Mrs. Newcomer continues a cheery outlook. She is proud of her Master Farm Homemaker Award and all the work that led to it.

She delights in showing visitors clippings of her writings, including those done on trains, buses, planes, and in hotel rooms. She laughs, "I never got more than $5 for an article, but it was a fulfilling outlet for me."

FARM COUPLE MAKES CHRISTMAS MERRIER
December, 1985

Christmas time is always a time for good will and good cheer. And, for Mr. and Mrs. Virgil Marshall, it was always a time to multiply their year 'round good deeds. For them, it was an opportunity to bring joy to shut-ins and "down-and-outers" as well as to their own loved ones.

An elderly Dallas County farm couple might well be described as the personification of the Christmas Spirit. Virgil and Mildred Marshall, now both 80, believe that "Peace on Earth and Good Will to All" begins with sharing blessings in their home community.

Because of their interest and activities, a happier Christmas will be enjoyed by many. Friends and neighbors, their church, retirement home residents, college students, down-and-outers, as well as their own children, grandchildren, and great-grandchildren will be the beneficiaries.

During the current Christmas season the Marshalls will lead sing-alongs for the Adel Acres senior citizens, conduct a worship service at Spurgeon Manor, and participate in the Panther Creek Church of the Brethren Christmas programs. The couple will also make hospital calls, visit nursing homes, attend Gideon prayer breakfasts, gather items for the Food Pantry, and become involved in any other community project where they can help.

This is a second marriage for both the Marshalls. Their first spouses died. Virgil and his first wife raised four adopted children. Mildred and her husband had two of their own. Today, as the Marshalls look forward to no less than three family Christmas reunions, they count 17 grandchildren and ten great-grandchildren between them.

Virgil's community service also includes a stint as Dallas County Farm Bureau president, superintendent of Sunday School, and work with the International Heifer Project.

Mildred, after serving as Dallas County deputy recorder several terms, became an Adel business woman. She says, "I bought a shoestore on a shoestring." After 19 years, she sold the store to go into sales work until she retired.

Service to others has always been one of Virgil's major goals. While a young hired man in Appanoose County, he resolved to be a "good Christian, useful citizen, and successful farmer." That he has achieved all three objectives is now eminently clear.

Relating "The Way It Was" for him in farming, he says that after earning wages several years, he bought a team, a few cows, and some machinery, was married, and then rented 60 acres in Dallas County where he still lives. In time, he bought another 100 acres in the Panther Creek community. A good steward of land and stock and a good neighbor, he did well and is now comfortably retired. A grandson, Ed Swinger, of Redfield, rents the 160 acres.

Mr. & Mrs. Virgil Marshall

As for community service and good citizenship, the Marshalls are shining examples, as evidenced by their many endeavors and by receiving the Merit Award for Citizenship.

The way it was . . .
1986

MANY REMEMBER 1910 VISIT OF HALLEY'S COMET
January, 1986

1986 was the year Halley's comet would return after a 76-year absence. Those who remembered seeing the celestial phenomenon in 1910 seemed anxious to view it again. Consequently, I went to the Madrid Home for the Aged in January to talk with residents in their 80s and 90s about their childhood recollections of the celebrated comet.

The long awaited return visit of Halley's comet has been widely heralded in recent weeks. The comet has been dimly visible high above the southwest horizon since late December. Some hardy souls braved the bitter cold on clear nights to get an early glimpse of the celestial phenomenon.

Next month, the famed comet will duck behind the sun so it will not be seen from planet Earth, but in March it will reappear and in April will put on its best show in this area.

Halley's comet appears in the heavens about every 76 years, and travels at incredible speeds as high as 62,500 mph. Its distinctive tail, said to be up to 100 million miles long, sets it apart from all other celestial sightings.

For most of us, Halley's 1986 "show" will be our first view of the celebrated comet, but for some of our elders, now in their 80s or 90s, it will be the second time around. It will also be an occasion to recall childhood memories of the excitement caused by Halley's comet many years ago.

A number of residents of the Madrid Home for the Aged disclosed vivid memories of "The Way It Was" back in 1910.

Lena Moffitt, 94, of Lorimor, recalls seeing it high in the sky. "It looked like a big bright star with a long, long tail," says Lena, adding, "I wasn't all that excited at first, but the papers were full of it and everyone was interested. Some were afraid it spelled doom, but nothing happened." She concluded, "I hope to see it again this spring."

Pearl Ingram, 87, who was living in Kentucky in 1910, says, "It was a big white star with a long tail and it caused quite a commotion. My father told me I'd see it again in 76 years and here I am looking forward to my second look."

Myrtle Cassell, 90, of Slater, says, "There was a lot of talk about it, but it didn't make much of an impression on me until a man in our area said it would spell the end of the world." She adds, "He solved his problem by crawling under his bed every night."

Nella Eihle, 82, was a little girl in North Dakota when the comet was last seen. She lived on a farm and tells how her father, brothers, sister, and she did a lot of Halley's comet gazing on clear nights. She points out, "There were a lot of stars in the sky, but there was no missing the comet with its long tail headed toward the east. It was quite a sight and I'm glad I'll see it again."

Oldest of the Madrid Home's 1910 "star gazers" is 99-year-old Ida Griffith, who grew up near Nevada, Iowa. She remembers the comet vividly. "People talked about its coming for weeks," points out Ida.

"We were on our farm and saw it often and in a different place each time. It really wasn't that big a deal, but it was interesting," she adds. She hopes to see the celestial display again this spring and is sure her children, five grandchildren, and five great-grandchildren will get a big kick out of the 1986 version of Halley's comet.

DEWEY JONTZ...INVOLVED WITH SHEEP FOR SEVEN DECADES
February 7, 1986

How a pair of twin lambs started Dewey Jontz on his way back to boyhood health and set the pattern for his life was documented in this column. As time went on, Jontz, the shepherd, became Jontz, the national sheep authority. This column listed details.

Over the past 40 years, sheep, lamb, and wool production has increased significantly in Iowa. No one person can be singled out as responsible for Iowa's rapid growth in sheep production, but Dewey Jontz, 78, of Runnells, has undeniably been a key leader in that progress.

Born on an Illinois farm, Jontz began his lifelong love affair with the sheep industry 70 years ago when he was a sickly eight-year old lad. An ewe on the farm produced two nice lambs, and soon the boy's illness ended.

Two years later, influenced by his County Farm Advisor, he enrolled in 4-H.

At age 12, and in 4-H, Jontz was offered two grade ewes for $5 each by a neighbor. Jontz earned the money to pay for them by plowing corn.

Dewey Jontz, nationally recognized shepherd.

When he was 17, another neighbor offered to take Dewey's best lambs on the show circuit. The entries did well, including winning a grand championship. The next year, young Jontz went on the circuit on his own. Traveling by train, he competed in 48 shows in the U.S. and Canada, winning countless awards.

In 1933, he was one of the three men invited to establish a flock of sheep on the President Monroe 1800 farm in Virginia. After achieving a 175% lamb crop from 500 Montana bred ewes, he left Virginia to join a British born shepherd on the 4800-acre DuPont farm in Pennsylvania, where he developed a show string that swept the International Stock Show in Chicago and earned him the nation's highest shepherd's award.

In 1938, Jontz accepted a position as the Iowa State College (now Iowa State University) shepherd. Jontz reorganized the sheep department and rapidly became popular with students and faculty alike. Five years later, he became secretary of the Iowa Sheep Association, which would later become a branch of the Iowa Department of Agriculture.

During his tenure, Jontz started lamb carcass evaluations, advocated shorter fleeced breeding stock, promoted lamb as a table delicacy, established ram testing stations, conducted sheep shearing schools, and originated FFA lamb projects. He also introduced border collie trials and demonstrated the talents of his sheep dogs before huge crowds at fairs and other events.

Jontz wrote a popular and practical shepherd's manual. He prompted the sale of pelts and wool products, developed a widely read newsletter — *Sheep Clippings* — promoted lamburgers, and directed the Iowa State Fair sheep show for 32 years.

A nationally acclaimed sheep judge, he has worked major shows throughout the U.S. and Canada. Meanwhile, his interest in border collie breeding and registering has developed into a nationwide enterprise involving over 5000 sheep dogs.

The Iowa Sheep Industry leader's achievements have not gone unnoticed. A huge trophy case in the living room of his small home is bulging with trophies, medals, plaques, and other mementos.

On his official retirement nine years ago, friends contributed a purse so he and his wife, Edith, could travel to Scotland and England to observe the sheep and border collie activities abroad. The 1984 Iowa State Fair sheep show was dedicated in his honor.

His son, Captain Dewey Jontz, Jr., of the Iowa State Patrol, says of his father, "He never quits, never even slows down, never takes a traditional vacation, just gives 100% effort in behalf of sheep and border collies."

MASTER FARMER OFFERS HOPE IN FARM CRISIS
March 1986

When I learned Herb Campbell was chosen as one of Iowa's Master Farmers and later named the first of more than 600 Master Pork Producers, I lost no time going to his Washington County Farm. In an hour's visit I quickly learned why he had been so highly recognized — as this column explains.

Many Iowa farmers are in danger of losing part or all of their farming operations. But, they can take heart from the experiences of Herbert Campbell, 75, who was named an Iowa Master Farmer in 1951.

Born in Lucas County, Campbell was raised in northern Missouri, and rode horseback 18 miles a day to attend the nearest high school at Seymour, Iowa. He won a football scholarship at Iowa Wesleyan College in Mt. Pleasant, where he met Neva Stacy, a Brighton farm girl.

When he married Neva in 1931, they resolved to own, instead of rent, land. Pooling their resources and borrowing heavily, they acquired 130 acres.

However enthusiastic and confident they may have been, things did not go well. They had borrowed at 7% interest. Then their bank closed. Gilts, for which Campbell paid $20 each, raised pigs that sold for less then 4¢ a pound. Corn plunged to 10¢ a bushel. Before the year ended they lost their farm and everything they had put into it.

"It was a blow and it hurt," says Campbell, "but we were young and decided it was not the end of the world." Within weeks they were able to rent back the land they had lost for $4 an acre.

By 1933, during the depth of the Depression, and just after their first child was born, Campbell was able to pick up some "off-the-farm" cash. He recalls, "I did almost anything to keep bread on the table."

Herb Campbell, Community Leader

He got $3 a week riding horseback to deliver Sunday papers. He did fencing for neighbors for $1.50 a day. In addition, he and his brother bought an abandoned railway bridge. The 40-foot poles were cut for corner posts and sold at a small profit.

Five years after losing their first farm, the Campbells had established a $500 line of credit. They were able to rent a hilly 290-acre tract ideal for raising sheep and hogs. Pasture rent was $5 an acre. Cropland was farmed on a 50-50 basis.

Hybrid corn was still a novelty, but Campbell bought 2 bushels at $7.50 each. Final yield were far above open pollenated varieties.

By 1941 Herb and Neva had $1500 to invest. A rough 210-acre place near Ainsworth was available for $8500. Nearby, another 80 could be had for $2500. The Campbells decided it was "then or never." Their $1500, plus a substantial bank loan, enabled them to become landowners a second time.

Because the farm was hilly, Herb immediately undertook a conservation program with emphasis on contouring, terracing, and building ponds and cement structures. He expanded his livestock program to 3000 sheep and 500 hogs. He became the first in the area to plant alfalfa and bromegrass, and use phosphate.

As the sons began showing an interest in farming, Herb and Neva bought another 240. The new farm was in Jefferson County and was operated with the help of a dependable hired man who later bought a Campbell farm.

The Campbell's second son, Bruce, now has taken over the operation. More land has been purchased. Minimum and no-till practices have been adopted, and the farm has been incorporated.

Over the years Herb has helped several families advance from hired hand to farm ownership, a contribution of which he is especially proud. He strongly believes hard work, a reasonable bank balance, diversification involving livestock and crop rotation, and respect for the land are basic essentials.

Asked about his favorite impressions over the years, Campbell emphasizes the need for conservation. "We need to remember," he points out, "we are only trustees of the land, and it behooves us to maintain its productivity."

TWO IOWA TULIP FESTIVALS NATIONALLY ACCLAIMED
April, 1986

Farm crisis or not, floral beauty, highlighted by the Pella and Orange City Tulip Festivals, continued to abide in Iowa in 1986. Hundreds of thousands of tulip and other gorgeous blooms began in late April and continued through the summer. They helped dismiss our financial troubles part of the time. The festivals were beautiful, exciting, and fun.

April and May showers and flowers have started to atone for the harsh winter months with their snow and cold. The beauty, aroma and freshness of those flowers has been a welcome contrast to the cruelties of the Midwestern farm crisis.

Focal point for flower lovers in Iowa next month will be the Tulip Festivals in Pella and Orange City. Pella's 51st annual celebration will be May 8, 9 and 10. The Orange City festival is May 15, 16 and 17th.

Both events are now nationally recognized, and attract huge crowds to admire the hundreds of thousands of gorgeously colorful tulip blooms grown from bulbs imported directly from Holland. Both communities have a rich Dutch heritage and make the most of it, not only during their festivals, but also year round.

Townspeople and neighboring farmers alike join in the celebration, which includes much pageantry. Operettas, coronation of a tulip queen, street scrubbing, burgomeister speeches, town criers, etc., are among the regular features. Many of the local enthusiasts wear the native dress of various Netherlands provinces, as well as wooden shoes. Dutch windmills are in motion during the celebration. Many merchants have rebuilt store fronts reminiscent of those seen in Holland. Colorful parades are a daily highlight, as are the evening operettas and folk dancing.

Some of the participants were born in the Netherlands. Many others are first generation Holland-Americans. Regardless of how recent their Dutch "connection" may be, residents in and around Pella and Orange City take great pride in their festivals and cooperate to a remarkable degree. Hundreds of homeowners plant tulips all along the fronts of their homes.

Some "old timers" have been a part of every festival. Among these are Peter Gaass and Mrs. Leonora Hettinga, grandchildren of Hendrik Scholte, founder of Pella. Mrs. Hettinga, now in her 70s, was the first Pella Tulip Queen. She recalls the occasion vividly. A student at Central College at the time, word came to her of her choice, with instructions to get a Dutch costume, wooden shoes, some Pella bologna and go with the Burgomeister to call on then Governor Herring to promote the Festival. The only problem was she had an important midterm exam that same day. However, the professors arranged for the test to be taken early, so Queen Leonora, after borrowing a costume and illfitting wooden shoes, made the trip to the Capitol and did the honors. Since then, Mrs. Hettinga has participated in every Festival and met all the 49 Tulip

Queens who have succeeded her. She also opens the Scholte home during Festival time.

Martha Lautenbach, 85, is another veteran Pella Tulip Time enthusiast who has participated in every festival. The former curator of the 23 room Scholte museum, Mrs. Lautenbach is a walking encyclopedia of Pella history, and her enthusiasm for Tulip Time knows no bounds.

In Orange City, the leading authorities on the Northwest Iowa community's famed Tulip Festival are Mr. & Mrs. Arie Vander Stoep. Arie, now 85, is the festival's official historian, but he quickly agrees his wife of 61 years, Leona, is the real authority.

Her Highness, The Tulip Queen.

With 13 large scrapbooks filled to overflowing, Mrs. Vander Stoep has every possible detail for instant reference. Carefully documented are the names and pictures of Tulip Queens, parade marshalls, wooden shoemakers, Dutch dance and drill leaders, programs and pageants, burgomeisters, parades, Netherlands costumes, high school bands, and everything else connected with the Orange City event.

Of special interest is documentation of the acquiring of an authentic Dutch street organ, first brought to Philadelphia from Holland and then acquired by and brought to Orange City. The rare instrument is only one of two in the U.S. An equally interesting account has been written about the construction of a Dutch Windmill.

This year marks the 46th annual Orange City Tulip Festival, where countless gorgeous tulips will be in full bloom in mid-May, and "volksparades", Dutch song reviews, Klompen (wooden shoe) dances, coronation of a queen and royal court, and colorful night time performances will be highlighted.

CLINTON COUNTY CATTLEMAN DEPLORES DECLINE IN NUMBERS
May 10, 1986

A chance to husk and scoop corn for 3¢ a bushel brought Leo Gannon to Clinton County a long time ago, and the few dollars earned doing that arduous work resulted in his becoming a farm renter and cattle feeder. Eventually, land was bought, and Gannon was able to join the nation's top cattlemen during the years when Clinton County dominated the Chicago International.

May Beef Month has lost some of its punch, and a veteran Clinton County cattleman joins thousands of others in lamenting the decline of cattle feeding in Iowa. But Leo Gannon, DeWitt, is not overly surprised.

Gannon, now 85, fed up to 1100 head during the years Iowa was a leading cattle feeding state and Clinton County one of the Midwest's leading counties in beef production.

"The change in transportation marked the beginning of the downfall," says Gannon. He explains that rail shipments were far less expensive than hauling by truck. "And," he adds, "everything has to be hauled by truck now." Rising production costs and poor returns — including too many years of actual losses — were also cited for the decline.

Gannon has been remarkably successful in almost every venture he has been involved in over his more than half a century of cattle feeding. After renting for several years, he and his brother, Mike, bought 400 acres for $160 in 1929. "However, we nearly lost it during the Depression," notes Gannon.

He eventually bought more land for prices ranging from $171 to $360 an acre, some of which sold for $4000 an acre in 1979. The remaining 820 acres has been divided equally between four sons — Bill, Dick, John, and Tom.

Three of the Gannon sons are still farming and feeding cattle. "It's nip and tuck now, but they're still hanging in there." says Gannon. He also has two daughters, one in Wisconsin and the other in California. There are 17 grandchildren and six great grandchildren.

Recalling "The Way It Was," Leo remembers that corn husking job — at 3¢ a bushel — brought him to Clinton County in 1919. His savings as a hired man were used to start farming, first as a renter, paying from $5 to $10 an acre, then as an owner. Cattle feeding was started at the beginning of his farming and continued for almost 50 years.

Gannon's eyes light up when he tells about the good feeders consistently obtained from the Doherty ranch in New Mexico. "They were the best," he proclaims. Calves, steers, and heifers were included in the large feeding enterprise, but steers generally made the most money. He also bought and sold thousands of feeder cattle.

A lover of horses, Leo always rode his favorite mount during his cattle feeding years. At one time, he had as many as 35 horses.

Mention the International Stock Show in Chicago and a broad smile crosses Gannon's face. "Clinton County, with feeders like Master Farmers Ferd and George Schmidt, almost always took the championships," he boasts. His own carloads often were among the top winners.

Leo Gannon, veteran feeder of prize cattle.

Later he helped judge the famed stock exposition three consecutive years. He says, "The press always wanted the results by noon, but with 200 carloads to place, I couldn't finish much before 5 o'clock."

Other pleasant memories Gannon recounts include a visit to Ireland with his daughters, and a private audience with the Pope in Rome, later followed by a visit to the Pope's farm, where he found emphasis on oxen and poultry.

Asked about his success as a farmer, feeder, father, churchman, and community worker, Gannon says, "Blame it on Irish luck, being in the right place at the right time, and having a good banker as a friend and partner." Neighbors say hard work, financial astuteness, and common sense also had a lot to do with Leo Gannon's accomplishments.

A HALF CENTURY OF SOIL CONSERVING EFFORTS
June, 1986

Among the nation's most dedicated soil conservation pioneers was Bill Davis, an enthusiastic supporter of Dr. Hugh Bennett, who, as head of the USDA Soil Erosion Service in the early '30s, became known as the "Father Of Soil Conservation." Davis started following Bennett's footsteps in 1935. This column verified the contributions he and other early leaders made to "nail down the topsoil and make the water work."

The day after Christmas 1935, William Davis signed on to work for what was then called the Soil Erosion Service. At the time, the nation was still reeling from the effects of the Depression and the devastating drought of 1934.

Hugh Bennett, known as the "Father of Soil Conservation," was fighting hard to stop soil erosion. Davis was eager to participate, thereby beginning a lifetime crusade in conservation.

At the 50th Anniversary Soil Conservation Jubilee held last fall in Marion County, Davis and several other conservation veterans mused about what has transpired during the five decades he has been involved.

Best known as "Bill", Davis, 82, recalled his first years in the regional office in Harrison County, Missouri, and then in Washington County, Iowa. "A new ethic in terms of land was needed and we accepted the challenge," says Bill.

Laying out contour lines, building waterways, establishing terraces, and similar early day soil saving practices were among Bill's first tasks. For a time, he was assigned to the Commodity Credit Corporation (CCC) at Red Oak, and later served as an area wildlife specialist.

The army engineers also "borrowed" him for several years before he started a Soil Conservation District in Dubuque County. Soon after that, he was moved to Iowa City to become an area conservationist for four counties, and finally he was assigned to Marion County, "where it all really began."

William Davis, dedicated conservationist.

"At first, there was tremendous enthusiasm," says Bill. "We were dedicated to the cause. World War II demands on the land became heavy, and farmers realized something needed to be done. Regrettably, somewhere along the line, the crusade slowed down. Then fence-row to fence-row farming to produce for export actually undid much of what we had accomplished."

Davis's sentiments were echoed by several others. Howard Chandler, 76, for example, has been a conservationist for 40 years and says, "It was disheartening to see our work destroyed. Our grasslands were plowed up, contouring and terracing ignored, and chemicals poured on. Now lakes are filling with sediment and there are no fish in the streams."

Alvin Van Zee, Pella, one of those honored at the jubilee for outstanding accomplishments in soil and water conservation and proper land use, has long advocated crop rotation and livestock production. In accepting his award, Van Zee said, "We're all in this together — city folks as well as farmers. It's been a big job to get the conservation ball rolling."

Lowell Johnson, 75, of near Knoxville, is one of Marion County's first soil commissioners. Among the first to build terraces, he has eight ponds on his 364 acres. Believed to be Iowa's original no-till farmer, Johnson undertook this system in the early 1950s before the term "no-till" was coined.

FRED SCHWENGEL...U.S. CAPITOL HISTORIAN
July 12, 1986

Every time anyone drives on one of our Interstate highways, it would be well to remember the former Iowa Congressman who had much to do with achieving those 43,000 miles of coast-to-coast thoroughfares. He was the late Fred Schwengel, who started out as a corn husking champion and would up as the Congressional choice for the presidency of the U.S. Capitol Historical Society.

When Fred Schwengel, former Iowa legislator and U.S. Congressman, was honored on his 80th birthday last month, Speaker of the House "Tip" O'Neill hailed him "Caretaker of the U.S. Capitol Building." It's a lofty title, richly deserved.

Born of immigrant parents on a farm in Franklin County, Schwengel has excelled at every task.

Confidant of eight U.S. Presidents, and respected by hundreds of fellow men and women in Congress, past and present, Fred Schwengel looks back on a multitude of achievements — personal, political, and public.

Recalling his contacts with top leaders, Schwengel particularly enjoys citing his first meeting with Harry Truman. It was at a Masonic meeting in Kansas City where the Iowan was introduced to the then Senator Truman as a fellow Baptist, fellow Mason, fellow historian, but unlike the senator, a Republican. "Truman's eyes twinkled," remembers Schwengel, "and then he said, 'Young man, out where I come from they'd call you a damned Republican.' Then he smiled and suggested we sit down and talk history awhile."

The Davenport Republican has often been at odds with party leaders. He was elected to the Iowa legislature against a party man. "I won by only 37 votes," says Fred, "so they called me 'Landslide Schwengel.'" He championed state aid for schools and won over the opposition of Governor Blue.

In Congress, Schwengel won a seat on the Public Works Committee early in his career and had a strong hand in placing the interstate highway system on a "Pay As You Pave" basis. "Our interstate highways now stretch over 43,000 miles and cost us $100 billion," says the former first district Congressman, then adds, "but estimates show it has saved countless lives and close to $500 billion in savings to motorists and truckers, so it's been an excellent investment." He is equally proud of his voting record on education, soil conservation, freedom of religion, and of being the founder of the National Capitol Historical Society which he now heads.

Despite the countless accolades he has received for his professional work and governmental statesmanship, memories of "The Way It Was" on the Franklin County farm and in the Chapin and Sheffield high schools, as well as in college, remain vivid. Fred recalls riding horseback 12 miles daily to Chapin High and as a sophomore being entered in an eight-hour long cornhusking contest in which he husked 184 bushels and was named North Iowa Champion.

At Sheffield, Fred was class president and became a one-man track team. So strong and fast was he that he singlehandedly won third place for Sheffield in the 1926 state track meet.

Fred Schwengel, U.S. Capitol historian.

On enrolling at Northeast Missouri Teachers College, Coach Don Faurot, later to become famous as head football coach for the University of Missouri, became Fred's coach and mentor. "I had never played football," explains Schwengel, "but Faurot spotted me, put me in a dummy scrimmage, and then sent me into the next day's lineup, telling me to wrestle down whoever caught the ball on the opposing team."

In any case, the young Iowan was a four-year first team player for Faurot, and was named a small college All American his senior year.

After graduating, Schwengel married his college sweetheart, Ethel Cassidy, and settled in Shelbina, Missouri, to coach and teach history. Several years later, after their son and daughter were born, the young couple moved to Davenport to undertake a highly successful insurance practice, prior to entering politics.

The Capitol Historical Society, under Schwengel's leadership, is now a thriving institution with a current half-million-dollar endowment, and $2 million in research funds, all from private gifts and grants.

As for its president, he remains a Lincolnesque figure of strength, health, and enthusiasm. On the morning of his 80th birthday, he rode a bicycle and did 1009 pushups. "I used to do 1010 every morning, but I've cut down a little," he apologizes.

Schwengel concludes, "I don't intend to retire until I'm 100, and by then I'm certain we'll have the Capitol Historical Society on solid footing so it can benefit the entire nation permanently."

SOME THINGS ABOUT THE STATE FAIR STAY THE SAME
August 9, 1986

As we all know, the State Fair has always displayed "everything." Few of the exhibits, however, are more attractive, or call for more painstaking effort, than Leah Keeler's prize winning quilts. This column dealt with her amazing needlecraft accomplishments and how she and her husband, Maurice, overcame countless obstacles.

During the 100 years the Iowa State Fair has been domiciled in Iowa's capitol city, countless dramatic changes have inevitably occurred. Horse-drawn carriages and steam trains bringing visitors in 1886 have been replaced by air-conditioned autos and jetliners. Women's warm hoop skirts have given way to cool shorts and slacks. 4-H and FFA youth now get headlines formerly given veteran showmen. The list of contrasts is endless.

While the changes have been great, some State Fair attractions remain much the same. Needlework entrants, for instance, must put in the same amount of painstaking, precise handwork as did their great-grandmothers. Leah Keeler, a Weldon farm homemaker and veteran State Fair exhibitor, is eloquent testimony to that.

Keeler, 1983 Best of Show winner, enters gorgeous examples of needlework art annually. Her quilts always measure 98 by 118 inches. Flowers, doves, baskets, and similar items are featured in 12 pastel colored quilt blocks. Borders are of darker shades of green, blue, or brown.

"I usually begin a quilt in September and finish in March," she says. By the time the last stitch is made, she will have used some 800 yards of thread. At an average of 11 stitches per inch, that figures to plying the needle about 317,000 times.

Quilting, however, is not Leah Keeler's only interest. She and her husband, Maurice, now 75, live on a Century Farm that has been in the Hall-Keeler family since 1860, when the grandfather acquired 160 acres for $900.

The Keelers were married in 1931. With a $200 nest egg, they started farming in Decatur County with an old kerosene stove, a bed, a couple of cows, a pair of mules, six horses, and a lot of old machinery.

Two daughters were born. Eulah West of Olathe, Kansas, has four sons. Connie Hook of Weldon has three children and has raised eight foster children.

Looking back over his 55 years of active farming, Maurice Keeler says the drought and chinch bugs of 1934 are probably his most unhappy memory. "It was 100° or higher many days, and we slept in the open yard at night. Our cattle had to be driven to water, and dust in the fields was four inches deep."

Many other vivid memories include $2 hogs, husking and scooping 80 bushels of "down" corn daily and then doing the milking, purchase of Henry Field's "mule corn" and the stir that early hybrid created, and the day their first child was born. Leah says, "We had 1000 chicks coming out of incubators, sold 90 dozen eggs at 8¢ a dozen, and welcomed Eulah all the same day."

After moving to Clarke County, the Keelers continued their community leadership that had started with the Decatur County Farm Bureau presidency. Leah was a long-time 4-H leader and women's chairperson. Recently, they have been deeply involved in the Weldon Centennial and with the Weldon Christian Church, now observing its 100th anniversary.

Part of the funds needed for the celebration are being raised by raffling a beautiful quilt with a strong Bible motif. As might be expected, Leah Keeler is a key motivator in the project.

FARM PROGRESS SHOW...
HISTORY OF FARMS RECALLED
September 13, 1986

It was quite a contrast from getting one cent a bushel for husking and scooping corn in drought-stricken 1930, to being parents of one of the 1986 Farm Progress Show hosts, but that's what happened to Noble Twedt. Other parents of the hosts of the '86 "World's Fair of Agriculture" also had fascinating stories to tell about "The Way It Was" in this account of "their times."

Given favorable weather, a quarter million or more visitors are expected at the Farm Progress Show near Alleman September 30 and October 1 and 2.

No one could be more interested and excited about this "World's Fair of Agriculture" than the senior members of the host families.

Mr. and Mrs. Noble Twedt of Huxley are the parents of Steve Twedt, operator of a 1400-acre grain and livestock farm, originally established in 1874, known as South Point.

Martha Stall of Ankeny is the mother of Dean Stall, whose 1000-acre stock farm is another important addition to the Farm Progress Show. Kathryn Law of Elkhart is the mother of Mrs. Dean Stall.

Mildred Holland, Huxley, is the mother of Jack Holland, who with his son, Steve, are providing a 1900-acre grain and livestock operation for the event, including the 70-acre Tent City.

Ruth Donaghy, Slater, is the great aunt of Tom Corey, a VoAg teacher in the Alleman school system, whose 150 acres is also a part of the site.

Loren Hildreth, Madrid, is the long-time owner of another farm in the project.

A boulder, bearing the words, "Century Farm", is prominently located on the Stall farmstead. Kathryn Law, 82, sold her interest in the farm to her daughter, Ruth, and son-in-law, Dean.

Noble Twedt, 76, who still runs the combine at harvest time, knows about farming the hard way. Forced by drought to come to Iowa from his native South Dakota in 1930, he picked corn for 1¢ a bushel and did his own scooping. He and Jeanette started farming in the drought year of 1934. "We didn't raise a single ear of corn that year," says Twedt. He then adds, "Quite a contrast from the 150 bushels or more to be harvested in the Farm Progress Show fields."

Martha Stall, 81, who along with her late husband, Milo, was once honored on a network radio broadcast for farming achievements, is also enthusiastic about the forthcoming event.

She hopes her daughter, Beverly, now living in Hawaii, will be able to get back for the excitement on brother Dean's farm.

Mildred Holland, 75, now lives in Huxley. She and her late husband farmed for 35 years, beginning in that difficult year of 1934.

Familiar scenes at a previous Farm Progress Show.

"It was meager living for a time," explains Mrs. Holland as she recalls "The Way It Was" back then. She says, "We had a cow, a few horses, some chickens, and we most certainly were not trying to keep up with the Vanderbilts or anyone else. We burned cobs and corn, made dresses out of feed sacks, worked hard, and assumed no debts. What we couldn't afford, we did without."

Mrs. Holland, along with Mrs. Twedt, will be in the center of things, working in one of the church food stands in Tent City.

Ruth Donaghy, Tom Corey's great-aunt, along with 86-year old Loren Hildreth, will observe the event from a different perspective. Both were born and raised on farms that have been in the Donaghy and Hildreth families for than 100 years. Their comments about the show will be in the next issue of *Wallaces Farmer.*

FARM PROGRESS SHOW...
SECOND NATIONAL FARM EVENT
September 27A, 1986

Henry A. Wallace, then editor of Wallaces Farmer, *chose the Alleman, Iowa, community as host for the first National Corn Husking Contest back in 1924. Sixty-two years later, the Alleman community again claimed the national farm spotlight with the Farm Progress Show. George Barnes remembered the '24 event well and was eagerly anticipating the '86 show.*

When the Farm Progress Show is held September 30, October 1 and 2, it will be the second time a national farm event has been hosted by the Alleman community.

In November, 1924, in a field across the road from Tent City, Henry A. Wallace, then editor of *Wallaces Farmer,* masterminded the first National Corn Husking Contest.

George Barnes, 78, recalls, "It was held on my father's farm. An early frost had hurt the corn, and much of it was down. The ears were big, but chaffy; but

Wallace thought our corn was better than that on his own farm near Johnston. I remember the excitement when the huskers came from Illinois and Nebraska to compete with Ben Grimmius and Fred Stanek, our Iowa champions."

The veteran Alleman farmer, who now lives at Madrid, adds, "It was a cold, windy day and everybody wore a heavy overcoat, or wished they had one. My two older brothers drove teams and my father joined John Wallace as a gleaner, but I just ran around having fun watching all six huskers slam those ears against the bangboards."

Official records kept by Wallace show Fred Stanek of Fort Dodge, triumphed over five other contestants. Virgil Archer, Nebraska, was second and Pearl Mansfield, Illinois, third. Grimmius, who earlier had beaten Stanek in the state match, was fourth.

The 1924 Alleman match was the forerunner of 18 national husking contests, some attracting crowds of 100,000 or more. And the national husking contests were, in fact, the forerunners of the Farm Progress Show.

The contrast between Alleman's "big day" in 1924 and the event the community will host this year will be about as great as the difference between husking "down" corn by hand and watching it pour out of combine spouts next week. Whereas some 200 persons shivered through the 1924 husking match, 200,000 or more visitors will attend the 1986 event.

And instead of husking hooks and pegs and horse-drawn wagons, the interest will focus on conservation tillage machines; modern, high-horsepower tractors, 4, 6, 8, and 12-row combines; hundreds of seed variety plots; fertilizer and herbicide demonstrations; and the latest in farm management information.

FARM PROGRESS SHOW...
TWO SHOW HOSTS HAVE RINGSIDE SEATS
September 27B, 1986

Two senior members of the proposed 1986 Farm Progress Show host families had a quiet time anticipating the event. They were Loren Hildreth, 86, and Ruth Donaghy, in her 70s. Both were raised in the Show area, where they had front row seats, and both still have land.

Two senior members in the four families hosting next week's Farm Progress Show near Alleman won't have far to go to witness the myriad of activities scheduled for the three-day agricultural extravaganza. Nor is there anyone who can better appreciate the march of farm progress achieved during their lifetime than these two individuals.

They are Loren Hildreth, 86, and Ruth Donaghy, now in her 70s. Both were born and raised on century-old family farms involved in this year's event. Both vividly recall "The Way It Was" in their younger years.

Hildreth, now a resident at the Madrid Home for the Aging, plans to reoccupy the large, attractive white stucco home where he was born and raised, and which he still owns. It is located close to Farm Progress Show manager Mark Wilson's headquarters. "I can see it all from my front porch," quips Hildreth, adding, "It's like having a seat on the 50-yard line."

Miss Donaghy, a great aunt of Tom Cory, one of the Farm Progress Show hosts, lives on what is known as Donaghy Road. "At one time, six Donaghy families had their homes on this mile-long stretch," says Ruth, as she reminisces about her family and the Donaghy farmland. She says, "My father, William Donaghy, came from Ireland in 1884 and settled here in Polk County. Four years later, he married Mary McGowan. There were 13 of us children, and I'm the youngest."

Copious family albums and meticulously kept farm records show Ruth's pride in her family and farm. The original Donaghy land was purchased in 1885. It was later divided among several children. Interesting reflections on years gone by are found in the diaries.

One notation refers to Alleman, with a 1911 population of 25, having one of the state's first consolidated school districts. Another sentence speaks of a graduation ring representing an entire week of cream sales.

Other references are to the McGowan log cabin, road work, stacking grain, threshing picnics, school board and jury duty, family cooperation to pay off the farm mortgage, grassland for nesting meadowlarks, brother Jack's blue ribbon horse-pulling team, and the Hickory Grove Ladies' Club.

An accomplished artist, Ruth Donaghy has painted many award winning pictures, most of them based on childhood memories on the farm. She now has a memento-packed small home on that farm.

Hildreth, now a widower, has two daughters — Myrna Nicols in Colorado and Maxine Beall in Maryland. Both are planning a homecoming for September 30 and October 1 and 2. "I wish all the grandchildren could come, too, to take in this exciting exposition." says Hildreth.

The 180-acre farm where he spent most of his life is now operated by the Holland families, Jack and Steve, co-hosts.

While farming himself, Hildreth believed in diversification. He fed cattle, sheep, and hogs, and had dairy cows. He says, "I know about hard work. It makes you appreciate what you have."

Hildreth enjoys reminiscing. He recalls the walking plow and the delight of switching to riding plows. When handling the binder, he always dumped bundles in a straight line for shocking.

On the subject of neighbors, Hildreth says those in the Alleman area are the "greatest", and adds, "Neighbors are what makes a community a great place to live." The Farm Progress Show octogenarian is still an avid sports fan. He enjoys fishing in Minnesota in the summer and mobile home living in Arizona in the winter. "But," he concludes, "for this fall, it's Farm Progress Show fever that 'grips me all the way,' and I am looking forward to next week's huge event with great anticipation."

TOWN OF COOPER HONORS ITS RETIREES AT A PARTY
October 26, 1986

It is not often a group of retirees is remembered in a special way, but the town of Cooper, Iowa, where TV's Johnny Carson is an honorary resident, did so in the Fall of '86. This column told of some of the highlights of the much-appreciated event.

Honoring farm retirees is rarely done, but the tiny town of Cooper, Iowa, did it in super style recently. The little Greene County town, where TV celebrity Johnny Carson was designated the hamlet's 51st citizen in 1981, staged an event that brought back smiles of joy and pride. It was a gala party honoring Franklin Township's retirees. Masterminded by a committee of local couples headed by Mr. and Mrs. George Meinecke, a potluck dinner opened the festivities.

Highlight of the evening was the awarding of citations to 92 retirees from farms, businesses, and the military. Each was awarded a neatly inscribed certificate.

Jack Anderson, former Cooper school principal, was emcee. Reverend Deb Mariya of the Methodist Church gave the invocation. Chris Toms, 12, and Mrs. and Mrs. Ken Monthei, entertained with songs. Mrs. Roy Monthei regaled the crowd of 170 with poetry written especially for the occasion. Program time did not permit sharing personal experiences and accomplishments, but there was much recalling of "The Way It Was" around heavily laden dining tables.

Grace Wadsworth, Jefferson, laughed when asked her age. "A woman never tells how old she is," Mrs. Wadsworth explained, adding, "I won't either, except to say I was born in 1900, so it can probably be figured out." A former teacher at Cooper, she said, "My only complaint is I have nothing to complain about."

Mabel Squires, also 86, now of Guthrie Center, described the retirement event as "a wonderful party and a great time to get reacquainted with former neighbors and boast about grandchildren."

"Deac" Hidelbaugh, 80, of Bagley, who had bought thousands of hogs in the Cooper area for 27 years, compared today's difficult times with the Depression years when hogs sold for $2.50. He says, "Just having a pair of shoes was a luxury."

Horace Burnell, 86, Jefferson, remembers farming in the '30s. To make ends meet, he became a contractor, and in WW II laid foundations for 175 large barracks at Fort Leonard Wood in Missouri. Later, he built 800 grain bins, each with capacity for 10,000 bushels. Eventually, he returned to Cooper to farm. Burnell says, "It was so nice of Cooper to do this."

Ort Meinecke, one of the military retirees honored, vividly remembers the foxholes of WW II. Other servicemen recognized were Don Stofer, WW II; Don Peer, WW II and Korea; Larry Cox, Korea; and Richard Smith, Vietnam and Lebanon.

Among those singled out was Mrs. Ellen Ure, whose 76th birthday that day brought forth a happy birthday song.

Oldest, and one of the most appreciative of all those present, was Mrs. Nellie Lawton, a farm wife, now 87.

Cooper's own poet laureate, Elsie Monthei, 75, brought the event to a fitting close with her clever original poetry. In addition to paying tribute to the country doctor, party telephone lines, "iron horse" (farm tractor), and other things, Monthei touched an especially responsive chord when she read about washday woes. "Their dryers were wires strung between trees — and in the wintertime, how those clothes did freeze."

The Cooper poetess concluded with, "Through memory lane we've traveled miles, and I hope you're all wearing happy smiles."

It was a hope that was fully realized and attested by a long, grateful round of applause.

36-YEAR VETERAN...MASTER FARM HOMEMAKER CONTINUES TO BE ACTIVE
November, 1986

For many years, November was the month when Iowa Master Homemakers were announced. I always tried to attend and to feature a past honoree in my column for the month. A regular attendee every year was Mrs. Rankin, so I arranged to feature her this month. I could not have chosen better.

Every Master Farm Homemaker strives to be worthy of the honor. New inductees, such as the three named this month, often look for a role model. Many in the group could serve in that capacity. However, few, if any, could do it better than a diminutive, silver-haired, Marion County Master Farm Homemaker named in 1950.

Mrs. Lester (Flossie) Rankin, 89, of Knoxville, is less than five feet tall; but when it comes to charm, wit, personality, ability, and sincerity, she has few peers. The mother of six, who now boasts 18 grandchildren, 14 great-grandchildren, and one great-great-grandchild, continues to be active in her favorite pastimes — housekeeping, cooking, and reading.

Flossie, as she is best known, has attended virtually all of the Iowa Master Farm Homemakers' gatherings since 1950. A former state president and secretary of the exclusive group, she delights in meeting the new honorees.

Happy Iowa Master Farm Homemaker.

Mrs. Rankin has participated in 16 national Master Farm Homemakers' Association meetings, including this year's session in South Dakota attended by 43 Iowans. She has also served as a national officer for five years.

On the international level, the Knoxville homemaker has been active in the Associated Country Women of the World, an organization started by her dear friend and Master Farm Homemaker class of 1930, the late Mrs. Raymond (Ruth) Sayre.

Remembering "The Way It Was", Flossie says, "When we were married in 1917 and moved to a 400-acre farm, we had no automobile, no running water, no electricity, no refrigerator, and no rural mail delivery." She goes on to recall farming with horses, caring for lambs and little pigs, picking corn by hand, putting up ice, home butchering, and often arising at 4 a.m. to begin cooking and baking for dinner and supper for 16 hungry threshing crewmen.

She also enjoys recalling how neighbors helped each other to add much to what she described as "the good life on Iowa farms."

Mrs. Rankin's eyes also twinkle as she recalls the years she served as a 4-H leader and county chairperson. She also speaks warmly of the country doctors who attended the farm home births of her six children, and of the neighborhood Zion church where the family always worshipped, and where her husband was a 76-year member before his death in 1984.

The widest smiles, however, are reserved for reflections about the family. She not only beams when she speaks of the children — Boyd, Pauline, Maxine, Genny, Joy, and Jobyna — but takes special delight in telling about the grandchildren, great-grandchildren, and the great-great-grandchild.

"They're scattered from coast to coast and into everything. One is an international skier, another a rodeo rider. Others are teachers, doctors, artists, farmers, students, and one even works for a zoo," she says proudly. Mrs. Rankin sums it up this way. "I love them all, just as I do all my fellow Master Farm Homemakers."

107-YEAR OLD RECALLS CHRISTMASES PAST
December, 1986

In planning my December columns, I always do a Christmas feature; and if possible, select an older person who had vivid memories of "Christmas Past." In 1986, I chose 107-year old Edith Smith, who could clearly recall happy Christmases back in the "'80s."

Most of us enjoy reflecting on Christmases past. However, Mrs. Edith Smith, a long-time Iowa farm homemaker, can "out-remember" almost anyone when it comes to recalling Christmases of long ago. She is now 107 and vividly remembers Christmases of 100 years ago.

"I'll never forget the first time I saw Santa Claus," she recalls, adding, "I was four years old and we were in church. Suddenly, Santa came 'ho-ho-ho-ing' down the aisle with his red suit and long whiskers, carrying a Christmas tree. I was so scared I jumped right into my father's lap and hung on to him all evening."

Now a resident of the Thomas Rest Home in Coon Rapids, Mrs. Smith has a remarkable memory and near-perfect sight and hearing. In speaking of her own childhood, she says, "My little brother and I would hang up our longest stockings on Christmas Eve, then pile out of bed and run down to see what Santa left. It usually was a doll for me and marbles and things for my brother."

She adds that back in those days, parents often made the toys given their children, including sleds and rocking horses. "One of the gifts I cherished the most was a dollhouse that had a little stove in it," asserts Mrs. Smith.

107-year-old Mrs. Edith Smith, oldest interviewee.

Nor are Mrs. Smith's memories limited to the long ago. She has perfect recall of her 18-year old great-grandson, John Cory, winning the 167-lb. class in the state wrestling tourney in 1985, where she was among those cheering the loudest.

Born near Victor in 1879, Mrs. Smith, whose maiden name was Albright, along with her parents and younger brother, moved to Audubon County, where he father and his brother leased a 160-acre farm in 1873. She recalls the big covered wagons and the horses used in making the move.

In 1894, a devastating drought caused the Albright family to lose their land. The father then started carrying mail on a rural route from Audubon to Guthrie Center, taking two days to make the round-trip by horse and buggy. Meanwhile, Edith's mother bought a restaurant, serving meals family style for 25¢ each. That venture also failed.

The family moved back to a rented farm in Guthrie County in 1896. Edith became a teacher at the Panora high school. She then taught in rural schools for six terms before marrying Aaron "Ernie" Smith a few days after the 1903 Christmas program.

The young couple started farming on their own. Money Edith had saved teaching was used for foundation cows to assure essential weekly cream checks.

In time, Ernie and Edith built a two-story home for less than $1000. Two children — Earl, now deceased, and Evelyn, now Mrs. Harry Cory — were born to the couple. The Smiths farmed for 60 years, adding to their holdings from time to time, and retiring to an apartment in the Cory home overlooking Lake Panorama.

Mr. and Mrs. Smith observed their 74th wedding anniversary before Ernie died at the age of 102. Today, Edith's greatest joy is in her four grandchildren, 17 great-grandchildren, and one great-great-grandchild.

The way it was . . .
1987

WEATHER OBSERVERS RECALL
JANUARY RECORDS
January, 1987

How cold would it get this first month of the new year? How much snow would fall? Those were two of the biggest questions Paul Waite, popular long-time State Climatologist, received daily, but could not answer until the month was over. At that time, the dozens of ever-faithful volunteer weather observers mentioned in this column gave him their reports.

How cold will it get this January?

How much snow will we have to shovel this winter?

These questions are on everyone's mind, but no one can answer them—for sure. However, if you talk with an Iowa co-op weather observer, you may get an indication based on statistical analyses made over many years. And while no one will get too far out on a snow covered, icy tree limb, some of those with years of experience studying weather patterns will venture a calculated guess that Jan. 1987 may not be too severe.

Paul Waite, state climatologist, shares that view. His bookshelves are crowded with volume upon volume of Iowa weather stats dating back to 1873. In a matter of moments he can tell you the high and low readings, precipitation amounts, wind velocity, etc., for any given date and any month in the past 114 years.

The records are voluminous and accurate, and Waite is quick to tell you Iowa's co-op weather observers, whose reports, often daily, but always weekly and monthly, are the basis for wagon loads of information.

"Our observers are scattered throughout the state, and they are the backbone of our climatology work," says Waite. "They are a dedicated lot, largely serve without pay, are faithful and prompt, and stay with us a long time."

Holding the record for having served the longest of any observer is Ross Forward, 87, of Sheldon. Before his retirement last year, he had been on the job each morning and evening for 61 years.

Oldest active observer now reporting to work is 88-year-old Earl Slife, who started studying weather in 1918 and became an official observer in 1926. In addition to reporting daily temp and precipitations, he also takes Missouri River readings. "Normally the Missouri runs about 4 ft. with 15 ft. as flood stage," says Slife, and then adds, "But after one 7 in. rain it shot up to 24.3 ft. It was a record, and it even surprised and scared me."

Some reports come from husband and wife teams. Mr. and Mrs. Alton Stohlmann, Williamsburg, were observers for 30 years before Alton died. Now his widow, Bertha, continues to submit reports, and points to striking contrasts from year to year. In 1982 their area had 21.4 in. of rain in May, June, and July, while the same months a year later produced only 9.47 in.

At Mapleton, a pair of sisters are Paul Waite's eyes and ears. Mrs. May Scheer has been reporting temperature and moisture amounts for 42 years. Meanwhile her sister, Mrs. Dorothy Pope, makes Missouri River readings.

"We look upon it as an opportunity to serve," says Mrs. Scheer. She studies the moon and stars, and in so doing learns ways to forecast what's ahead. She looks for a reasonably moderate winter.

"Money could never buy the dedication we get from our observers," says Waite. "Their dedication is a service for the community, state, and nation."

Looking at "The Way It Was" Waite points out that the winter of 1912 recorded the state's bitterest cold, with Washta registering 47° below zero.

January temperatures for Iowa average 17.3°, but last January we had a mild 24° average.

As for January snowfall, the heavy snowfall of 1979 brought the most snow ever, with an average of 20 in. statewide.

IOWA'S OLDEST MASTER PORK PRODUCER
February, 1987

Master Pork Producers are always named early in the year. It occurred to me it would be interesting to find the oldest of these so honored over the years since four of us started the project back in 1942. In the search, I found 101-year-old Ben Knutson, and recorded his interesting story in this column.

Except for a minor cycling mishap last fall, Ben Knutson, Radcliffe, has been doing just fine since his 100th birthday observance about a year ago.

The veteran Hardin county Master Pork Producer and his wife of more than 50 years still live in their own home, where they enjoy reading, feeding birds, maintaining church interests, and reminiscing about a century of farm progress.

The Radcliffe centenarian looks back on "The Way It Was" when a span of mules was a major source of farm power and hand labor the order of the times.

101-year-old Ben Knudsen cycling with his great-granddaughter.

Ben has been a hard-working farmer all his life. Beginning as a small boy milking cows and feeding pigs, he was doing a man's work at age 14.

After working with his father for many years, he started farming on what is now a Century Farm in 1910 when he could buy the necessary second-hand machinery for a total of $ 150.

Ten years later he acquired one of the first farm tractors made— an IH Titan. However, when the Depression began, he returned to using horses and mules. Then in the late 1930s he traded a span of mules plus $325 to get a John Deere G. P. tractor.

The Knutsons were among the first to produce hybrid corn. They also were pioneers in mulch-tillage, ridge-till, and in growing crown vetch.

In 1947 Ben and his younger son, Caleb, entered into a partnership.

Livestock has always been a major enterprise. At one time they had eight purebred polled Herefords. They also fed some crossbred cattle.

Hog production was always Knutson's main undertaking. Beginning in the early 1900s with money earned husking corn at 2½¢ a bushel, Ben invested $15 in a Chester White boar. From that modest start the project grew steadily. Caleb and his youngest son, Ben II, now feed 1500 head annually. In 1966 statewide recognition came when Ben, then 80, and in his 50th year as a producer, and Caleb, were named Iowa Master Pork Producers.

Ben continued to go to the farm daily, driving his car and the tractor until, at age 95, he had eye surgery. He was then given a "three-wheeler" bike, which now serves as his personal transportation.

Ben's first wife died suddenly when he was in his 40s, leaving him with three youngsters. Three years later he married Gertrude Bjerkstran, who raised, and later adopted, the children.

Besides Caleb, there is an older son, Glen, and a daughter, Rhoda. There are 13 grandchildren and 16 great-grandchildren.

Ben's recipe for longevity: "Gertie's loving care and her flare for good nutrition, hard work, living in a good neighborhood, and choosing the right ancestors. My father also lived to be 100."

About farming's future, Ben says, "I'm afraid it's not too bright." As to his concern about today's troubled farm economy, and the loss of farms, he says, "I'd rather have a neighbor than the neighbor's farm."

1949 MASTER FARMER PIONEERED CONSERVATION
March, 1987

Friends who nominated Dale Blackwell for the title of Master Farmer in 1949 knew what they were doing. They knew their neighbor to be a man who would step in wherever any community job needed to be done, and he would do it. They also knew how much he loved the land and how diligently he would work to conserve his own soil and that on many other farms.

In 1949, when friends of Dale Blackwell nominated him for the Iowa Master Farmer award, they said, "Dale Blackwell's business is farming, but his hobbies are people and good will."

They were right, and also prophetic.

When Dale and his wife, Nadine, were selected he was only 40 years old. Despite his youth, he had already established himself as a good farmer who did a lot of clear thinking and right living. But Blackwell's activities up to then were only the beginning of a long career underscored by community service.

After buying a 400-acre farm in 1940, the Davis county farmer soon became concerned about soil and water conservation. In the mid 40s he was one of three named to the original Board of County Soil commissioners, and for the next 18 years served as district treasurer.

An outspoken advocate of terracing and contouring, Blackwell has continued those practices to this day. Even as late as last December he installed another $3000 worth of terracing on his land.

Dale Blackwell, Southern Iowa Master Farmer.

In addition to his conservation efforts, Blackwell has greatly exceeded the community contributions for which he was cited in 1949. A partial listing of his services include nine years on the Davis county Board of Supervisors, president of the township school board, and a nine-year stint on the Davis county school board.

Other community efforts' included the presidency of the Davis County Agricultural Society and the Davis county fair board. He also did organizational work in what was to become Tenco, a 10 county extension association from which evolved Indian Hills College, now a trade school near Ottumwa, with some 2000 students.

Recently, partially because of Nadine's health, the Blackwells have become less active in community and church.

The activities and interests of their four children and 10 grandchildren, as well as his own seed distribution business, keep the Master Farmer busy.

Rex, the older son, who was named an Outstanding Young Farmer in 1966, now operates close to 2000 acres and feeds large numbers of hogs and cattle.

Jim, the younger son, also farms, but on a smaller scale because of extensive shop and auto/ tractor repair work.

The older daughter, Betty Fairchild, her husband, and children all work for Rockwell at Cedar Rapids. The younger, Connie Steinkruger, serves in a medical clinic, and is married to a Davis county magistrate judge.

Dale, now 78, and his wife still live on the home farm. He has no desire to live in the city.

Looking at today's farming picture, Blackwell says, "We are in a time of heavy adjustments. High inflation got things way out of hand. We've taught other countries how to produce and now they are competing with us. Government programs with high price supports were a part of our undoing. We may be too domineering, but if our president talked more peace and less preparation for war, that might help all of us."

GERMAN IMMIGRANT BECAME SUCCESSFUL CATTLE FEEDER
May 9, 1987

It's a long way from Schleswig-Holstein, Germany, to buying a 400-acre Iowa farm and feeding 500 cattle and 300 hogs a year, but that's the route Lorenz Bahnsen took. This column tells how he did it, with the help of a loving wife and six children.

Lorenz Bahnsen was a wagonmaker's apprentice in Schleswig-Holstein, Germany. But farm wagons were rapidly being replaced by motorized trucks, and the 18-year-old Lorenz could not get a job.

An older brother, Bernhardt, had already left Germany for Clinton, Iowa.

Lorenz wrote to his brother, lamenting his jobless plight. Bernhardt knew Henry Hansen, a farmer in need of a hired man. Hansen sent Lorenz money for ocean passage. The young German arrived in Clinton county to spend the next 12 years working for Hansen.

In 1937 Lorenz married Elsie Carter. Hansen gave the young couple a home on a 120-acre farm he owned near Goose Lake, along with two cows and a few hogs. Bahnsen continued to work as a hired hand 4 more years. Then, with Hansen's help, he rented the farm on a 50-50 basis. A team of horses and used machinery were purchased, including a John Deere tractor for $80. In the meantime Elsie gave birth to Lorraine, the first of their six children.

After 9 years, Lorenz told Hansen he would like a larger place. Hansen replied, "I've got 400 acres near Low Moor. Is that big enough?" Lorenz and Elsie figured it was.

The move meant some drastic changes. Much tiling had to be done. Large ponds were drained. Disappointed duck hunters showed up that fall asking, "Where are the ponds?" A new crawler type tractor was purchased. A hired man was engaged. Some 200 feeder cattle were bought in South Dakota, and 250 hogs were raised.

Eventually the Bahnsens bought the 400 acres, paying $320 per acre, and increased their feeding operations to 500 or more Hereford or crossbred cattle and 300 hogs a year.

Feeders weighing 300 pounds, were usually purchased in Texas and several Western states. They were fed out to 1200 pounds, then sold in Chicago. Bahnsen always rode in the caboose to go in with his cattle. On seeing him in the yard, commission men would ask, "Where's your pen, Lorenz?" and then pay him a bonus.

"Our banker was our partner," says Bahnson, now 78. "We worked hard, didn't have much automation, bought a lot of corn from neighbors and concentrates from the cooperative, did a lot of grinding, had two silos, and always tried to buy and sell right." He adds, "We were lucky because the times were right, and we only lost money one or two years."

Lorenz and Elsie take real pride in their six children and nine grandchildren, now scattered in five states. Loretta and Lorraine are the oldest. Nancy, Iowa's Favorite Farmer's Daughter in 1965, came next, followed by the youngest sister, Wilma, Iowa Beef Queen in 1968. The sons are Larry, who now operates the home farm, and Robert.

Lorenz has been back to his homeland five times to visit two sisters, but always rejoices when he returns home to Clinton county. He was president of Clinton County's Cattlemen's Association in 1964 and '65, heavily promoting May Beef Month during that time. He retired in 1974.

What's ahead in the cattle business for Iowa? Bahnsen says, "I don't think it will ever be as big, or as good, as when I was feeding. Interest rates are too high."

139 YEAR-OLD WINDMILL SYMBOLIZES DANISH HERITAGE
May 23, 1987

Danish windmills are a rarity in America, but at Elk Horn, Iowa, 50,000 or more visitors annually admire a windmill brought over from Denmark. The story of its acquisition, shipment to Iowa, and faultless reconstruction, led by Harvey Sornson, is fascinating — as reviewed here in this column.

Iowa has its own "Little Denmark" in Elk Horn, a Shelby County town of 755 people. Many are of Danish descent.

Last year close to 50,000 persons from virtually every state in the union, and a dozen or more foreign countries, found a warm *welkommen* (welcome) awaiting them as they visited Elk Horn to see the Danish windmill, a towering landmark, and to enjoy Danish food at the nearby Danish Inn.

The mill was transported from Denmark to Iowa a dozen years ago and is the culmination of an "impossible dream" nurtured by Harvey Sornson, well-known Elk Horn - Kimballton area farmer and conservationist.

The fascinating story has its genesis in 1974, when Sornson and his wife, Dagmar, visited their parents' homeland in Denmark. Danish mills had intrigued Sornson from boyhood. Realizing the mills were rapidly being dismantled, Sornson thought he'd like to take one of them back to Iowa.

Sornson discussed his hopes with Warren Jacobsen, an Elk Horn realtor and cattleman, who quickly saw the value of Harvey's dream.

Within days, Jacobsen and Sornson were able to convince other Elk Horn "Vikings" that an authentic Danish mill not only could be a tremendous tourist attraction, but it would also salute the town's proud Danish heritage. Henry Petersen, Danish cousin of Milo Anderson, who was visiting Iowa, learned of an available mill built in Jutland in 1848. The price for the 60-ft. mill, its dismantling, and shipment to New York, would be $30,000. In less than a week Elk Horn townspeople and neighboring farmers raised that sum.

Trans-Atlantic phone conferences were made courtesy of the Marne-Elk Horn telephone company, with Howard Sornson as translator. In October dismantling of the mill was started, with every piece carefully numbered. A scale model was built to correspond to the original mill.

A flatbed truck was loaded with the 22-tons of windmill parts, then put on a ship bound for New York. The mill reached Elk Horn on Feb. 4, 1976.

A Danish windmill comes to Danish Iowa town.

That same day the first Elk Horn miracle occurred. When truckers demanded $100 a day for unloading, "Slim" Jensen brought a boom truck over, and everybody joined in to unload the 44,000 pounds of parts by nightfall.

Rebuilding a 127-year-old foreign mill without a single blueprint is no small challenge. The dismantlers in Denmark said it couldn't be done. They did not reckon with the tenacity and genius of Harvey Sornson, Gerald Brewer, Carl Bonnesen, LeRoy Christiansen, Jim Sporleder, Warren Jacobsen, Howard Hansen, and many other Shelby and Audubon county Danes.

Meanwhile, hundreds of donors contributed a total of $100,000 for the project.

It took some doing to raise the heavy timbers, restructure wings, hoist the windshafts and brake wheels, gears, and fantail to the top, but Elk Horn's Vikings did it with zest.

Within 10 months the "miracle of Elk Horn" had been achieved. The mill that "couldn't be rebuilt" stood tall and proud, ready to grind wheat into flour, an everlasting symbol of a small Iowa community's determination and dedication.

Sornson's dream lives on. He continues his more than 40 years in conservation work, helps stage Kimballton's annual husking matches, boosts plans for the National Danish Immigrant Museum soon to become another Elk Horn international attraction, and reminds everyone of Elk Horn's "Tivoli Days," when Iowa's Danish windmill will receive the focus of thousands of visitors.

ALLAMAKEE COUNTY DAIRYMEN CELEBRATE JUNE DAIRY MONTH
June, 1987

June Dairy Month is ostensibly a month to promote dairying and dairy products, but it is also a time for dairymen to get together to tell interesting stories and exchange experiences. One day, I went to Allamakee County, an Iowa dairy center, to meet with four dairymen and get their comments.

June Dairy Month is a great time for longtime dairymen to do some reminiscing and some looking ahead to 1987 Dairy Month festivities, and that's what happened recently in Waukon, a northeast Iowa dairying center.

Mr. and Mrs. Karl Simmons were hosts. Dairymen in addition to Karl, 78, were twins Willard and Harold Fritz, 75, and Walter Winke, 72.

"If I had to do it—dairying— all over again, I'd operate the same way," opined Karl Simmons. "We were proud of our Shorthorns and later our Holsteins and of the way they produced," he added.

The twins, Willard and Harold, agreed. Their view was, "We must have liked dairying or we wouldn't have been at it so many years."

Winke said, "It's a 365-day-a-year job, and it wasn't always easy, but it's steady income as well as steady work."

Simmons got into the dairying business when his father died in 1922. Karl was still in high school, but he soon had charge of the family's 24-cow herd.

He recalls, "We started with some good Shorthorns and one-legged milkstools, but we worked our way up to a fine herd of more than 100 Holsteins. The Simmonses have a daughter, a son, and two grandchildren.

Walter Winke's career started with a mixed herd of 15 cows, but he gradually got into Guernseys, 35 of which are now registered.

Three daughters and a son, Ken, helped with the Winke herd through the years. Ken now operates the farm and manages the Guernsey herd. Ten grandchildren enjoy coming to Grandpa's farm, now a 103-year-old Century Farm.

Community service seems to go along with dairy interests. Winke has served as DHIA president, board member for the Ludlow Creamery, as well as an officer in the church, telephone company, and other organizations.

Karl Simmons has been active in his church council, and in Mutual Insurance Association work, as well as being president of the Allamakee County DHIA and the northeast Iowa Holstein-Friesian Association.

The Fritzes have been active participants and leaders in their church, DHIA, and the Jersey Cattle Club. We will have a more complete report on their dairying achievements and their escapades as twins in baseball, dance band, and other interesting and amusing activities in a future "The Way It Was" column.

As for June Dairy Month, the Fritz brothers join Simmons and Winke in enthusiastically endorsing the nationwide dairy promotion, and in looking forward to Allamakee County's annual Dairy Month festivities June 19 and 20 in Waukon.

NINETY-YEAR-OLD REFLECTS ON SEVERAL CAREERS
July, 1987

Today there is a tendency for people to change careers frequently, often within a few years' time. While changing jobs was nothing new to 90-year-old J.R. Underwood, the time between his various changes often lasted many years — and greater service to students and farmers was always the reason.

A legend in his own time is an accolade rarely used, but in the case of 90-year-old J. R. Underwood, Davenport, it fits like a husking glove. "JR" as he is best known, is a veteran of several careers and, although supposedly retired now, he continues to serve Iowa farm families.

To summarize Underwood's activities and accomplishments over 7 decades is virtually "mission impossible." An ambitious Palo Alto County farm lad, his first work was farming with his father. Then came WWI naval service. Next, he became an intense Iowa State College student.

First of his major careers was as a $2500 a year vo ag teacher, after which he became a high school superintendent at $4000 a year.

While an ag instructor at Clarinda, he met and married pretty Ruth Austin, a native of Illinois. Soon after, he became vo ag director at Corning.

Then JR was chosen superintendent at Bridgewater, before going to the superintendency at Wall Lake, a position that lasted 11 years. While there, four daughters, Onnalee, Lois, Miriam, and Virginia were born.

Underwood also served as superintendent of schools at Missouri Valley and Yarmouth, but after 26 years as a teacher and school administrator, he joined the extension service as county director in Scott county.

That position lasted for 21 years, and earned him the highest recognition attainable in his field —USDA's Distinguished Service Award.

Far more important than the high USDA citation and the many other recognitions he received were the contributions he made in many areas.

J.R. Underwood, esteemed county extension agent, popular broadcaster, treasured friend.

In addition to routine services for farmers, gardeners, conservationists, and others, he worked to unify all branches of the extension program and to coordinate community activities involving urban as well as rural residents. A strong leader in his own right, he emphasized leadership among youth and saw the county's 4-H membership more than triple during his tenure.

Recalling his years as a county agent, JR says, "We regularly worked 16 hours a day, with meetings virtually every night. That sort of dedication no longer seems to exist."

At age 70, with several highly successful careers behind him, JR declined the rocking chair. Offers from banks, dairy associations, and other groups quickly developed. After some deliberation he chose to become a farm broadcaster for WOC-Davenport, originating as many as nine homey, authoritative radio and TV programs daily.

Highlight of his broadcasting career, however, was when WALL ACES FARMER chose him to be an NBC "Today Show" spokesman at the 1977 Farm Progress Show. JR says, "Working with Jane Pauley was a delight, even though she was a bit squeamish about holding George Gollinghorst's squealing piglet. I heard from all over the country after that show," he adds.

Speaking of "The Way It Was," Underwood recalls walking behind a plow drawn by two horses, and using a one-row cultivator. "In my lifetime I've seen more changes and progress in agriculture than was made in all prior recorded history," he adds.

Quick to give his wife credit for much of his success, JR, now the grandfather of nine, emphasizes, "A public servant's wife and children have to sacrifice a lot, but Ruth and the girls supported me every step of the way."

There is some question as to whether Underwood is actually retired now, or ever will be. Many still seek his counsel. Meanwhile the veteran educator, county agent, and broadcaster has become an avid gardener and remains active in his church and many other organizations. "I manage to keep out of mischief by keeping busy," concludes JR.

INDIANOLA GARDENER REMAINS VETERAN STATE FAIR WINNER
August 8, 1987

Down at Indianola, the Pemble family has a heritage of State Fair and other major winnings. Vince Pemble, now in his 80s, is the third of five generations to claim trophies and blue ribbons. Don't ask him how many. They number more than many persons can count.

If Vincent Pemble of Indianola wins a major award at the Iowa State Fair later this month it will not be a new experience. Vince, as he is best known, won his first championship as a toddler and has been claiming purple banners, plaques, and trophies ever since.

Born on a Dallas county farm, Vince and his parents moved to Indianola in 1915. His mother entered him in the Warren County Fair baby contest, where Vince won his first trophy.

With six children, Vince's parents decided a large garden would be one way to keep everyone busy. "One hundred yards of rhubarb, plus 500 of asparagus, lots of strawberries and other crops kept us all well occupied," recalls Vince.

By the mid-1920s Vince was a 4-H member, growing many garden crops. In 1927, just 60 years ago, he won his first blue ribbon at the Iowa State Fair.

Vince enrolled in horticulture at Iowa State College in 1932. Within months he won the ISC Hort Show championship and other awards. The next year, when Pemble was only 20, Iowa State Fair secretary A. R. Corey asked him to help manage the Horticulture Department.

After graduation in 1937 Pemble went to Connecticut to conduct germination tests for Associated Seed Growers. He then returned to Indianola to join his father and brother in the Pemble and Sons Hardware Company, and to marry his college sweetheart, Marian Hoppe.

In 1940 the Pembles had their first full fruit harvest. But their success was short-lived. Soon after harvest the devastating Armistice Day freeze killed 75% of the trees. New root stock had to be planted and countless hundreds of budding grafts were made. Eight years later the orchard was again in full production.

During the interim the family experienced both sorrow and happiness. WWII saw Vince's youngest brother join the Marine Flying Corps only to be lost over the Pacific. Meanwhile, Marian and Vince welcomed three little ones. Richard, now head of biology at Moorehead State, and twins, John and Joan. John now is on the governor's staff in Minnesota, while Joan is a hospital dieti-

Champion vegetable grower and exhibitor, Vincent Pemble.

cian in Des Moines and a housewife and gardener in Indianola. They also raised two other children, brothers James and Dennis Mathes. The Pembles now boast six grandchildren.

Today, Vincent Pemble is considered the State Fair's senior horticulture exhibitor. After winning that first blue ribbon 60 years ago, he has missed showing at only two State Fairs since then. Although now in his mid-70s he is caring for a city-blockwide garden involving 250 tomato plants, 10 varieties of potatoes, huge tracts of squash, melons, sweet corn, and virtually all other types of vegetables grown in this area, as well as remarkable crops of peaches, apples, and even blue plums grafted on an apricot branch.

Vince is the third of five generations of State Fair exhibitors. His daughter, Joan Craven, and grandsons Stephen and Paul, are also State Fair winners.

MASTER FARM HOMEMAKER SERVES ON WORLD MISSIONS
August 22, 1987

If there were a contest to determine the Master Iowa Farm Homemaker with the largest number of experiences, widest travels, and most energy, Evelyn Livingstone would certainly be one of the finalists. The Anamosa farm widow has done more, seen more, and helped more people, then the average person can imagine. The following brief summary is positive proof.

With only limited space available, recounting the past and present activities of Master Homemakers virtually becomes "mission impossible."

Evelyn Livingstone, Anamosa, named a Master Farm Homemaker in 1954, is a classic case in point.

Born a city girl, the daughter of a physician and with two uncles as pastors, Evelyn seemed destined to be a nurse or a church worker. All that changed abruptly when Robert Livingstone, a tall, handsome, young dairyman came calling. Before long Evelyn was a farm wife with little experience, a home not yet modern, a herd of Holsteins in the barns, and boundless energy.

Homemaking skills were quickly learned, although sometimes the hard way. Three daughters, Jean, Lois, and Doris, were welcomed. Church and community service beckoned.

The oldest daughter, now Jean Brown, of North Carolina, describes her mother as a perpetual dynamo. She recalls, "Her days on the farm were spent running the household and helping outside. She was forever giving us and Dad loving care and cooking, cleaning, washing, canning hundreds of quarts of food, refinishing furniture, papering walls, and whatever else was needed."

"Outside she helped with milking, separating cream, raising chickens, tending garden, and assisting Dad in the fields."

"Evenings, after we girls were in bed, she would do crocheting, knitting, quilting, sewing dresses, hooking rugs, and painting. She also found time to mount 151 Indian arrow heads we found."

Mrs. Evelyn Livingston, happy Master Farm Homemaker.

"Busy as she was at home, she still managed to be involved in many community programs, as night school board member, county 4-H chairperson, hosting foreign exchange students from Finland, Greece, and Iran, serving as Sunday School teacher, Farm Bureau Women's chair, singing in the womens chorus, volunteering at the hospital and in nursing homes, and once she even got into politics as a campaign manager."

"She was also Anamosa's official hostess to 383 newcomers to the city, and became involved in weddings, baptisms, adoptions, and Christmas coffees."

Little wonder that Zoe Murphy and the Iowa Master Farm Homemaker judges chose Evelyn Livingstone as a 1954 Master Farm Homemaker. Her election as state president also came as no surprise.

Widowed while still quite young, she left the farm after 26 years. Since then the Jones county Master Farm Homemaker has plunged into many other meaningful projects. She was an early supporter for, and now life member of ACWW (Associated Country Women of the World) and has attended almost all the organization's Tri-ennial World Conferences, including those in Australia, Africa, India, Europe, and Canada. She has also traveled widely on her own from Alaska to China.

In more recent years Mrs. Livingstone has centered her energies on the World Gospel Mission, a volunteer work program. Although already in her 70s, she has served in Bolivia, Guatemala, Japan, India, Honduras, and elsewhere, often up to a year. Gospel Mission volunteers pay their own travel, meal, and lodging costs, and do everything from laying bricks to teaching classes.

Evelyn says, "I've found this exciting and fulfilling, just as I enjoyed my association with Master Farm Homemakers and the Country Women of the World."

Most of all, however, Evelyn, exudes pride in her family. In addition to Jean and Bruce Brown, of North Carolina, who have adopted 10 mountain children; she mentions Lois, married to James Wild, who have three children, two of whom work with their father on a 2000-acre farm near Anamosa; and Doris, a teacher, who married Wayne Larson, a land appraiser. They have two children. "That adds up to 15 grandchildren altogether," boasts Evelyn. A few years ago she had one of the best times of her entire, fascinating life when she and her three daughters took an 8000 mile bus tour together.

TONS OF FOOD ORDERED FOR FARM PROGRESS SHOW
September 12, 1987

Although dismayed when the 1986 Farm Progress was totally rained out, Alleman community residents were undaunted in preparing for their "second chance", set for September, 1987. In fact, more than 700 volunteers in 15 food tents prepared for a "Bigger and Better" event than ever, as this column reveals.

Food is a universal concern, but for the 200,000 visitors expected for the Farm Progress Show near Alleman, Iowa, Sept. 29, 30, and Oct. 1, there's ample assurance that no one need go hungry. The show will be held on the Holland, Twedt, Stahl, and Cory farms.

Many tons of food have been ordered to satisfy the heartiest of appetites, and thousands of gallons of drinks will be available to quench every thirst.

Quantities of food to be delivercd to the site a mile east of Alleman are almost unbelievable. Greg Stensland of Huxley, general chairman of the Farm Progress Show food committee, offers this impressive list:

- 12,000 lb. hamburger
- 12,000 lb. pork patties
- 10,000 lb. ham
- 11,000 dz. hamburger buns
- 30,000 pies
- 20,000 caramel nut rolls
- 1,200 lb. cheese
- 2,000 lb. hot dogs
- 1,000 dz. hog dog buns
- 20,000 cartons whole milk
- 30,000 cartons chocolate milk
- 30,000 cartons orange juice
- 25,000 frosty malts
- 40,000 packets of potato chips

"Also," says Stensland, "we will have countless packages of coffee and hot chocolate, and huge supplies of ketchup, mustard, and other condiments." Moreover, 700 wooden palettes will be needed on which to place equipment.

Six huge food tents, each with four entryways for the public and one express line for exhibitors, will be conveniently located in the center area of Tent City. Each has four long serving counters for rapid dispensing of food and drink, as well as four long standup eating bars outside. An additional seventh tent will serve exhibitors only.

Each food tent will also have two roving pickup trucks carrying sack lunches and drinks to demonstration fields and elsewhere.

An army of 700 volunteers, all involved with local churches and ranging in age from 16 to 85, will operate the seven food tents from 6 a.m. and continuing to 6 p.m.

Each tent has elected its own chairperson to direct the activities of 99 other workers— including grilling food, keeping coffee hot, making sandwiches, serving the customers, and cashiering.

As is true of all the countless other volunteers of the Farm Progress Show, none of the 700 food area workers receives pay. Whatever profits are derived from food sales are shared by the 15 cooperating churches.

A Farm Progress Show photo.

"Prices will be the same at every tent," says Stensland. "And," he adds, "they will be reasonable." Samples of the costs are: Hamburgers, pork patties, and ham and cheese sandwiches, each $1.25; hot dogs and pies, $1 each. Cinnamon rolls and malts, 75¢, and coffee and all other drinks 50¢ each. Sack lunches, available at the food tents and from the roving pickups, will be $3, and will include a ham and cheese sandwich, pie, chips, and a drink.

Thanks to 700 volunteers from 15 churches it will be "food aplenty" at this year's Farm Progress Show.

VETERAN SHOW EXHIBITORS RECALL PAST EXPERIENCES
September 26, 1987

However disappointed the 300 exhibitors may have been in September, 1986, when the Farm Progress Show had to be called off because of excessive and endless rains, they were right back for the 1987 "Agricultural World's Fair." Not only were they back, but they had a lot of tales to tell. Here are a few.

Over the years, Farm Progress Show visitors have enjoyed looking over the hundreds of exhibits and displays annually in what is called Tent City. This year will be no exception, with no less than 300 exhibits already all set up for the Sept. 29, 30, and Oct. 1 farm extravaganza on the Holland, Twedt, Stahl, and Corey farms near Alleman.

Memories of last year's rainout are still vivid, and exhibitors last week were not only busy preparing for a rainproof show, but also swapping tales about their experiences last year and at Farm Progress Shows of days gone by.

Don Mills, of Pioneer Hi-Bred International and a farm show exhibit veteran of some 40 years, says, "Late the night before last year's show was to start we got word tents were blowing down. We rushed out through the mud to see the devastation between lightning flashes, tried propping up the tents, and asked ourselves, 'What are we doing out in this downpour'?"

Mills well recalls the first Farm Progress Show in Iowa. "Back then," he recollects, "we designed our displays on napkins while settled around coffee tables. At the '59 show on Elijah's farm near Clarence we had a small tent, showed 11 samples of double cross hybrids, had a few Hy-Line chicks, and a display showing the history of corn."

"Contrast that with the eight lots we'll have at Alleman, featuring our latest hybrids along with soybeans, wheat, alfalfa, inoculants, free popcorn, a fountain, park benches, and some flowers to further enhance our display."

Farm Progress Show exhibitor, Don Mills.

Pioneer has exhibited at every Farm Progress Show and Don has been to 18 of them, including all those held in Iowa.

The Pioneer representative also recalls many unusual situations. "At Clarence in 1959 rain came in the final hour so we couldn't get exhibits out for several days. At Washington in 1977 trucks could not get in the fields so we had to hand-carry all display material. At Vincent in 1974 a cold wave struck suddenly."

Asked his most unforgettable experience Don responds, "It was one of the Van Horne shows. The Clay County Fair wouldn't release us 'til 8 p.m. Sunday. I got home to Ankeny after midnight. At 2 a.m. my wife went into labor. We rushed to the hospital. An hour later, little Polly, our fourth child was born. I went home, changed, got a cup of coffee, and drove to Van Horne in time to open the exhibit at 8 a.m. Tuesday morning."

Whatever difficulties might be encountered in connection with a farm show exhibit, Mills is quick to point out the rewards far overshadow the problems. "And," he adds, "of all the shows you can go to, the Farm Progress Shows are the best because they are so farm oriented."

That opinion seems to be reflected by many other Farm Progress Show exhibitors. Dennis Tatge, president of TOK-O-WIK, a Kansas livestock equipment manufacturer, says, "We've been at 28 Farm Progress Shows and regard them as the World's Fair of Farming."

Another veteran of Farm Progress Shows is Leo Olson, of DeKalb, Ill., now retired but with vivid memories of the first 20 or more Farm Progress Shows. For 40 years Olson headed the advertising department for what was originally the DeKalb Agricultural Association, now DeKalb-Pfizer Genetics.

"At those first shows we had relatively small exhibits, mainly devoted to introducing our leading hybrid corn numbers and DeKalb hybrid chickens, but as time went on our exhibit continued to expand until we had a gigantic tent 100 ft. wide and 300 ft., long, displaying our newer corn hybrids, as well as hogs, wheat, alfalfa, sorghum, and other products," recalls Olson.

He concludes, "The Farm Progress Show is totally agriculturally oriented. We always look forward to it. They've become a national institution."

Sharing Olson's view are the leaders of a Fulton, Mo., firm, the Danuser Machine Company, maker of posthole diggers, post drivers, log splitters, and original equipment for 1000 other firms. Earl O'Rourke, general sales manager for Danuser, says, "If our company were limited to only one exhibit a year we would choose the Farm Progress Show."

Mills, Olson, O'Rourke, and Tatge speak for only four of the more than 300 exhibitors who will convert the Holland alfalfa field into a huge Tent City near Alleman Sept. 29, 30, and Oct. 1.

WORLD AG EXPO TOPIC
October, 1987

When Wallaces Farmer editor, Monte Sesker, asked me to write a column about plowing matches in preparation for the 1988 World Ag Expo, I was fairly well-prepared. I am credited with having originated the National Plowing Matches, which drew hundreds of thousands of persons in their "Hey-Day" and I have also been involved in World Matches around the globe.

National and international farm spotlights will be focusing on Iowa next Sept. 7-10 when the 1988 World Ag Expo will be held on a 1000 acre Amana Colonies tract in Iowa.

The expo promises a myriad of attractions for both rural and urban visitors. Plans include a 60 acre exhibit area, harvest demonstrations similar to those at Farm Progress Shows, home and family programs, and conservation tillage demonstrations. Also on the schedule are ethnic group activities, old and new world crafts, seed, herbicide, and fertilizer plots, delicious Amana style food, a Cairn of Peace, plus state, national, and World Plowing Matches as featured events.

Staging plowing competitions in the heart of no-till farming country may raise eyebrows and pose questions. Some farmers have abandoned moldboard plows entirely. Conservationists often blame soil losses on the plow. Economists regard plowing as an unnecessary consumer of fuel and time.

Why then conduct a worldwide plowing event?

The question can be answered in several ways. While some sloping soils obviously are not suited to plowing, many other areas continue to depend on the plow for incorporating manure and plant growth into the soil, preparing an ideal seedbed, and controlling weeds.

Historically, the plow looms large. It is mankind's most ancient and best known tool of the land. It remains a worldwide symbol of agriculture, as seen in the seal of USDA, and on the National FFA and other emblems.

While the earliest plows were nothing more than forked sticks pulled by slaves through stony soil, the evolution of the plow is a dramatic story. First known improvement over the forked stick came in the late 1500s AD when a Dutch farmer devised a pointed, wooden moldboard drawn by oxen. In 1720, Joseph Foljamke of Great Britain nailed iron strips on his wooden plow's landslide. Some 65 years later another Englishman, Robert Ramsome, a name still revered in plowing circles, introduced a cast-iron share. And an American, Charles Newbold, of New Jersey, patented a cast-iron moldboard. Acceptance, however, was slow because farmers feared the metal moldboards would poison the soil.

In the early 1800s, John Lane, John Deere, and James Oliver collectively developed the steel moldboard plow. Deere's plow, perfected at Grand Detour, Ill., in 1837, became the standard on most farms. This plow did not poison land, and it scoured well, resulting in clean-cut furrows.

As for plowing matches, the story is equally dramatic. Back in the 1 700s, ploughing competitions began on the British Isles. Booted and bearded farmers took their oxen and crude plows to a nearby point and held a contest. The matches were both social and educational events.

In 1802 a Scottish paper reported "ploughs drawn by Galloway heifers." By 1818 the Scottish Land Society was offering prizes for the "best ploughman."

Since then plowing contests have been a meaningful attraction in many parts of the world. By the mid-1800s oxen began giving way to horses. Steam engines entered the picture in the 1800s. By 1925 the modern tractor had taken over.

Meanwhile, plows changed from the cumbersome, single-share, walking plow, to the sulky, riding plow and 2 and 3-bottom horsedrawn gang plows.

Plowing match fever quickly spread to the European continent and Scandinavia, and eventually went into Canada, and down to Australia, and New Zealand. By the late 1880s the move had reached the US. Wheatland, Plainfleld, and Big Rock became Illinois hotbeds. Long Grove, Cherokee, and Martensdale were pioneer Iowa plowing communities.

As a farm editor and broadcaster back in 1938, while national husking matches were at their zenith, I expressed concern about their future. I was convinced mechanical pickers would soon sound the death knell for husking contests. Our WHO manager, Joe Maland, agreed. We discussed special events where farmers could continue to be "king for a day." A national plowing match, with emphasis on the soil, would do that.

In 1939 WHO conducted its first interstate contest. Around 8000 persons came to Mitchellville, Iowa, on a dusty, windy day to watch plowmen compete with both horses and tractors.

The following year, 14,000 interested persons came to Boone, Iowa, to watch 25 contestants vie for the state plowing crown.

By 1941 the matches were attracting national attention. Some 21,000 attended the contest near Albia, Iowa. *Life* magazine carried a three-page spread.

The matches were canceled during WWII, but resumed in 1945 with emphasis on contour plowing as a means of restoring war depleted soils. By

1946, at Pleasantville, Iowa, the matches were national in scope with emphasis on conservation, and with champion plowmen coming from many states from then on. Ellsworth, Iowa, was host in 1947, and in 1948 the match near Dexter, Iowa, was highlighted by President Harry Truman's "Give 'em hell" speech and his tour of the plowing and conservation demonstrations.

Since then, National Plowing Matches and Conservation Days have been held annually.

In 1953 a world match was staged in Canada and was so well received there that the colorful spectacle has been held every year since with contests as far away as Australia, Finland, and Zimbabwe.

All told, 33 world contests have been conducted in 20 countries around the globe, including the US —1957 in Ohio and 1972 in Minnesota. The world matches at Amana next year make a fair bid to top any of the past, both in terms of participation, attractions, color, and activity. Mark Moser, director of Ag Expo '88, says preparations are being made for as many as 200,000 or more visitors. The 50 or more world competitors, all national champions in their own right, will be royally entertained. Visitors are assured much activity along with the matches.

Iowa will determine its state champions Sept. 7, 1988. The national champions will be named the following day. Then on Sept. 9 and 10 spectators will see world class plowmen from up to 30 countries from New Zealand to Finland, Yugoslavia, and Zimbabwe. They will match furrows in their determined effort to win the coveted Golden Plough, symbolizing the world championship, and to help dedicate the Cairn of Peace — a monument embodying the World Plowing Match motto "Peace Cultivates the Fields."

NORTHEAST IOWA COUPLE RECALLS BARN RAISING
October, 1987

Barn raisings were a major event back in pioneer days, but Mr. and Mrs. Dave Flage revived it when they needed help to replace a tumble-down shed with a new dairy barn. They told about how it occurred some time after starting married life on a farm, after being on teachers' salaries so low no modern day teacher could believe them.

When Mr. and Mrs. Dave Flage of near Waukon hear complaints about teachers' salaries being too low, they can't help but make some comparisons. Average beginning annual salary for Iowa teachers is now $14,159. In the late '30s when the Flages were teaching, Dave, a University of Iowa graduate and track star, received $70 a month as a high school math teacher. Gladys, who taught all eight grades in a country school, was paid $50 a month.

However low their teaching income may have been, the Flages, by frugality and hard work, have become another example of the American Dream. Today they own 240 acres and have raised and educated six children.

The road has not always been easy. There was no large nest egg from their combined teaching earnings. Moreover, a $10,000 debt hung over their heads after purchasing 70 acres and a nearby small farmstead with an old house and tumbledown barn. After acquiring a few horses and some hogs, they put together a duke's mixture herd of eight cows to provide for weekly cream checks badly needed to pay bills. Gladys also had a flock of hens and sold or traded eggs for groceries.

First priority was getting running water and a bathroom in the old house. Next problem was the old barn, totally unsuited for dairying. Replacing it would be costly.

To meet that challenge, Dave contracted with a neighbor for $100 worth of timber "on the stump." Then with the help of some nephews and an old crosscut saw, 300 logs were cut and hauled to the sawmill to be converted into beams and boards.

The next step was an old-fashioned barn raising involving some 50 neighbors and their wives. They made short work of the building task, and enjoyed the pork roast feast and pie supper that followed.

With the new modern dairy setup, the mixed breed cows were replaced by a high producing, purebred Brown Swiss herd. Not only were the dairy checks much larger, but as the children grew to 4-H age the Flage Brown Swiss cattle won high awards at local Canton exhibits, and at county, All-Iowa, and State Fair shows.

The Flages': 50 neighbors help with their "barn raising"

Gladys did her part by serving as 4-H dairy leader, while Dave made community contributions on the school and REC boards and in their church.

As the years sped on, the children grew up, graduated from college, and went out on their own, so the herd was dispersed.

Now retired, and with Mark Palmer as their hard working tenant, the Flages count their blessings. They are proud of their accomplishments, and of their three daughters, Ruth, Sharon, and Carol, and their three sons, Mark, David and Steve. Not surprisingly, Dave and Gladys also do a bit of modest boasting about their 10 grandchildren.

WWI VETERANS RECALL ARMISTICE DAY
November, 1987

The 11th hour of the 11th day of the 11th month of 1918 will never be forgotten by the thousands of U.S. Doughboys over in Europe on that eventful day. It marked the end of World War I. Two Iowans with good reason to remember it are Amil Laschonsky and Raymond Block, both 92 when this was written.

When Veteran's Day was observed nationwide earlier this month many "old-timers" recalled that Nov. 11 once was known as Armistice Day. Especially was this true of some 3000 Iowa WWI veterans who vividly recall that it was on the 11th hour of the 11th day of November, 1918, when Kaiser Wilhelm's vaunted German army surrendered to Allied Forces.

No less than 119,213 Iowans answered their country's call to service, many of whom eventually served "over there." Of these, 3576 paid the supreme sacrifice.

Among the surviving "doughboys," as they were affectionately called, is Amil Laschansky, of Clarence, now 92, and the current Commander of Iowa's WWI Veterans Association. He was one of those to man the 6-in. guns in the fierce battles in the Argonne Forest and at Bella Woods.

On his return from service he started farming in Nebraska, married, then came to Iowa to farm near Delmar and later become Cedar County surveyor.

Now Regional Commander of an eight-state WWI veterans organization, he and his wife were among a small group chosen to go to France this summer to observe the 70th anniversary of the US entry into WWI. His son, Melvin, now deceased, was a WWII veteran.

Another WWI veteran with many recollections—and a permanent reminder of that 1918 conflict is Raymond Brock, now 92, of Winterset, a long-time Madison County auditor. Brock, who lost a leg when his unit was shelled less than a month before the armistice, first enlisted in the Mexican Border War in 1916.

Lt. Raymond Brock, a WWI Rainbow Division officer in France.

Early in WWI, Private Brock re-enlisted and was made Corporal while the national guard was encamped at the State Fairgrounds in Aug. 1917. He soon found himself a member of the famed Rainbow Division, was promoted to Sergeant, and was on a cattle boat converted to a troopship headed for France in November.

By Thanksgiving the Madison county farm youth was in Alsace Loraine and not long afterward, the young infantryman was in the trenches going "over the top" and struggling with gas masks against the enemy's poisonous fumes. In July 1918, Brock was in the thick of it near Champagne, where many of his buddies were killed.

Soon after being promoted, Brock again was in heavy fighting in the Argonne forest, and, as an officer, led his unit in the fierce struggle. It was there that his right leg was shattered by a German shell. Medics provided first aid during the night but stretcher bearers could not get him to a field hospital until morning. Later, after being transferred to a base hospital, gangrene set in and the leg had to be amputated.

Brock was married in 1920 and the couple observed their 65th wedding anniversary with their son and daughter, six grandchildren, and three great-grandchildren in 1985.

CHRISTMAS REUNIONS SINCE EARLY 1900S
December, 1987

Christmas family reunions started in the early 1900s continue for the Peterson family of Dayton, Iowa. Always held in their large farm home as long as their parents, Chris and Christina, were living, it was a gala event for the 13 Peterson children. Since their parents' passing, they now meet in a church the first Sunday in December, with nine of the 13, and many grandchildren, continuing the traditions.

As the Christmas holiday season approaches, virtually all families look forward to a time of togetherness.

Few families, however, have enjoyed Christmas season reunions more enthusiastically, or in greater numbers, than the Petersons of Dayton, Iowa. Their annual Christmastime gatherings date back to the early 1900s when Christian Peterson, a native of Denmark, his wife, Christina, and their growing family, started a tradition that continues to this day.

There were 13 children born in the Peterson farm home. Laura, the oldest, is 96, and along with three of her sisters, Frances, 89, Edna, 87, and Mabel, 85, lives at Friendship Haven, a Fort Dodge retirement center.

All four sisters, along with five other surviving members of the family, enjoy recalling "The Way It Was" at those long ago yuletide observances.

Laura, who married Peter Nelson in 1914, remembers helping her mother bundle up younger sisters and brothers for a 4-mile bobsled ride to church. She says, "We would all pile onto a bed of straw in the sleigh, cover ourselves with warm blankets, and put our feet on a bed of hot stones."

Frances, who later married Ivan Slater, remembers the drive was made very early because the service, called "Julotta," began at 5 a.m. Edna, who married Ed McCullough, recalls the sermons were very long.

Mabel, who later became the wife of George Tomlinson, says, "The service included Christmas carols by us youngsters." She adds, "The men and boys sat on one side of the aisle and the women and girls on the other."

In recording the family history, Mabel also tells that their father, after arriving from Denmark, worked as a hired man for $7 a month for several years before marrying Christina and buying an 80-acre farm where their children were born.

As time went on, Christmas observances in the farm home took on added significance. A tree, cut in a nearby woodlot, was decorated by all the children. There was no fireplace, so 13 pairs of stockings were hung over doorknobs, bed posts, and almost anything else.

Four of the Peterson sisters with brothers Ralph, left, and Kenneth, right. Sisters are Laura Nelson, now 102, Frances Slater, Edna McCollough, and Mable Tomlinson.

Toys were largely handmade by Chris himself. Meanwhile the busy mother did a lot of baking. "Her cookies and other goodies were always a treat and disappeared quickly," says Mabel. She also recalls that for many years Chris gave every grandchild a silver dollar at Christmastime.

Other Peterson sons and daughters still living include: Ralph, 82 retired Dayton farmer; Earl, 79, a WWII veteran and the first in the family to graduate from college, now a retired ag advisor at Hillsboro, Illinois; Melvin, 77, also a veteran and a retired Fort Dodge electrician; Dorothy Smith, 75, who lives in California; and Kenneth, 73, who farmed the home place before turning it over to his son, Craig. Four others of the original 13 have died.

While Chris and Christina were living, the Peterson reunions were always at the parents' home. Since their passing the annual pre-Christmas gatherings are held at a Dayton church, usually on the first Sunday in December.

"That first Sunday in December is always marked off on our calendars," says Laura. She adds, "It's such a happy day for all of us when we can reminisce and pay tribute to the memory of our parents who gave us so many Merry Christmases."

The way it was . . .
1988

VETERAN MASTER PORK PRODUCER SALUTES NEW HONOREES
January, 1988

As 1988 dawned, plans for honoring another group of Master Pork Producers were being made. Joe Ludwig, 76, one of the few remaining members of the first group of "Masters" recognized in 1982, eagerly awaited word of the '88 winners. In a visit with him, I soon learned why he had been one of the first to be chosen.

Later this month, on Jan. 27, another group of outstanding Iowa hog producers will be honored. The Master Pork Producer citation will be awarded to some 25 swine raisers at the annual Iowa Pork Producers convention.

The "Masters" project has been conducted continuously since 1942. To date more than 1100 Iowa farmers have been singled out for their hog raising and marketing accomplishments.

Among the veteran producers previously honored is Joe Ludwig, 76, of Fort Atkinson. Ludwig, who was among those recognized in, that first year 46 years ago, says, "I'm eagerly looking forward to learning who will be named this year and to congratulate them on their achievements. It's a real honor, but they will find they will be on the spot from now on."

Ludwig lives on a Century Farm that has been in the family for 130 years. At their father's passing, Joe and his brothers, Martin and Edward, took over until Joe went on his own. Hog raising has been a main enterprise on the 430-acre tract for more than a century.

Master Pork Producer, Joe Ludwig.

During his own active years, the northeast Iowa farmer raised and fed out up to 1000 hogs a year. His nephews, Dave and Bill, now operate the farm and feed out 1500 head a year.

A graduate of the Iowa State College herdsman's course, Joe Ludwig worked closely with the late E. L. Quaife, one of the originators of the Master Pork Producer project, as well as with E. J. Weigle, long-time Winnishiek county extension director. "Their counsel was invaluable," says Joe.

Various breeds were involved in the Ludwig enterprise with Poland China, Chester White, Duroc, and Landrace all involved, as well as crossbreds.

Boar testing stations are held in high regard by the veteran hog raiser. He served on the New Hampton Station's board of directors for a number of years and says, "I always bought tested boars and was pleased with the results."

Ludwig hogs were raised outdoors on "clean ground," rotated annually. Pens were painstakingly cleaned between each spring and fall farrowing. Disease problems were virtually nonexistent.

Meticulous records were kept. Feed was mixed on the farm. Heat lamps were used with fall litters. Marketing was done when the shoats reached 215 lb. Most sales were on a grade-and-yield program.

Asked for his views on the pork industry, the Winnishiek county farmer says, "The year 1986 and most of 1987 were good for raisers, but cheap corn and good hog prices may result in some dismaying overproduction in the immediate future." He quickly adds, "However, those fellows to be honored later this month are all pretty solid and sound, and will be a credit to the industry in which Iowa leads the nation."

'THE WAY IT WAS' MARKS 10TH ANNIVERSARY
February 23, 1988

"THE WAY IT WAS" *entered its tenth year this year. A review of the number and kinds of columns carried monthly — and twice monthly on occasion — seemed to be in order. Here is that anniversary report.*

Ten years ago last month Monte Sesker, *WALLACES FARMER* editor, gave me an opportunity to write a feature about an elderly Iowan. "Let's give it a try" were his words. As a senior citizen myself, I welcomed the challenge and called the article "The Way It Was."

That first article centered on Albert Weston, then an agile 90, who remembered Indians roving around farm homes, scaring small boys "half to death," and how his father plowed an endless furrow around 160 acres of land when all farm work was done without machinery.

Although happy to reminisce, Weston seemed even more intrigued by the continuing march of farm progress, never missing a Farm Progress Show.

The Weston story must have gotten "The Way It Was" off to a good start. Now, 120 columns and articles later, the record shows 203 Iowans 75 years old or older from 68 counties have been featured. I am most grateful to Monte and to Frank Holdmeyer, Joanne Couey, and other editors for their encouragement, help, and patience. I am similarly appreciative of our *WALLACES FARMER* readers who by their comments and letters have been a constant inspiration.

Equally gratifying is the magnificent cooperation given me by those interviewed and their response and appreciation. Fifty thousand or more miles have gone on the odometer. There have been countless phone calls, thousands of pictures, and endless hours devoted to writing.

Every "old timer" had an interesting story to tell. Never, however, could I have anticipated the countless fascinating anecdotes. For example, V.B. Hamilton recalled that he was a direct descendent of Patrick Henry. A native of Tennessee, V.B., on graduating from Iowa State University, became so enthralled with Iowa he remained here the rest of his life.

There are many others. Carl Marcue was 87, a double amputee in his fourth major career. He jokingly wondered what he would undertake after he got to be 100.

Mrs. Raymond Sayre, related her experiences as ACWW leader, of riding elephants in India, camels in Egypt, and ox carts in Ceylon, as well as about her efforts for country women around the globe. The irrepressible Clarence Hill gave me a few lessons in journalism as well as a lot of chuckles in recalling amusing anecdotes about his efforts as an ag innovator, grandfather clock maker, and raconteur.

Oldest person interviewed was 107-year-old Edith Smith, whose keen memory recalled "Christmas Past" over 100 years ago. Ernle Thompkins, at 101, complained he couldn't find enough takers for the delicious, abundant, free vegetables produced in his garden that year. And 100-year-old B.W. Knudson, Iowa's oldest pork producer, was also featured.

At least a dozen Master Farmers and almost that many Master Farm Homemakers have been recognized in "The Way It Was." The same is true of cattlemen, dairymen, pork producers, sheep and lamb raisers, horsemen, poultry raisers, champion plowmen and cornhuskers, religious leaders, weather observers, Farm Progress Show hosts, war veterans, pioneer county agents, teachers, legislators, conservationists, crop specialists, authors, and retirement center residents.

Finally, in the 10-year series last December, the four Peterson sisters, aged 96, 89, 87, and 85, all living in the Fort Dodge Friendship Haven, told their memories of Christmas past.

Many more features could be mentioned, and many more are contemplated.

With 10 candles now on our "The Way It Was" cake I look forward to visiting and acknowledging many more indomitable Iowa "golden agers."

AMANA COLONIES WILL SHOWCASE AMERICAN AGRICULTURE
February, 1988

When the International Leaders of the World Plowing Organization chose the Amana Colonies in Iowa to host their 1988 World Plowing Match, they chose wisely. And when U.S. officials and WALLACES FARMER *editors learned of the choice, they quickly expanded it to become a World Agriculture Expo. This column tells of some of the countless attractions the Amanas could provide to show off American Agriculture at its best.*

When World Ag Expo officials and International plowing match leaders selected Iowa's Amana Colonies as the site for their 1988 exposition and competitions they chose wisely and well.

Situated in the heart of corn and soybean country. and in a leading livestock production and dairying area, the Amanas will show off American agriculture

Bringing in the bales instead of the sheaves.

200

at its best. Moreover, residents of the Amana Colonies, already accustomed to annually hosting tens of thousands of visitors, will provide their guests with the warmest kind of hospitality.

The Amana Colonies involve seven villages and 26,000 acres of farmland and timber. They are located in east central Iowa some 20 miles west of Iowa City. Interstate Highway 80 intersects some of the Amana landholdings, thereby making them readily accessible to travelers and tourists.

Competitors in the upcoming World Plowing Contest, along with their galleries of supporters, as well as contestants in the national plowing and husking matches and their fans, will revel in the Amanas' pleasant rural setting as will other expo visitors. Large herds of cattle roam the rolling pasturelands. Fertile valleys produce near record yields of corn and soybeans. Woodlands add much beauty to the area and abound in wildlife. A 200 acre lily lake with 10,000 or more yellow blooms is a special attraction, as is a dam built by Indians centuries ago.

Amana Colonies street scene.

The history of the Amanas is fascinating, and a story of faith. Bound together by common religious beliefs back in the 18th century, ancestors of today's Amana residents suffered severe persecution in Germany. To escape further harm, they pooled their resources for passage to America In 1844 and settled on a 5000-acre tract near Buffalo, N. Y. Ten years later, as the rapidly growing city encroached on their land, the "Inspirationalists," as they were then known, made the long ox trek to Iowa, establishing a communal way of life at Amana.

The pioneer settlers, after purchasing the 25,000 acres of land, immediately set forth to build the seven colonies, each of which remains today. All have the name Amana — East Amana, Amana, Middle Amana, High Amana, West Amana, South Amana, and Upper South Amana. Homes, churches, schools, mills, shops, and barns were built, most of them still in good repair today. When the railroads came through nearby Homestead in 1861, the Amanas' elders acquired that small village as well, thus obtaining access to rail shipments.

A monumental task—the digging of a 7-mile long canal to provide water power—was also undertaken and completed. Soon woolen mills, furniture factories, meat plants, wineries, and other enterprises were flourishing.

New Enterprises

Although the Amanas' communal system worked reasonably well for many years, 1932 saw a dramatic change from the "one for all and all for one" concept to total American free enterprise. The transition, made by popular vote, quickly gave rise to many new ventures.

Restaurants replaced communal kitchens. Production in the woolen mills, furniture factories, and other enterprises increased as a new spirit penetrated the Amanas.

Among the new enterprises was the establishment of the refrigeration plant, which came about when an Iowa City businessman asked an Amana craftsman to make a beverage cooler. From that small beginning in 1934, Amana Refrigeration was born. Today, the Amana firm is a national leader in the home appliance field, employing some 2400 persons annually and selling the Amana products in all 50 states and 120 foreign countries.

Farming, however, remains the Amanas' biggest business. In fertile fields where the sod was first broken by oxen-drawn prairie breaker plows in the 1850s, and later tilled by horse-drawn machinery, modern tractors now power equipment over 11,000 acres of cropland.

As much as a half million bushels of corn, as well as countless thousands of bushels of soybeans and oats are produced annually, along with alfalfa and other hay crops. Six thousand acres are in pasture. About 7000 Hereford, Angus, and Charolais cattle, along with 10,000 hogs, are fed out each year.

Another 7000 acres of land are now in woodland preserve. Streams and ponds provide some good fishing.

Amana foods, and wines are far famed. World Ag Expo visitors will find the community's obsession for homemade food perfection a special bonus.

Generous family-style servings of prime beef, Amana ham, country fried chicken, wiener schnitzel, bratwurst, sauerbraten, and other popular dishes will be provided In each of the seven food tents in expo's 50-acre tent city, as well as in a dozen or more eating places in the seven villages.

Most of the wholesome meats served to visitors will come from the Amana Meat Market and the tasty fresh breads from the Amana Bakery.

WALLACES FARMER is one of six major sponsors of World Ag Expo. Future issues will include updates on the activities, displays, competitions, schedules, program plans, and other information pertaining to the worldwide farm event.

"KING CORN" SPECIAL TRAINS IN EARLY 1900S
March 8, 1988

At the beginning of this century, an interesting project united corn, America's major farm crop, with railway trains, the nation's foremost transportation system. It was known as "King Corn Special", and found dozens of corn specialists riding various railway parlor cars from town to town dispensing corn improvement information to thousands of farmers.

Trains have always been a source of fascination for farm families. Billions of tons of grain went to market by rail. Countless millions of cattle, hogs, and sheep were shipped to meat packing centers. Coal, wood, groceries, machinery, and other supplies came to farm communities by way of rail.

One of the most novel, and educational, uses of the railways occurred in Iowa shortly after the turn of the century. Called the "King Corn Seed Corn Specials," they involved five major rail companies and served a large number of farmers.

Shortly before he passed away at age 99, Martin Mosher, Iowa's first county agent, gave me a day-by-day diary of one of the 1905 corn "specials." It is fascinating reading, pointing out that Iowa corn yields averaged between 30 and 40 bu./acre. but that 100-bu./acre yields could be achieved with proper practices and management.

A killing frost early in the fall of 1904 resulted in severe damage to seed germination, Realizing the severity of the problem, the legendary P. G. Holden, Iowa corn specialist, suggested using train stops as a means of alerting farmers to the dangers facing them.

Mosher was one of the first corn experts drafted to join Holden in the undertaking. The corn special started on Feb. 13, with the Chicago, Milwaukee, and St. Paul train making 14 stops that day.

Lectures and demonstrations on seed corn testing, planting suggestions, corn uses, improving yields, and other topics were made from the train's rear car platform.

Brass bands frequently welcomed the traveling lecturers. As many as 200 teams of horses hitched to wagons or buggies were counted in some towns along the way, along with saddle horses.

Each rail line took from a week to 14 days of travel. Full schedules were maintained Monday through Saturday. From 12 to 16 stops were made every day.

Biggest single day was March 29, when more than 2000 persons were warned about germination problems. Largest crowd at any one stop totalled over 700 persons at LeMars in northwest Iowa, Crowds of 500 or more also were often encountered. Smallest turnout was at Wall Lake where only six were counted. Walcott found only 21 men at that stop, and as Mosher noted, "They all talked German."

When all was said and done, 882 lectures had been presented to 108,023 farm people at 546 Iowa railroad stations in the 43-day period of the King Corn run.

Thousands of farmers benefitted from corn train meetings with Ames college professors.

INTERNATIONAL ATTRACTION
March 22, 1988

Rarely in a farm writer's lifetime does he or she have an opportunity to become involved in an international agricultural event in which there is participation from almost all over the world. Yet this is what has happened to me by way of the World Plowing Organization headquartered in England. A long-time friendship with Alfred Hall, WPO Director, with whom I have been associated since the 1953 International Plowing Contest in Canada, plus the part I played in getting the 1988 World Competition to Iowa, prompted Wallaces Farmer Editor Monte Sesker to invite me to write this preview for the International Plowing Event sponsored by the World Ag Expo.

The World Ag Expo, which will be staged in Iowa's Amana Colonies Sept. 7-10, 1988, seems appropriately named. Aside from the Winter Olympics held at Calgary, Alta., Can., earlier this year, it is doubtful many other 1988 events in the Northern Hemisphere will be more international in scope.

Billed as a "Worldwide Celebration of Agriculture," the central

Albert Hall, Secretary General of the World Plowing Organization.

highlight of the Amana farm extravaganza will be the World Plowing Matches. Last held in the U.S. in 1972, and not scheduled for this country again until the year 2010, the contests are often referred to as "The Plowing Olympics."

Champion plowmen from no less than 26 countries will vie for the coveted Golden Plough. Competitors, all national champions in their own right, will come from as far north as Finland, as far south as New Zealand, as far east as Yugoslavia, and as far west as Tasmania.

Overseeing the myriad of details involved in staging a worldwide match is Alfred Hall, of Cumbria, England, founder of the international contest. No less than 18 countries will be represented by judges who must determine the winners. A dozen other nations will provide stewards and timekeepers.

Presiding over the annual meeting of the World Plowing Organization (WPO), sponsor of the event, will be Airie Stehauer of Holland. Vice presidents include Franz Geiger, Austria, and Lawrence McMillan, Canada. Phil Palmer, England, is treasurer and Hall serves as general secretary. U.S. representation on the world board — and host country director — is Glen Brown, Minnesota dairyman and poultry raiser.

Visitors are expected from all over the world, and representatives of foreign equipment manufacturers and plows are also expected to attend, especially those whose equipment will be in use. Included among those involved in previous years are tractors made by Fiat of Italy, Renault of France, Carraro of Portugal, Massey Ferguson of Australia and Canada, Belarus MTX of Hungary, Cassell of Switzerland, and Zetor of Czechoslovakia.

At the World Plowing Match land ends.

The international theme will not be limited to just the plowing events. Expo planners are arranging for musical and dancing ethnic groups from Iowa representing various European, Balkan, Scandinavian, and African cultures.

Hosting the visiting plowmen, coaches, WPO officials, and other foreign visitors is a major U.S. involvement. A group known as the Ambassadors is taking on this king-sized opportunity to extend Iowa hospitality, arrange lodging, tours, parades, banquets, and entertainment, as well as translators for competitors and officials.

Amana area restauranteurs will also have a major responsibility to make sure all visitors are introduced to the famous family-style German-American Amana foods.

Hundreds of volunteers from the Amana, Iowa City, Cedar Rapids, Kalona, and other east central Iowa areas will assist in staging what will be one of this year's major farm attractions with its many international aspects.

The worldwide goal of peace will be heavily underscored at the 1988 Ag Expo.

Moreover, WPO officials are deeply involved in the cause of peace. Their list of objectives includes these words, "By means of improving the skill of plowing worldwide, fellowship and understanding amongst the people of all nations will be encouraged."

When addressing competitors, officials, and spectators, General Secretary Hall regularly quotes the WPO's Latin motto, "Pax Añva Colat." Translated it means "Cultivate Our Fields in Peace."

With that in mind, a Cairn of Peace has been dedicated since the competition's inception at Cobourg, Ont., Can., in 1953. Each cairn is located in or near the plowing field, and serves as a symbolic and permanent reminder of that country's part in achieving the goal of world peace.

On Sept. 10, the 35th International Cairn of Peace will be dedicated at Amana. It will be a lasting reminder of the universal

Five of the expert judges from 18 foreign countries whose difficult task it was to choose a previous year's winner.

dream that peace and brotherhood will, indeed, plow the world's fields. Equally important, it will also serve as a 20th Century expression of the biblical command to "beat spears into pruning hoods and swords into plowshares."

IOWA FARMER DEGREE WON 60 YEARS AGO
April 12, 1988

In my six decades as a farm writer, columnist and broadcaster, I've found many "firsts". One of the most unusual of all was to learn that Ralph Gruenwold, a vo-ag student at Maquoketa before the Future Farmers of America were organized, was one of the first 13 persons to win the coveted Iowa FFA Farmer Degree. Here's the story.

At the recent Iowa Future Farmers of America (FFA) Leadership Conference, 195 members received the Iowa Farmer Degree. This prestigious award is presented only to the top Iowa Vocational Agriculture students, based on FFA achievements and academics.

The recognition, awarded annually since 1929, brought back pleasant memories to thousands of Iowans who have won the award since then. Ralph Gruenwold, 76, Ankeny, has especially happy recollections.

Gruenwold was a hard-working student at Maquoketa, one of Iowa's pioneer vo-ag schools. On graduation in 1928, he was one of the five named to receive an Outstanding Iowa Ag Student award.

FFA chapters were not officially established in Iowa until 1929. One of the first moves by the newly formed Iowa Vocational Agriculture Teachers Association (IVATA) was to establish the Iowa Farmer Degree as a major FFA award.

Soon after its organization in 1929, the IVATA decreed that the 13 students who had received the Outstanding Iowa Student award in previous years would be the first to receive the Iowa Farmer Degree.

"That was 60 years ago," remembers Gruenwold, "and I've cherished that honor ever since."

After a short stint in farming and graduation from a junior college in 1930, Gruenwold taught country school for 3 years. The $60 per month salary received as a teacher during the mid '30s was welcome but not enough to establish a home and family. Accordingly, Gruenwold enrolled in Iowa State University, graduating from ag education courses in 1937. That fall he became Lytton, Iowa's vo-ag teacher, starting a 34-year career involving hundreds of FFA members in four different schools.

In 1940 the young vo-ag teacher transferred to Marengo, where he spent 5 years instructing one of Iowa's largest FFA chapters.

Near the close of WWII, Gruenwold and his wife, the former Kathryn Zelle, both took teaching assignments at Story City. Here Ralph initiated a summer travel study tour that took his FFA members as far east as New York City.

Ralph Gruenwold, one of Iowa's first FFA members.

Final assignment in his long vo-ag career was at Tipton, where he was a teacher and vo-ag chapter advisor for 26 years. Tragically, the Gruenwolds' only son, Dale, who had already earned an Iowa Farmer Degree, was killed in an accident while en route to the Iowa State Fair.

Now retired, Ralph Gruenwold looks back on his long vo-ag teaching career, proud and happy of the achievements of many of his FFA members. Of all his recognitions, receiving one of Iowa's first 13 Iowa Farmer Degrees still brings him a special sense of pride.

WOMEN'S CLUB CELEBRATES 90TH YEAR
May, 1988

Not many organization chapters or clubs can boast 90 years of continuous existence, but the Webster "Daughters of Ceres" can. Organized in what is now the Living History Farms mansion, the club is still going strong. Pauline Wipperman, granddaughter of a founder, tells that Mrs. Henry Wallace, wife of the WALLACES FARMER editor, was state president and spoke at the Chapter's first meeting May 19, 1898.

In Greek mythology, Ceres is known as the Goddess of Agriculture. Thus, the name "Daughters of Ceres" was a happy choice for a rural women's club organized late in the last century.

Mrs. Henry Wallace, wife of the beloved "Uncle Henry," the founding publisher of *WALLACES FARMER*, was one of the club's founders and was named the first state president.

Women's Lib had not yet been heard of, but farm women joyously embraced the new organization. Chapters in various areas of the state were soon established.

On May 19, 1898, a group of central Iowa farm wives met at the home of Mrs. Martin Flynn—now the stately Living History Farms mansion — to form the seventh chapter in Iowa. Known now as the Webster Daughters of Ceres, the club has been active throughout the past 9 decades and continues to meet monthly.

This month the group will celebrate its 90th anniversary in the Church of the Land on the Living History Farms, a stone's throw from where their great-grandmothers first met in 1898.

Five generations are now accounted for at some meetings. Oldest is Cora Schafer, 98, who became a member in the early 1900s. Her daughter, Mrs. Margaret Taylor, Grimes, a 57-year member, attends regularly.

Oldest active member today is Mrs. Mabel Baer, whose mother was another early member. Mrs. Baer says, "It's been about 60 years of enjoyable membership for me." Mrs. Berneda Milligan, Urbandale, can claim a half century of active participation.

Pauline Wipperman, Grimes, one of the most enthusiastic of the group, whose grandmother, Mrs. John Anderson, was a founder, started attending 50 years ago.

Now Pauline's daughter, Mrs. Carol Calvert, and granddaughter, 4-year-old Lindsey, a 5th generation Daughter of Ceres, also attend.

Three others have been members 45 years. They are Joyce Kocheiser, Grimes; Maxine Loose, Redfield, and Betty Nelson, Urbandale. Mrs. Laura Ward, also Urbandale, has participated more than 40 years. Mrs. Edna Bartlett, Grimes, is the newest member.

Minutes of the monthly meetings of the central Iowa unit have

Iowa Daughters of Ceres attending a meeting during 90th year of organization.

been carefully preserved. At the club's very first meeting, secretary Emma Terhune bespoke the membership's appreciation of nature with references to Mrs. Flynn's country home, majestic trees, blooming shrubs, and twittering birds.

The May 19, 1898, minutes also tell that the state president, Mrs. Wallace, was in attendance and spoke briefly on the organization's benefit as applied to farm life. Twenty-one women are listed as charter members. Mrs. C.W. Stewart was named first president.

From the outset, club objectives were to help others. Sewing clothes for needy children (as many as 130 garments in a single year), helping the Iowa Girl's School at Mitchellville, providing Thanksgiving and Christmas dinners for the poor, serving the Red Cross before, during, and after war years have been among the club's major projects from its inception, and continue to this day.

Through all these 90 years each meeting opens with a recitation of the Lord's Prayer, and concludes with the serving of refreshments repeatedly described as "delicious. "

Sociability also rates as a high club goal. Mrs. Wipperman points out, "We are just like family, and have a great time at our meetings." The anniversary celebration, highlighted by the distribution of a 90-year history written by Mrs. Wipperman, will be a potluck lunch with husbands and friends invited.

SPECIAL EVENTS ADDED TO WORLD AG EXPO
May 17, 1988

As the time for the World Ag Expo and World Plowing Matches approached, more and more attractions were added to and scheduled for the International Agricultural Extravaganza. Listed in this column are a number of the exciting new developments.

You name it and if it has anything to do with the farm and home the World Ag Expo, to be held in Iowa's Amana Colonies Sept. 7 - 10, will have it.

Mark Moser, expo director, says "The World Ag Expo will be an international celebration of agriculture and things are rapidly falling into place." One look at the 1000-acre field site, with its new Welcome Center and its 60-acre tent— city layout, will convince anyone the expo will be an exciting, enlightening, and enjoyable "once in a lifetime" event.

Although state, national, and world plowing competition will serve as expo centerpieces, a dozen or more special events and attractions during the 4-day farm show will also be of widespread interest to the anticipated 150,000 or more visitors. Some of them are:

Sheepdog Trials

This will be one of the major side attractions in which 50 or more dogs, some from as far away as California and Pennsylvania, will follow their owner's voice and whistle commands as they drive lambs from an open field through a long, intricate course into a small pen. Cash purses will be augmented by special mementos by Iowa artists. Jim Lynch of Prole, president of the Iowa Border Collie Association, will be in charge, assisted by Kristi Feltz, Iowa City, the secretary, and other IBCA members.

Sheep dog trials were one of the special events planned.

Cornhusking Contests

Iowa representatives for the National Corn Husking Matches slated for Illinois in October will be determined on expo opening day, Sept. 7, in a field near the center of the exhibit area and along the shuttle bus route. Winners in five classes will be determined. National rules will apply. National champions of previous years will demonstrate their husking skills on Sept. 8, 9, and 10. Mr. and Mrs. Vincent King, of the Living History Farms, Des Moines, and Bob Ferguson, president of the Iowa huskers, have charge, aided by the Living History Farms Harvest Festival Committee.

Rural Craft Fair

Visitors interested in rural crafts will find the expo to be a Utopia. No less than 175 crafters will have 190 booths in two huge tents. Woodworking, needlework, ceramics, metalwork, jewelry, garments from wool, and many other crafts will be on display. R. C. Eichacker, Amana, has charge and reports some participants coming from as far away as Tennessee.

Horses, Mules, and Oxen

Expo officials have set aside a 40-acre tract to enable Iowa and Minnesota horsemen and "mule skinners" to stage dozens of demonstrations of farming in "yesteryear." Six-horse-hitches on 3-bottom gang plows, as well as demonstrations involving 2-bottom gangs, 1-bottom sulkies, and 14-in. walking plows, will start the exhibitions, followed by horses and mules on discs, harrows, planters, drills, cultivators, and other turn-of-the-century machines. Horses will include Belgians, Percherons, and Clydesdales. Several mule teams and a yoke or two of oxen will be in action. Some Iowa horsemen will compete in the State Plow Match, Sept. 7. Walter Long, Strawberry Point, and Harold Mulford, Iowa City, have charge.

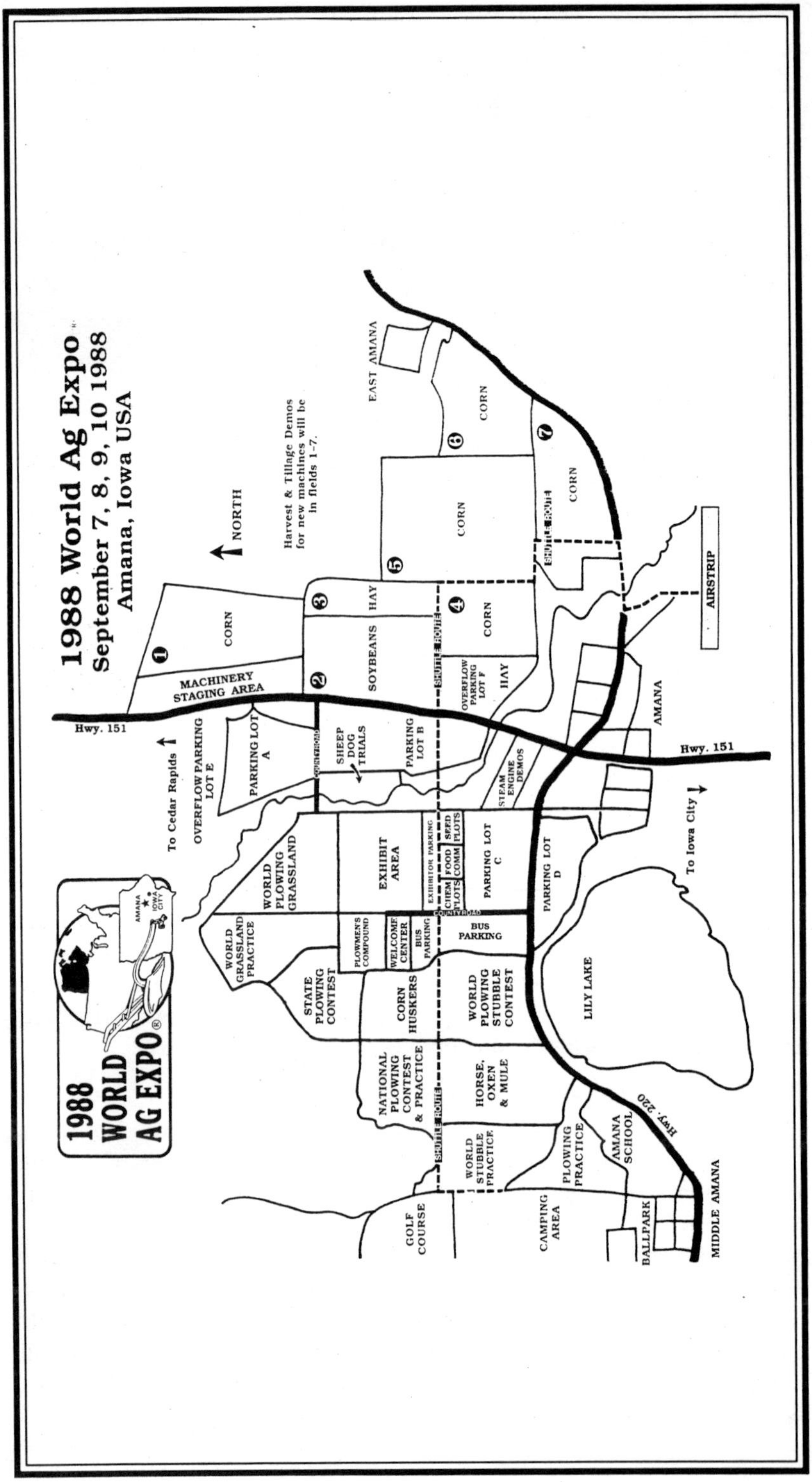

1988 World Ag Expo
September 7, 8, 9, 10 1988
Amana, Iowa USA
1988 WORLD AG EXPO®
AMANA
IOWA CITY
NORTH
Harvest & Tillage Demos for new machines will be in fields 1-7.
EAST AMANA
CORN
HAY
SOYBEANS
MACHINERY STAGING AREA
Hwy. 151
To Cedar Rapids
OVERFLOW PARKING LOT E
PARKING LOT A
SHEEP DOG TRIALS
PARKING LOT B
OVERFLOW PARKING LOT F
SHUTTLE ROUTE
STEAM ENGINE DEMOS
AMANA
AIRSTRIP
To Iowa City
WORLD PLOWING GRASSLAND
WORLD GRASSLAND PRACTICE
EXHIBIT AREA
EXHIBITOR PARKING
CHEM PLOTS
FOOD COMM
SEED PLOTS
PARKING LOT C
PARKING LOT D
COUNTY ROAD
PLOWMEN'S COMPOUND
WELCOME CENTER
BUS PARKING
STATE PLOWING CONTEST
CORN HUSKERS
WORLD PLOWING STUBBLE CONTEST
LILY LAKE
NATIONAL PLOWING CONTEST & PRACTICE
HORSE, OXEN & MULE
WORLD STUBBLE PRACTICE
PLOWING PRACTICE
AMANA SCHOOL
Hwy. 220
GOLF COURSE
CAMPING AREA
BALLPARK
MIDDLE AMANA

Threshing/Steam Plowing

No celebration of farming can be complete without steam threshing and other grain harvest activities. Thanks to the Midwest Old Steam Threshers Association (MOSTA) of Mt. Pleasant, the Amana event will not only have threshing machines powered by steam engines in action, but gasoline engines and antique tractors on display, plus a unique "steam plowing" performance. Jim Adams, of MOSTA, says the 1988 Midwest Threshers Reunion at Mt. Pleasant, an outstanding annual national farm show, ends two weeks before expo begins, thus enabling Mt. Pleasant officials to get machines and volunteers to Amana for threshing and steam plowing exhibitions daily.

Inventors Showcase

Farm minded "Thomas Edisons" of today will have a heyday at the World Ag Expo, where an Inventors Showcase is planned. Amateur farm inventors are invited to compete for a $1000 first prize, with $500 to second place, and $250 for third. Sponsored by the Merchant's National Bank (MNB) of Cedar Rapids, the Inventors Showcase will be directed by Doug Keiper, of MNB, who reports, "We need farm inventions of all sorts. Only a few applications have been received so far. So, get yours in." Deadline is May 31.

Avenue of Progress

For expo visitors interested in the relentless forward march of progress in agriculture, the Avenue of Progress is a "made-to-order" feature. Farm machines of the late 1800s will be on display in the same area with the 100,000 4-wheel drives, massive horsepower, giant tractors of 1988. Essentially, the Avenue will portray a century of progress in farm mechanization. Andy Appleton, representing Merchant's National Bank of Cedar Rapids, Avenue of Progress sponsor, and Roger Mohr, Vail, Iowa, are in charge.

Special Ag Topics

A new and challenging addition to expo is the Special Ag Topics program. Plans include discussions on "Ag Products for the Future," "Marketing: World Strategy," "Ag Chemicals and Our Environment," and "High Technology For World Agriculture." Jerry DeWitt, Iowa State University associate director of extension, and Ann Harrison, East Central Iowa extension service, have charge.

All-Iowa Ag Tent

Many Iowa agricultural service and commodity organizations will participate in the expo. *WALLACES FARMER,* one of the six major sponsors of the World Ag Expo, is sponsoring and coordinating the ALL IOWA project. Monte Sesker, Editor of *WALLACES FARMER,* is in charge and expects many commodity and ag service groups to join in by the deadline day, July 1.

Living History

An especially interesting feature for the expo is being presented by the Living History Farms, widely known Iowa historical and tourist attraction. The display will portray a pioneer family making an overnight stop en route to a new home. A covered wagon with needed provisions —flour, salt, sugar, and various foods, utensils, tools, seeds, portable forge, and furniture—is included. Miriam Dunlap, Living History Farms public relations director, is in charge.

Ag Forum

Because 1988 is a presidential election year, presidential candidates are among national figures considered for the Ag Forum. Ag policy will be the topic assigned presidential aspirants if they agree to attend. World trade policies, red meat in diets, and global water policies are other topics under consideration by the Ag Forum committee headed by Stan Butt of Amana. Protein Blenders, Inc., Iowa City, is forum sponsor.

GUERNSEY HEIFERS INSTEAD OF WAGES
June 21, 1988

Livestock in lieu of wages was a common story for hired men in the "Trying Thirties". Clyde Core well remembered receiving 12 Guernsey heifers for five years of hard farm work. Strange as it may sound today, those 12 heifers started him on his way as a successful dairyman and conservation-minded Master Farmer.

Clyde Core, Master Farmer and dedicated soil conservationist.

Twelve Guernsey heifers given him in lieu of 5 years' wages during the Depression enabled Clyde Core, Pleasantville, to launch a dairy career in the 1930s. Core eventually branched out into other livestock and turkey production and became a tireless community worker. By 1950 he was given the Iowa Master Farmer award by *WALLACES FARMER*.

Core, who is 80, clearly remembers his boyhood ambition to be a good farmer. His father operated 590 acres where Red Rock Lake is now located. Cattle, hogs, sheep, ducks, chickens, geese, and a barnful of Clydesdale horses, along with a lot of fieldwork, kept everyone in the family busy. At 12, Clyde was already adept at handling the "Jenny Lind" walking cultivator and other machinery.

In 1930, Clyde's studies at Iowa State College were cut short when the farm's big stock barn burned. The next year he and his Knoxville High School sweetheart, Wilma Maddy, were married. They moved into a hired man's log house, bought a team, an old plow, planter, cultivator, and wagon, rented 35 acres of land, and grew their first crop of corn.

Hardships in the early 1930s were commonplace. Every drop of water had to be pumped by hand. There was no electricity. Eggs were traded for groceries. Drouth and chinch bugs devastated crops. Hogs were $2.50/cwt. However, the Cores and thousands like them carried on, convinced better times were ahead — and they were.

By 1933 Clyde and Wilma were able to rent a larger farm, and with his father's gift of the 12 heifers, started their Guernsey herd. After joining a cow test association they increased their rolling herd average to about 400 lb. of butterfat. One cow, Susan, topped 600 lb.

After several years, the herd was increased to 25 or more good producers. In 1942, the Cores, now the parents of three children, purchased 240 acres south of Pleasantville.

Purebred Angus cattle, market hogs, and a flock of 4500 turkeys were then added to their operation. Terraces, contouring, waterways, and other soil conserving practices were quickly adopted.

While he is too modest to talk about his own community contributions, neighbors are quick to point out that he was a pioneer conservationist, a member of the Pleasantville and Marion county school boards, a Sunday School teacher, extension council chairman, and president of the County Farm Bureau, Angus Association, and the Pleasantville State Bank.

Clyde and Wilma now spend part of each year visiting Richard, Ronald, and Nancy, their spouses, and their seven grandchildren in Texas, Florida, and Iowa.

AMANA'S EARLY YEARS RECALLED
July 12, 1988

1988 was the year of the World Ag Expo. More than 300,000 persons attended the four-day event sponsored by WALLACES FARMER *and five other organizations. Incredible 20th Century farm progress was displayed on all sides, and nobody noted that more than 85-year-old Rudolph Blechschmidt and 77-year-old Helen Rind, as they compared the 1988 machinery with early Amana years as they knew them.*

The latest census count shows 2505 persons call the Amana Colonies, site of the World Ag Expo scheduled for Sept. 7-10, home. Included are a number of elderly residents, who vividly remember when the seven widely known east central Iowa villages embraced a communal "one for all and all for one" system.

Among those who recall what life was like before the change to a free enterprise society in 1932 are 85-year-old Rudolph Blechschmidt of East Amana and 77-year-old Helena Rind of Middle Amana.

Blechschmidt, known as "Rudie" to all, served as a teacher 19 years, a woolen mill foreman 23 years, and for the past 20 years, a clock works technician in a furniture store.

Rind, now retired, was a woolen mills employee 50 years, serving first in the spooling department and then as a receptionist and guide. In 1983 she enrolled in a high school equivalency course at Williamsburg. She graduated at age 72.

Recollections of their childhood and teen years in the colonies are fascinating. Both emphasize that religion, discipline, and hard work were the corner stones in the Amanas from 1856, when the communal group, then known as the Society of True Inspiration, left Ebenezer, N.Y., to settle in Iowa in the 1920s.

Blechschmidt remembers Amana communal society.

German was the only language spoken. Virtually everyone attended 11 church services a week. Food was served in communal kitchens.

One person, either a man or woman, was regarded as a "prophet— with something akin to divine powers. Elders were carefully chosen, largely on the basis of their devoutness. Marriage, though necessarily tolerated, was not particularly encouraged because a single person could devote more time to religious study. In church or other assemblies, women and girls sat on one side, men and boys on the other.

Farming was the main enterprise on the colonies' 25,000 acre holdings. Manufacture of woolen goods was also a major enterprise and fine furniture was manufactured. Oxen furnished the power for farming for many years.

A grade school education was available to every child, but girls were totally denied high school. Only especially studious boys like Blechschmidt were allowed to go to a high school outside the colonies.

Rudie remembers the communal system well. He tended orchards and worked in potato fields. In the fall he helped husk corn alongside a "teamster." He also helped with livestock. Sheep, beef and dairy cattle, and hogs were all raised.

In his late teens he was chosen by the elders to go to Williamsburg High School.

Helena recalls childhood pleasures such as walking in the woods, picking flowers, fishing, sledding, and skating. At 14 she was assigned to the communal kitchens. The girls took turns cooking, dishwashing, and washing tables. She also remembers endless sermonettes by the elders and how hard it was to stay quiet.

Asked how they felt about the change from communal life, Helena and Rudie both welcomed it.

Both marvel at the progress from ox cart to the modern Amana Refrigeration plant.

Asked about World Ag Expo both are hopeful it will be a success.

PEARSON RECALLS A HALF CENTURY
OF PLOWING MATCHES
August 9, 1988

The World Ag Expo, in which I was deeply involved because of my experience with plowing contests and my acquaintanceship with champion plowmen from all over the world, prompted a column on U.S. plowing match history. Chosen to discuss this was 75-year-old "Bill" Pearson, who had used four Percherons on a gang plow to score winnings in the first National in 1939, and came back 40 years later to become a tractor plow class winner.

Well over 100 plowmen, including national champions from 26 countries, will be seen in action at the state, national, and world contests to be held during the World Ag Expo at Amana, Iowa, Sept. 7-10. Among them will be William Pearson of Mitchellville, now nearing his 75th birthday.

Not only is Bill, as he is known to all, the oldest contestant, but he is also one of the most popular. He will be competing in the state match Wednesday, Sept. 7, and there is little doubt he will be the sentimental favorite.

For Bill Pearson it all started back in 1939, when the nation's first interstate contest was held near Mitchellville. Not only was he a competitor himself but two of his grandfathers were also in the contest. Interestingly, one of them, 83-year-old W. W. Pearson, who placed second in the 1939 walking plow match, had broken the prairie sod in that same field more than a half century before. Colonel Stark, 78, one of Bill's maternal grandparents, also placed.

Meanwhile, Bill himself, then a Percheron breeder, put four of his best "blacks" on his sulky plow to place 5th in the horse-drawn section of the matches, and found himself hooked.

As the years unfolded the 5 ft. 7 in. Bill Pearson became a stalwart worker and competitor. Although a busy farmer, he was always ready to help. In 1949, in the national near Runnells, he rode a horse all day on traffic control, while his wife, Ruth, baked 149 pies for the food tents. In 1956, near Colfax, with President Eisenhower and Sen. Stevenson making their presidential pitches, Bill again was a mounted traffic "cop."

Subsequently, he was elected to the Iowa Plowmen's board of directors, and, along with his wife, took on numerous major committee responsibilities. After participation in several state contests, he has served as a judge in national contests held in recent years, and he was involved in the 1986 World Matches in Canada.

Bill Pearson, plowing match competitor 1939-1992.

In 1979 it was Bill's "Big Year." The national matches returned to Iowa that year and were held in Marshall county. It was just 40 years after Pearson had competed in the horse-drawn matches at Mitchellville.

By now his Percherons were gone so Bill entered the tractor class, placing third in exceedingly tough competition.

Looking back over a half century of farming on his own, Bill is proud to be the third generation of Pearsons on a Century Farm established by his grandfather 107 years ago.

Asked his assessment of moldboard plows and plowing matches, Bill replies, "Plowing matches are exciting and fun, and although the moldboard plow has been bad-mouthed a lot, there is still a place for it on many farms."

MASTER FARM HOMEMAKERS
September 13, 1988

Once our World Ag Expo responsibilities were over, it seemed good to get back to normalcy. Master Homemakers have always had a high priority in my book, so for this column I featured Mrs. Lorene Robie, recipient of the high recognition in 1958. I invite you to read her interesting story.

Now that the World Ag Expo, with its World Plowing Championship and other exciting attractions, is history, and the 1988 Farm Progress Show at West Brooklyn, Ill., is still 2 weeks away, we can settle down to some matters of the moment.

The effects of the drouth, adjusting livestock programs, and that quadrennial American circus, the presidential campaign, come to mind.

We can also reflect on this year's Iowa State Fair results, and on the recent honoring of the WALLACES FARMER sponsored Iowa Master Farm Homemakers.

Lorene Robie

Not only are congratulations due the 1988 honorees, but also all the other 238 Master Farm Homemakers honored in the past.

Among that illustrious group is Lorene Robie of Clarion, wife of Floyd Robie, her high school sweetheart. She was honored in 1958.

Lorene Bell gained her homemaking experience early on. Oldest of six children, she was only 16 when her mother died. She sacrificed one day of high school a week to do the washing, ironing, cleaning, canning, cooking, etc. She also was in school plays, chorus, varsity basketball, and she became county 4-H vice president.

After graduation she taught all eight grades in a one room country school for several years, for $65 a month, and continued teaching after she and Floyd were married in 1934.

A busy farm wife for more than 50 years, mother of three, grandmother of 11, she is a dedicated community worker.

In 1939 the Robies were one of three out of 250 Wright county couples to receive a Tenant Purchase Loan.

Recalling "The Way It Was" back then, the Robies say that of the maximum allowable $12,000 loan, they spent $8100 to purchase 90 acres of land, $1000 more on a barn, hog pen, and chicken house, and another $600 to make home improvements. Even so, there was no plumbing, running water, or electricity.

The first of three daughters, Beth, now Mrs. William Wunder, was born in 1938. Later, after moving to their tenant purchase home, Mary, now Mrs. Roger Kallem, and JoAnne, now Mrs. Robert Olson, arrived. Mary and her family now live on the farm acquired through the Tenant Purchase Program.

Soon Lorene found herself leader of the Dayton Dandies 4-H Club. Then the county 4-H committee called, as did the Wright County Rural Women's Chorus. the Drama Club, the Presbyterian church, the UPW Association, the Farm Bureau, and other organizations. She answered every call, but her family always received priority.

Lorene is also chairperson of a schoolhouse museum, the building in which the late O.H. Benson, former Wright county superintendent of schools, is credited with coining the 4-H emblem.

Another project is family genealogy. She has carefully researched family histories and painstakingly duplicated them so that every Robie and Bell family member has access to a copy.

Regarding the 1958 Master Farm Homemaker award, Lorene, a former secretary and treasurer of the Master Farm Homemakers Guild, says, "I was both surprised and humble. I know I am really only a representative of thousands of other homemakers who have done their utmost for their families and communities." She adds, "And I also know there can be no Master Farm Homemaker without a loving and supporting husband and children."

FARM SAFETY LEADERS HELP SAVE LIVES
October 11, 1988

Mrs Clarence Miller, farm and home safety leader.

In farm circles, there is nothing more important than farm safety. Two leaders in this worthy program include Mrs. Clarence Miller, Story City farm wife, and Dr. Dale Hull, ISU Agricultural Engineer. This article touched on some of their many contributions.

With the corn and soybean harvest season in full swing, farm safety should be uppermost in everyone's mind. Caution may be even more important this year because of the drouth. Poor crops will create unusual and perhaps stressful conditions.

Looking back over the years, records show few farm families have escaped the trauma of some family member or neighbor being involved in an accident.

For years little was done to prevent accidents, but in 1943 a small group of editors, weary of having to report tragedy caused by farm accidents, formed a farm safety committee, now recognized statewide as the Iowa Farm Safety Council.

Within a few years the council had convinced Iowa State University to add Norval Wardle, a farm safety engineer, to the staff. Under Wardle's leadership, studies were made relating to many farm accidents including harvest time injuries and deaths, slow moving vehicle dangers, proper warning devices, silage gas dangers, first aid on farms, rural fire prevention, etc.

In time several safety committees were organized. Chairpersons were carefully chosen. Many safety workers served tirelessly, but two names stand out. They are Dale Hull, of Ames, former ISU extension farm safety specialist, and Mrs. Clarence Miller, a Story City farmwife.

Both have been members of the council since its inception, and continue their interest in farm and home safety today. Mrs. Miller, 75, has been especially active in the home safety committee and in promoting safety through 4-H. She is a strong supporter of safety workshops. She continually stresses care, capability, and correct approach to safety.

Hull, 76, is the personification of farm safety. One of his most vivid recollections is working out safety rules for the WMT National Mechanical Corn Husking Matches, as well as the WHO Plowing Contests.

Hull was also a pioneer in developing portable corrals for cattle, tractor driver training programs, establishment of safety awards, plowing match rules, soil conservation techniques, and fire prevention work. His major contribution, however, probably would be his work with Rollover Protective Structures (ROPS), whereby uncounted lives have been saved.

Both Mrs. Miller and Hull are pleased with the progress made in the realm of farm safety the past 45 years. Hull says, "When I first started holding safety meetings, there were bound to be several persons present wearing artificial limbs, the result of a farm accident. Thank God, that's less true today."

Dale Hull, Iowa Ag Engineer and farm safety specialist.

SHE HAS VOTED IN EVERY ELECTION SINCE 1920
November 6, 1988

There is probably no one with a better voting record than 100-year-old Helen Schooler of Carlisle, Iowa. On November 8, 1988, she cast a presidential election ballot for the 18th time. It would have been an even more impressive record if Women's Suffrage had been enacted earlier.

An estimated one hundred million Americans are expected to cast their ballot for president before the polls close Tuesday evening, Nov. 8. One of the most enthusiastic of all of them will be 100-year-old Helen Schooler of Carlisle. Moreover, when she exercises her right of franchise, she will be one of a very few to set a unique record in the history of American elections.

When Schooler pulls that lever in the 1988 general election, It will mark the 18th time she has voted for a president of the US. "It would have been my 20th time if I could have had my way," says the Warren county centenarian. "But remember the Women's Suffrage Act was not passed until 1919. Thus, there was no way I, or any other woman, could cast a ballot until 1920."

Not only has Schooler voted in every presidential election since women received the right to vote. She has also voted in every state election held the past 68 years. What's more, she has also cast her ballot in virtually every primary election, as well as in county and municipal elections. It's estimated she has cast her vote as many as 100 or more times.

"Voting is a privilege," Schooler asserts emphatically. "It's what America is all about."

Born Helen Sheiberger on a farm in Page county In 1888, she studied to be a teacher and in 1909 moved to Warren county to teach the upper four grades in the Scotch Ridge country school. Her salary was $40 a month plus board and room on a nearby farm.

Scheiberger's teaching career was short-lived, however. Soon after she came to Warren county, a handsome young Scotch Ridge area farmer took special note of the pretty new schoolmarm. Soon he was courting her. Romance quickly turned to serious future plans, and by the next year it was wedding bells ringing instead of school bells.

"I traded the books and blackboard for cooking, sewing, making butter, raising chickens and then children, and helping my young husband," says Schooler.

Two daughters were welcomed into the Schooler farm home. One is Mrs. Louise Johnson of Carlisle, who keeps a close eye on her mother. The other is Mrs. Eleanor Reynolds of Estherville.

The couple farmed until Arthur died in 1949. Originally 120 acres when established by Peter Schooler, a Scottish immigrant in 1882, the farm now totals 355 acres and is one of Iowa's Century Farms. Schooler continues to take an active interest in the farm, and has high praise for her tenants, Mr. and Mrs. Jim Penick. She also proudly reports her 1988 corn will average over 130 bu., asserting, "That's not bad for a drouth year."

100-year-old Helen Schooler.

Schooler says the 1934 and 1936 drouths were much worse than the drouth of '88. "Chinch bugs and other insects struck hard," she opines, "and there was no drouth insurance or government help to bail us out." She recalls trading eggs for groceries, planting a large garden, canning countless quarts of vegetables and fruits, and serving dinners to hungry threshermen.

Although away from the farm many years, Mrs. Schooler is still an avid gardener. She raises more than she needs for herself, so gives a lot to the Carlisle Care Center.

Although marking her 100th birthday last January, Shooler still cooks her own meals and cares for her own tidy, ranch style house, garden, and flowers. She is proud of her three grandchildren and three great-grandchildren.

Asked about her recipe for longevity, Mrs. Schooler has a brief, authoritative reply: "Just work hard and don't ever stop working," she concludes.

As for the '88 presidential candidates, Schooler is not enthusiastic. She says presidential candidates and political parties have changed greatly in recent years. "They make all kinds of promises, then wait for Congress to tell them what to do," she adds.

CHRISTMAS REUNIONS OUTGREW FARM HOME
December, 1988

Christmas reunions for the Ober Anderson family of Winnebago County have always been special. By 1988, the family included 10 children and their spouses, 28 grandchildren and 7 great-grandchildren. As time went on, there wasn't room for everyone in the farm house. That the Anderson's have been a most fortunate family is seen in the fact that by 1988 not a single death had occurred in more than 50 years.

Christmas is a time of joy and family togetherness. Gift giving—and receiving—may be the big thing for children and grandchildren, but for adults, the family reunion gets top priority.

Few Christmastime family gatherings can surpass the Ober Anderson family reunions in Winnebago county. At first it was Ober, now 86, and Myrtle, 81, and their children, eventually numbering ten, who celebrated Christmas together. Spouses were added, then grandchildren, and more recently, great-grandchildren.

For many years the Christmas gatherings were in the cozy, but small, farmhouse near Thompson. However, as time went on, the farmhouse living room seemed to get even smaller and the Christmas dining area larger and larger.

By 1977, when the Andersons observed their 50th wedding anniversary, 50 family members assembled and the celebration had to be moved to Bethany Lutheran Church in Thompson where neighbors and friends could join in the festivities. Today, 10 children and their spouses, 28 grandchildren, and 7 great-grandchildren make up the family circle.

Few families have been as fortunate as the Andersons. Except for the loss of one child in infancy many years ago, there has not been a single death or serious mishap in the family in more than 50 years. "We are most fortunate," says Myrtle, "especially when we think of some of the boys who went to war."

Mrs. Anderson has no problem ticking off the children's names in the order of their arrival. Elois, now Mrs. Arvin Qualley of near Lake Mills, is the oldest, followed by Orvis, of Austin, Minn.; Duane, Enid, Okla.; Norma, now Mrs. Roger Thompson, Lake Mills; Ober J., Ankeny; Leona, now Mrs. Robert Lacroix, Monument, Colo.; Donovan, Aurora, Colo.; Marlene, now Mrs. Ray McLaurin, Vicksburg, Miss.; Lynn, Castle Rock, Colo.; and Gary, Victoria, Tex. All 10 graduated from Thompson High School. Several graduated from college.

Mrs. Anderson has kept a complete record of every year's Christmas reunion highlights. Listed are the dates of the various family members' arrivals for the holidays, how many assembled, what activities were involved, what gifts were given, major highlights noted, when departures took place, etc.

War service and overseas teaching assignments sometimes precluded some from being home for Christmas. In those instances tape recordings from and to the absent ones helped fill the void, with everyone, including grandchildren, taking part.

Gift exchanges were always a highlight, but sometimes the presents were homemade. During the Depression, Myrtle's sewing machine seldom stopped running. Attractive dresses were made from feed sacks for the girls. Stocking caps were knitted for the boys. Ober's worn out, well-laundered socks became monkeys and other animal toys. Doll dresses were sewn for the little girls. Bathrobes pillows, rugs, doilies, and other items were made. A grab bag was fllled. Monetary gifts, however, were limited to $ 1.

The Ober Andersons, parents of children in leadership.

Ober remembers that there was one Christmas when Myrtle was not up to making something for everyone.

"Times were difficult that year," he says, "but we just couldn't disappoint the kids at Christmas. I went to the store and bought small gifts on credit and paid it back that spring."

Ober and Myrtle Anderson are also well versed on "The Way It Was" in years gone by.

First they rented, did all farm work with horses, fed cattle bought for 1½¢/lb., traded eggs for groceries, helped break broncos to work, fed hogs and sheep as well as cattle, and eventually, in 1943, bought 160 acres near Thompson for $110/acre. They still own that farm.

They have been active in the Lutheran Church ever since their marriage 61 years ago, with Myrtle serving as Ladies Aid president and circle leader. Ober, meanwhile, was on the school board a long time, was a corn sealer in AAA days, and was Winnebago county ASCS committee chairman several years.

Though no longer able to have the whole family home for Christmas, the Andersons' greatest joy now is to have children, grandchildren, and great-grandchildren, now scattered throughout the US, drop in for a visit anytime of the year.

The way it was . . .
1989

IOWA'S SMALLEST BANK ONE OF NATION'S SAFEST
January 10, 1989

Fear of bank closings is a universal concern among savers, but not for patrons of Iowa's smallest bank. It's the Lucas Farmers and Miners Savings Bank which was 100 years old in 1988, and where 88 year old Gerald Baker was the third generation of a conservative banking family to head the institution. Incidentally, their largest loan loss ever was $20.

The Farmers and Miners State Bank at Lucas, Iowa, may not have an impressive building by most banking standards. It has no new furniture. Files are old and its safe is an antique. Total assets are listed at less than $3.5 million. However, when it comes to solvency and security, Gerald, "Jerry" Baker, the bank's 88-year-old president and cashier, his two employees, and his several hundred depositors can all smile confidently.

In the face of recent farm crises, and predictions of more bank failures ahead, Baker says, "Tell everyone that if there's a single customer of the bank the least bit nervous about his savings, I wish he or she would come right in so I can give him his money."

That Baker's stewardship of the millions of dollars in his care has been the best is attributed to the conservative manner in which loans were made during the 1970s land boom. While many other bank officers were eagerly lending big bucks at high interest, Baker kept saying, "Land prices are too high. There's no way crop yields will pay the interest on $3000 to $4000/acre land." So certain was he that land values would eventually tumble, as they did in the 1920s and '30s, that he declined to make any farm or real estate loans.

A tireless and dedicated bank official, Baker works 6 days a week In the small brick building next to an abandoned tavern. He dresses neatly, is always clean shaven, knows every customer personally, and has a warm smile and friendly word for everyone.

Baker is the third generation to operate the bank. His recollections of "The Way It Was" are interesting. He tells how his grandfather, J. Clark Baker, bought the bank from the Mallory family in 1886 when coal mining was a major industry in the Lucas area.

"He paid $100 for the bank and all he needed was a safe," says Jerry. Nevertheless, 10 depositors started savings accounts totalling $2289.45 the first day. Deposits that first year totalled over $21,000.

After the elder Baker's death, his son, Norman, took over and conservative policies continued to prevail. Norman Baker's biggest loan was $500. Virtually every loan was well secured, but Jerry tells of one his father made that turned sour. "It was for $20, and the borrower mortgaged three hogs. However, one was sold to buy feed for the other two. Then one of them died and the other was butchered for winter meat. The result was the $20 loan was never repaid."

In 1922 Jerry Baker joined the firm. "It was on-the-job training," says the bank president, who soon installed a Burroughs bookkeeping machine to replace the hand-written ledgers.

Following up on the policies of his father and grandfather, Jerry says, "No promise was ever broken." He declined to lend on homes because he never wanted to foreclose on a family. He never solicited loans and repeatedly urged customers "not to borrow if they could get along without it."

VETERAN SEEDS MAN RECALLS WALLACE'S ADVICE
February 14, 1989

How Wallaces Farmer *editor, Henry A. Wallace influenced his life is the dramatic story Carl Blom told me one winter day in Newton. The meeting with the future Secretary of Agriculture and U.S. Vice President took place at a corn show; and, as the column recalls, made quite a difference for the Bloms.*

One of Iowa's pioneer corn breeders, 80-year-old Carl Blom of Newton, vividly recalls meeting Henry A. Wallace at a Sigourney corn show in the early 1930s—and the impact it had on his future.

"It was while he was editor of *WALLACES FARMER* and shortly before he became U.S. Secretary of Agriculture," says Blom. "H.A.," as he was best known, was judging the show." My brother, Everett, and I had gone over several thousand ears of our Black's Improved Yellow Dent to enter samples in the 30, 10, and single ear classes. It was beautiful corn and we were delighted to see Wallace place our entries so high. Then he came over to me and asked, 'Young man, is this your corn?' and then praised us on our samples."

During the visit the famed editor spoke enthusiastically about hybrid corn, which was then still a novelty.

Blom adds, "Wallace went on to say hybrids were the biggest improvement ever achieved in the history of corn production, citing Lester Pfister who had made a million dollars developing inbreds. Then, when he asked if we might be interested in growing hybrids, I eagerly responded. He explained how to get inbreds from experiment stations to make the single and double crosses."

The Newton octogenarian delights in recalling how the man who eventually became vice president of the U.S. inspired him to go into hybrid seed production.

Mr. & Mrs. Carl Blom at home in Newton.

In recalling "The Way It Was" in his boyhood, Blom first speaks of his father. "He was the 13th child in a Holland family, and an immigrant who became a Keokuk county farmer and producer of open pollinated seed corn."

"While husking we put the best looking ears in a box on the side of the bangboard wagon, placed them in twin hangers or Korn King wire racks to dry, then rag doll tested for germination, tip, butt, shell, and graded the best and sold the seed for $2/bu," he adds.

Once in the seed business themselves, the Blom brothers quickly learned the merits of various inbreds. Among those he remembers best was a Pfister inbred for which he paid $2/lb.

In 1936 Carl married Lois Abram, the pretty girl he met at the Union Chapel church near Delta. Lois laughs when asked about their honeymoon. "We spent it shelling and grading seed corn," she replies.

The young couple worked from daylight till dark. He was in the fields, in the seed house, and at chores. She was caring for their three young sons, raising 1000 chickens annually, tending large gardens, and providing meals for the family and hired help.

As time went on the Blom brothers seed firm purchased certified single cross seed stock from the Iowa State College Experiment Station, and from Black's, Holden's, MiddleKoop's, and other leading seed specialists.

Buying rundown farms, improving them, and selling them became his favorite hobby. All told 15 were purchased, including the River View Farm of 1476 acres that he later sold to the state as a prison farm. He still owns three and says, "If Lois would let me I'd buy and improve some more."

The Bloms now enjoy four grandchildren, have been active in their church, on school boards, and are 50-year members of the Farm Bureau. They enjoy traveling and have retired to a beautiful ranchstyle home in Newton. Carl continues to pursue his farming interests.

FRANKLIN COUNTY
CHEESE AND CRACKERS CLUB
March 14, 1989

"Cheese and Crackers" is the name of a Franklin County club. One day, founding members Willard Latham, Verald Brown, and Clarence Thompson invited me to sample cheese, crackers and other goodies Evy Latham set out, and to learn about the club. This report tells about the club's interesting beginning 50 years ago, its fraternal connection, and a half century of lively discussions.

Compared to hors d'oeuvres or caviar, cheese and crackers may not sound exotic, but to a group of Franklin county farmers and agribusiness leaders it has special appeal.

It was some 50 years ago when some of the late V.B. Hamilton's "boys" decided to meet occasionally to recall Hamilton's 4-H judging team coaching achievements and his wide-ranging philosophical pronouncements.

Willard Latham, 76, widely known Alexander, Iowa seedsman, was first to host the group.

We all respected 'Ham' for his teachings, coaching, and inspiration. He was a great leader, not only as county agent, but also of our 4-H programs, as

Willard Latham, farm seed specialist.

Iowa Farm Bureau secretary. Farmer's Hybrid Company president. and a member of the Board of Regents," says Latham.

Others attending that first meeting in 1940 were the late J.S. Van Wert, farmer and hybrid seed producer; Verald Brown, purebred hog breeder; Ted Dohrman, farmer; Ted's brother, Ben, now deceased; A.J. Markam, farmer, also deceased; and Clarence Thompson, farm manager.

Hamilton himself was made an honorary member early on and attended many meetings until his death in 1978.

As time went on, more and more of Hamilton's admirers joined the group, which continues to meet several times a year. Wives join in and serve as hostesses. Children are also invited. "At times it gets pretty lively and noisy," says Latham.

All told, more than 50 have become eligible for membership. Many are former members of Hamilton's 22 state, national, and international livestock, dairy, and crops judging teams. All are also members of Alpha Gamma Rho (AGR) fraternity at Ames, where Hamilton was an early leader.

In speaking of the fraternal connection, Brown jokes "Ham" always took his teams for workouts at ISU. "None of us had money for hotel rooms so he put us up in his fraternity dormitory. We thought it was a hotel. Anyway, our coach never told us about other fraternities so when it was time for college, we all pledged AGR."

At their first gatherings Evy Latham and other hostesses put on big spreads. The members soon decided their wives were going to too much trouble so they voted to have only cheese and crackers—thus the name "Cheese and Crackers Club." Over the years a great many varieties of cheese and brands of crackers and other goodies have shown up.

Close to 30 of the members, mostly farmers, still live in Franklin county. Those living elsewhere in Iowa or out of state are not forgotten in meeting discussions. Sons and grandsons of the early members now outnumber the founders.

Verald Brown, purebreed hog breeder.

All agree the club helps relive the pleasure of college fun and accomplishments.

Ted Dohrman, 81, says, "'Cheese and Crackers' has been a means of retaining close contact with many Franklin county ISU alums." Clarence Thompson, now the oldest member at 83. says, "Over the years our meetings are always happily anticipated and fun." Jay Van Wert, son of one of the founders and father of one of the younger members, reports, "We often discuss markets and try to guess where prices will be a year ahead."

"It makes for really close fellowship," opines Latham.

"The club is a meaningful extension of happy years at the university and enables us to settle the problems of the world in general, and those in agriculture in particular," concludes Verald Brown, 75.

The club expects to have the largest of all county delegations at AGR's 75th anniversary celebration in Ames, April 7-9. "We'll show them what brotherhood is all about," says Latham.

THOUGHTS FROM THE GOVERNOR'S GRANDMOTHER
April 11, 1989

Virtually every Iowan knows about their Governor's activities and accomplishments. However, not everyone knows about Terry Branstad's capable parents and dynamic grandmother, Hazel, who was 91 when I met her. It didn't take long to realize where some of the Governor's leadership and resilience came from as she told about a deadly avalanche in Norway and the resultant family move to Iowa. This column is replete with Grandma Branstad's fascinating story.

With Iowa's legislature now past its midway mark, Gov. Branstad is busier than ever signing or vetoing bills, promoting foreign sales of Iowa farm products, and sparring with the Democrats.

All Iowans are interested in the governor's decisions, but no one is watching his every move more closely than charming, 91-year-old Lake Mills resident Hazel Branstad, his grandmother.

"He loves his politics, but it's a hard job. I feel sorry for him and pray for him all the time," says Mrs. Branstad.

Hazel Branstad is a remarkable person in her own right. Still active in her church, she visits daily, and helps friends in the Lake Mills Care Center. She also vividly recalls "The Way It Was" while she was a farm homemaker, and loves to reminisce about five generations of Branstads.

"They originally were farmers in Norway," she relates, and adds, "but their land was poor and mountainous. Then one bitterly cold day when some of them were milking, an avalanche struck, killing six persons working in the barn." It was then the governor's great-great-grandmother told the remaining family members, "There is no future for my sons in Norway. We will go to America."

With Andrew, the governor's great-grandfather, in charge, the family set forth on the torturous 6 week crossing of the Atlantic. "And they had to take along their own food supplies," says Hazel.

After reaching Winnebago county, Andrew and his wife, Dorte, bought a farm south of Leland for $3.50/acre .

Highly religious, the family held church services in their farm home until the governor's great-grandmother decided it was time for Leland to have a church. The Branstad family offered to pay half the costs. Others quickly agreed to pay the rest and Leland soon had a Lutheran church

Andrew later paid $ 12.50/ acre for 160 acres 5 miles north of Forest City. This is now a Century farm, operated by Monte Branstad, the governor's younger brother, where four generations of Branstads, including the governor, were born.

Two of Andrew and Dorte's sons, Hilmer and Karl, rented the farm in 1916. This was farmed with horses until a steelwheeled Farmall was bought in 1939.

Her husband, Hilmer, in addition to farming, became a community leader, serving as president of the local bank, farm co-op, church board, creamery, and the school Hazel Branstad of Lake Mills, grandmother of the governor, likes to reminisce about five generations of Branstads. She stands between the governor's parents, Mr. and Mrs. Edward Branstad.

Mrs. Hazel Branstad, grandmother of Iowa's Governor.

Hazel, whose maiden name was Peterson, married Karl in 1917, only to lose her new husband in the 1918 flu epidemic. A year later, she married Hilmer, and they eventually bought the farm and lived there until 1946.

Four children blessed this union — Karl, Helene, Edward, and Hubert. In 1946, Edward married Rita Garland of Forest City, and they then took over the farm where Terry, now the governor, and Monte, now the farm's operator, were raised.

In recalling her own 30 years on the farm, Hazel tells about carrying pails of water to her large flock of chickens, milking by hand, husking corn, watering and feeding hogs and cattle, and welcoming rural electrification.

Leadership seems to be an inborn trait in the Branstad family. Following in Hilmer's footsteps, Edward has also served his community well, including many years as an ASCS office manager and on farm co-op and other boards.

Regarding the governor, grandmother Hazel proudly states, "He was always a worker and a good boy, often reading the Bible." She points out Terry's interest in politics started in the eighth grade and increased during high school and college. "He always enjoyed talking politics with older people; and when he came back from service, he went to college at Drake so he could be near the Legislature," she remembers.

BOOK WRITTEN FROM MOTHER'S FARM JOURNALS
May, 1989

One of ten children deeply devoted to their mother, Edith Zobrist is an attractive farm homemaker and enthusiastic 4-H booster who refused to let a severe illness stop her. While suffering from, and overcoming, cancer, she wrote a book based on daily journals kept by her mother, a pioneer homemaker. Entitled "Home Life On The Prairie", the book is briefly summarized in this column.

Whether the carnation worn that day was white or red, Mother's Day had a special meaning to all of us.

A Dallas county homemaker, Edith Zobrist, puts it this way. "Because my mother influenced my life so greatly, both while she lived, and to this day, I have come to realize the power of a mother's love is eternal." And Zobrist had good reason to rejoice at last month's observance. She has overcome a debilitating illness. Her husband's health is improved. The three grandchildren are all "doing fine," and a book she has written about farm life in the early 1900s has been published and acclaimed.

Entitled *Home Life on the Prairie,* it's essentially a family history, based on entries in journals kept by Edith's mother, Manchia Miller Blood, mother of 10. It's 181 pages and 196 pictures, along with diagrams and maps, graphically portray the trials and triumphs of farm life, and "The Way It Was" on Minnesota and Iowa farms soon after the turn of the century.

Zobrist says the journals used for the daily diary entries date back to 1902, when Ira and Manchia Blood and three small daughters set forth from Runnells, Iowa, by covered wagon to the farm they would homestead near Wheaton, Minn., 500 miles away. Edith found journals after her mother's death.

The journals tell of good times and bad as experienced by the family and their neighbors. Not included, however, is the tragic period reported in the book by Edith when Ira Blood lost both his wife, and his farm, in one week.

Zobrist, who wrote much of the book when she was very ill, credits her husband, Herman, along with her son-in-law and daughter, Mr. and Mrs. Robert Kelley, with much help and encouragement.

Edith does her writing in a remodeled attic room she calls her "Sky Lab," and where another book is now being contemplated.

Mrs. Edith Zobrist, lifelong 4-H enthusiast.

Pictures of her daughter, Suzanne, and son, Dale, and the grandchildren — Leanne, Kevin, and Ryan—adorn the walls.

Gazing out of the window at the pastoral scenes outside, the Dallas county homemaker concludes, "I'm grateful to God for growing up in a large family, and for the joy of living in the country most of my life—a privilege I treasure to this day."

MASTER FARMERS CONTRIBUTE TO 4-H
June, 1989

Master Farmers are regularly associated with 4-H and other worthy projects. Dozens listed in this column have contributed generously to the Iowa 4-H Foundation. Three, along with their wives, have donated $1000 each. They are Wayne and Margaret Northey, Joe and Duffy Lyon, and Howard and Lois Hill, who all told their reasons for such strong support.

Wayne Northey, farm leader.

Elsewhere in this issue of *WALLACES FARMER*, Melva Berkland has written about the Iowa 4-H Foundation, a privately funded "Investment in Youth" program now in its 40th year.

During the four decades, millions of dollars have been contributed to the foundation by corporations, individuals, banks, and by 4-H members themselves. Included in the list of major donors is a formidable group of Iowa Master Farmers.

Three of them, along with their wives, have contributed $1000 each. They are E. Howard and Lois Hill; Joe and Duffy Lyon; and Wayne and Martha Northey. Twenty-one others have contributed $400 each.

Hill, of Minburn, who was named a Master Farmer in 1946, served as the vice president of the foundation during its first 20 years, and has maintained a continuous interest ever since.

"The 4-H camp has meant a great deal to our family and to me personally. My three daughters and several of their children have spent many happy days in that beautiful setting," says Hill.

Lyon, of Toledo, a Jersey breeder, was named a Master Farmer in 1983. He and his wife, Duffy, widely known as a sculptor of the famous Iowa State Fair butter cows, and now a trustee of the 4-H Foundation, have nine children, all of whom were in 4-H. "The 4-H Foundation is one of the great institutions in Iowa. Our nine children, and my late brother Howard's thirteen, all benefited from 4-H membership. We look upon the

Great grandfather E. Howard Hill with great-grandson Drew Joslin.

State Fair Butter Cow Sculptor, Norma "Duffy" Lyon and husband Joe Lyon, National Dairy Leader.

foundation as a real 'Investment in Youth,'" believes Lyon.

Northey, of Spirit Lake, was designated a Master Farmer in 1987. His wife, Margaret, is one of Hill's daughters. "The Iowa 4-H Foundation is contributing in a significant way to the future of Iowa by providing growth experiences for many Iowa 4-H'ers. Even with all out great natural resources in Iowa, I'm sure we all agree our youth are our greatest resource," points out Northey.

Other Iowa Master Farmers, all of whom have contributed $400 or more to the foundation, include Leigh Curran, Mason City; Norman Barker, LeMars; Roy Keppy, Davenport; the late Herb Pike, Whiting; Ken Showalter, Hampton; George Busch, Allison; Dale Sorenson, Harlan; Ferris Gray, Bedford; the late Bob Joslin, Clarence; Loren Eddy, Centerville; Richard Kuecker, Algona; James Sage, Waterloo; brothers John and Lawrence Wall, Iowa City; David Williams, Villisca; Allen Korsland, Eagle Grove; the late Howard Lyon, Toledo; Loren Schuett, Holstean; brothers Richard and Wilford Groves, Kamrar and Webster City; Charles Bjustrom, Whittemore; Lloyd Martin, Marion; and Donald Burt, Marshalltown.

Trustees serving the foundation now, in addition to Duffy Lyon, include Loren Kruse, son of Master Farmer Donovan Kruse.

Previously serving as trustees, in addition to Hill, are Leigh Curran and Norman Barker, as well as Ferris Gray's wife, Patsy, and David Williams' brother, Don.

Florene Swanson of Galt, executive director of the Iowa 4-H Foundation, says the 4-H 400 Donor Plan is the most popular of the various programs for contributing. Payments of $40 annually can be made over a 10-year period. Other donor plans include the 4-H 1000, 4-H 4000, and 4-H 10,000 plans.

Four $10,000 donations are credited to Mr. and Mrs. William Applegate, Waterloo; Larry Dietz, Kansas City; Ronald and Florence Swanson, Galt; and Don and Sheryl Williams, Villisca.

Three $4000 contributions have come from Mr. and Mrs. William Berkland, Ames; Pioneer Hi-Bred International, Inc., Johnston; and Ed and Grace Tubbs, Maquoketa. At last count, some fifty $1000 contributions have been received.

The 4-H 400 Club now includes some 2000 members. Contributions of lesser amounts add hundreds more names to the foundation's supporters.

June 25 has been set as the date of the 40th Anniversary celebration at the 4-H Camp near Madrid. All donors and their families and friends are invited.

BARGER RECALLS 75 YEARS OF EXTENSION WORK
July, 1989

As the U.S. Department of Agriculture marked the 75th anniversary of its Extension Service in 1989, it seemed logical to write about a long-time Extension Service member and leader. To illustrate the best in the nationwide Extension effort, I chose Paul Barger of Blackhawk County. I could not have chosen better.

In this 75th year of the extension service in the U.S., it seems appropriate to recognize one of the thousands of long-time county agents often described as the "front line soldiers of extension programs."

Paul Barger, 88, has not only observed extension efforts throughout all these years, but has also served in county, state, regional, and national extension positions.

On graduation from Iowa State College he found work on an Angus farm in California.

In 1927, Barger returned to Iowa as Madison county agent, and married Mildred Dawny.

He soon set up an extension supervised cow testing association and had all 16 townships organized in Farm Bureau activities with each also boasting a 4-H club. He stressed the cow-calf program, pasture improvement, and hired a home demonstration agent.

Then in 1930 Barger became Black Hawk county's top farm advisor. After serving as Iowa president, the National County Agents' Association tapped him for major committee chairmanships, all of which were handled with distinction. He was named national secretary-treasurer in 1950 and national president in 1963.

The *Waterloo Courier* induced Paul to write a weekly garden column, which he still writes.

He also gave daily reports of farm interest over radio station KWWL. After his retirement from extension in 1966, Paul became a radio and TV farm director.

He continues to thrive on work at the Bargers' "Shangri La" retirement home they built along the Cedar River near La Porte City.

Named "The Trees" the several acre tract called for intense erosion control and unique architecture.

Barger says, "It's unending work, but I regard it as an 'extension' of extension days when every day and 6 evenings a week were devoted to helping farm families." The eminent former county agent concludes, "In these 75 years, extension has made a great contribution to all Americans. I'm glad I was privileged to be a part of that service most of that time."

Paul Barger, National County Agricultural Agents Leader.

TOWN GIRL BECAME A
MASTER FARM HOMEMAKER
September 12, 1989

How a full-fledged city girl who became "terrified" at the thought of becoming a farm wife wound up as a Master Farm Homemaker was the interesting story told in this feature. Mrs. Howard Heffernan told of how her concern turned to delight as she adjusted to life on the farm.

Many of the four Iowa Master Farm Homemakers named last month will tell you of their surprise at being named a member of the select group of Iowa women. However, none could have been more unsuspecting of the high honor than was Mrs. Howard Heffernan when she learned of her selection in 1968.

"I didn't even know there was such a project," says the former Brehmer county homemaker, who now lives in Sioux City. "I was flabbergasted when they told me I had been chosen one of the six to be recognized that year, and I must admit to some tears when I realized the high honor bestowed on me."

Alvesta Davey was a town girl living in Waterloo when she met Howard Heffernan, a John Deere employee, at a church singles group meeting she had helped organize in 1935.

She and Howard married in 1936. Soon after their marriage, Howard expressed the desire to become a farmer, although he had no farming experience. "I didn't know the first thing about farming and was horrified at the prospect of leaving the city," says Alvesta. Nevertheless, she soon found herself on an 80-acre farm helping care for 1000 laying hens, as well as the first two of their five children.

When Howard's father realized his son much preferred raising corn and hogs to repairing tires, he helped the young couple rent a larger farm, get a team of horses, a Fordson tractor, some machinery, and a few sows.

Mrs. Heffernan

Shortly after becoming a full fledged farm wife, Alvesta suddenly found she loved her new role. "In addition to raising the children, Jean, Bill, Karen, Keith, and Ann, I helped Howard in the fields and around the cattle and hogs, including cultivating 70 acres of corn one long day. And that was after I had gotten the youngsters their breakfast and before I attended an 8 p.m. farm meeting that evening," says Mrs. Heffernan. She also remembers often riding her favorite horse to round up the Angus herd.

The Heffernans were pioneers in hog confinement operations and sold some 2000 porkers a year. "We paid back all of the loan and were able to put four of our children through college," she says proudly.

Busy as she was with her family and helping her husband, the Brehmer county homemaker also was remarkably active in community and state service projects. She served her Methodist church in many ways, was president of Brehmer County's Farm Bureau Women, served as a state vice president, was active as a member of the Associated County Women of the World, was on the County Extension Council, and was a 4-H leader many years.

The 1968 Master Farm Homemaker, who is now 78, has not stopped being a community worker. She is a member of a northwest Iowa district Alzheimer's disease board and regularly takes her Sunrise Manor Retirement Center neighbors on drives and out to dinner. And as if that were not enough, a trip to Alaska is also on her 1989 schedule.

Mrs. Heffernan's greatest joy, however, still centers around the children and her nine grandchildren. Daughter Jean is a medical technician. Son Bill is in the University of Missouri Rural Sociology Department and is president of the American Rural Sociology Society. Keith is Gov. Branstad's representative for the National Governor's Association. Karen is on the Sioux City Community College staff and Ann, the youngest, is a computer analyst. "I love to visit them and those nine precious grandchildren," she concludes.

TENANT PURCHASE PIONEERS ON SAME FARM 50 YEARS
November 14, 1989

The desire for farm renters to become land owners is always strong. Thus it was that soon after their marriage and living on a rented farm, David and Grace Williams looked into the Tenant Purchase (TP) program created by President Roosevelt and Secretary of Agriculture Wallace in the 1930s. They applied for, and received, a TP loan. This column told about their experiences and successes.

Thanksgiving is usually a special day in Iowa farm homes. Gratitude for family, good health, and the completion of another harvest are always good reasons for giving thanks. And, for a veteran Henry county farm family, this year's Thanksgiving Day will be special.

David Williams, 91, and his wife, Grace, 85, marked their 65th wedding anniversary this year, and are also celebrating the 50th year of ownership of one of Iowa's first Tenant Purchase farms.

The Tenant Purchase loan program, known as TP, was one of several highly popular federal programs launched by Pres. Franklin Roosevelt on the advice of Henry Wallace, FDR's Secretary of Agriculture, and a former *WALLACES FARMER* editor.

In 1938, David and Grace Williams rented land near Winfield. Anxious to be on their own, they eagerly read about the TP project in *WALLACES FARMER* and *IOWA HOMESTEAD*, as *WALLACES FARMER* was called at the time. "It sounded too good to be true, but we went for it," recalls Dave.

By 1939, nine Iowa counties were in the program directed by the Farm Security Administration (FSA). Plans were made to enroll selected tenants in

21 more counties, including Henry county. David and Grace Williams were among scores of applicants, and to their great joy, were one of the 12 couples chosen.

The farm available to them was 120 acres near Mt. Pleasant. They paid $85/acre, and obtained a 40year loan at 4.3% interest.

Grace was especially pleased because she now had a large, nearly new, frame home for the family, which included a son, Morris, now an X-ray technician at a Washington county hospital, daughters, Leila, Mrs. John Carlo of Ottumwa, and Carol, Mrs. Robert Mills of Cypress, Tex.

In their first year, corn averaged only 45 bu./acre. Hogs were the main enterprise then, but they were determined to increase their income base so a 30-cow dairy herd was established. "That meant we had to work 365 days a year," says David, adding, "and when Morris left for the armed services in World War II, I had to do all that milking alone."

Mr. & Mrs. David Williams, successful tenant purchase pioneers.

The dairy and hog enterprises did well and one year the corn averaged 209 bu./acre. The loan was repaid ahead of time. Dave retired some years ago and started enjoying golf with old-time friends.

All through the years David and Grace have been active in community endeavors. David was on the school board 12 years, including a difficult consolidation period. He was a long-time Farmers Co-op Elevator director, and was president of the county Farmers Union (FU), as well as a delegate to state and FU conventions.

Meanwhile, Grace has busied herself with the children, four grandchildren, two great-grandchildren, and with church activities, the garden and flowers, the chicken flock, and in the home.

Not only are the Williamses one of the first Iowa TP families, but they are among the very few who still live on their TP farm.

FAMILY QUILT A TREASURED CHRISTMAS GIFT
December, 1989

Christmas presents come in all shapes, sizes and forms, but the one Blanche Hildreth, 87, when this was written, received a few years ago was one of the most novel anyone can imagine. It was a quilt made up of 20 blocks from 20 grandchildren, each representing a grandchild's favorite memory of Grandmother. Read on.

Blanche Hildreth, 87, of Rockwell City, vividly recalls past activities and events by way of an unusual Christmas gift she received a few years ago.

The gift is in the form of a handmade quilt portraying a special memory about "Grandma" held by each of her 20 grandchildren, two of whom have

Blanche Hildreth

since been fatally injured in auto mishaps. Centerpiece of the quilt is a large block depicting a family tree. Blanche and her late husband, Carroll, represent the main trunk, with five large branches symbolizing the five Hildreth children and their spouses: Richard and his wife, Ardith; Donald and Dorothy, Eugene and Doris, Noel and Ruth, and Carolyne, the wife of Phil Drennan.

Twigs on the five branches represent the 20 grandchildren, almost all of whom are now married and have children of their own. In fact, Blanche now boasts 34 great grandchildren.

As for the Christmas quilt below, and on each side of the center block are 20 cleverly hand-embroidered blocks, each depicting a special remembrance by each grandchild.

Twin grandsons, Galen and Gilbert Hildreth, chose farming scenes and Christmas candles for their contribution, while Steve Drennan's block shows his favorite breakfast dish at Grandma's — oatmeal and raisins.

Among the granddaughters, Sandy Feld used a 4-H emblem to depict her grandmother's dedication as a 4-H leader. Linda Swedlund's block portrays a sewing machine, and Vicky Roby's block shows a beautiful dress Blanche made.

The pies that Grandma Hildreth baked brought back fond memories to Randy Hildreth and his cousin, Rohn, now deceased, so each of them has a pie on his contribution. Meanwhile, David, the older grandchild, who was also an auto accident victim since the quilt was presented, put milk cans on his block, while Michael Drennan centers on another farm scene showing sheep and a windmill. Craig Hildreth wrote the word "Grandma" with a special memory for each letter.

Cheryl Johnson becomes poetic with one of Blanche's bedtime comments, and Lori Hildreth delineates an Indian costume her grandmother made.

Mrs. Hildreth, artist with quilts.

Tony Hildreth and his cousin, Joy Bell Anderson, will always remember the delicious pancakes Blanche served, so stacks of pancakes enhance their blocks. With the grandsons outnumbering the granddaughters 11 to 9, Dennis Hildreth "rubbed-it-in" by placing a boy's likeness on the quilt.

Debbie O'Toole remembers the wonderful birthday cakes Blanche always baked, so her contribution was the likeness of a birthday cake. Donna Jean Hildreth is the 20th grandchild, so she simply placed the number 20 on her block.

Holidays were always observed at the Hildreth farm so the quilt also has a beautiful cornucopia for Thanksgiving, hearts for Valentine's Day, an Easter breakfast scene, and a ''Christmas is Family'' slogan.

All the designs were carefully planned by the grandchildren themselves. Daughter, Carolyne Drennan, directed the final hand stitching done so immaculately by 15 members of a Manson, Iowa, quilting club.

The way it was . . .
1 9 9 0

FAMILY HISTORY FASCINATES LEW MORRIS
January 9, 1990

Family history can be an intriguing subject and a challenging project. There is probably no one who knew this better than Lewis E. Morris, who had spent many years of researching and recording forebearers on both sides of the Atlantic. This column indicated the magnitude of the undertaking and the result.

Lew Morris researches family history.

Lewis Ecroyd Morris, a Madison county farmer, has a rich agricultural family heritage. His father, Lew Morris, Sr., was named an Iowa Master Farmer, and his mother an Iowa Master Farm Homemaker. Most of his ancestors were of the landed gentry in England or Wales, as far back as the 14th century, or became farmers once they started emigrating to the U.S. in the 1600s. He has records of forebearers dating back to the 1300s, and has become involved in updating the "family tree."

Morris, 75, has taken a keen interest in genealogy for many years and has traced some branches of his own family through 17 generations. He first became involved while a teenager when the Morris family received a letter from a distant relative inquiring about Iowa members of the family.

The fact that his middle name is Ecroyd prompted Morris to work with that maternal side of his father's family first. Thirteen years after he started in 1966, Morris finally had a relatively complete record, dating back to the year 1381 and including more than 4000 names.

In the course of this research he was greatly aided by detailed records kept by forebears in England and Wales. He reports finding 22 different spellings of the name Ecroyd.

Bible records, lengthy letters, diaries, land deeds, maps, financial accounts, and other documents, some dating back 500 or more years, were carefully studied.

A priceless letter, written by his father, before the elder Morris died in 1950, was also of special value.

Similar work was done on the Warner family, also on the maternal side, with records dating back to 1660. A good start has also been made on the Morris paternal side of the family.

Finally, in 1979, Morris was able to complete a 459-page hard-cover book with well over 100 pictures in which 353 family histories are summarized. The book lists 398 surnames and 1435 individuals on the Ecroyd side.

An entire basement room in the Morris farm home near Earlham is literally filled with family and farm records. A hand-painted Ecroyd family crest with three stag heads, an oak wreath, chevrons on a shield, and the words, "In Truth —Victory" is on the wall.

Many farmers in the family owned sizeable tracts of land. Others were gamekeepers, doctors, ministers, lawyers, or owners of pubs or inns. Many were in the military. Still others served in the British government. "You name it, and we have them," says Morris.

Of special interest to many readers is the fact that much of the Living History Farm land in Iowa was originally the Lewis Morris farm.

VETERAN LAWMAKERS EXPRESS THEIR CONCERNS
February, 1990

Three Legislators with years of experience in the Iowa Senate and House of Representatives took time out to tell me their concerns. They were Senator Joe Coleman, a Democrat in his ninth term in the upper chamber; Senator Norm Goodwin, a Republican, oldest of all the lawmakers, and Representative Wendell Pellet, a Republican in his 20th year on Capitol Hill.

Most Iowa Capitol Hill observers expect the 1990 General Assembly to become the preliminary round in the fight for Iowa's governorship. With five Democrats aspiring for Republican Gov. Branstad's job, the predictions for political bloodletting may easily materialize. But there are other questions facing lawmakers that will also demand attention.

Three General Assembly veterans point out that taxes, spending plans school issues, agricultural questions, drugs, teen pregnancies, and other major issues should also be addressed.

Comments on these questions were made by: Sen. Joseph Coleman of Clare, a farmer now in his ninth consecutive term; Sen. Norman Goodwin of Clinton, the oldest of this year's lawmakers; and Rep. Wendell Pellett, now in his 20th consecutive year in the House.

All three agree that the major agricultural issues include a number of livestock questions. Among them are: carcass disposal, contract feeding, the Packers and Stockyard Act, livestock co-ops, taxes on buildings, and renewal of a $350,000 appropriation to the Iowa Extension Service for programs to improve efficiency in livestock production.

Other issues to be dealt with include farm property taxes, agricultural bankruptcy forfeiture, farm safety, soil conservation, mediation services, and a $2 million appropriation to Iowa's Agriculture Experiment Station.

Sen. Coleman, a Democrat, bemoans the drastic increases in state spending. "When I was a freshman here in 1956, we authorized a $ 125 million budget. This year the governor's budget calls for $3 billion plus. That's not good news for taxpayers, and especially property tax payers."

Rep. Pellett, a Republican, is also worried about ever-increasing spending. During his first session, which was in 1970, the budget was $550 million, only about one sixth of what it is today. "The governor's 1990 budget had to be put in two workbooks totalling more than 1200 pages and weighing 5 lb., 9 oz.," he laments.

Three widely known, influential Iowa lawmakers, Norm Goodwin, Coleman, and Wendell Pellet.

Pellett, a farmer, says property taxes will continue to be "astronomical" because every lawmaker has a pet project he feels must be passed, as compared to only major legislation in years past.

Sen. Goodwin, also a Republican, is deeply concerned about the continuing trend toward gambling. "We are fast becoming a leading gambling state, and I do not believe that we can gamble ourselves into prosperity," he asserts. Even though he represents a Mississippi River district, he has had the courage to vigorously oppose riverboat gambling and is convinced most Iowans agree.

THE DELICATE BALANCE
March 13, 1990

The Iowa State Historical Building is one of Iowa's newest and largest attractions. Not only does it house countless historical displays, but it also offers many educational exhibits, including a special 1990 highlight called, "The Delicate Balance." This column explained this fascinating feature.

"Boy, this building would hold a lot of hay!"

That is not an uncommon statement heard when a group of farmers first enter the State Historical Building located just west of Iowa's State Capitol. The spacious building occupies most of an entire city block and has 220,000 sq. ft. of floor space.

Both short-term and permanent exhibits are on the Historical Building schedule. Recently, the Smithsonian's "Pioneer America" display delighted visitors for several months.

On long-term display are pictures of those chosen for the prestigious Iowa Award, including Henry A. Wallace, former editor of *WALLACES FARMER*.

Meanwhile, a permanent exhibit entitled *"The Delicate Balance"* is now the featured attraction. The exhibit is exceedingly timely as it addresses environmental, conservation, and other concerns.

"The Delicate Balance" takes a look at all of Iowa's natural resources, their availability, continuous change, and our own relationship with the environment.

First to catch visitors' attention is an Iowa soil profile that places the state in a geological context, beginning with the Precambrian Era 600 million years ago.

Also of great interest to old and young alike are exhibits relating to prehistoric animals and plants, including a 6 ft. long tusk of an ancient Wooly Mammoth.

Indian life is outlined in a huge showcase with its arrowheads, spears, stone mauls, war clubs, peace pipes, pottery, beaded jackets, feathered headdresses, and deerskin dresses.

Opposite the Indian showcase, modern Iowa history begins to unfold in exhibits and pictures of yokes of oxen on prairie breaker plows. Also highlighted are the old 1860 steamboats and paddle wheels and their landing ports along the Mississippi. Grinding wheat, rye flour, and corn meal is seen In the massive millstones— some of red granite — weighing hundreds of pounds.

Stewardship is heavily emphasized. Exhibits show the bounty of Iowa soil — and the frightening problems caused by its misuse. By turning a large wooden "Dial A Century" knob, visitors note that Iowa's rich top soil averaged 14 in. in depth in 1850, only 8 1/2 in. in 1950, and is down to 7 in. now.

Spotlighted is an article on the cover of the May 9, 1936, *WALLACES FARMER* which points out that Iowa originally had 25% of all the Class A land in the nation. But, 35% of that had already eroded into the Gulf of Mexico.

The editorial appealed for more acres into grassland, improving rotations, and putting a stop to overgrazing. The editorial went on, "Every farmer knows what to do, although it is difficult to shift out of cash crops to grassland."

Soil Conservation Service pictures help tell the grim story of soil loss, and a video presentation further nails down the need to use soil saving practices.

Finally, a living History Farm's quote by Pope John Paul II, made in 1979, underscores the need for better land stewardship. "Conserve this land well, so that your children, and generations after them, will inherit an even richer land than was entrusted to you."

A coal mining shaft showing miners at their dangerous work, and tools of their trade, plus a picture of Ottumwa's famous "Coal Palace" of one hundred years ago, adds to the interest of the exhibit.

The attractions seen at the Historical Building's *"The Delicate Balance"* exhibit are endless. Breaking plows with 10-ft. beams in deep prairie grass, sod huts, log cabins, ox yokes, maple syrup making, swimming suits where no skin is revealed, the wild rose and other state symbols, wagon wheels, appreciation and management of game, harness, stump blowers, perfectly mounted bison, elk, prairie chickens, and wild turkeys common in pioneer times, are a few of the appealing displays.

And, just in case you think minimum-till farming is a new technique, think again. Back in the mid-1800s when the "prairie buster" plow was doing spring plowing, and before the next three furrows were turned, a Moravia, Iowa, grandfather, with the help of a youngster or two, put four kernels of corn a few feet apart at every third furrow slice. Nothing more was done until October when they harvested 30 to 40 bu./acre, and there's an ear of "sod corn" preserved since 1860 in the display to prove the point.

All state historical exhibits are free to the public. The building is open daily except Monday. "The Delicate Balance" will be on permanent display for at least five years.

MANDERS RECALLS MAJOR LEAGUE BASEBALL CAREER
April 10, 1990

Iowa has had its share of Major League Baseball stars, most of whom grew up on a farm and first played "cow pasture" baseball. One of them was Hal Manders, who was signed by the Detroit Tigers shortly after pitching a no-hitter for Iowa "U" against Notre Dame. This column told about Hal's great record with Detroit and his return to the farm.

Hal Manders, major league pitcher, Iowa farmer.

Every spring. when the words "Play Ball" are intoned on the baseball diamonds of America, Harold Manders, retired Dallas county farmer, finds his thoughts quickly turning from corn and beans to our national pastime— and little wonder. Hal, as he is best known, was himself a minor and major league pitcher.

Along with other 10 and 11 year olds, he shagged foul balls at his grandfather's Booneville ball diamond every Sunday afternoon. "We'd get a nickel for every foul ball we could bring in, and that would buy a big bottle of pop," explains the former Detroit Tigers pitching star.

One of the boys joining in the Sunday afternoon fun was Manders' cousin, none other than Bob Feller, of near Van Meter, later to rewrite major league history books as "Rapid Robert," the Cleveland Indians strikeout king.

Hal and Bob were almost inseparable as boys. and they retain that same close relationship to this day.

Moreover, their interest and accomplishments on the ball diamond were closely linked. By the time Hal was 15 and Bob 14 they were on the Oak View team playing with the men. Manders' uncle, William Feller, who was Bob's father, had created a fine diamond on Feller's farm.

The boys helped with the building of the diamond. They cut poles for the backstop from the nearby timber, then bought rolls of chicken wire 150 ft. long and 6 ft. wide to complete the job. When they were finished it was called the Oak View ballfield.

While on the Waukee High School ball team, young Manders was giving fans and teammates a preview of the future when he pitched a no-hitter against Yale. fanning 21 batters in the first seven innings.

L. M. Peet, a Des Moines insurance leader, had formed a Farmers Union team that used the Oak View diamond. The young cousins were soon regulars on that team, and did their share in winning the Iowa Semi-Pro championship.

Hal chose to enroll at the University of Iowa, where he was a standout pitcher, while Bob went directly to the majors even before finishing high school. However. baseball scouts were watching both of the cousins. Soon after pitching a no-hitter against Notre Dame, Hal signed on with the Detroit Tigers.

As is almost always true of newly signed players, Hal soon was sent to Beaumont, Texas, where he won 10 and lost only four games. The next year he went to Evansville, Ind., in the Three I League (Iowa-Illinois-lndiana), where he not only compiled another good record, and was a major factor in Evansville winning the Three I league pennant, but more importantly met his future wife, Marabel Cross.

They were married in 1941, by which time Hal was a regular starter in Detroit. Their son, Bob, now a decorated NASA Space Program aeronautical engineer, was born two years later.

Hal continued pitching for the Tigers through 1942, but was told he would be drafted for WWII service in the early spring of 1943. His draft board ordered him home to the farm near Dallas Center, but did not conscript him. Consequently, he and Marabel farmed with Hal's father in 1943, 1944, and 1945, after which he returned to Detroit in 1946. He pitched there and at Buffalo, where he won 10 and lost only four that season and the next. He also played in the minors at Alexandria, La., where he won 10 and lost three games in 10 weeks. In the Southern League of Knoxville he won more games than all the other pitchers put together.

Hal Manders, former major leaguer, now an Iowa farmer.

All the while Hal and Marabel regarded Adel and Dallas county as their home, and spent the off-season working with his father.

When Hal was 29, and knowing his father's health was failing, he hung up his spikes to become a full time farmer for the next 35 years.

He continued with the Manders' purebred Hampshire hogs, and became a director of the Iowa Hampshire Assn. He also had a cow-calf herd, and raised corn and soybeans.

Following heart by-pass surgery in 1979 Hal and Marabel bought an attractive ranch home in Dallas Center and rented their farm to Dale Meyers.

When asked about the recent standoff between players and owners, Manders says, "It's almost obscene."

As for $3 million-plus salaries some pitchers now receive, Hal says, "They are superstars only because eight other players have hit and fielded well. I never forgot that whatever success I had on the ball diamond was due to the efforts of my teammates."

HAGEN — A LEADING DAIRY PROMOTER
May 8, 1990

Al Hagen evidently was a born leader. He was involved in several careers and made a success of every one. For many years, he was one of the nation's dedicated dairy leaders. Al was one of my closest friends. I shared his interests, reveled in his successes, gloried in his honors, and saluted him in this column.

When Al Hagen, 79. well known former Iowa dairy leader, notes that June Dairy Month is almost upon us, memories of his own involvement in dairy promotion come back clear and strong.

Hagen was raised on a traditional Franklin county family farm and attended Alexander Consolidated School. He now lives in retirement in Colorado.

Livestock on the Hagen farm included 15 shorthorn cows. While sitting on that one legged stool milking those cows some 65 years ago he could not have envisioned the diverse career ahead of him, nor his eventual dedication to dairy promotion.

He enrolled in Iowa State College, and after two years, in the depths of the depression, got a job teaching and coaching at Lanesboro. He finally obtained his degree in Agriculture Education in 1935 and became my closest friend.

Upon graduation he taught Vocational Agriculture at Adams, Minn., where he married Margaret Dunn. On his return from service in WWII, Hagen was named Humboldt county extension director. The Hagen family also included a daughter, Janice, and son, Keith.

Al Hagen in his "view room" in his Colorado "Shangra La."

In the mid-forties the Iowa Dairy Industry Commission was created by the Iowa legislature. Its purpose was to promote dairy foods by way of a two-month checkoff. Iowa's dairy farmers, however, expanded the program with a 10 month voluntary checkoff. This program eventually resulted in the formation of the American Dairy Assn. of Iowa with Hagen in charge.

Now with a state agency and a state organization, both financed by dairy farmers, it was common sense that the two be coordinated into one program. This was accomplished by pooling the checkoff funds into one budget.

Hagen says his dairymen developed the first commodity promotion program in Iowa, and all other commodities have followed suit.

During his 20-year tenure in the realm of dairying, Hagen structured and coordinated various dairy organizations and always made certain that dairy promotion was advancing the dairy producers' cause.

"During the 1960s there was much reorganization among dairy cooperatives. It was time for state promotion programs to adjust accordingly," says Hagen.

Nationally, dairy leaders recognized the need for coordinating dairy promotion — advertising, merchandising, nutrition education, and research, together in one organization. Thus, the United Dairy Industry Assn. was formed. Dairy leaders of Missouri, Iowa, Nebraska, and Kansas then put their programs together into what was called Midland United Dairy Industry Assn., with Hagen named an executive vice-president.

During the two decades he served as a spokesman for dairy promotion, Hagen also had a strong hand in building a new dairy center in Ankeny where many dairy groups now office.

Prior to his 1974 retirement he was the recipient of the Keeting Dairy Leadership Award, and was presented with some of ISU's highest honors, including the Alumni Medal, Distinguished Graduate Award, and the President's Medal. He served as president of the ISU Alumni Assn. and was named Cy's Favorite Alum.

KOOS IS CONSERVATIONIST AND HISTORIAN
June 12, 1990

Soil conservation is one of the most universal necessities and challenges in America. The annual loss of precious top soil is frightening. Ervin Koos had realized this for a long time. This feature told of some of the things he had done in conserving soil at home and over the state, as well as recording Master Farmer history.

Ervin Koos is a dedicated soil conservationist. His interest in conservation began more than 50 years ago when he was renting 320 acres north of Walnut, Iowa. Then, when he bought the 160-acre rundown farm in 1950, where the Kooses now live near Shelby, he immediately began building terraces that could be maintained by the moldboard plow.

At that time he contracted for three-forths of a mile of terraces at 7 cents a running foot. "That was a good time to put in terraces," explains Koos. "Today it would be closer to $1 per foot."

The Pottawattamie County Master Farmer eventually rented 380 additional acres of cropland for his farm.

In the area of conservation, he not only contoured and terraced his fields, but also established wide waterways and put in tile inlets. He now has three miles of terraces on the 160 acres. They are mostly the parallel-seeded, back-slope, type.

Koos' interest in conservation has not been limited to his own farm. He served on the East Pottawattamie County Soils District committee several years before being named chairman. He was also active in the Macedonia watershed movement where all conservation work was done with farmer-owned equipment.

In the early 1970s, Koos became president of the Iowa Association of Soil Conservation District Commissioners and in 1975 was elected to the board of the National Soil and Water Conservation Districts Association.

His record of service also includes 14 years on the Governor's Commission on Conservation of Natural Resources.

Ervin Koos, Master Farmer and historian.

As historian for the Iowa Master Farmer Club, Koos has been especially interested in the club's scholarship program, first mentioned in 1952 with the appointment of a scholarship committee to make recommendations.

The following year the committee recommended raising their annual dues from $2 to $5 per year to provide a scholarship for an Iowa State University student. By 1956, $200 was raised and Louis Thompson, Jr., a journalism student, was named the winner.

Koos' records show that in 1960, the club voted to provide two $200 scholarships working in conjunction with the University's Alumni Achievement Fund. In 1972, *WALLACES FARMER* began matching the club's scholarship gift fund. The amount was raised to $600 per scholarship in 1982.

To date, 60 scholarships have been awarded. Of this total, 55 of them have gone to Iowans, four to out-of-state students, and one to a youth in England. The total amount given toward Master Farmers-*WALLACES FARMER* journalism scholarships now has exceeded $20,000.

Koos and his wife, Iona, have one son, David, of Harlan, Iowa, and two daughters, Kathleen of Walnut, and Karen, of Crafton, Maryland.

CLARION RURAL SCHOOL BIRTHPLACE OF 4-H EMBLEM
July, 1990

The 4-H Emblem is one of the best-known youth emblems in the world. How, where, and when this significant symbol came into being was the interesting subject of this column.

If you are, or ever have been, involved in 4-H programs, or attended a one-room rural school, Clarion, Iowa, has an attraction that will interest you. It's called the 4-H School House Museum, and is the actual birthplace of the 4-H emblem.

The museum is located in Clarion on Highway 3. Fully restored to its original condition with desks, stove, blackboard, school bell, etc., it is filled with 4-H memorabilia dating back to the beginning of the program for farm youths.

Open every afternoon during June, July, and August, it is a paradise of nostalgia for anyone familiar with 4-H and one-room schools. There is no admission charge.

The story about the genesis of the 4-H emblem is both interesting and inspiring.

Early in this century, the exodus of young people from farms was alarming. O.H. Benson, the Wright County superintendent of schools, undertook a survey which revealed 91 percent of the farm boys, and 89 percent of the girls, were planning to leave the land.

Appalled at these findings, Benson established projects and programs designed to dignify farm life. Corn and pig projects were formed for boys. Gardening, baking, canning, and similar projects were formed for the girls. School courses in home economics, agriculture, and manual training were introduced in connection with the junior clubs, Benson used a three-leaf clover emblem as a membership badge.

While making visitations in schools one day in the spring of 1907, Superintendent Benson stopped at Lake Township #6 in Wright County. As he was tying his horse to the hitching post, he noticed the teacher and all her pupils in a nearby clover patch looking for four-leaf clovers.

Still holding a bouquet of four-leaf clovers given him by the youths, Benson told the class about the 4-Square program he was trying to develop through education — a program involving head, hand, heart, and health.

Then, glancing as his clover leaves, he went to the blackboard, took a piece of chalk, and drew a large four-leaf clover. Next, he placed a large letter "H" in each of the four leaves, explaining one "H" was for head, for clearer thinking; another for hands, for larger service; a third for heart, for greater loyalty; and the last for health, for better living.

As the children copied the picture and the lesson about the four H's, Benson suddenly realized that here in a one-room country school, under the leadership of a rural teacher, out of a clover field in full bloom, and from the hands, hearts, and minds of farm girls and boys, the emblem he had been seeking was right there on the school blackboard.

BEE EXHIBIT A STATE FAIR ATTRACTION
August 14, 1990

Most of us give bees a wide berth. About all some people know about bees is that they sting. However, the fact is bees are highly beneficial. Without the cross-pollination done by bees, many crops and fruits could not exist. This column quoted Glen Stanley and other leading apiarist re: the value of bees.

State Fair visitors always find the beekeepers displays on the second floor of Agricultural Hall a most interesting exhibit. In addition to the bottles of pure liquid honey, beeswax, honeycombs, candles, cream honey, other honey products, and recipe books in the exhibit, the sight of live bees working hard under glass "supers" is always a fascinating attraction.

Two men who have had much to do in making the State Fair apiary display so interesting are Glen Stanley, 73, whose beekeeping activities are with his brother Loyd, 74, in Gilbert, and Albert "Andy" Andriano, also 73, of near Cumming. Between the three of them, Glen, Loyd, and Andy boast a heritage of beekeeping that exceeds 250 years.

Andriano tells of his grandfather's work with bees in Italy over 100 years ago. Stanley and his brother are the fourth generation of beekeepers, beginning with their great grandparents' families in England more than 150 years ago.

Andriano, a former State Fair bee exhibit winner, has been raising bees himself for more than 50 years, and now has 30 hives on his own 86-acre farm where he grows soybeans, corn, berries of all kinds, apples, pears, plums, and other fruits, as well as vegetables. In addition to the bees Andy has on his own farm, he has 88 additional colonies of bees on six nearby farm locations. "The bees make a big difference in our farm and fruit crop yields by their work in cross pollination," he says.

Both Stanleys were in the service — Lloyd in the Navy and Glen in the Army in WWII for four years. Following the war the brothers joined their father in the honey producing enterprise at Gilbert, Iowa. Today the Stanley brothers have had as many as 1,300 hives of colonies located on some 30 farms in Story, Hamilton, and Boone counties. Glen recalls one year when the partners produced and processed a quarter million pounds of honey.

In addition to his interest in the Gilbert operation, Glen has served as Iowa Bee Inspector 12 years and as State Apiarist 27 years. During that period he served under seven Iowa Secretaries of Agriculture— Thornburg, Linn, Spry, Liddy, Owen, Lounsberry, and Cochran. This is a claim few, if any, Iowans can match. He also directed the State Fair honey exhibit.

Glen Stanley, Iowa's leading bee expert.

By virtue of his personal and professional experiences, Stanley has become a walking encyclopedia on the nature of bees and their importance in agriculture and to humankind.

He stresses the fact that cross pollination is necessary to produce soybeans, alfalfa, and all other legumes, almost all fruits, as well as melons and flowers, and is largely achieved by honey bees.

Stanley, who was president of America's Bee Inspectors in 1963, says that Iowa's 80,000 or more colonies of bees contribute some $10 million to the state's economy in the form of sales of honey and other products, and employment in the processing of bee products.

"And, the increase in yields of soybeans, fruits, and melons accounts for at least another $20 million," he adds.

The former State Apiarist points out that each of Iowa's 80,000 or more beehives houses about 65,000 bees. Each hive has a single "queen" bee. A hive also houses several thousand drones. These are male bees, a few of which mate with the queen. All the others are female bees, known as "worker" bees, who seek nectar in fruits, flowers, legumes, soybeans, and other plants. By flitting from one plant or flower to another they achieve cross pollination so essential to a final crop.

Worker bees may fly as many as five or six miles seeking nectar, but always return to their own hive. The worker bees work so hard they seldom survive more than six weeks. Thus, the queen bee must lay an average of 2,000 eggs per day in order to maintain the worker bee population.

Stanley says indiscriminant use of pesticides and herbicides can be a death knell for bees. Farmers using dangerous pesticides are urged to notify beekeepers in their area so the bees can be confined briefly, or moved if necessary.

Stanley says the drought of 1988 resulted in one of the best years on record for honey production in Iowa, but that this year, with so much rain, will find the honey harvest much lower. Honey now retails at about $1.50 per pound. Stanley remembers one year when he and his brother loaded an entire rail car with honey destined for Wisconsin, for which they received a paltry $4^1/_2$ cents per pound. John Johnson now directs the State Fair honey exhibit.

AMANA COUPLE MARRIED 70 YEARS INTERESTED IN FARM PROGRESS SHOW
September 11, 1990

The 1990 Farm Progress Show was held in Amana, so it was logical to search out some long-time Amana residents for a column. Mr. and Mrs. Philipp Mittlebach, who had recently celebrated their 70th wedding anniversary, were the ideal guests to tell about the old days in Amana and "The change" in 1932.

When tons of food and thousands of gallons of beverages are dispensed at the 1990 Farm Progress Show near Amana, Iowa, no one will be more interested in the spectacle than Mr. and Mrs. Philipp Mittlebach, a South Amana couple, Philipp, 93, and Clara, 92, recently observed their 70th wedding anniversary.

The Mittlebachs are the oldest couple in Amana and both can vividly recall when they too had a lot to do with large quantities of food. Philipp was a youthful field worker in the old Amana Colonies era, and Clara worked in one of the community kitchens then serving everyone living or working in the colonies at the time.

In recalling his part in food production, Philipp remembers helping plant 10 acres of potatoes by hand. "Someone would plow a furrow, and then we boys planted the potato seed pieces 25 in. apart in the bottom of the furrow. Next, someone would cover the potato pieces with a plow and we would stomp over the loose soil." he says.

Of course there were dozens of other tasks in Amana's fields for boys and young men in the early 1900s. Mittlebach says food production was always paramount. He refers to work in the orchards, plowing fields, planting, hoeing, cultivating and harvesting corn, haying, reaping, shocking, and threshing and hauling grain.

Philipp also recalls some bitterly cold winter days when he helped haul logs over the snow in bobsleds, and later chopped wood for the six community kitchens.

Meanwhile, Clara tells how, at age 14, she and other young girls were put to work in the community kitchens. Along with two other 14 year olds she

Mr. & Mrs. Philipp Mittlebach of South Amana, Iowa, remembers the colonies when they still had communal

learned to cook, can, handle dishes, and properly set tables under the direction of an older woman known as the senior cook.

The clanging of a large dinner bell announced the meals at 6 a.m., 11 a.m., and 6 p.m. Everyone in the colonies ate their breakfast (friestook), lunch (mittag). and supper (abendsfest) in the community kitchens, with the exception of families with small children who would come to the kitchen to procure their food and eat at home.

Menus were anything but fancy and were the same every week. Potatoes were served with every noon and evening meal. Pork, ham and bacon, along with boiled beef, were standard items. Cherries, peaches, and grapes were served in season, as were vegetables. There was never any dessert. Saturday meals were often made up of leftovers.

Forty people could be seated at a time. The men were always served first. Then the children and. finally, the women.

There was no compensation for Amana Colonies labor and services for anyone as long as the communal system prevailed. However, at Christmas time each kitchen worker received a gift of $1.

After their marriage, the Mittlebachs had two children: a son, George. now a member of the Amana Society Board of Directors. and a daughter. Mrs. Lusia Langlas, who lives in nearby Williamsburg. There are three grandchildren.

After his early field work experience, Philipp continued work in the food area as a store clerk. Later, under the tutelage of Heinrich Koch, a German wagonmaster, he became an accomplished wagon maker. At times he was also called upon to make furniture, and frequently, a needed coffin.

Mrs. Mittlebach looks back at "The Change" in 1932, when the Amana Colonies changed to the free enterprise system with "great joy." "We began to live like everyone else then.'' she states.

As time went on Philipp, who had learned to drive, became involved with a Marengo bulk oil plant and for 27 years was a popular oil truck driver.

The Mittlebachs look forward with great anticipation to the Farm Progress Show Sept. 25, 26, and 27, and will look on with awe when the six 1990 model community kitchens (food tents operated by five community church groups and by the Iowa City Chamber of Commerce) dispense their food and drink.

HUSKING CHAMPION CONVERTS CORN TO FUEL
October 9, 1990

Elmer Carlson is a legendary figure in American corn husking circles. I was one of the first to interview him when he won the 1935 state title on my father-in-law's farm near Davenport and again when he won the national match in Indiana. Because I knew him well, it was no surprise to me when he came up with the 1990 idea of converting our huge corn surplus into fuel for autos, tractors and Persian Gulf tanks.

With war clouds hanging heavy over the Persian Gulf, Iowa corn prices hovering around $2 per bu.. and gasoline up near $1.50 per gal. Elmer Carlson, legendary figure in corn husking circles, has pushed aside his husking hook and picked up his pencil to do some figuring. What the 81 year-old former champion has come up with is mind boggling.

Refuting USDA figures which claim use of corn for alcohol is uneconomical, Carlson insists if all our surplus production of corn and other starchy crops were converted into alcohol-based fuels, the price of corn could be increased to more than $3 per bu. Carlson's figures are based on a national yield of 120 bu. per acre and on the statistics the USDA Office of Energy used to assert that it does not pay to convert grain into alcohol.

"We are now importing more than $80 billion worth of fossil fuels, most of it where war now seems imminent," asserts Carlson. "By using our price depressing surplus corn, and other crops, we no longer would be dependent on foreign oil. Income to farmers would significantly increase, subsidies could be reduced, and our national economy could stabilize." he adds.

Elmer Carlson is one of the few surviving national champions of the grueling 80-minute corn husking contests originated in the early 1920s by Henry A. Wallace, then the editor of *WALLACES FARMER*. Carlson became state and national champion in 1935.

Later the Audubon husker was involved in many other enterprises and projects. He originated the Carlson Champion Hybrids seed firm, imported breeding hogs from Europe, was a candidate for Iowa Secretary of Agriculture, once made a run for Congress, went on foreign missions and farmed

While a small boy he started going to the husking field with his father. By the time he was 14 he had his own team and wagon. "Before my 15th birthday, I put 90 bu. against those bangboards in one day," says Carlson.

After a few years Carlson won the county match, and was doing well in the district contest

National champion corn husker, Elmer Carlson.

near Ames. "I had corn running over the sideboards, and thought I'd won, but Henry Wallace was field judge. When he saw I'd left a lot of 'ribbons' on, he

253

checked my deductions carefully and I finished second from the bottom," confesses Carlson.

1935 again found Carlson the county winner, and he set a new Iowa record to win the state contest on the Hahn farm near Davenport, Iowa. He knew he had a good shot at the national title. In Indiana, stripped to the waist, the "Audubon Iowa Flash," as he was being called, husked 41.52 bu. to set a new national record and claim the crown.

Retiring undefeated the next year, Carlson proudly watched his 38-year-old brother, Carl, win the state and then the 1936 national match to gain his own place in husking history.

Carlson continues to live in Audubon. He has two daughters and five grandchildren. He continues to promote ethanol, the "Purple Train," etc.

AABERG HELPED CONQUER ANIMAL DISEASES
November 13, 1990

"The Way It Was" columns often tell of the struggle some people must suffer before they find their place and success in life. Few people could endure as much hardship as the man highlighted in this column — Herman Aaberg, whom some readers will remember as Iowa's Assistant Secretary of Agriculture, and later the American Farm Bureau Livestock and Marketing Director.

Ever since the farm crisis of the early 1980s, the word "survivor" has become a familiar term. This column is about a veteran agricultural leader who not only survived two deadly diseases as a youth, but has also conquered other overwhelming challenges to not only benefit agriculture, but all Americans as well.

He is Herman Aaberg, 88, whose life story began in a small makeshift building on a Nebraska farm. The youngest of 11 children of Norwegian pioneers, he miraculously survived an appendicitis attack as a boy. Later, as a youth, after losing his mother, three sisters, and a brother to tuberculosis (TB), he contracted the dread disease himself. Isolated in a small tent, and with many prayers, young Aaberg survived the odds. Those prayers were answered so he could help in the fight to eradicate TB.

At age 21, determined to get an education, Aaberg decided to enroll in the two-year ag course at Iowa State College (ISC) for students without high school diplomas. He sold his crops, mules, and machinery for $3,000, one-third of which he gave his father. He loaned $1,000 to a brother and set the rest aside for college and other expenses.

Aaberg suddenly became very ill with diphtheria. Two of his brothers had contracted the disease at a bullfight in Mexico. "Had it not been for another brother, Oscar, who scraped my throat repeatedly, I would have choked to death," says Aaberg.

At ISC, Aaberg had a rough beginning, but finished second from the top in his class. He participated in wrestling and boxing, and because of his ability as a swimmer, saved three persons from drowning. He also found time to court Iris Leith and become engaged to her. On graduation day, he wanted to celebrate with his bride-to-be, but his funds were down to 16 cents. "We celebrated anyway. I bought four hot dogs and took her on a picnic," he says.

After graduation, Aaberg became a $65 per month Cow Test Association Director in the Lake Mills-Scoville area, going from farm to farm by horse and buggy. He married Iris in 1925.

The next year, he was named Winnebago County, Iowa, extension director, winning out over six other applicants. He immediately went to work setting up yield and fertilizer plots, livestock disease control, and saw Iowa totally eradicate TB, thereby striking back at the disease that nearly cost him his life as a youth.

Aaberg's successes in Winnebago County, Iowa, led to his selection as county agent in Sioux County, Iowa. While there he was chosen Iowa's Assistant Secretary of Agriculture, a position he held from 1933-37, four of Iowa's most difficult years for farmers.

After losing the race for Iowa Secretary of Agriculture, he later described it as "the best thing that happened in my career".

Aaberg directed the farm committee to re-elect President Roosevelt. After that, he was named Iowa's representative on the Chicago Producers Commission Company, to supervise $3 million in loans.

During WW II, the Iowan joined the American Farm Bureau (AFB) as director of livestock and market research. It was in this capacity his prayers to eradicate tuberculosis in cattle and in hog cholera were answered. The AFB position enabled Aaberg to wage total war on these two major killers of livestock — and humans — and save farmers an estimated $100 million.

Many honors and awards have come to the 88-year old ag leader. Latest of these was the Iowa Farm Bureau's Distinguished Service Award. However, the veteran fighter against animal diseases considers his part in the eradication of TB and cholera as his crowning achievement. "God spared me as a youth so I could become a benefactor to mankind in my own small way," he concludes.

NINETY-EIGHT YEAR OLD KATE PLAMBECK RECALLS CHRISTMAS PAST
December, 1990

Our names are spelled the same and our forebearers came from the same part of the world, but our relationship is hard to trace. However, Kate Plambeck and I have things in common. One is spelling bees. When I was 13, I went down in the county contest and when Kate was 96, she won the State Fair spelling matches. The great-grandmother of 40 and great-great "grandma" of several more loved to tell about very different Christmases long ago.

For most senior citizens, "Christmas Past" means recalling memories of the 1920s, but for Kate Plambeck of Portsmouth, Iowa, childhood Yuletide recollections take her back to the mid-1890s.

Plambeck, a distant relative of mine by marriage, remembers when an orange in the stockings hung above the fireplace was a once-a-year treat to be savored for hours on Christmas Eve.

"We didn't even have a Christmas tree," says the 98-year-old former Harrison and Shelby County farm homemaker. "But, each of us children received one nice gift on Christmas day," she adds.

Now, more than nine decades later, Plambeck reflects on the 95 Christmas holidays she can remember, highlighted by those she and her husband, Harry, shared with their five children.

"Our Christmas dinners on the farm were always happy events when we had turkey with all the trimmings topped off with raspberry pie," she says. Nor did the sacred day go by without the family attending church.

Kate Plambeck, champion speller at age 96.

There are now 37 grandchildren and more than 40 great-grandchildren, as well as a number of great-great-grandchildren.

This year, Plambeck will observe the holiday at the home of her son, Bill, who farms near Persia, Iowa, and is the father of nine and grandfather of several.

Three of her children, Dennis, Doris, and Max, have passed away.

Bill, and Donna, her youngest, who lives in Omaha, visit several times a week.

By almost any standard, 98-year-old Plambeck must be regarded as a remarkable woman. Born in 1892 in the tiny village of Yorkshire, she was an excellent student in country school, and although unable to go to high school, was admitted to the Woodbine Normal School to earn a teaching certificate. She taught rural schools until marriage and resumed teaching after having raised her family. She retired from the classroom at age 78 and the past 20 years has tutored children in math, reading, and spelling.

In 1988, when she was 96, she entered the Iowa State Fair Spelling Bee and was the winner.

Plambeck joined the Portsmouth quilting Club when she was 80. She is also a member of the Catholic Daughters and was secretary of the Golden Pioneer's Club for 17 years.

"I don't want to sit around and do nothing," concludes the 98-year-old matriarch.

The way it was . . .
1991

WWI VETERAN RECALLS SEVERE
NORTHWEST IOWA WINTERS
January 22, 1991

In 1991, Orval Barnes was 98, and his boyhood recollections of how cold it got in his native extreme Northwest Iowa were as vivid as the day the mercury dropped through the bottom. Those memories made a good January column, as did his recollections of WWI and all that happened to him then and in the seven decades since then.

However cold it may get this winter, it's not likely it will be any more severe than some of the winters 98-year-old Orval Barnes can recall. Barnes, a native of Lyon County in northwest Iowa, spent the first 21 years of his life on a farm near George, not far from the Minnesota border. He remembers January and February readings that frequently dropped down to 30 degrees below zero, and on occasion plunged to 40 degrees or more below.

Official weather bureau records show Washta, Iowa, experiencing an Arctic-like 47 degrees below on Jan. 12, 1947.

"As for snow, we used bobsleds for transportation every winter and roads were often totally blocked," says Barnes. He tells of cutting fence wires so they could go through open fields to detour past the huge road drifts and says at times the snow was almost as deep as the fence posts. "We were frequently snowbound out there on the farm," notes Barnes.

He smiles, though, as he thinks back of the little gray mare on the cutter he used in his courting days. "It got rather late before I left my future wife's house," admits Barnes, who sometimes fell asleep on his way home. "But Vernie, that little mare, always found the way home."

After leaving the farm he took business administration courses at the Old Highland Park College in Des Moines and assumed a teaching assignment at the Cherokee High School.

During WWI, Barnes enlisted in a development battalion. Poor eyesight kept him from more dangerous duty, but his services proved important elsewhere. Musically inclined, he was a cornetist in the Camp Dodge Band. However, while with the band at an Elkhart performance he fell victim to the deadly Spanish influenza then claiming so many lives. Hospitalized in an old tuberculosis clinic, he became seriously ill. His father was called, along with a neighbor whose son was also afflicted. The neighbor's son died, as did hundreds of WWI doughboys, but Barnes survived.

Back on his feet, after two weeks in quarantine, he was tapped by the camp commander shortly after the Armistice to serve in the headquarters

Orval Barnes, 100-year-old-poet.

office. "I was a good penman so they promoted me to corporal to sign discharge papers, including my own," says Barnes.

After discharge, Barnes resumed teaching at Cherokee, then came to Des Moines, first to teach at Old West High and then at Roosevelt High as a business administration instructor for 37 years.

After a seven-year engagement, Barnes married Ethel Rhodes, his childhood sweetheart, in 1920. He tells about a trip the young couple made soon after in an old Model T Ford. They traversed 6,000 miles to the West Coast and back. "There were virtually no paved roads back then," says Barnes, as he recalls heavy rains which meant pulling through miles of mud.

"We found only one tourist cabin on the whole trip," he remembers. That was in New Mexico and cost $1.50 per night. The Iowa couple had a tent which they used every night except for the New Mexico stay, sleeping on folding army cots. However, Barnes considered the grueling trip highly educational because, in addition to his regular assignments to handle classes in typing, bookkeeping, penmanship, and shorthand, school officials also asked him to teach a class in geography.

Poetry became Barnes' hobby after retirement. He has written hundreds of poems and published four books called *Musing In Verse*. Included in volume one is his first poem entitled, *Autumn Leaves,* inspired when he was raking leaves.

Opening verse reads as follows—
Leaves falling swirl and dips,
Scoot along on a windy trip,
Stop and slide, then rise again
Without a thought of where they've been,
Until at last behind a tree
Or rock or bush, no longer free,
They halt to see a wintery rest,
Content to hide where it seems best.

His poems deal with a multitude of subjects and run the gamut of all human emotions as well as much of nature—trees, flowers, birds, and animals. One of his latest is entitled "Pigs."

Now a widower, the former teacher continues an active interest in WWI history, the American Legion, Masonry, the Shrine, and the Methodist Church. He also corresponds with 27 nieces and nephews, as well as with some 30 other relatives.

IOWA ORNITHOLOGIST IDENTIFIES HUNDREDS OF BIRDS
February 28, 1991

Most of us recognize robins, meadowlarks, wrens, bluebirds, crows, bluejays, and a dozen or so other common birds, but that's not even a start for a Pleasantville, Iowa, ornithologist. She is Gladys Black and the number of birds she recognizes and records on Iowa field trips is phenomenal.

Gladys Black of Pleasantville, Iowa, has been observing and studying birds for more than 75 years. She has recently helped compile an official listing of more than 300 species seen in the Lake Red Rock area between Knoxville and Pella. Affectionately known as "Iowa's Bird Lady," Black, 82, became interested in birds at an early age.

"By the time I was seven, my mother claimed I was able to correctly identify at least 25 species," says the well-known Iowa ornithologist.

When the U.S. Army Corps of Engineers recently published a booklet called *Lake Red Rock, a Feather Magnet,* Black served as advisor, and personally identified almost all of the 301 species listed. This winter she was elated to add two more—an Ivory Gull and a Pacific Loon.

Born on a Marion County, Iowa, farm long before ag chemicals started to decimate bird populations, the former Gladys Bowery recalls ideal bird nesting sites.

"As a small child I remember seeing turkey buzzards at Red Rock Bluff, and prairie chickens and wild turkeys in nearby meadows," she notes.

Biology was her favorite subject when she graduated from Pleasantville High School at age 17. She then attended the Mercy Hospital School of Nursing in Des Moines, became a registered nurse, took public health courses at the University of Minnesota, and then assumed a position as Clarke County Public Health Nurse.

In 1940 she returned to the U of M to get a degree. After WWII started, she married Wayne Black, a restaurant business administrator. After her husband was called into military service, the couple left for Robbins Air Force Base in Georgia.

While in Georgia, Black was a volunteer in Girl Scout programs, gardening and community rose planting projects, Episcopal Church guilds, and assumed the presidency of a Federated Garden Club.

In 1950 her husband suffered a heart attack and passed away a few years later, so Black returned to Iowa to take care of her mother and resume her bird watching interests. When Red Rock Lake was established in 1969, that interest blossomed into full flower.

"It took only five days for the lake to fill. Migrating patterns changed immediately, and thousands of birds came flocking in," explains Black. Very shortly she had identified more than 200 species of birds in the area.

In addition to observing, studying, and writing about birds, the Pleasantville ornithologist undertook intensive nesting studies and banding work wherein as many as 900 birds were banded in a single year. Bluebird trails were also established.

Along with Beth Brown, Clarke County, Iowa, Conservation Board naturalist, and Tim Shantz, Marion County's naturalist, she now takes birds to schools, hospitals, nursing homes, etc. Her pet barred owl, "Stryxie," a sparrow hawk called "Killy," and "Bubba," a great horned owl, have been star performers.

Still another way in which the Pleasantville octogenarian is helping her feathered friends is to take injured birds brought to her home to Mark Poell, a kindly Pleasantville veterinarian, for "patching up." She also leads numerous birdwatching tours.

A current major project in which Black is involved is known as "Eagles Days", to be held March 8, 9, 10 at Pella and nearby. Hundreds of school children and adults will come to hear Marilyn Obermire, a farm wife, and other naturalists, tell about the hundred or more Bald Eagles now wintering below the old Iron Bridge on the Des Moines River south of the Red Rock Dam.

Black is active in nature conservancy projects, and a Fellow in the Iowa Academy of Sciences. She has received an honorary doctorate from Simpson College, and has been inducted into the Iowa Women's Hall of Fame.

Gladys Black has identified more than 300 birds in Iowa.

WAR MUSEUM WILL RECALL IOWAN'S MILITARY EXPLOITS
March, 1991

Iowa has always stood tall in terms of men and women serving in our armed forces, beginning with the Civil War and on through the Persian Gulf. Acts of heroism have been countless. Many of those in uniform have paid the supreme sacrifice. Now plans are underway to erect an Iowa War Museum. General Edward Bird is leading the effort.

The Persian Gulf War has dominated our thoughts for the past several months. Virtually every Midwest community has seen some of its sons and daughters sent to the sand of Saudi Arabia. Some Iowa communities with strong National Guard units have dozens of their members involved. All told, by late February, Iowa counted more than 3,200 troops in the struggle against Iraq.

Allied air supremacy, directed by General Horner of Iowa, not only knocked out countless enemy military installations, but also enable the United States and other ground forces to fully mobilize to finish off Saddam Hussein.

Recollections of experiences with exploits in previous wars are being heard wherever farmers gather for their morning coffee, or wherever else veterans of WWII, Korea, or Vietnam may get together. And in Veterans Administration hospitals, old soldiers who were in the trenches in WWI shake their heads in disbelief as they watch their TV sets and learn of the computerized radar and other technology used to win wars today.

Meanwhile, all America seems determined to prove its patriotism. The Stars and Stripes have been waving proudly everywhere. Yellow ribbons are equally evident. And, so unlike the unforgivable receptions given Vietnam War returnees, a hero's welcome awaits everyone returning from the Persian Gulf.

Still another pleasant surprise will be experienced by those engaged in the Middle East crisis who have been enduring enemy fire, desert sandstorms. unappealing chow. and cold showers. A group of Iowa veterans have announced plans to establish a museum where Desert Storm's contribution to this nation's defense and freedom will be acknowledged, along with that of soldiers of all previous wars in which Iowans have participated .

General Ed Bird, military museum mastermind.

Known as the Gold Star Museum, it will be located at Camp Dodge, and financed entirely by private and corporate contributions. Its purpose will be to portray events that helped shape the destiny of our state, the nation, and the world.

All branches of military service, plus the Iowa State Patrol, will be represented. National defense contributions, both by civilians and the military, will be highlighted, including emphasis on agriculture's contributions to war and peace. Artifacts, mementos, historic letters, etc., will be displayed. A research library focusing on Iowa's military history from the Civil War of the 1860s, to the Persian Gulf struggle of 1991 is planned, as are explorations into the impact of peace and peace movements, and recognition of military chaplains.

Officers and directors of an Iowa National Guard organization, known as the Gold Star Memorial Association, are in charge. Heading the project is 76-year-old Brig. Gen. Edward Bird, a battle-tested and battle-scarred Iowa veteran of WWII. Another leader of the project is Gen. Harold Thompson, whose organizational skills first surfaced during Pope John Paul's 1979 Iowa visit.

Now retired, Gen. Bird has a proud record of service in WWII where he re-enlisted in Iowa's National Guard in early 1940. He passed a second lieutenant exam in July of that year and reported for full-time duty with the famous "Red Bull" (34th Infantry) Division in early 1941. While at Camp Claiborne he was promoted to first lieutenant and was in training when Pearl Harbor was struck, whereupon he was ordered to take charge of our anti-tank company. Then, in 1941, Lt. Bird was promoted to captain and, after being shipped to North Ireland, was placed in charge of a rifle company.

Capt. Bird was one of the first to land in North Africa in late 1942, and, with only 50 men, forced an enemy unit of over 1,000 to surrender.

In September 1943, Bird was one of those intrepid Americans at Salerno, Italy, and in Cassino, where the fighting was fierce. By now the Iowan had been promoted to lieutenant colonel and, as commander of the 2nd Battalion of the 168th Infantry, was in the thick of it on bloody Mt. Plantino. While on forward reconnaissance there. he was severely wounded.

After stays in Italian and U.S. hospitals, Col. Bird returned to combat duty in the Voges Mountains in late 1944. I met Col. Bird while I was a war correspondent in Germany. It was in Nuremberg where mopping up was taking place, and where the colonel took me under his wing (no pun intended). Sniper fire could be heard every few seconds. Ever mindful of my safety, the Iowa veteran of many battles found a protected spot on the ledge of a badly damaged building where he described the action we were witnessing. Later I got one of my best interviews of the war from him, and to this day I regard him as my personal WWII hero.

WINSLOWS HAVE THE BEST OF TWO WORLDS
April, 1991

After years of arduous labor farming and raising livestock, many midwestern farm people become "snowbirds" by going South for the winter. Mr. and Mrs. Francis Winslow are among those who relax in Arizona' s sunshine. While in Arizona they always make new friends to be added to the many they have back in Iowa.

To be named an Iowa Master Pork Producer is an achievement only 25 top hog raisers realize annually.

To be selected an Iowa Distinguished Dairyman is an honor accorded only a few of the state's best dairymen.

And to be designated an Iowa Master Farmer is the ultimate lifetime recognition any farm family can attain.

Yet, there is one Iowa farmer on whom all of these honors has been bestowed.

He is Francis Winslow, 77, of Grundy County, Iowa. He was named Master Swine Producer in 1942, the first year hog raisers were singled out for special recognition. Some 20 years later Winslow was accorded the Distinguished Dairyman award. Then in 1967 the highest of all farm accolades—WALLACES FARMER Iowa Master Farmer award— was conferred on the Grundy County farmer.

The Francis Winslows, Iowa "Snowbirds"

Winslow was a 16-year-old high school senior when his father passed away in February, 1930. The entire burden of managing and operating a 240-acre rented farm fell on his young shoulders.

In essence, young Winslow was carrying on the farming for his newly widowed mother. His higher education would be attained the hard way, "learning by doing" on the farm.

The depression years were difficult, but the family survived. In 1931, a friend talked Francis into a double date. The girl he called was Dorothy Miller, a rural school teacher. Five years later wedding bells rang in her farm home.

Now fully on their own, the young couple enlarged the barn, started replacing grade Holsteins with purebreds, and undertook a hog crossbreeding program involving Yorkshires, Hampshires, and Berkshires.

Two daughters were welcomed—Francine, now Mrs. Lee Gruenhaupt of Waukon, the mother of three, and Carolyn, now Mrs. Loren Miller, the mother of five.

The young couple rented until 1951 when they bought the 240 acres on contract. It was paid for within seven years.

Despite his high recognition as a Master Pork Producer, Francis' main interest was in the dairy herd. DHIA testing constantly helped improve production. Several cows won top awards.

In addition to his other honors, Francis Winslow is also a Master Corn Grower based on a yield of well over 160 bu. per acre.

In 1980 the Winslows retired from active farming. The farm is now operated by Jim and Dick Lynch on a crop share program. "That enables me to join in decision making," says Francis.

When it comes to community service, the Winslows have done more than their share. They have been active in farm organizations, Grundy County Fair, the extension council, PTA board, 4-H leadership and their church.

McNUTT ONE OF MANY WORLD PORK CONGRESS VOLUNTEERS
May, 1991

Promotion of pork products becomes a top priority at the World Pork Congress and similar national and international gatherings. One of the leading supporters constantly seeking to improve the image of pork is Iowa's Paul McNutt. Beginning on the county level, his dedication has taken him into state responsibilities, and to key roles on national and international pork promotion boards.

Among the hundreds who will be giving tirelessly of their time and talents at the World Pork Expo May 31, June 1 and 2 in Des Moines is Paul McNutt, 76, of near Iowa City. The Johnson County, Iowa, Master Pork Producer has been a pioneer in pork organizations and pork promotions, and is still quite involved in finishing out 2,500 hogs per year.

McNutt's assignment at the World Pork Expo will be in the political action area, a project designed to impress upon congressmen and legislators the magnitude and economic importance of the nation's pork industry. It's also designed to enhance the image of pork to American housewives and food retailers.

Paul McNutt, a leader in Iowa and National Pork Producers Associations.

McNutt first organized the Johnson County Pork Producers Association in the early 1950s. Since then he has been highly influential as president of the Iowa Pork Producers Council (NPPC) and the National Pork Producers Council.

McNutt also served the National Livestock and Meat Board a number of years and was a pioneer worker in pork promotion programs and in achieving the voluntary, and now legislative, pork checkoff. Currently he is a member of the NPPC's PAC board.

In addition to his involvement with swine industry projects, McNutt has been extremely active in community and farm programs, as Rotary district governor, Mercy Hospital advisory board, County Farm Bureau president, P.T.A. president, Iowa State Bank director, Methodist Church boards, Farm House fraternity, Johnson County Fair president, American Friends Service, and other organizations.

In 1965 McNutt was named an Iowa Master Pork Producer, and to no one's surprise, he was designated a WALLACES FARMER Iowa Master Farmer the following year.

Born and raised on an O'Brien County farm in northwest Iowa, McNutt became an active 4-H member, graduated from high school at 16, worked on the farm several years and, at 21, entered Iowa State College (ISC).

On graduation in 1938, McNutt was named Scott County Club Agent, serving with distinction until 1941, when he was promoted to Plymouth County extension agent. McNutt married Mary Kaldera that spring, but soon after he was called to service in WWII.

McNutt had the opportunity to regain his county agent position, or join with ISC's Herb Howell in the farm management field. "Both offers were appealing," says McNutt. "But Mary and I wanted to farm, and her father said he'd loan us two horses, some machinery, and money, so we started farming."

By the time he was named a Master Pork Producer, the number of pigs marketed numbered close to 1,200. Since then a confinement feeding system has been established, and the number marketed is around 2,500 annually.

The McNutts' youngest son, John, their herdsman, Steve Phillips, and part-time helpers, Earl Grazel and John Sponan, do most of the work with the hogs and the 900 acres of land now known as Elmira Farms, Inc. "I'm still hanging in there, and get to do most of the marketing and some of the field work," says McNutt.

Oldest of the family's children is James McNutt, a veterinarian at West Branch. The daughter, Mrs. Martha Port, 1969 Iowa Pork Queen, lives in Cedar Falls. There are now eight grandchildren.

1954 MASTER FARMER ASSUMES MANY RESPONSIBILITIES
June, 1991

The exemplification of community service is found in the person of Wayne Keith, former vice president of the Iowa Farm Bureau, who holds the distinction of having been selected for two of Iowa's highest farm recognitions — Master Farmer and Master Swine Producer. His contributions to his community have been almost endless, but his greatest pride is in his remarkable family.

Wayne Keith, 83, retired Kossuth County, Iowa farmer, is the exemplification of the oft heard comment, "With recognition comes responsibility." Named an Iowa Master Farmers in 1954, Keith, who was then already active in many community endeavors, became a dedicated statewide agricultural leader.

Best known for his many years in Farm Bureau work where he served eight years as Iowa vice-president, he's been involved with countless organizations.

In 1968 he was elected State Senator. During his four years as Senator, Keith became chairman of the tax study committee to achieve property tax relief. "We had a $43 million problem," says Keith.

For 15 years Keith farmed with his father on a 50-50 basis. They farrowed and finished over 500 hogs per year. Keith was named an Iowa Master Swine Producer in 1943. In addition, some 50 steers were fed annually, 15 cows milked daily, about 50 ewes and their lambs placed on rough ground, and a 500-hen laying flock was kept.

Father of three daughters — Jane, Mary, and Margaret, and a son, Edgar—Keith is immensely proud of his children, all living in Iowa. He also boasts 12 grandchildren, five of them raised on the home farm, the children of Edgar and his wife, Joyce. And there now are eight great-grandchildren.

Wayne Keith, long-time Iowa Farm Bureau Vice President.

The family farming tradition looms large in the Keith family. His grandfather first bought some of the land in 1881, thus making part of the present holding a Century Farm. His father, Lynn, bought it in 1904. Keith was the third generation to farm it. His son, Edgar, with whom he farmed 15 years on a 50-50 basis, now owns 478 acres, and rents another 500 or more from Wayne. Edgar's daughter, Loralei, and her husband, Al Koenecke, now are involved— the fifth generation on the same farm.

Soil conservation has always been a priority. Today, there are more than 28,000 ft. of terraces, along with grassed waterways, as well as rotation cropping and pasture management to help nail down the topsoil.

Although Keith has much to be proud of, his greatest joy was to watch his son, Edgar, and daughter-in-law, Joyce, receive the Master Farmer recognition in 1988. "That was even better than when I got the award myself," concludes Wayne.

Keith has the distinction of being one of *WALLACES FARMER* S longest continuous subscribers for more than 70 years.

HAMMERLY'S CONTRIBUTIONS SPAN EIGHT DECADES
July, 1991

An 80 year member of the national Grange and more than 70 years of American Farm Bureau membership is rock-solid proof of Lawrence Hammerly's dedication to farm organizations. Moreover, his 80 years of community involvement and service prompted me to write this column.

In my many years of writing "The Way It Was", it has been my privilege to report the activities and accomplishments of hundreds of remarkable senior citizens. Occasionally I find persons or a couple that could well qualify as "incredible old timers."

Ninety-four-year-old Lawrence Hammerly, who lives just north of Newton, is in that special category. A brief summary reveals that he has been...

- A hired man, tenant farmer, and landowner.
- An active Grange member since 1912.
- A soldier in WWI.
- A dairy producer since 1920.
- A soil conservation pioneer.
- Farm Bureau 71 years.
- A 20-year 4-H leader.
- Rotarian since 1961.
- Longtime school board member.
- A 1956 National Soil Conservation Field Days leader.

Hammerly has had a world of farming experiences.

Hammerly wasn't merely a "joiner" of organizations. He played an active leadership role.

During his 79 years in the Grange, he has served as overseer and on drill teams. In 4-H he helped establish the Jasper County 4-H Achievement Show in the 1930s, and was treasurer many years. In the Farm Bureau he was county secretary and voting delegate. In the Wittenberg church he held every office and headed the building committee. As for the school board, the Jasper County farmer was secretary on both the township and county level.

Hammerly's major contribution, however, has been his pioneering work in soil and water conservation. When the Soil District program was in its infancy, his was one of five farms chosen as a demonstration farm where strip cropping, terracing, contouring, and other conservation work was already underway.

Hammerly's roots run deep in Jasper County. His great-grandparents emigrated from Canada to homestead a treeless section of $1.25-per-acre land near Newton in 1855, and then bought a nearby wooded 80-acre tract for fuel and logs. Three years after the purchase, his great-grandfather, Charles Watt, drowned while fording Indian Creek, leaving his wife to raise their 12 children.

One of the 12 was Hammerly's grandfather, William Watt, who acquired the land and raised a family of eight. One was a daughter, Estella, who married J. Nelson Hammerly.

Shortly after WWI, the senior Hammerly mortgaged the section homesteaded by his grandparents in order to buy additional land. He lost everything in the Great Depression except for 80 acres.

That 80 is now a part of the farm owned and operated by Hammerly's daughter and son-in-law, Harriet and Robert Smith.

As for Hammerly, he attended Iowa State College at Ames for one year, then entered WWI. Soon after his discharge in 1919, he married Lucille Scott of Scott County. A year later they rented 240 acres when corn was selling at $2.40 per bu., only to see it plunge to 40 cents per bu. in 1921.

Five children were born to Lawrence and Lucille, including a son, Raymond, who farmed with his father many years.

IOWA STATE FAIR A HORSESHOE PITCHING MECCA
August, 1991

They sometimes call horseshoe pitching "barnyard golf". While the comparison to golf may be a bit far-fetched, horseshoe pitchers at the State Fair are no less dedicated to their favorite sport than Arnold Palmer, Lee Trevino, or Greg Norman trying for holes-in-one on the golf links. Marion Lange, Bondurant farmer, told why.

Historians reveal horseshoe pitching is an age-old sport first practiced by the Romans. It has long been played in our own country. Records show during the Revolutionary War both Colonial and British troops found it a relaxing diversion.

In Iowa, horseshoe pitching has been a favorite farm sport since the first horse-drawn Conestoga wagons entered the state. It still remains a popular pastime at fairs and other events. as well as in urban parks and farmyards. At the Iowa State Fair, horseshoe pitching tourneys have been held since the exposition's outset. In 1921, it became the site of Iowa's annual state championship, as well as a number of world championships.

Dozens of Iowans have become nationally recognized players. Among them is Marion Lange, longtime Bondurant farmer who was introduced to the sport when he was only 12.

Marion Lange, National Champion horseshoe pitcher.

"My father and I were at the State Fair horse barn when we saw a huge crowd assembled nearby," says Lange, "When we got there Frank Jackson of Kellerton and Frank Lundin of New London were throwing ringer after ringer vying for the world title. I decided that was the sport for me." he adds.

From that day on Lange has had an unending love affair with the game. Now 78, he has been involved for 66 years as player, state champion, national tournament finalist, coach, Iowa Horseshoe Pitching Association president, state fair tournament director, promoter of a national horseshoe museum, enthusiast for every phase of the game, and 1987 inductee in the national "Horseshoe Pitchers Hall of Fame."

Lange recalls some of the legendary figures in the game. "Putt Mossman of Eldora could lay on countless ringers while blindfolded, and was a daredevil motorcyclist to boot." The former Bondurant farmer beat 10-time national champion Ted Allen of Colorado during the 1954 World Tourney at Salt Lake City, only to lose the next match to California's Guy Zimmerman, who tossed 17 consecutive double ringers to go on to the title. Currently, Lange is active in a $40,000 nine-court year-round horseshoe arena project at Eldora.

During his active career from boyhood through 1989, Lange won the Iowa Open Class Championship twice, as well as the four-state tourney two times. In addition, he won dozens of invitational meets, and once was rated 16th best player in the nation.

His most cherished victory, however, was at the Altoona Centennial where hundreds of personal friends were cheering him on to triumph. Over the years he has won countless trophies, many of which he is now giving away to winners of youth contests.

Great players he has pitched against, in addition to Jackson, Lundin, Mossman, and Allen, include Carl Steinfelt of New York and Iowa champions Dale Dixon, Des Moines; Harold Shaw, What Cheer; John Paxton, Ottumwa; Hugh and Francis Rogers, Cedar Falls; Lincoln Taylor, Grand River; and Glen Hinton, Maquoketa, who won the Iowa title 18 times.

While State Fair horseshoe superintendent, he introduced daily horseshoe pitching events, a practice now being continued annually by Chet Foster, Ankeny, the current superintendent.

Play at the Iowa State Fair begins on Wednesday, Aug. 14, with the Iowa championship to be decided on Sunday, Aug. 25. Kevin Cone, an Alta, Iowa farmer, who is only 28 years old and a third generation horseshoe pitcher, is the current defending champion.

MASTER FARM HOMEMAKER "CARRIES ON" THE TRADITION
September, 1991

Annually, a select few Master Farm Homemakers are recognized by Wallaces Farmer. Back in 1954, Mrs. Caroline Ingels was one of those honored. Her work as a homemaker, teacher, 4-H leader, and in other community projects continued here at home, but soon she also found herself participating in international efforts in behalf of farm women elsewhere in the world.

To be chosen an Iowa Master Farm Homemaker not only means the highest recognition attainable by a farm woman, but it also calls for continued responsibilities in leadership.

Virtually all of the 252 Iowa Master Farm Homemakers named since 1928 have accepted that challenge. An outstanding example is Caroline Ingels, of Maynard, Iowa, named to the select group in 1956.

Ingels was one of eight children including two sets of twins, in the John Wallace family near Williamsburg, Iowa. As the oldest, she learned homemaking responsibilities early, and her mother's leadership in the community set a good example.

While at Iowa State College in the early 1930s, she met John Ingels at a campus 4-H party. They were married in 1937, soon after both had graduated. Earlier, John had done farm work and had been a cow tester, and then became a Carnation Milk Company field man. Meanwhile, Caroline taught home economics at Jesup.

Their first home was in Waverly where their oldest daughter, Lois, was born. Later two more children, Harold and Alice, were welcomed.

In 1942 John became County Agent in Carroll County, and in 1945 the couple began their farming career by renting land near Maynard in Fayette County.

Like most other farm wives of that time, Caroline was responsible for the chickens and eggs, as well as a large garden. She also helped with the milking and in the field. She laughs about her first field assignment, saying, "I was to drive the horses on the wagon with an endgate seeder, but I got so frustrated counting rows I told John to do the driving himself and I would shovel the oats into the seeder."

Shortly after becoming a farm wife, Ingels became involved in community service as a 4-H leader, Sunday School teacher,

Mrs. John Ingels, Iowa Master Farm Homemaker, International Farm Women's Delegate.

county fair judge, host of foreign exchange students, and a leader in the Presbyterian Church, among other things.

With college approaching for three children, Caroline supplemented the family's farm income by teaching at Fayette, Oran, Maynard, and West Central. She also found herself more involved than ever in church, community, state, and national leadership roles.

Space does not permit us to list all of Ingel's contributions. However, she indeed has "carried on" in the best tradition of an Iowa Master Farm Homemaker.

BACHMAN HUSKED 271 BUSHELS OF CORN IN A SINGLE DAY
October, 1991

Back in the days of husking corn by hand and bringing in and scooping 100 bushels a day, it was considered a good day's work. I personally never did better than 90, but there were those who threw well over 100 bushels against the bangboard. This column cited Earl Bachman's almost unbelievable husking feat.

October is synonymous with the nation's corn harvest. Billions of bushels of the golden grain will be combined before the end of this month. Yields vary greatly.

Nostalgia also always enters the scene during every harvest season. Old-timers recall their hand husking prowess. Nine Corn Belt states have revived the art of hand husking. State matches have determined entrants for the 1991 national contest at Kimballton, Iowa.

Paul Christensen, president of the Iowa Corn Huskers Association, says everything is ready. About 100 persons will vie for trophies in youth, women's, senior citizen's, and men's open classes.

As compared to the gruelling 80 minute contests H.A. Wallace, editor of WALLACES FARMER, and later U.S. secretary of agriculture and vice president, started in 1924, today's championships are decided in 30-minute time periods.

Nostalgic arguments about the stamina and achievements of the hand huskers of the 1920s, 1930s, and 1940s compared to today's winners inevitably are common. The boast of "shucking" 100 bu. or more a day in those years is often heard. There is no denying that was a good day's work in fields of open pollinated corn where stalks were often down and yields less than half that of today's hybrids.

Whether today's national champions could measure up to the Fred Staneks and other husking

Earl Bachman held world corn husking record.

"giants" of the past will probably never be answered. Nor will achievements of some young huskers back then ever be equaled.

Take Earl Bachman, of near Crawfordsville, Iowa, who will be 75 next month. Back in 1939, when he was 22 and husking for 6 cents per bu. on the Joe Garver farm near Lowpoint, Ill., Bachman went out early one October morning, and by noon had already picked three loads totaling 168 bu. After a hearty lunch and a half hour's rest, he picked two more loads, making a total of 271 bu. in a 10 1/2-hour period. Many believe he set a world's record that day.

The extraordinary record Bachman made was verified by the check by Garver for $16.25 for the intense day of work.

The corn in which the record was made was an early hybrid planted in rows 100 rods long, yielding 82 bu. per acre.

Bachman isn't the only good husker in the family. His father went out every morning. By 9:30 a.m. he would have a first wagon full, and then fill the second by noon. What is even more amazing is that Earl's 14-year-old sister brought in 108 bu. in one day, and his younger brother, Louis, envious of his big sister's accomplishment, managed a 111-bu. load in a single day when only 13. No wonder Bachman, who started husking when he was just 10, and did 115 bu. when he was only 12, went on to set the 1939 mark, which may stand as the world's best.

Now the owner of more than 350 acres of top Washington County farmland, with 280 in corn this year, Bachman still has the husking peg with which he set the 1939 record. He recently showed it to this reporter while standing by one of his two 4-row combines. "That peg," he says, "let me do 271 bu. in a 10 1/2-hour day. This machine enables me to do 3,000 bu. in one afternoon. Times have changed!"

MILLIONS RAISED FOR SOUTHEAST IOWA CHURCHES AND PARISHES
November, 1991

Raising money for churches and parishes is something in which most of us become involved. However, the modest funds raised in most communities are "peanuts" compared to what some Catholic and Protestant leaders raise through annual auctions in Southeast Iowa. In some instances, the totals annually reach $150,000 or more and millions have been raised over the years. To learn how they did it, read on.

Thanksgiving always comes early in two southeast Iowa communities. Denmark and St. Paul, both in Lee County, annually conduct their "God's Portion" and "God's Acre" sales in October. The outpouring of generosity seen at these events bespeaks a Thanksgiving expression for the year's blessings.

The Denmark community started it all in 1947. Since then, dozens of Protestant churches and Catholic parishes have benefited.

In Denmark, the spirit of ecumenism has prevailed since the beginning. In fact, twelve different churches and parishes have shared in Denmark's "God's Portion" sales over the past 44 years. The 1991 participants are the Denmark

Congregational United Church of Christ and the Augusta St. Mary's Catholic parish.

The history of the Lee County auctions is fascinating.

Back in 1947, the Denmark church was searching for ways to increase community interest and help with finances. Newcomers to the church, Mr. and Mrs. Art Meyers, suggested a harvest festival. Farmers in the community offered to donate produce. Thus the name, "God's Portion," was coined. So favorable was the response that plans were made for an annual sale. Over the 44 years, the Denmark auctions have resulted in more than $775,000 for missions, church, building projects, and other needs.

About a dozen miles west of Denmark is the little town of St. Paul, a Catholic community centered around St. James parish, now in its 153rd year. Bishop Maurice Dingman is a St. James alumnus, as are two other monsignors, six priests, and no less than 38 nuns.

Among leaders in St. Paul's record "God's Acre" sale were Al Menke and Al Overberg.

St. Paul's first sale was in 1953, when Father Schaefer cleaned out the attic in the parish rectory and several farmers brought in an acre's yield of corn. Because area farmers had donated produce from one of their acres, St. Paul chose the name, "God's Acre," for its auction. The first year's proceeds came to only $600. The 1990 all-time record was $93,000. The 1991 total was more than $89,500. More than 500 donors contribute annually. Primary beneficiary is the Marquette Parochial School made up of students from St. Paul, Houghton, and West Point.

A report provided by Al Overberg, 87-year-old St. Paul farmer, who has given an acre's yield of corn every year since the sale started, lists 832 separate donations in a single year.

Each sale has its side attractions. Denmark, with Don Blanchard as 1991 chairman, had Boy Scouts do the flag raising, followed by prayers, booth displays, a colorful parade, lunch, and games for children before the sale began. John Gorham was this year's Master of Ceremonies. A service of Thanksgiving was held the day after the sale.

At St. Paul, where Albert Menke and Tom Klesener were 1991 cochairs, a community dinner and dance preceded the sale, and the Rosary Society served 1,265 turkey dinners and countless sandwiches at the auction.

A craft stand added $2,000 to the day's total. Business enterprises in Ft. Madison, Mt. Hammill, Houghton, Mt. Pleasant, West Point, Donnellson, and other nearby communities, added thousands more dollars.

Prices paid at the sales often are high. Mary Menke reports corn brought $3 per bu. this year. Soybeans sold for up to $7. A quilt at St. Pauls made by Agnes Merschman, went for $1,500. A ham dinner for eight brought $500.

A CENTURY OF MEMORIES
December, 1991

101-year old Rona Schaff of Eldridge never seems to have to worry about something to do. The long-time Wallaces Farmer *reader has painstakingly made dozens of beautiful afghans. All her many grandchildren and great-grandchildren have received one of her treasures. During a delightful visit, I was told about her ten decades of interesting memories. I was also intrigued by the skillful way she used her needle and yarn, totally unaware she was making another beautiful afghan as a much-appreciated Christmas present for me.*

Rona Schaff, Eldridge, Iowa, celebrated her 100th birthday late last month. She received hundreds of congratulatory cards and notes, including one from President Bush. At an open house on the big day, four generations joined in the celebration. Reminiscing by the remarkable Scott County centenarian was the highlight of the event. Blessed with almost total recall, Rona remembers Christmases in the late 1800s, the coming of Rural Free Delivery in 1901, the community's first automobile, neighbor youths going to France in World War I, the advent of radio some 70 years ago, and many other historic occasions.

"Aunt Rona," as she is known to countless friends, as well as to all members of her large family, says, "When I was a small girl, Christmas wasn't such a 'big deal.' We had no Christmas tree, no church to attend, and no big family gatherings. Girls got a doll almost every Christmas and boys got skates, hobby horses, and tools.

Rona's parents were Peter and Hanchen Schneckloth, pioneer farmers in their neighborhood. She had one brother, Herbert, who was an outstanding farmer and horseman, and was named an Iowa Master Farmer by WALLACES FARMER in 1939. Rona married Hugo Schaff, also a farmer, and became the mother of four daughters and two sons. Only one of her children, Lois, is still living. She has 21 grandchildren and 31 great-grandchildren.

Mrs. Rona Schaff, centarian.

One great-grandson, John Brown, served in the Persian Gulf War. A nephew, Don Schneckloth, is a nationally recognized Belgian horse showman. A niece, Fern Hahn, was named an Iowa Master Farm Homemaker in 1959. A son-in-law, Henry Koch, is well known in Iowa sheep circles.

Among her grandchildren are teachers, school administrators, farmers, nurses, doctors, homemakers, lawyers, realtors, building contractors, bankers, conservationists, photographers, decorated war veterans, and others in various professions or businesses. Rona is proud of all of them. A great-granddaughter, Dawn Nichols, lives in Alaska and will be presenting Rona with her first great-great-grandchild in the near future.

For many years Rona has made her home with a caring daughter-in-law, Angie Schaff, to whom she is most grateful.

The Schaffs were active in 4-H leadership roles and otherwise in their community, but Rona's major interest has been in genealogy. No less than five large loose-leaf books, filled with family records dating back to the 1700s, are proof of family history data.

In 1922 Rona started planning for family reunions. The first family picnic was held in 1928, and was so well attended that the gathering has been held every year since, with Rona the official chronicler. Her records show 1977 to have been the biggest year, with some 500 family members in attendance.

Among the childhood memories that stand out are the dancing classes held in the community Turner Hall at the turn of the century.

Although her formal education stopped at graduation from 8th grade in country school, she continued to read books throughout her life, and laughs about reading early Sears Roebuck catalogs.

She is a dyed-in-the-wool Chicago Cubs fan, so she continues to listen and watch TV throughout the baseball season.

While most people her age, and many of those younger, are content just sitting in a rocking chair, the Eldridge centenarian has better things to do. Every day she works on afghans for grandchildren and great-grandchildren. She manages to complete about one a month, and has already made close to fifty. "It takes 165 stitches every time I go across," explains Rona, adding, "and I'll just keep on making them until I run out of great-grandchildren.'

The way it was . . .
1992

HAGEN ONE OF IOWA'S FIRST MASTER SWINE PRODUCERS
January, 1992

An innovator in swine production ideas, Walter Hagen not only became a member of the first class of "Masters" to be honored in 1942, but whose ideas pioneered better hog production for many neighbors as well. In addition, Hagen was one of the first to recognize and meet the challenge of soil conservation.

"Walt" Hagen, Master Pork Producer, master conservationist, dedicated forester.

When Walter Hagen first learned that a Master Pork Producer project would be undertaken in Iowa, he little dreamed that he would be one of the original group to be so honored.

There were only 12 sows in Hagen's 1942 herd, but they farrowed 108 pigs for an average of nine per sow. An average of eight per litter were weaned, and almost all those were raised. The daily rate of gain was 1.26 lbs.

As for innovation, Hagen was a pioneer in crossbreeding for vigor, confinement programs, use of farrowing crates, farrowing stalls, side rails, corner heat lamps, clipping tails, and administering iron shots and antibiotics.

He also helped sponsor barn meetings where hog raisers could meet with swine specialists and exchange experiences.

Hagen's work in soil and water conservation overshadows everything else, however. One day when his father was attending a farm sale, Hagen had a neighbor with a "whirlwind plow" build broadbased terraces. When the elder Hagen saw what had been done to his field, he was furious. Later, however, he was so impressed with the increased yields and erosion control that he demanded all future cultivated crops on the farm be planted "on the contour."

A "fanatic" on conservation, Hagen first served as county soil commissioner, then for 12 years on the State Soil and Water Committee. For the past 14 years he hosted Allamakee County sixth graders on his farm, stressing the importance of conservation.

LEAP YEAR BIRTHDAYS
A SOURCE OF MUCH FUN
February 22, 1992

When Lillian Buckley's birthday arrived on the last day of February, 1992, exactly 88 years after she first saw the light of day, she actually only celebrated her 22nd birthday. February 29th babies get older, of course, and Mrs. Buckley, now living in a retirement center, was a prime example. This tells how.

Lillian Buckley was born in 1904. However, she will only mark her 22nd birthday later this month. The reason, of course, is that the petite, attractive widow, who lives at Wesley Acres, a Des Moines retirement center, was a baby, born on Feb. 29th, so she only has an actual birthday only every four years.

"It doesn't bother me a bit that I don't have as many birthdays as other people," says Buckley, who has lived an interesting life and continues to do so.

Born in Pocahontas, Iowa, one of six children of Bohemian parents, she spoke only Bohemian until she started school at age six. Her father was a shoemaker. He had come to America as a teenager in order to avoid being drafted into the Bohemian (now Czechoslovakian) army. Her family was very frugal, and, at 13, Buckley started earning wages as an evening telephone operator. "We fibbed a bit about my age," she admits. "But we needed the money," she adds.

Lillian Buckley has a February 29th Birthday and is either 22 or 88 years old.

In high school her best friend was a Laurens farm girl, Anna Bovansky. One day when they compared notes, they discovered both had been born on the same Leap Year day.

All three of her brothers went to college and Buckley had the same desire, but the Depression intervened. Instead, she attended a business college in Quincy, IL. In the meantime she fell madly in love with a young man who was subsequently sent overseas during WWI and was killed.

On returning from Quincy, the Maytag Co., Newton, Iowa, called her for a "temporary" job. She accepted with some misgivings. Forty-two years later she was still there. Her work in the "temporary" job was so outstanding that she was soon promoted. Eventually, she became secretary to Verne Martin, sales manager, and after his retirement, to his successor Clare Ely. "I watched Maytag grow from a small company to an internationally recognized Iowa industry," concludes Buckley.

Leap Year day, as well as the calendar, has an interesting history. Hebrews had crude calendars 3,700 years before our present calendar, which is based on the year Christ was born.

The very first calendars were based on seasons. Later, astronomers concluded it took 365 days for the earth to make one revolution around the sun. However, in 47 B.C. Julius Caesar learned the year was actually 365 1/4 days. To correct this, he added one extra day every four years. thus, Feb. 29 was instituted.

It was later learned, however, a year actually is only 365.2422 days. Therefore, over the centuries, by 1582, the difference had produced a 10-day surplus. Pope Gregory then decreed Leap Year, with its Feb. 29, would be observed every fourth year except in century years divisible by 400. This means the year 2000 will not be a Leap Year.

Even so, there is a discrepancy of split seconds and attempts are now being made to correct this with leap seconds.

Meanwhile, according to tradition, this is the year when women have priority rights on proposing marriage, so all bachelors had best beware!

While at Maytag she noticed a handsome, but shy, widower named Laurel Buckley, who was raised on a farm near Reasnor. Apparently he also noticed her. In time, after they were formally introduced by Laurel's brother, Ivan, a Jasper County farmer and stockman, wedding bells rang. In the meantime, Laurel had bought half interest in a bank at Monroe, Iowa, where he served as president.

The couple made their home in Newton until his death. Both enjoyed gardening and visiting farms. In the early 1980s, Buckley moved to Wesley Acres where she pursues her knitting and crocheting hobbies.

"I've knitted over 100 washrags and many baby booties for our gift shop," says Buckley. Proceeds from the shop go to Wesley Acres projects. Other hobbies include reading and travel. She has seen much of Europe, and was once in Czechoslovakia, the native home of her parents and grandparents, where both grandfathers were ministers .

Buckley jokes about an Octogenarian having only a limited number of birthdays, and has no intention to make a "big deal" of her 22nd birthday this Feb.29.

This writer is also a Leap Year baby and will celebrate my 21st actual birthday on the last day of this month. Unlike Buckley, l have always celebrated on March 1, "moving day" on Iowa farms when I was a boy. Also unlike Buckley, I've told people I want them to help me celebrate my 21st this year. I'm a bit worried now, though. If a lot of them come, where will I put them in our small condo?

We travel in good company, Jimmy Dorsey, bandleader; Home Run King, Al Rosen and popular singer, Dinah Shore are Feb. 29 babies, as are more than 100,000 others.

A VERMEER FAMILY LEGACY
March 28, 1992

Pella, Iowa, is known far and wide for its Tulip Festival, Dutch customs and accomplishments, and its industrious, conservative residents, most of them bearing names straight out of Holland. That was firmly re-established for me when I spent a few hours with the Vermeers (sometimes known as Ver Meer). This column told about the family and some of their achievements.

When Pella's 57th annual "Tulip Time" takes place May 7-9, tens of thousands of visitors from near and far will enjoy countless gorgeous tulips, Volks parades, operettas, and other program features. Inevitably, some will also look into the Pella directory and when they do, Dutch names from Aalbers to Zylstra will dominate the pages. Few names, however, are better known than Vermeer or VerMeer.

First to bring that name to the Pella community was Brant Vermeer who arrived In Pella In 1856, along with his wife, Teunetje, and their sons.

Shortly after arriving, Brant bought 80 acres northeast of Pella. A small log cabin located on the tract became their humble home for the next 12 years.

The family has prospered over the years and today—seven generations later—there are 800 or more living descendants of the courageous immigrant couple. What is equally impressive is that 70 percent of those descendants now make their homes In Iowa.

The Vermeer cousins of Pella: Gary, Bernie, Anthony, and Tunis.

A Vermeer family history was compiled In 1963 by Gary and Harry Vermeer, great grandsons of Brant and Teunetje. Updated last year by Gary's son, Stanley, Mrs. John VanderHart, and Prof. J. C. Vanden Bosch, the book contains 233 pages and lists every family member.

Farming is the Vermeer family's dominant occupation, beginning with great-great.-great-grandfather Brant. "We stick close to the soil," opined 77-year-old Anthony Vermeer.

Proof of the agrarian bent of the Vermeer family is seen in a 1963 Marion County plat which shows 30 or more Vermeer farms owned and operated within a few miles of where Brant, the pioneer, bought his 80 acres a century earlier.

Based on my visit with four Vermeer cousins, I have concluded all aspects of Midwest farming are represented. Whereas, Anthony was primarily a cattle feeder, his son, Owen, is a pork producer. Tunis (Tudor) Vermeer, also 77, has concentrated on a much smaller acreage where he has also fed livestock. Another cousin, Bernie, 72, has 160 acres where dairying was long the mainstay. Still another cousin, Gary 73, has a 1,400-acre grain farming enterprise.

Although Jan Vermeer, the 17th century painter, may be the most famous Vermeer in world history, Gary is undoubtedly the best known of all of the Vermeers of today by virtue of his inventive genius. He and another cousin, Ralph, founded the Vermeer Mfg. Co. in 1948.

The meteoric rise of the Pella firm is almost a Believe It or Not" story. Tired of scooping corn, Gary designed a mechanical wagon hoist In 1947. Neighbors saw the hoist work and immediately asked Gary to build some for them.

Soon thereafter a portable power take off drive was designed for hammer mills and corn shellers. This, too, met with immediate success. Developed next were a ditcher for tiling and a boom-type sprinkler.

In 1956 a hay conditioner was perfected, and more than 5,000 were sold. Next came a low-cost stump cutter followed by a tree mover. By now the Vermeer plant was employing several hundred workers.

In the early 1970s a new concept in haying was conceived and, with it, Gary Vermeer revolutionized haymaking. He introduced the round baler for convenient outdoor storage and easy wintertime feeding. More than 80,000 of the Pella-made machines are now in use throughout the world, and the "little shop" of 1948 has grown to seven large plants covering around 1 million sq. ft., and provides employment for 1,200 Iowans.

As for the Vermeer and VerMeer surnames, they apparently will go on forever. "Our family seems to specialize in boys," says Anthony, who has two sons and a daughter, and six grandchildren, five of them boys. Tunis also had two sons and a daughter, but the girls beat the boys in the grandchildren department, five to four. Gary has two sons and a daughter. Bernie has three sons, five grandsons, and only two granddaughters. "Boys are to be expected in our family. Great-grandfather had seven sons and grandfather had five," says Bernie.

Records show that almost every member of the family, beginning with the pioneers who came to Pella 135 years ago, has been, or is, a devout member of the Dutch or Christian Reformed Church.

Community pride also looms large in the family, as seen in service through beef, pork, and dairy associations, farm co-ops, Chamber of Commerce, service clubs, Tulip Time days, and other organizations. Mary Vermeer, now Mrs. Lyle Borg, was both a Tulip and Dairy queen.

When the four cousins were asked the surnames of the women they married, they listed DeZwarte, Vander Wal, Van Llenden, and Van Gorp. Asked the surnames of the women their sons married they replied with Bogaard, Verschure, Steenhoek, Van Wyngarden, De Boer, DeJong, and Brand. Meanwhile, their daughters married men whose names were Engelhoven, Terborg, and Andringa.

105-YEAR OLD FARM WIFE
RECALLS PIONEER DAYS
April, 1992

When a person has passed the hundred year mark and has a clear mind like 105-year old Effie Greiner, events spanning an entire century come cascading back. Thanks to her children, Lyman, Glenn, and Mrs. Ruby Nail, I got to hear her tell of the early days on pioneer Iowa and Minnesota farms.

Effie Fedlie Doolittle Greiner is 105 years old. She is a popular resident at the Southfield Care Center in Webster City, Iowa, where she is surrounded by family pictures and mementos of her long, interesting, and exciting life.

Born on a Hamilton County farm on March 5, 1887, she vividly recalls pioneer hardships, her country school days, high school, enrolling in the first teacher's class at State Normal School in Cedar Falls (now University of Northern Iowa), and then teaching in Liberty Township rural schools.

'My contract was for $36.88 a month, and for that 'big check' I had to do the janitorial work, 'fire up' the stove every morning, keep a pail filled with fresh water, and do all the teaching," she recalls.

After a couple of years of teaching, romance entered the picture. A handsome young neighbor, Charles Greiner, found excuses to bring library books to the Doolittle farm. Courtship ended with marriage on Jan. 17, 1906. All the neighbors came over that night to stage a long and loud shivaree. Then on March 1, the traditional "moving day," they loaded their possessions into a straw-laden bobsled to start their housekeeping and farming career on a rented farm.

Two years later they bought a small farm and welcomed their firstborn, a son, Loren. Good crops and good prices then enabled them to buy a larger farm in Minnesota. A second son, Lyman, arrived just in time to make the move north. Two years later, in early 1913, a baby girl, Hester, was added to the family.

Greiner vividly remembers two unforgettable experiences in Minnesota. One was choosing to remain in the frame house with her three babies when horses with long cables pulled the building to a new location 50 rods away, nearer to the main road.

The second experience was a terrible storm on July 2, 1913, when a promising crop was totally ruined during the 30-minute hailstorm, which also killed chickens and pigs, devastated outbuildings, destroyed the garden, and smashed house windows, while lightning killed horses and cows.

Having lost so much in the storm, the family moved to Litchfield, Minn., to operate a butcher shop. Soon thereafter, in March 1914, another girl, Ruby, was born, and yearnings to return to Iowa were being felt. On March 1, 1917, the family, now numbering six, resettled on a Greiner farm near Blairsburg, Iowa, where another son, Glenn, arrived soon after the move. Still another boy, Esley, was born later.

A month after returning to Iowa, World War I broke out. Rationing of flour, sugar, and meat was immediately ordered. "It was hard to bake bread and we substituted honey for sugar and grew cane for molasses," says Greiner.

In the mid-1920s a purebred Holstein herd was started, and the children entered 4-H. Greiner became a Liberty Lassies 4-H leader.

All the children went to high school in Blairsburg, Iowa, and all later married. Several followed their father's footsteps at Iowa State College. During World War II Loren and Esley served overseas. Glenn became a farmer and still is. Hester and her husband moved to Idaho. Ruby became a teacher in several schools, and a rural school advocate, as well as a community and church leader. She has written a humorous book, *Home Remedies*. Lyman taught school for several terms, then farmed for many years.

105-year-old Effie Greiner and three of her children, Lyman, Ruby and Glenn.

As for Effie Greiner, she became president of the Iowa Women's Relief Corps when she was 80. She remains active in her Rebekah Lodge and Lutheran Church. She enjoys recalling the "good old days," and likes to tell about her 84-year-old sewing machine that "never missed a stitch."

Keeping busy and serving veterans groups has been Effie Greiner's passion. She has belonged to Daughters of the American Revolution, American Legion Auxiliary, and several other groups serving veterans of all wars.

Most of all, Greiner is grateful that all of her six children are alive and well, and that she can count 16 grandchildren, 40 great-grandchildren, and 16 or 17 great-great-grandchildren, some as far away as Alaska.

H.B. WALLACE AND HIS ARIZONA CACTUS RANCH
May, 1992

It's a far cry from directing an Iowa project involving millions of Hy-Line baby chicks and high-producing laying hens to creating a cactus ranch in Arizona, but that's what H.B. Wallace has done. Wallace, fourth generation member of the famous Wallaces Farmer *publishing family, has become as enthusiastic about cacti as he once was about chickens.*

A widely known former Iowan, Henry Browne Wallace, great grandson of the beloved "Uncle Henry" Wallace who founded WALLACES FARMER 137 years ago, now lives near Scottsdale, Ariz. Wallace, who is remembered by thousands of Midwest families as the developer of the Hy-Line chickens, these days takes great pride in the 20-acre "Cactus Ranch" he has developed.

"H.B.", as he is best known, has a rich heritage. Not only is he "Uncle Henry's" great-grandson, but his grandfather, Henry Cantwell Wallace, "H.C." for short, was editor of WALLACES FARMER from 1916 to 1921, when he was appointed U.S. secretary of agriculture. Then H.B.'s father, Henry Agard,

H.B. Wallace on his Arizona cactus ranch.

popularly known as "H.A.", became the highly respected WALLACES FARMER editor in 1924 until 1933, when he, too, was designated U.S. secretary of agriculture in the "F.D.R." cabinet, and later served as U.S. vice president.

"H.B.", now 76, and I have been close friends and fraternity brothers for half a century.

Annually I visit his "spread" where he has more than 700 species of cacti, plus many other desert plants, trees, shrubs, and flowers. He is also involved with the University of Arizona in a project centered on leguminous desert plants that may have significant value in the future.

Wallace's cacti range from 30 ft. tall Saquaros to some species only 1 in. high. Dozens of prickly pear, barrel cactus, and other commonly known domestic species share space with hundreds of exotic cacti from South and Central America and the Galapago Islands. Many other plants in H.B.'s collection are native to Australia, Africa, Kuwait, and elsewhere .

Variety and color abound throughout the area. The cactus plants themselves are of every shade of green, with some showing blue, orange, brown, or purple hues. The blossoms range from white to deep red with delicate pink, yellow, green, lavender, purple, and magenta adding to an extravaganza of beauty. One species from Argentina has spines 6 in. long. A few are virtually spineless. Still others, like the "Teddy Bear" Cholla variety, must be given a wide berth.

Palo Verde, Ironwood, Mesquite, Joshua, and other native desert trees, as well as a large selection of exotic trees, shrubs, and greenery add greatly to Wallace's "Desert Wonderland."

H.B.'s wife, Jocelyn, adds much beautiful variety to the tract with her love for roses and flowers.

This past winter's soaking rains have given the entire desert a new lease on life. Seeds dormant for years have now germinated. Water, however, is always a problem. H.B. has partially solved the problem by installing loops of leach pipe around many species.

High, strong fences have been built around part of the six acres already planted to help keep out deer, desert rabbits, pack rats, and other animals that thrive on cacti. Meanwhile, desert wrens, orioles, woodpeckers, cardinals, thrashers, and other birds nest in the area.

Unpredictable low temperatures are of great concern. Winter readings as low as 13 degrees have been registered on the Wallace property. To overcome this threat, H.B. has built a 6,000 sq. ft. pavilion which houses over 350 of the most cold susceptible species. Large, automatic louvers make up the ceiling and automatically follow the sun, thus assuring every plant daily sunshine. However, when temperatures drop below 35 degrees, the louvers automatically close to conserve heat, curtains are rolled down the side, while three furnaces instantly kick on at 32 degrees to provide warmth.

Humus and a 14-14-14 slow release fertilizer, plus sulphur, is added to the natural soil to assure growth. Three reliable workmen help Wallace with planting, watering, fertilizing, maintenance, and innumerable other tasks.

H.B. has been a benefactor of many projects. A champion gardener and dahlia grower during his years in Des Moines, he helped the late Corwyn Hicks, Iowa State University horticulturist, establish the Iowa Dahlia Society. He is also a major donor for the Living History Farms and has contributed generously to cancer, heart, and mercury poisoning research. Of special note is how he has helped to get the University of Arizona desert legume project effectively started. The Wallace Genetic Foundation, originally founded by H.A. Wallace, enabled the university to start seeking leguminous plants with potential value in landscaping, medicine, and food from deserts all over the world.

Currently, Wallace is planting, testing, and evaluating the leguminous plants provided by the university.

COUNTY EXTENSION DIRECTOR THRIVES ON VARIETY
July, 1992

Marvin Smart has lived up to his last name in any number of ways. However, before getting "smart enough" to go to college, he tried many lines of endeavor. Then, after becoming Warren County extension Director, he stayed on that job 24 years before entering the international field to help others.

If variety is the "spice of life," Marvin Smart, longtime Warren County extension director, must feel quite "spicy."

Beginning as a helper on his father's farm, then attending an Ottumwa business college as a teenager, he had worked in a funeral home, waited on tables, served as a hired farmhand, fought chinch bugs in the mid-1930s, was a truckline billing clerk, and served the War Department in Washington, D.C. as a medical records clerk all before he reached the age of 21. Nor did the variety of jobs stop then.

He returned to Iowa in 1938 to serve as a paymaster on the Missouri River stabilization project earning $120 a month. However, when he saw the size of the engineers paychecks, he decided it was time for Smart to get "smarter," so he enrolled at Iowa State College (ISC).

While at Ames, he attended Wesley Foundation, where he met Mary Simmerman. They were married in 1941.

When World War II broke out later that year, Marvin elected to do "alternative service" with an American Friends Committee and the Mennonites.

Transferred to Cleveland, he was assigned to manage a large dairy herd at a mental hospital for $15 a month.

After the war was over, he re-enrolled at ISC, with ag education as his major. On graduation in 1947, he became Vo Ag Director at Monroe with 47 FFA members in his class, and 50 farmers in night school

Mr. & Mrs. Marvin Smart with one of their 50th wedding anniversary gifts.

Corn was selling as high as $3.48 per bu. in the early 1950s when Charles Craig, a successful Palmyra cattle and hog feeder, offered Smart a 30 percent interest to manage the operation.

After several years of success on the Craigs' farm, Smart was able to rent 240 acres from Art Vander Ploeg near Melcher."

Unfortunately, drought struck the first year. Consequently, Smart's yields were poor.

"We survived, thanks to the milk checks from our 30-cow-herd, and from the hogs," says Smart. But the next year when hog prices dropped to $7.50 or less, and milk plunged to $4 a hundredweight, we had to throw in the towel."

The next venture was to become a Farm Service tank wagon driver, and then, in 1968, came the opportunity to serve as county extension director for Warren County, a position he held for 24 years.

With Mary's help, he gave 4-H leadership high priority, but he also worked hard in many other areas including home improvements, farm management, farm business analysis, community development, soil and water conservation, pork and beef associations, County Fair, and a dozen other projects. Smart was also a recognized horticulturist.

In 1980 he resigned his county extension director position, must to the regret of hundreds of Warren County residents. However, he did not stop serving his fellow man. He and Mary went overseas for several years to help people in third world countries improve food production.

VETERAN EXHIBITORS PREPARE FOR STATE FAIR
August, 1992

If there were a first prize for State Fair winning exhibitors, Harold Goecke would certainly be in the running for it. Beginning in 1923 as a 4-H beef club member, he had been exhibiting at fairs and shows throughout the Midwest since that time. He and his wife, Kay, spent many long hours preparing prize entries, as this column sought to prove.

Iowa's 134th annual State Fair is slated for Aug. 20th through the 30th.

Once again it will be a blue ribbon extravaganza. The finest of everything produced in the state will be on display—as well as the best that some of the other states have to offer.

In the Agricultural Hall, where more than 300,000 visitors will view farm crops, orchard, garden, floral, FFA, apiary, conservation, fanners' market, and countless other exhibits, competition will be keen. Newcomers will mix with veterans in the bid to win the purple ribbons and coveted plaques.

Among those almost certain to give everyone a run for their money are Harold Goecke and his wife, Kay, who live near State Center and devote countless hours to selecting grains and vegetables for the critical eyes of the judges.

A World War II veteran, Goecke served 3 1/2 years in the U.S. Field Artillery's 10th Mountain Division as an ammunition truck driver in Italy. "The Alps are beautiful, but driving in those blackouts with no lights didn't offer much chance to appreciate them," he notes.

Goecke is also a true veteran of show rings and exhibit places. He first participated in state fair competition in 1923, when he was showing in Marshall County's champion baby beef groups. After he started farming and cattle raising on his own, he entered champion carloads at the International Livestock Show in Chicago, Ill. as early as 1938.

After the Chicago exposition closed, Goecke started concentrating on corn and other farm crop exhibits. For the past 25 years, he has been entering top quality grains and vegetables at the State Fair.

Last year the State Center farmer won a total of 14 trophies, including the top awards at the state fair where he enters in every class for farm crops and potatoes, as well as entering most vegetable classes.

He has also been a winner at the Central Iowa Fair in Marshalltown, Clay County Fair in Spencer, Mississippi Valley Fair at Davenport, All-Iowa Fair at Cedar Rapids, and many other Iowa exhibitions. Moreover, he has topped the American Royal Show in Kansas City with his corn and soybeans.

Hard work and thoroughness are policies that have made Goecke a winner. Summer visitors to his farm will find dozens of small plots of corn, soybeans, oats, barley, wheat, rye, clover, grasses and forage crops of all kinds, melons, eight kinds of potatoes, as well as several vegetable gardens. It is from these plots that he critically selects his final exhibits.

Mr. & Mrs. Harold Goecke, Iowa State Fair champion exhibitors.

Kay, who also shows winning entries, helps him with final selections. "It's a hectic day and night task for a week before fair time," says the former city girl from Ohio who had much to learn when she married Harold.

One experience was with 1,000 laying hens.

"Harold told me I should talk to them when gathering eggs," she says. "So when I entered the laying house I'd say, 'Good morning, girls, have you had a good day, etc. etc.', and when I'd leave I'd always say something like, 'Now girls, let's see you do a good job again tomorrow.'"

Nor can there be any question that the Goeckes have achieved results for their intensive efforts. Anyone entering their large, nicely kept farm home will see rooms full of trophies, plaques, certificates, and other mementos of their achievements. Kay estimates Harold has won "well over 100" in the past 70 years.

ANTIQUES FASCINATE
MASTER FARM HOMEMAKER
September, 1992

When Mrs. Joe Gray was named an Iowa Master Farm homemaker back in 1959, she was considered the personification of a community worker. While her efforts in helping in the community continued, along with her duties as a farm wife, a new interest in collecting antiques developed — and with it a successful business under the interesting name "Maxine's Henhouse Antiques".

Earlier this month when four Iowa farm women — Patricia Carney of Guthrie County; Esther Frandson, Story County; Norma Hager, Black Hawk County; and Shirley Pennington, Floyd County, were named Iowa Master Farm Homemakers by WALLACES FARMER, quite a few farm wives previously honored were there to applaud.

Among those attending was Maxine Gray, Mahaska County, who was honored in 1959. Gray and her husband, Joe, still live on the farm Joe's grandfather bought in 1864. Joe's father became the owner in 1900 and Joe and Maxine, who were married in 1938, took over in 1952.

In the 128 years the Gray family has owned the land, there have been a myriad of changes, both in farming practices and in personal interest.

When she was named a Master Farm Homemaker, Gray had already served many years as a 4-H leader, Sunday school superintendent, Methodist Church Circle chairperson, extension council member, and in other community endeavors.

Moreover she had raised a stalwart son, Kenneth, who lost his life in an auto accident a few years ago, and a daughter, now Emily Alsop, a teacher. Gray also had charge of the farm chicken flock and garden, did lots of canning, and helped on the farm at haying and harvest time.

After her induction into the select Master Farm Homemakers' state-wide organization, she added other responsibilities, serving as a member of the Iowa Extension Advisory Council and as a judge in Pioneer Hall at the state fair, as well as becoming involved in the International Farm Youth Exchange (IFYE), programs. Moreover, she was rapidly developing an interest in genealogy and became fascinated with antiques.

Mrs. Joe Gray, Master Farm Homemaker and collector of antiques.

For several years the Mahaska County homemaker studied journals and books centered on antiques. Soon friends began asking her to procure special items for them, a friendly service for which she never charged a penny.

After the Grays hosted a Centennial Farm celebration in 1964, Joe also became very interested in Maxine's projects.

In 1966, Evelyn Anderson of Des Moines, Maxine's sister-in-law, urged her to go into business. Joe concurred and said, "You've always gone to the henhouse, so why don't you call it 'Maxine's Henhouse Antiques'?" So, instead of renting a building in town, the couple cleaned, repainted, remodeled, and air conditioned the chicken house, and the budding antique business was started.

Meanwhile, Joe continued to farm 200 acres, but took time out to join his wife on extended buying trips. Soon, in addition to the henhouse, the barn where horses, cattle, and sheep were once housed, began to fill with pioneer farm tools.

By 1968 the business began to flourish. "I'd be planting corn or something and every little while I'd get the call to come in and help load stuff into a buyer's car or pickup," recalls Joe. "So in 1971 I rented the land to Ken VanGilst on a 50-50 basis."

Since then both Joe and Maxine have devoted most of the last 20 years to the antique business and to travel on Friendship Force, People to People, and personal tours of foreign countries. Now the Grays have cut back on the antique project considerably.

"We are still dabbling in it," says Maxine, who has some items at the Pella Antique Mall and works with Patty Lamberson, Phyllis Power, and Dee Talbert in a shop in Oskaloosa, but "Maxine's Henhouse" is closed.

Some antiques are family heirlooms and will never be sold. One example is a beautiful Pink Slag berry bowl with six sauce dishes that were given Joe's parents at their wedding in 1900. It is now their property and worth a couple thousand dollars. It will remain in the Gray family forever.

Maxine points out reproductions have been coming in fast, and warns potential buyers to make sure what they pay dearly for is the "real thing."

By her knowledge of authentic items, Maxine has been able to help many people avoid costly mistakes during her years of "antiquing."

COMMUNITY LEADER BEFORE AND AFTER MASTER FARMER AWARD
October, 1992

Wallaces Farmer has long had a slogan, "Good Farming, Right Living, Clear Thinking", and one of the many perfect examples of that credo is Elmer Hamann, named a Master farmer in 1963. In the 30 years that have followed, the Scott County Farmer has stood very tall in community service. This column emphasized some of Hamann's countless contributions.

Scott County's Elmer Hamann, now 82, was named a Master Farmer back in 1963. He is a good example of the "right stuff" Master Farmer judges are looking for.

Starting out as a hired man at $25 a month, then managing the farm where he was working, later renting that farm, and eventually purchasing a farm of his own, Hamann has personified the longtime WALLACES FARMER slogan, "Good Farming, Right Living, Clear Thinking."

Soon after he and his wife, Ruth, were married in 1936, they were able to rent a 175-acre farm for $8 an acre and buy seven horses and some machinery. Later, he bought a 10-year-old tractor, a few sows, and 24 dairy cows. Soon thereafter. using artificial insemination, he upgraded the herd. Dairy Herd Improvement Association (DHIA) records weeded out poor producers. There was no upright silo on the farm, so Hamann made one of the first surface silos. He was also named to the county DHIA board.

Hamann also became involved in the 1940 National Corn Husking Contest sponsored by WALLACES FARMER. He says, "I was the 'gofer' for all kinds of projects including guarding the husking lands and helping with the National Plowing Match."

Mr. & Mrs. Elmer Hamann, Scott County Community Leaders.

Successful as farm renters, the Hamanns decided to buy 160 acres where dairying could be continued on a larger scale and where various innovations were undertaken. He was the first in the county to install a milking parlor, and to undertake a modern pipeline, bulk milk tank operation.

The terracing which was started on the rented farm was continued on his own.

Another innovation of Hamman's was a corn drying project. He had quite a lot of bin room for shelled corn, so he bought an old box car in Illinois, hauled it to his farm near Eldridge, opened up one end, and installed an oil-fired burner. A tractor belt-driven fan on the burner drove heat through the newly harvested corn, resulting in a good, marketable product.

With their children growing up, church, school, and 4-H leadership activities were undertaken. So were other obligations. Elmer served several years on the Farmers Home Administration Board, was county Farm Bureau president, voting director, and delegate to the American Farm Bureau convention. He was also Eldridge Farmers Institute chairman.

Other leadership responsibilities included serving on a County Soil Conservation panel, member of Brucellosis Eradication committee, June Dairy Month chairman, County Extension Council member, and as Scott County Farm Service Company president. "We had $3 million in sales, and one year 1,600 customers shared $65,000 in dividends," he says.

Hamann's greatest satisfaction, however, comes from his involvement in helping start and build the North Scott Community School, which serves a 210 square mile area. He was president of the board when the $1,100,000 project was completed in 1957.

Meanwhile Ruth, herself a former 4-H champion, served as an active 4-H leader for 10 years and later chaired the county 4-H committee. She has also been active on the Merit Mothers Association and has been a director of the Scott County "Porkettes" organization.

Mrs. Hamann also served as Scott County Farm Bureau Women's chairman and is on the local Lutheran Church Council.

After Hamann was named a Master Farmer, he continued right on with his farming and community endeavors. A farrow-to-finish hog enterprise was greatly expanded and about 100 head of feeder cattle finished out annually. Hamann also became an Iowa Master Corn Grower in 1971.

In time, Hamann was elected an Eldridge Bank director and became involved in politics as a presidential elector. He has also served both Rotary and Kiwanis service projects, was elected vice president of the Scott County Pork Producers, and served on the church council.

Looking back over the years, Elmer Hamann credits his neighbor and 1941 Master Farmer, the late Herbert Schneckloth, as his inspiration for community service and farming excellence. "He was a fine neighbor and a great teacher," says Hamann.

100-YEAR OLD IOWAN RECALLS SERVING IN WW I
November, 1992

Armistice Day is observed every November 11th. It is a day set aside to pay tribute to all who wore a U.S. uniform in any one of many wars in which this nation has engaged. WW I veterans are rapidly being called to their final reward. This column saluted 100-year-old Bill Boian, who constantly remembers his WW I "buddies."

Each year, at the 11th hour of the 11th day of the 11th month, the end of World War I is internationally observed with a minute of silence. Relatively few veterans of the 1917-18 conflict were left to join in this year's Armistice Day celebration at 11 a.m. on Nov. 11th. However, one who well remembers the moment the German command surrendered to the Allies is 100-year-old Bill Boian of Des Moines, Iowa, who enlisted in the struggle in early 1918 to make the world "safe for Democracy."

It was July 20, 1892, when the Ernest Boian family welcomed a bouncing boy they promptly named Wilbur. Since then, "Bill," as everybody knows him now, has seen the U.S. population grow from less than 50 million persons to more than 250 million, and to go through seven wars —Spanish-American, Mexican, World War 1, in which he had such a heroic part, World War 11, Korea, Vietnam, and the Persian Gulf.

Moreover, the Iowa centenarian has watched electricity and atomic power revolutionize industry, "sweat shops" give way to 40-hour weeks, livery stables replaced by a garage at every home, airports displace train stations, tractors and combines instead of horses and scythes on farms, 5-cent a loaf bread to $1 a loaf, and land costs rise from $10 an acre to $1,000.

Still physically active at 100 and gifted with a remarkable memory, he enjoys recalling his World War adventures.

"I was given a bad time by the draft board when I tried to enlist in early 1918, but finally got in as a buck private." he says. First assigned to feed horses and then haul coal before he was put on guard duty, he will never forget the night he was given a loaded revolver to guard a murderer. He also vividly remembers the tragic toll taken by the Spanish flu that winter.

"We were in the 88th Division at Camp Dodge and were soon taken to Camp Gordon in Georgia, where we trained going up Stone Mountain with full pack, rifle, and gas mask, and where rations were fat meat, boiled potatoes, and beans which we didn't like much," says Boian.

Placed in the 82nd Division with orders to get "over there" as soon as possible, the U.S. "doughboys," as they were known, were loudly cheered at every train station enroute.

After landing at LeHavre in France, they were moved to a defense sector as German troops neared Paris. "We were in the thick of it from then on," says Boian, who well remembers the train cars taking them to the front. "We stole a keg of wine and had a good time on the way," adds the veteran.

He vividly remembers Chateau Thiery and its trenches where he became a battlefield observer, fought to keep telephone lines open during shellings, endured a 30-day siege without a bath, and then moved on to the St. Mihiel battlefields, where he remembers seeing an aerial "dog fight" in which a German flyer believed to be Capt. Richthofen, the "Red Baron," downed an American plane and pilot.

Finally, Boian went with his 82nd Division buddies into the Allies' victorious battles in the Meuse-Argonne Forest campaigns, where he remembers a few close calls, the result of poison gas attacks.

When the German surrender came on Nov. 11, 1918, the Iowa veteran was too weary to join his fellow soldiers in raiding liquor supplies and in celebrating. Instead, he checked into a hospital with a severe cold, but refused to stay. On returning to his outfit, he and the others awakened at 4 a.m. the next morning and were taken to Paris to march for Gen. Pershing. "We weren't all that enthusiastic," he says.

100-year-old Bill Boin with his WWI helmet.

Pleasant memories are revived as he recalls the return home by ship with no U-boats to worry about, then getting $60 in discharge pay at Camp Dix just before the happy train ride back to Iowa. "That," says the 100-year-old veteran, "was the best part of the war."

For his services, Boian received several awards, one of them from the French Government. A self-educated person, he eventually became head of the engineering and drafting departments of a leading Des Moines steel company building bridges, barges, and buildings. To this day, the 100-year-old veteran remains exceedingly well fit physically, drives his car daily to visit his hospitalized wife, and still attends lodge, Shrine, and other meetings regularly after his 80 years of Masonic membership.

Asked for his recipe for a long, healthy life, the centenarian says, "use moderation in all things."

IOWA COMMUNITIES SPREAD CHRISTMAS JOY
December, 1992

This was the final feature in my 15 year resume of 170 "The Way It Was" columns listed in this book. It serves as a most appropriate closing highlight. The Humboldt and Dakota City residents, led by Kiwanis Club members, have established a massive annual "Holiday Wonderland". To appreciate the magnitude of their "Christmasland" and other appealing attractions, this column called for "must reading".

Christmas came early again this year to two north central Iowa communities whose residents are sharing their Yuletide joys with thousands of visitors.

All this month, the citizens of Humboldt and Dakota City are staging their annual "Holiday Wonderland" with many displays centered on the Christmas theme. Included are a mammoth "Christmasland" exhibit, Candy Cane Lane, an Avenue of Greeting Cards, a Tree of Life, the Mill Farm House featuring "Christmas Past," a breathtaking "Hillside Spectacles", and an untold number of private homes and farmsteads ablaze with the spirit of Christmas.

Mrs. Donna Wind and Fred Meyer, volunteers in Santa's workshop at Humboldt's Christmasland.

Led by two Kiwanis Clubs, this marks the 12th season for the event that has attracted more than 40,000 visitors from almost every state and several foreign countries.

Fred Meyer, 77, a Humboldt businessman and a Kiwanian, is credited with being the event's originator. "We started with eight holiday season figures in 1980, and it's been growing by leaps and bounds ever since, thanks to hundreds of volunteers and various organizations," he explains.

Bernice Smith, 97, is one of Holiday Wonderland's most enthusiastic boosters. "It's a wonderful attraction for children, as well as adults, to enjoy," says the former history teacher.

"Christmasland" is an indoor exhibit in a large building where visitors can see a huge array of animated characters and animals. Included are an impressive Nativity scene, a Charles Dickens-era miniature city, Santa's Workshop, animated deer and other woodland creatures, a North Pole polar bear and South

Pole penguins, carolers singing favorite Christmas carols, a new display of Teddy Bears and—of course—Santa himself.

The Kiwanians spend endless hours and sizable sums of money—about $30,000—readying, maintaining, lighting, and hosting Christmasland. Donna Wind and Wayne Miner are cochairs.

The Faith United Methodist Church sponsors a Tree Walk involving more than 70 lighted trees, while Our Saviour's Lutheran Church has large trees on its grounds colorfully lighted.

One neighborhood puts up dozens of 8-ft. high greeting cards, each with an appropriate Christmas message. Another community calls itself "Candy Cane Lane" with huge painted canes amid elaborate Yuletide decorations. Elsewhere, huge wreaths, whirling snowflakes, icicles, and gold glitter add to the attractions.

On a high hill near the Dakota City Farmer's Elevator, Marlyn Forte has arranged a "Hillside Spectacular" involving thousands of lights and innumerable Christmas scenes. And near the Des Moines river, the 13-room Mill Farm House has the calendar turned back 100 years so as to relive "Christmas Past."

The "Tree of Life" sponsored by the Humboldt County Hospice enables people to memorialize or recognize someone by contributing to a colored light. Funds raised are used by Hospice for terminally ill patients and their families and the Good Neighbor Respite Service.

Large, unique highway signs direct visitors to the displays. Hours for most of the lighted displays are 6 p.m. to 10 p.m. except for Christmasland which closes at 8:30 p.m. and is not open Sunday and Monday. Guided tours can be arranged for any afternoon. There is no admission charge, but donations are welcomed at some attractions.

Children love to give Santa their "orders," but one year "Mac" McArthur, in his Santa suit, had a strange request. A boy afflicted with epilepsy said, "If there is a Santa, I wish he would let me survive an operation in St. Paul next week." McArthur was stunned, but assured the lad Santa would help, then arranged for prayer circles and followed through on the delicate and successful surgery. The boy has now returned to normalcy and McArthur says, "That helps make everything we do here seem worthwhile."

The way it was . . .
1993

The preceding fifteen chapters in this book represent my first fifteen years of "The Way It Was". By no means have these more than 170 columns ended my writing efforts.

In this chapter, readers will find summaries of columns already written in 1993 and those yet to be published this year, as well as some planned for 1994 and beyond.

In addition, my pen and typewriter, along with Ruth Schultz's word processor, will continue to turn out feature stories for various other publications. Among them are *SICKLE & SHEAF,* the Alpha Gamma Rho (AGR) quarterly magazine; the *IOWA HORTICULTURIST,* a bi-monthly publication by the Iowa Horticultural Society; *HILLTOP NEWS,* a weekly newsletter for some 300 Scottish Rite Park Retirement Center residents; and several other publications.

Moreover, more than a hundred broadcast scripts will be written annually for the garden program my wife, Laura, and I present twice weekly on Radio Station KRNT, Des Moines. More than 50 others will be prepared for my weekly farm commentary on Radio Station WMT, Cedar Rapids. Dozens more scripts for nationwide use will be prepared for hundreds of other radio stations across the United States in connection with my assignment as chairman of the National Association of Farm Broadcasters' (NAFB) Farm-City Week committee.

And, as though that were not enough to convince anyone I am still trying to keep active, let me add that a number of chapters have already been written for my tenth book. This next book undoubtedly will be one of the most ambitious projects I have ever undertaken. It will deal with the incredible progress made in the world of Agriculture in this amazing 20th Century.

I realize, of course, that many of my friends question the wisdom of a person in his mid-eighties keeping so busy. I am well aware there are easier ways to spend the so-called retirement years. I'm frequently reminded that "all work and no play makes Jack a dull boy." However, "all play and no work" does not appeal to some of us. In any case, if doing some creative work in the "golden years" brings pleasure and satisfaction, perhaps it should not be totally frowned upon. In writing *THE WAY IT WAS,* I have come across many men and women who have continued to make meaningful contributions well into their 80s and 90s and several beyond their 100th birthday.

January, 1993

Turning now to summaries of 1993 columns already published, my January effort did not feature any one person. Instead, it was in the form of a review in which I dealt with what had transpired in the past.

The initial meeting with *WALLACES FARMER's* young editor, Monte Sesker, was described in which it was agreed older persons merited some special recognition. A brief mention was made about the first person to be featured, Albert Weston, retired farmer, then 90. Weston's story included many interesting recollections of pioneer days.

Counts were made and reported. Totals showed 174 columns written over the 15-year period involving 358 persons. More than eighty Iowa counties were included, as well as fifteen different states and ten foreign countries.

Over 150 of those featured were in their 80s, with several dozen in their 90s, and eight were 100 years old or older. The oldest was 107. Mention was made of their remarkably clear memories.

Some 80,000 miles were covered, countless telephone calls were made, and hundreds of letters written to achieve the more than 170 columns.

Singled out were a few special persons. One was 97-year-old Fred Metzger, father of 14, grandfather of 84, and great-grandfather of 148. For my interview, the family sent over a 73-year-old son to make sure "Grampa" was accurate in his recollections. Instead of the elder Metzger being mistaken, he corrected the 73-year-old son three times.

Herb discussing a special column with Governor Branstad.

February, 1993

My second 1993 column featured two persons. One was Mrs. Herbert Johnson, Charles City farm housewife who had served as the head of Iowa's Farm Bureau women several years and was named an Iowa Master Farm Homemaker. The other was Collins Bower of Cass County, Iowa, a District Farm Bureau Director for several years.

Mrs. Johnson — Thelma to all — served as the Farm Bureau Women's chairperson six years and was involved in national and international, as well as state leadership. She attended triennial Associated Country Women of the World meetings in Ireland, Canada, Norway, Africa, Australia, Germany and the United States.

Mrs. Herbert Johnson, Master Farm Homemaker and Farm Bureau Women's Chairperson.

However great her state and other responsibilities were, she never failed to give her husband and family of four children, nine grandchildren, two great-grandchildren, and two adopted Chilean children top priority. She was also a 4-H leader fourteen years. After starting on a small rented farm 50 years ago, the Johnsons now own and operate 800 acres with their son.

Collins Bower and his wife farm 540 acres, but Bower has spent much time on his Farm Bureau District responsibilities, serving twelve Southwest Iowa counties.

Collins Bower, veteran Farm Bureau leader.

The Bureau's "grass roots" policies and its stand on farm inequities first drew Bower into the organization 42 years ago. Subsequently, he became a township director, county vice president, president, and voting delegate, before being named a district director.

Bower is pleased at what farm organizations have accomplished over the years, but makes it clear there are many issues still ahead. Among them are rural health care, farm insurance needs, livestock welfare, the increasing trend of women working away from home, farm exports, and the possibility of heavily increased farm imports from Russia, China, and elsewhere.

March, 1993

March, 1993, was a big month for *"THE WAY IT WAS"*. Two features were prepared and published.

The first was a story about a Northwest Iowa swine breeder and his wife, Mr. & Mrs. Lawrence Peters, who I met in January at the Iowa Pork Producers Congress, where Lawrence was awarded the Association's highest honor. The feature was headed *"A Half Century of Seed Stock Production,"* and told of 50 years of effort in the hog business, starting out in 1943 with one crossbred sow and winding up with being named the top Iowa Seed Stock Producer in 1993.

Mr. & Mrs. Lawrence Peters, Pork Producer Honorees.

Lawrence, now 75, says he had two major ambitions in his early 20s. One was to marry the prettiest girl in Woodbury County and the other was to start farming with her. Both were realized in 1943, but the farming was on a small and rented scale, with borrowed machinery, a team of horses, a couple cows, and that one crossbred sow. Her litter sold for only 6¢ a pound.

From that year on, things went better. First, six sows produced good litters that sold much better. Next, purebreds entered the picture. Soon a Poland China herd was established, and the rest is history.

The Polands did well. Land was bought. The Peters' hogs were entered in Iowa Swine Testing Stations and made fabulous records. Soon boars from the herd sold for $500 and the demand continues strong to this day.

There's much more in the published column, but this brief summary would not be complete without pointing out the Peters have four children, and have been a credit to their community. Lawrence has been a Little League coach, county fair director, and Pork Producer leader, while Phyllis has been active in her community club and church, as well as a proud grandmother of six. Over the years, they have improved hilly land with conservation practices, and built a lovely home on a neat farmstead. Lawrence gives Phyllis much credit for their success, to which she laughingly quips, "That's right, after the hogs and bowling, I always come first."

April, 1993

In April, 1993, the column switched completely from Agricultural things to Ornithology. Some readers might have said, "We went to the birds."

Actually, that's just what was done. My wife and I live at Scottish Rite Park, a large 12-story retirement center with some 300 other people. Many of them are "bird watchers". Our next door sixth floor neighbors are Mr. & Mrs. William "Bill" Yaggy, and Bill is one of the most dedicated bird lovers I know.

Many readers will remember the name, "Yaggy", because the Yaggy family established a Farmers Mutual Insurance Association in 1874. Hail, flood, tornado, and other coverage was applied. I know, because hail insurance benefits came to my farm from the Yaggy's firm several times.

Wm. "Bill" Yaggy, the "Birdman"

Bill, now 84, followed his father as chief executive of the firm many years. Always soft-spoken, he was a popular C.E.O. However, insurance was not his only interest.

While still a relatively young man 50 years ago, Bill became involved in feeding birds and has done so ever since. Every day of the year, he gets up about 5:00 AM to provide feed and water for dozens of species of feathered friends. Four feeders are filled each day, along with a bird bath heated all fall, winter and spring. "Birds," he says, "need water as much as feed."

Raccoons and squirrels, of course, are always ready to steal feed put out for birds, so Yaggy has made numerous devices to discourage the four-footed thieves. And to help pacify the squirrels, he puts out corn in another area for them.

Known as the "bird man" by all his neighbors, he says he has no idea how many thousands of birds he has fed or how many "tons" of feed he has put out at his own expense, or how many "oceans" of water he has provided. He continues to do so lovingly because, in addition to all his neighbors and business acquaintances, he has won so many feathered friends.

May, 1993

Raymond Baker, internationally recognized corn breeder.

One of the most interesting and challenging stories I have ever undertaken was to write about Raymond Baker, a hybrid corn pioneer - now internationally recognized. The story was featured in the May, 1993 issue of *WALLACES FARMER*.

Baker is a long-time friend who I first got to know in college during the genesis years of hybrid corn. It was long before I realized the revolution in corn production he and others had started.

To summarize that column is a difficult challenge. *WALLACES FARMER* editors used almost every word I wrote to make it a two-page piece, the longest I had ever written.

A relatively poor Ringgold County farm youth, Baker had to buckle down hard to get to college. He enrolled in a two-year Ag Course at Iowa State College (now ISU) where our mentor, Prof. Paul Henson, waxed enthusiastic about hybrid corn. Raymond caught on fast. Most of the rest of us didn't.

The next thing that happened was a chance meeting at the Iowa Corn Show with Henry A. Wallace, editor of *WALLACES FARMER*. Both were checking over entries in the corn division. When Wallace noted young Baker's interest in hybrid corn, he immediately took a deep interest in the young man. It was the beginning of a lifelong friendship that blossomed into one of the most significant relationships in the hybrid corn industry.

Because of that chance meeting, Baker was given some of Wallace's experimental seeds. However, because he had to attend classes at Ames, he relied on his father to plant them, but the elder Baker got too busy to do so. Fortunately, however, his mother planted the plot. After cultivating, detasselling and harvesting the plot, he made an entry in the state corn yield test, and to everyone's amazement, won the southern Iowa trophy and became forever "hooked" on hybrid corn. His mother, meanwhile, became the unsung heroine of the budding hybrid corn industry. That surprising accomplishment in the state yield contest marked the beginning of Baker's career as a corn breeder. Not many years later, he became a key associate in Wallace's Hi-Bred Corn Company.

The road to success, however, was not covered with golden bricks. There were lean years ahead. Wallace had invested so heavily in starting his fledgling company that there was little left for salaries. In fact, Baker worked as a hired man on a Wallace farm with little pay. While doing so, he kept abreast of the corn breeding project.

In return, he received ten shares of Hi-Bred Corn stock in lieu of salary. Then the depressing early '30s struck. Corn dipped down to a lowly 10¢ a bushel. Baker found it necessary to borrow from his father to provide for his growing family.

When Wallace was named Secretary of Agriculture in 1933, he had to sever relations with his corn company. Now Baker's responsibilities became awesome. Nor did two years of drought and a killing early frost help. Nevertheless, Baker "kept the faith".

Not only did he lead the corn breeding work to new heights, but he also had to oversee the expansion of plants and research facilities.

However difficult and discouraging it may have been for the onetime southern Iowa 4-H pig club member, he never wavered from his belief that hybrid corn was the wave of the future.

By 1936, enough farmers had seen how hybrid corn could withstand drought and other adversities. They had noted its yielding potential and they wanted it for themselves. From then on, it was mostly "all down hill" for Baker and others who never lost faith in the hybrid principle.

Today, Baker is recognized the world over as one of the pre-eminent pioneer corn breeders. He continues to have an office at Pioneer International. Meanwhile, his ten shares of stock, along with additional stock acquired, have grown to the point where the one time college youth who worked in experimental corn fields for 25¢ an hour, was able to make a million dollar contribution for agronomy work at Iowa State University.

June, 1993

Merle Travis, conservationist.

Merle Travis, now 83, has long been in the forefront in the realm of Iowa soil conservation. He was the subject for our June 1993 issue column.

Travis is a long-time Taylor County farmer. He became involved in the conservation challenge back in the 1930s, when his County Agent, Bob Davies, a long-time friend of mine, fast-talked him into using birdsfoot trefoil to help hold and enrich the soil. Not long thereafter, Davies sought out Travis and two other leading farmers for the purpose of forming a Soil Conservation District. The trio went to a CCC camp to make application and receive authorization. That was 50 years ago, and for 40 of those years, Travis served as District Chairman.

The Taylor County conservationist has practiced what he preached. He was one of the first to put his plow to building terraces. He did contour farming and established grassed waterways. Multiflora windbreaks were also established. Equally important, he helped neighbors establish conservation practices.

I got to know Merle best when he was named chairman of the 1954 Iowa Soil Conservation Days and Plowing Matches sponsored in part by WHO. No one could have done a better job.

Nor were his talents limited to his home county. Governor Hoegh named him to his Agricultural Board. The Iowa Soil and Water Conservation Association chose Travis as their state president. He was named "Iowa Soil Conservationist Of The Year" one year and chosen "Watershed Man Of The Year" the next.

To top it all off, my friend, Merle Travis, the hands-on pioneer conservationist, was named an Iowa Master Farmer, and you can't get a higher honor than that in the Hawkeye State.

July, 1993

When it comes to writing *"The Way It Was"* columns, under no circumstances do we limit ourselves to farming achievements and contributions. The July, 1993 column verifies that.

Our guest was Armetta Keeney, a State Fair champion pie baker in every sense of the word. She has an outstanding record of accomplishments over a period of years at the Fair.

Nor can competition at the Iowa Fair be taken lightly. Food and Nutrition Department entries often reach 7000 or more and vie for some 24,500 in premiums.

Armetta Keeney, pie baking champion.

Friends and relatives who had tasted Mrs. Keeney's lemon pie at family, community, or county events, insisted she enter the State Fair competition. Somewhat hesitatingly, she finally did so some 20 years ago. She entered only a single lemon pie and when she looked over the other 14 in the class, she sort of wished she hadn't. The judge took one bite out of each pie; and after tasting hers, lost no time putting a blue ribbon on it.

Since then, she has been entering pies and other baked goods every year and has won many top awards. Blue ribbons have been claimed on her custard, rhubarb, apple, pear, apricot, peanut butter, chocolate, and other pies, in addition to her famous lemon pies. In addition she has won awards on casseroles, cakes, breads, and other entries.

This year, at the 1993 Fair, she took 22 awards, including nine blue ribbons and the Sweepstakes Award in the pie division.

In addition, Armetta has been named "Cook Of The Year" by *Country Magazine,* and has served as guest baking artist at the Living History Farms. However, despite many offers, Mrs. Keeney will not become a professional baker. She says turning professional would prevent her from competing and would no longer let her do things for her community, such as baking for her church events where her skills once netted $185 for the treasury.

Armetta has also been a 4-H leader, is active in the Missionary Society, and enjoys bringing pies to the senior citizen's group. You can be assured we senior citizens love to have her come.

August, 1993

Almost every August, our column centers on some aspect of the Iowa State Fair. It's a way to help promote the venerable exposition, now in its 135th year. Many aspects of the Fair have been publicized in this way. Last year, it was the Harold Goeckes' long time record of accomplishments in Ag Hall. Another year, it was Vince Pemble, champion gardener from Indianola. Still another year, Roy Heathershaw, Ag Department Superintendent, and Frank Goecke, long-time corn show winner, were recognized. Leah Keeler, Weldon, Iowa, needlepoint artist and State Fair quilt contest winner was also featured.

This year, the August 1993 issue column took a new turn. Harold Peterson, the State Fair's gardener, was highlighted along with his fabulous array of flower beds planted earlier in 1993.

A quiet 77-year old "no nonsense" gardener, who always wears a big hat, Peterson was a farmer and hog raiser on 310 acres in Audubon County until his doctor told him he had to quit or suffer unbearable asthma. Then he applied for a State Fair job and was placed in the maintenance department.

Harold Peterson, State Fair Gardener.

Soon after he was hired, he noticed only a few flower beds on the more than 250 acres. After suggesting there should be more, he was given the job of getting it done.

That was 26 years ago. Today, there must be 60 or more beds of flowers on the grounds, each a classic in floral beauty. Dozens of kinds of flowers from little petunias to tall cannas are planted every spring, and are in full bloom every Fair week. The immensity of the job is seen in the fact that 5000 or more canna roots are dug up every fall and replanted early every spring. Composting, weeding, trimming shrubs, as well as planting, keeps a four-person crew busy throughout the season.

Peterson himself also spends many hours in the wintertime planning just what flowers are to be used to enhance the different beds in the coming summer.

The result is that the Iowa State Fair can rightfully boast it is the prettiest, as well as the best, State Fair in the nation.

September, 1993

The September 1993 issue obviously needed to center on the Farm Progress Show slated for the Amana Colonies later in the month, where this book would first go on sale.

Art Selzer, an Amana historian and a long-time friend, along with his wife, Marie, again came to the rescue with help and advice.

In dealing with this column, I chose an 86-year-old Amana area farm woman and an 81-year-old farmer as my guests.

Mrs. Anna Moennich, who lives with her son, Theodore, Jr., and his wife, Caroline, on a farm southwest of the Colonies, told about coming to Iowa from Germany during that country's hideous years of depression and inflation soon after WW I. She explained about adjusting to the Amana communal life before "The Change" in 1932, and how great a difference life became. The column summarizes how she and her late husband, Theodore, both worked hard to make a success of their farming venture, and the good life that resulted.

Gottfried Steinmetz, who sold his land to the Amana Society, adds an interesting note to the September column with his enthusiasm for the Farm Progress Show, where 200,000 or more visitors will see a multitude of new developments in Agriculture. Mr. Steinmetz also touches on some unique rural mail boxes he has created, and some other things he has done.

OTHER COLUMNS PLANNED FOR 1993

Columns planned for the period after the 1993 Farm Progress Show promise to be highly interesting.

In October, Ernest Heidecker, 82, highly successful Kossuth County farmer and champion "before and after" corn husker will be featured.

The November column originally was to highlight a 97-year-old horseman. However, when he suffered a broken leg shortly before the scheduled interview, new plans had to be made quickly. Good fortune again befell *"The Way It Was "* in the person of 101-year-old Mrs. Ralph Stoeber, whose remarkable story, related during a Master Farm Homemaker meeting, will grace the November issue.

December's column will center on a unique Christmas season attraction at Algona. Wes Bartlett, 78, past president of Kiwanis International will tell of the unusual display, as well as recall a few Kiwanis Club accomplishments.

The following pages briefly summarize some of the highlights of these three upcoming 1993 columns as they were being prepared for *WALLACES FARMER* readers.

October, 1993

Ernest Heidecker, 82, of near Lakota, is a remarkable man who has done some remarkable things.

Ernie, as he is known, began working on farms away from home when he was only 16, and he is still working hard 66 years later. He served as a hired man for five years, and then began thinking about farming on his own. That dream came true in 1934 soon after his marriage to Pauline Jontz.

They moved onto a 160-acre crop share rented farm, but drought and other adversities ended that project. Then, an

Ernie Heidecker, champion corn husker.

uncle rented them a better 160-acre tract for $6 an acre. A little money was made and saved that year. Heidecker started buying land and has increased his holdings to where he, along with his son, Marvin, grandson, Greg, and nephew, Ivan, now operate 2250 acres, almost all of it owned by the Heidecker Corporation.

There has also been quite a change in the harvesting procedure. Back in the '30s, Ernie husked all his corn by hand. The husking hook cost about 60 cents, and Ernie husked 100 bushels a day or better.

Today, the husking hook is still being used in husking matches for Senior Citizens, but not in Heidecker's fields. Instead, an eight-row Massey-Ferguson picker-sheller, costing well over $100,000 new, can harvest about 1800 bushels an hour and well over 15,000 a day. "Times have changed," says Ernie.

In addition to changes in the corn harvesting, there are some other things different. When he started out, Ernie had a couple of teams of horses. Today, he has a fleet of tractors, including one four-wheel drive Massey-Ferguson.

One thing hasn't changed though. That's Heidecker's spirit of competitiveness seen in his hand-husking skills in corn fields. Since 1986, when he picked up hand-husking where he left off in 1940, he has been the unbeatable senior champion in Iowa, Indiana, Minnesota, Illinois and other states. A total of 21 large trophies now adorn shelves in the Heidecker home. Mrs. Heidecker, three children, nine grandchildren and eleven great-grandchildren and many neighbors are all rightfully proud of Ernie.

November, 1993

It was my good fortune to meet 101-year-old Mrs. Ralph Stoeber of Charles City at the Iowa Master Farm Homemaker's awards ceremony this fall. Mrs. Stoeber had good reason to be in attendance. Her granddaughter, Mrs. Cyndie Schenkloth, was one of four outstanding Iowa farm wives to be inducted into the select circle. Earlier, Mrs. Stoeber's daughter, Mrs. Thelma Johnson, had been accorded the same high honor. Thus, Mrs. Stoeber was introduced as Mother of Master Farm Homemakers.

Proud as she rightfully is of her daughter and granddaughter, the Charles City centenarian is very soft-spoken and shies away from the limelight. Yet, in visiting with her, I learned of much of her pioneer spirit.

Elaboration on her accomplishments must wait until the November issue, but a few items and experiences can be told now.

Born in Illinois, she came to Iowa when she was only eight years old. She enjoyed country school and reading books, but there was no high school or college. As a teenager, she helped with cooking, baby sitting, milking and herding cows. She also enjoyed horseback riding and community events. Her heart beat faster when young Ralph Stoeber paid $4 for her box at the school box social, but he had to borrow money to pay for it. They were married and started farming near Charles City. Their first three babies were lost at childbirth. There were no doctors to help. Later, a son, now Army Colonel Wesley Stoeber, and a daughter, Thelma, were welcomed. On the farm, Mrs. Stoeber helped with the milking, feeding, and field work. She frequently drove four-horse hitches and helped husk corn. When automobiles first came out, she learned to drive right away. "We were on mud roads and they were terrible," says Mrs. Stoeber. She remembers the pretty hats ladies always wore to church. Drought years with chinch bugs and grasshoppers are recalled. The Stoeber's lost a farm during the depression, but started up again near Huxley.

President Teddy Roosevelt is the first president she remembers. She also recalls Presidents Taft, Wilson, Harding, Hoover and FDR.

This year's terrible flooding gave her much concern, but her biggest worry is today's young people. "They want the money, but they're not willing to work for it." Nevertheless, Mrs. Stoeber looks forward to doing some more traveling. "I enjoyed Hawaii a lot," says the smiling centenarian, who says Kentucky is about the only state she has missed.

With her apparent good health, and her enthusiasm and spirit, I'm sure anything Mrs. Stoeber wants to do she'll get it done with "flying colors."

December, 1993

Wes Bartlett, Past President Kiwanis International.

Concluding my 1993 series of *"The Way It Was"* efforts will be the December column featuring Wesley Bartlett, 78, of Algona, Iowa. He has been a consummate community worker and leader for more than 50 years and is an enthusiastic spokesman for an internationally recognized Nativity Scene made by German prisoners of war some 49 years ago.

The Algona attraction is placed on display every Christmas season and is viewed by thousands. Bartlett tells how homesick WW II prisoners, dead tired of the long war, and in a camp near Algona, sought to ease their loneliness and frustration by turning to thoughts of peace. Their answer was in spending long hours in creating nativity scenes out of concrete.

Bartlett explains that a non-commissioned German army officer, Eduard Kalb, was the leader. Thoughts of home and of earlier happy Yuletide festivities in his home church inspired him to undertake the project on which he and fellow prisoners worked many months.

The Algona community worker's enthusiasm for his city's Christmas attraction is quite understandable. Even before acquiring a furniture store in Algona in the mid-40s, the Parsons College graduate, who had taken further training at Iowa "U", had established himself as a leader.

At the Primghar and Eagle Grove high schools, he taught math, science, physical education, biology and chemistry. At Eagle Grove, he also became athletic director before going to Eagle Grove Junior College to serve as the Navy's V-7 training instructor for fledgling WW II Navy pilots. Later, he taught electrical engineering for the Navy at Iowa City and in Ames.

It did not take long for Bartlett to become involved in community work in

Algona after arriving there in 1945. He soon found himself serving on the Board of Education, as well as on the Kossuth County Hospital Board, Algona City Board, Armory Building Committee, and other groups. He was also made chairman of a North Iowa Study Council.

He also became a member of the Algona Kiwanis Club, a service organization. He was soon named president of the club, then, in 1951, chosen Lieutenant Governor for Northwest Iowa, and to no one's surprise, he was elected Governor of the 7000 member Nebraska-Iowa District and to several Kiwanis International committee chairmanships.

So effective was his work on the Kiwanis International Board that he was elected trustee in 1964, vice president in 1968, and president in 1971. That position of international responsibility took him and his wife, Mary, to many parts of the world as head of the 350,000 member organization dedicated to community service.

FUTURE PLANS AND HOPES

Many other columns I hope to write are "on the drawing board".

Among them is a feature about Sherry Fisher, a long-time Iowa leader in many areas, who has taken on an impressive gardening hobby and is now referred to as Iowa's "Tomato King" by his Scottish Rite Park neighbors. Sherry, a long-time friend of the late "Ding" Darling, and a leader in the foundation for the famous Des Moines Register cartoonist, enjoys surprising his friends with red, ripe, juicy tomatoes soon after mid-June.

Sherry Fisher, civic leader and tomato "king".

The column will tell about how he achieves his annual tomato "firsts", and more importantly, it will tell of his many accomplishments in civic and state organizations.

Another column under consideration will be one of a personal nature, and will tell about the five Jagerson Brothers, four of whom are war veterans,

The Five Jagerson Brothers Sunny View Farm Tenants.

Mr. & Mrs. Ratloff.

who have worked together on their own, and on rented farms, for many years. One of those rented farms is my own Sunny View Farm in Boone County, on which Harold Jagerson and his wife, Mary, have lived for 35 years. It's to be a down-to-earth column to which a great many readers can relate.

These are only two of a dozen or more *"The Way It Was"* features on the horizon. Others presently under consideration for future issues include a couple in Humboldt County, the Ratloffs, who have done a tremendous job of drainage in which might well be considered a wetland farm. Besides listing some of their efficient, modern, up-to-the-minute farming accomplishments, there is one more unique aspect I will include in their story. It's the fact that Mrs. Ratloff still raises 500 laying hens every year, and the demand for the eggs from her flock is phenomenal.

Gene Meyer, a former Clayton County 4-H champion, has been a *Hoard's Dairyman Magazine* editor for many years. His story includes many fascinating experiences with the National Dairy Farmer's publication.

Present plans are for Robert Jardon, 79, oldest Master Farmer ever named, to be highlighted in June, 1994. Mr. & Mrs. Jardon raised eleven children and

Master Farmers, Mr. & Mrs. Robert Jardon.

have a highly-recognized farming and dairying operation in extreme Southwest Iowa. Three sons are involved in the 900-acre farm and with the herd of 88 registered Holstein cows. They speak proudly of a rolling herd average of nearly 23,000 pounds of milk annually.

The Grotto of Redemption at West Bend, Iowa, said to be the largest grotto in the world, and its long-time curator, Reverend L.H. Greuving, is another feature I hope to include in future writings.

An interesting community historical museum at Madrid, where Margaret Keeghly and Leonard Ackerlund, who was one of my long-time farm neighbors, work hard to preserve local history. This will also be featured in *WALLACES FARMER* in 1994.

Still others under consideration are Ernie Metzger, Northwest Iowa, whose 97-year-old father, Fred, gave me such a fascinating interview several years ago. Ernie is one of fourteen children and has a large family, and has a lot of amusing anecdotes to tell.

Bill Lemke, Waterloo, who is a leading historian about mechanical corn pickers is also scheduled.

A feature on Flying Farmers is also planned, as well as more stories about Master Farmers and Master Farm Homemakers, and others who have made significant contributions.

Still another column I am eagerly anticipating concerns Bob Feller, the famed Cleveland Indians' baseball pitcher. I have known Bob since he was a member of the Iowa Farmers Union team in his mid-teens. He was already

Bob Feller and his cousin, Hal Manders, photographed on the day they pitched for batting practice in Chicago.

"mowing down" opposing batters back then.

After he reaches his 75th birthday, I hope to write a column about Feller's meteoric career, and about the happy relationship between him and his cousin, Hal Manders, another Dallas County farm youth who made it "big" in the major leagues. In fact, the two continue to work together on an antique farm machinery project, as well as in the Bob Feller Museum program planned for the Hall of Famer in his home town of Van Meter.

It must be crystal clear to every reader that if my hopes to do these and other future columns materialize, I have my work cut out for me. Moreover, as mentioned earlier, in addition to the contemplated columns for *WALLACES FARMER*, there is another project that will keep me busy for many months to come. That is the book currently expected to be written under the title, *"AGRICULTURE'S INCREDIBLE PROGRESS IN THIS AMAZING 20TH CENTURY."* It will be my tenth book and unquestionably the most challenging. Among the revolutionary changes in farming to be chronicled will be the transitions from hand labor to machines, from horses to tractors, development of hybrid corn, forming of national farm organizations, 4-H Clubs, FFA programs, and much more.

Among significant developments to be chronicled are rural electrification, mechanical corn pickers and grain combines, early soil and water conservation efforts, government farm programs, hemp production in WW II, and other war-related developments. Other chapters will center on national Conservation Days and Plowing Matches, State Fair farm emphases, importation of so-called exotic breeds of cattle and hogs, livestock disease control, land booms and busts, and computerized farming. These are some of the things, along with many others, that made farm history in this 20th century, and will be included in the new book.

God Willing, I expect to get the job done before any thought is given to retiring my pencil — and eraser. However, I must add, considering what happened to Iowa and other Midwest farmers during the deluges of 1993, my next book will be written, "If," according to an old saying, "the creeks — and rivers — don't run over" as we have seen only too vividly — and tragically — this year.